Principles of Insurance:
Life, Health, and Annuities

Second Edition

LOMA (Life Office Management Association, Inc.) is an international association founded in 1924. LOMA is committed to a business partnership with its worldwide members in the insurance and financial services industry to improve their management and operations through quality employee development, research, information sharing, and related products and services. Among LOMA's activities is the sponsorship of the FLMI Insurance Education Program—an educational program intended primarily for home office and branch office employees.

The *FLMI Insurance Education Program* consists of two levels—Level I, *Fundamentals of Life and Health Insurance,* and Level II, *Functional Aspects of Life and Health Insurance.* Level I is designed to help students achieve a working knowledge of the life and health insurance business. Level II is designed to provide a more detailed understanding of life and health insurance and related business and management subjects. Students who complete Level I receive a certificate. Students who complete both levels earn the designation Fellow, Life Management Institute (FLMI) and receive a diploma.

Statement of Purpose: LOMA Educational Programs Testing and Designations

Examinations described in the *LOMA Insurance Education Catalog* are designed solely to measure whether students have successfully completed the relevant assigned curriculum, and the attainment of the FLMI and other LOMA designations indicates only that all examinations in the given curriculum have been successfully completed. In no way shall a student's completion of a given LOMA course or attainment of the FLMI or other LOMA designation be construed to mean that LOMA in any way certifies that student's competence, training, or ability to perform any given task. LOMA's examinations are to be used solely for general educational purposes, and no other use of the examinations or program is authorized or intended by LOMA. Furthermore, it is in no way the intention of the LOMA Curriculum and Examinations staff to describe the standard of appropriate conduct in any field of the insurance and financial services industry, and LOMA expressly repudiates any attempt to so use the curriculum and examinations. Any such assessment of student competence or industry standards of conduct should instead be based on independent professional inquiry and the advice of competent professional counsel.

Principles of Insurance: Life, Health, and Annuities

Second Edition

Harriett E. Jones, J.D., FLMI, ACS
Dani L. Long, FLMI, ALHC

FLMI Insurance Education Program
Life Management Institute LOMA
Atlanta, Georgia

FLMI 280 Text

Authors:	Harriett E. Jones, J.D., FLMI, ACS Dani L. Long, FLMI, ALHC
Manuscript Editor:	Gene Stone, FLMI, ACS, CLU
Exam Editor:	Kelly W. Neeley, FLMI, ACS, AIAA, ALHC
Project Manager:	Joyce Abrams Fleming, J.D., FLMI, ACS, AIAA, ALHC HIA, MHP
Production/Editorial Manager:	Stephanie Philippo
Copyeditor:	Robert D. Land, FLMI, ACS
Production/Print Coordinator:	Cara Taylor Gaskins
Permissions Coordinator:	Michon Wise
Index:	Gail Liss
Cover Design:	Jackie Taylor; Michelle Stone Weathers
Typography:	BJ Nemeth, Puffin Typography

FLMI 280 Quik Review

Authors:	Barbara Foxenberger Brown, FLMI, ACS Tom Lundin Jr., FLMI, ACS, AIAA, PAHM
Project Manager:	Jane Lightcap Brown, FLMI, ALHC, ACS
Production/Editorial Manager:	Stephanie Philippo
Technical Development:	Keith Hesser
Production Coordinator:	Cara Taylor Gaskins
Special thanks to:	Susan Abbot, FLMI, ALHC, Claims Consultant/ Education Coordinator, John Hancock Signature Services and Karla McPherson, Business Analyst, John Hancock Mutual Life Insurance Company, who developed the original concept and prototype for the FLMI 280 Quik Review presentation.

07 06 05 04 03 02 01   10 9 8 7 6 5 4 3

While a great deal of care has been taken to provide accurate, current, and authoritative information in regard to the subject matter covered in this book, the ideas, suggestions, general principles, conclusions, and any other information presented here are for general educational purposes only. This text is sold with the understanding that it is neither designed nor intended to provide the reader with legal, accounting, investment, marketing, or other types of professional business management advice. If legal advice or other expert assistance is required, the services of a competent professional should be sought.

ISBN 1-57974-029-4

Library of Congress Catalog Card Number 99-73129

Printed in the United States of America

Contents

Preface

The life and health insurance and financial services industry has undergone many changes since 1996, when the first edition of *Principles of Insurance: Life, Health, and Annuities* was published. Like that text, this second edition is designed to give readers an understanding of the basic principles that underlie the operation of life and health insurance companies. The text describes the most widely marketed products of the life and health insurance industry, and it explains how those products operate.

Acknowledgements

LOMA's Education Division has assembled a team of writers, editors, and production staff who work together closely to create educational publications such as this textbook. This staff team, however, depends on the work of industry professionals who give their time and knowledge to help ensure that LOMA's educational publications are as accurate and complete as possible. We first thank the industry experts who helped us develop the original edition of *Principles of Insurance*, from which this second edition was developed. The original panel included

- Linda K. Borden, ACS

- Gail L. Cobin, FLMI, ACS, CLU, LUTCF

- Peter F. Headley, CLU, ChFC, FLMI, RHU

- Paul Kibler, FLMI, CLU, FALU

- Patricia A. Lombard, FLMI, CEBS, QPA

- David Lee Nelson, Ed.D.

- Nancy C. Nichols, FLMI, ALHC, CEBS

- John E. (Jack) Schroeder, FLMI, HIA, ACS

- Robert (Bob) Wilson, FSA, FCIA

On behalf of LOMA, we particularly want to thank the members of the textbook review panel who read and commented on the manuscript for this second edition, answered many author questions, and provided ideas and documents for supporting materials. These individuals were extremely generous in sharing their time and industry experience with the authors, who were privileged to work with them.

Textbook Review Panel

- Robert Ahlschwede, CLU, FLMI, Compliance Manager, Annuities, CNA Life Companies

- Jeanne M. Clarke, FLMI, ACS, 2nd Vice President, Corporate Project Management, Unity Mutual Life Insurance Company

- Mark K. Fujita, C.A., FLMI/M, ACS, CIA, Director of Quality Service, The Canada Life Assurance Company

- Judy Heard, FLMI, CLU, AALU, Director, Benefits Administration/ Relocation, Nationwide Life Insurance Company

- Jerry Hogya, FLMI, Manager, Systems Reconciliation and Maintenance, Mutual of Omaha

- Nancy C. Nichols, FLMI, ALHC, CEBS, Help Desk Officer, Fortis Information Technology

LOMA Staff

Many of LOMA's Education Division staff members worked to create this textbook. We especially want to thank William H. Rabel, Ph.D., FLMI, CLU, Senior Vice President, Education Division and Dennis W. Goodwin, FLMI, ACS, HIA, Assistant Vice President, Insurance & Financial Services Programs, for their guidance of the FLMI Insurance Education Program and their support and encouragement of the Division's staff. Joyce Abrams Fleming, J.D., FLMI, ACS, AIAA, ALHC, HIA, MHP, Director, Insurance & Financial Services Programs, ably directed this textbook project, and the authors appreciate her willingness and ability to provide creative ideas and helpful suggestions. The project's editor, Gene Stone, FLMI, ACS, CLU, Senior Associate, made invaluable improvements to the text and cheerfully helped assure the text's accuracy and readability. Kelly W. Neeley, FLMI, ACS, AIAA, ALHC, Senior Associate, Examinations Department, also reviewed the manuscript and made many helpful suggestions. Robert D. Land, FLMI, ACS, served as copyeditor and prepared the index.

The production staff, lead by Stephanie Philippo, Director, Editorial/Production/Intellectual Property Management, worked tirelessly to complete this project on time. Michon Wise, Editorial/Permissions Coordinator, assured that we received necessary permissions. Cara Taylor Gaskins, Production Coordinator, managed the typesetting process and arranged for the printing. Aurelia Kennedy-Hemphill, Administrative Assistant, provided administrative support through all stages of the project.

Harriett E. Jones, J.D., FLMI, ACS
Dani L. Long, FLMI, ALHC
Atlanta, Georgia
1999

Introduction

The purpose of *Principles of Insurance: Life, Health, and Annuities,* Second Edition, is to describe the life and health insurance industry and the products provided by life and health insurance companies in the United States and Canada. The text, which is designed for students who are preparing for LOMA's FLMI Course 280 examination, is divided into two parts.

- Part 1 (Chapters 1–13) provides an introduction to the principles of risk and insurance and describes the operation of individual life insurance policies.

- Part 2 (Chapters 14–23) describes the principles of group insurance, the operation of group life insurance policies, and the features and types of health insurance coverages that are available in the United States and Canada.

Suggestions for Studying This Book

Several features have been included in this book to help you organize your studies, reinforce your understanding of the materials, and prepare you for the FLMI 280 examination. As we describe each of these features, we will give you suggestions for studying the material.

- **Chapter Outline.** The first page of each chapter contains an outline of the chapter. Review this outline to get an overview of the material that will be covered and scan through the chapter to familiarize yourself with how the information is presented. By looking at the headings and figures, you will get an idea of how various subjects relate to each other.

- **Learning Objectives.** The first page of each chapter also contains a list of learning objectives to help you focus your studies. Before reading each chapter, review these learning objectives. Then, as you read the chapter, look for material that will help you meet the learning objectives.

- **Key Terms.** Because this is an introductory text, it requires no prior knowledge of insurance terms and concepts. Each insurance term is defined or explained when it is first used. Important insurance terminology is highlighted in ***bold italic*** type when the term is first used or defined and is included in a list of key terms at the end of the chapter. All key terms are also included in a comprehensive glossary at the end of the book. As you read each chapter, pay special attention to these key terms.

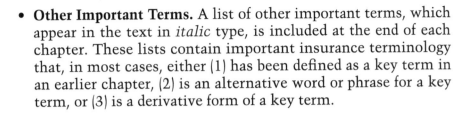

- **Other Important Terms.** A list of other important terms, which appear in the text in *italic* type, is included at the end of each chapter. These lists contain important insurance terminology that, in most cases, either (1) has been defined as a key term in an earlier chapter, (2) is an alternative word or phrase for a key term, or (3) is a derivative form of a key term.

- **Insights.** Insights—excerpts from industry publications and other sources—appear throughout the text and are designed to amplify the text's description of certain topics. These Insights should help you get a better feel for the life and health insurance industry.

In addition, we have included insurance cartoons and interesting statistics or "Fast Facts" within the chapters to round out the presentation of material and enhance the learning experience.

Using LOMA Study Aids

LOMA has developed a variety of study aids, designed to help students prepare for the FLMI 280 examination. LOMA recommends that you use all of the study aids available for this course. **Studies indicate that students who use LOMA study aids consistently perform significantly better on FLMI Program examinations than other students.**

Using the Prep Pak for This Course

In addition to this book, LOMA's *Prep Pak for FLMI 280** is assigned reading for students preparing for the FLMI Program examination. Used along with this textbook, the Prep Pak will help you master the course material. Included in the Prep Pak are chapter review exercises, practice exam questions, a full-scale sample examination in both paper and electronic format, and answers to all of the questions in the Prep Pak.

Using the CD-ROM Accompanying This Text

The CD-ROM found on the inside back cover of this text contains a Quik Review, which is an interactive review of the materials found in this text and is designed for both instructors and students studying for

---

* The Prep Pak may be revised periodically. To ensure that you are studying from the correct text, check the current LOMA Insurance Education Catalog for a description of the texts assigned for the examination for which you are preparing.

the FLMI 280 examination. The CD-ROM also provides students with a sample whole life insurance policy and a sample flexible premium annuity, which are two of the insurance products described in this text.

Using *LOMA's Handbook of Insurance Policy Forms*

LOMA's Handbook of Insurance Policy Forms (available October 1999) is suggested reading for the FLMI 280 course. This handbook is a reference tool to provide students and other insurance and financial services industry professionals with examples of the insurance and annuity products that we describe in this text. Sample policy forms include a range of individual life insurance, health insurance, and annuity products. The handbook also includes a sample group insurance master contract and a certificate of insurance provided to the individuals insured under the group contract.

1

Introduction and Individual Life Insurance

CHAPTER 1

The Life and Health Insurance Industry

After reading this chapter, you should be able to

- Distinguish among the three types of business organizations and explain why insurance companies must be organized as corporations

- Identify how stock insurers differ from mutual insurers

- Describe the financial services industry and how insurance companies function within that industry

- Identify the major types of life and health insurance products

T he life and health insurance industry plays a major role in the economies of both the United States and Canada. At the end of 1996, residents of the United States and Canada had total life insurance coverage of almost $15 trillion.[1] That same year, U.S. and Canadian insurers paid out over $100 billion in health insurance policy benefits.[2] In this chapter, we take a brief look at insurance companies as business organizations by describing how insurers are organized and how they fit within the larger context of the U.S. and Canadian economies. We also provide an overview of the types of products that life and health insurance companies sell; we will describe these products throughout this text. Finally, we describe some other life and health insurance providers that operate in the United States and Canada.

Insurance Companies as Business Organizations

A *business* can be defined as an organization established for the purpose of producing goods or services that consumers want or need and then selling those goods or services, typically for a profit. **Profit** is the money, or revenue, that a business receives for its products or services *minus* the costs it incurred to produce the goods or deliver the services. As a business, an insurance company typically has a responsibility to its owners to operate profitably.

Each business organization is structured in one of three ways: (1) as a sole proprietorship, (2) as a partnership, or (3) as a corporation. A **sole proprietorship** is owned and operated by one individual. The owner reaps all profits and is personally responsible for all the debts of the business. If the business fails, the owner's personal property may be used to pay the debts of the business. If the owner becomes disabled or dies, the business usually closes its doors.

A **partnership** is a business that is owned by two or more people, who are known as the *partners*. The partners reap the profits and are personally responsible for the debts of the business. If one of the partners dies or withdraws from the business, the partnership generally dissolves, although the remaining partners may form a new partnership.

For our discussion, we're primarily concerned with the corporate form of business. A **corporation** is a legal entity that is created by the authority of a governmental unit and that is separate and distinct from the people who own it. A corporation has two major characteristics that set it apart from a sole proprietorship and a partnership. First, a corporation is a legal entity that is separate from its owners. As a result, a corporation can sue or be sued, can enter into contracts, and can own property. The corporation's debts and liabilities belong to the corporation itself, not to its owners. The owners are not personally responsible for the corporation's debts. The second difference is that the corporation continues beyond the death of any or all of its owners. This second characteristic of the corporation provides an element of stability and permanence that a sole proprietorship and partnership cannot guarantee. This stability makes the corporation the ideal form of business organization for an insurance company. Because insurance companies must be permanent and stable organizations, laws in the United States and Canada require insurance companies to operate as corporations.

Types of Insurance Company Organizations

Even though they must be corporations, life and health insurance companies have some flexibility in how they are organized to do business. Typically, however, insurers are organized as either stock companies or mutual companies.

Stock Insurance Companies

The majority of life and health insurance companies are established and organized as stock companies. A **stock insurance company** is an insurance company that is owned by the people and organizations that purchase shares of the company's stock. The investors who purchase *stock*—ownership shares—in the corporation are known as the *stockholders.* From time to time, a portion of the company's operating profits may be distributed to these stockholders in the form of *stockholder dividends.*

Mutual Insurance Companies

Life and health insurance companies can also be organized as mutual companies. A **mutual insurance company** is an insurance company that is owned by its policyowners, and a portion of the company's operating profits are from time to time distributed to these policyowners in the form of *policy dividends.* We describe policy dividends in more detail in Chapter 6.

Before a mutual company can be formed, a certain number of policies must be sold in advance to provide the funds the company needs to begin operations. Because most people are reluctant to purchase a product from a company that does not yet exist, most mutual companies in existence today began many years ago as stock companies and later converted to mutual companies. This process of converting from a stock company to a mutual company is called *mutualization.* One advantage that a stock company gains from the process of mutualization is that a mutual company cannot be bought by another company since a mutual company has no stock to sell.

During the late 1990s, a number of U.S. and Canadian mutual companies reorganized as stock companies through the process of *demutualization.* The primary reason a mutual insurer might wish to demutualize is that, as a stock company, it can more easily raise operating funds because it can issue additional shares of stock to the public. Stock insurers also have greater flexibility than mutual insurers in buying and operating other types of companies.

Even though stock insurers greatly outnumber mutual insurers, mutual insurers provide a significant amount of the life insurance in force in the United States and Canada. (See Figure 1-1, which depicts the concentrations of stock, mutual, and fraternal companies in the insurance industry. We describe fraternal companies later in the chapter.) Mutual insurers account for a significant amount of life insurance in force because they are generally older and larger than stock insurers.

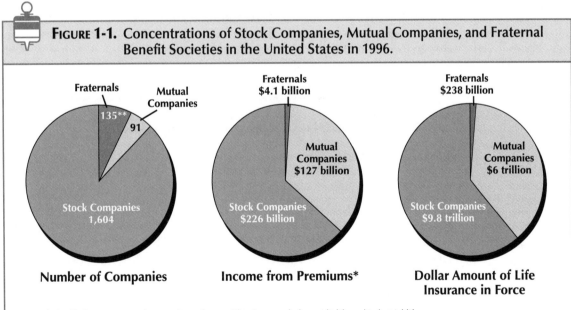

FIGURE 1-1. Concentrations of Stock Companies, Mutual Companies, and Fraternal Benefit Societies in the United States in 1996.

Fraternals — Mutual Companies
135** — 91
Stock Companies 1,604
Number of Companies

Fraternals $4.1 billion
Mutual Companies $127 billion
Stock Companies $226 billion
Income from Premiums*

Fraternals $238 billion
Mutual Companies $6 trillion
Stock Companies $9.8 trillion
Dollar Amount of Life Insurance in Force

* Includes life insurance premiums and annuity considerations; excludes credit life and industrial life.
** Number of fraternals who filed annual statements with the NAIC in 1996.

Source: ACLI, *1997 Life Insurance Fact Book* (Washington, D.C., American Council of Life Insurance, 1997), 34–35; National Fraternal Congress of America.

Organizational Operations

As a final topic in our look at insurance companies as business organizations, we'll define some terms that are commonly used to refer to the physical or geographic aspects of an insurer's operating structure. The headquarters of any insurance company is generally referred to as the company's **home office** or *head office* and is often located in the state or province in which the company was incorporated to do business. In addition, the home office is usually the location of all the company's executive offices.

Because insurance companies vary significantly in size, the geographic arrangement of their office locations also varies. For example, very large insurance companies may have regional offices in addition to the home office. A **regional office** is generally charged with many of the same functions and operations as the home office but is geographically closer to the market it serves and generally reports to the home office.

Within each geographic region, a company may have field offices. A **field office** is an insurance company's local sales office. The home office and regional office typically provide support services to the field office. Some field offices are classified as *branch offices* while others are classified as *agency offices*, depending on how they are organized and what the working relationship is with the home office.

These structural aspects of insurance organizations vary widely from one company to another, depending on the size of the company's operations and the geographic markets it serves.

Insurance Companies as Financial Intermediaries

> **FAST FACT**
>
> By the end of 1997, assets of U.S. life insurance companies totaled $2.6 trillion. Assets of Canadian life insurance companies totaled more than $165 billion.[3]

Insurance companies are financial intermediaries that function in the economy as part of the financial services industry. A **financial intermediary** is an organization that helps to channel funds through an economy by accepting the surplus money of savers and supplying that money to borrowers who pay to use the money. The **financial services industry** is made up of various kinds of financial intermediaries that help consumers and business organizations save, borrow, invest, and otherwise manage money.

Insurance companies are among the most important financial intermediaries in North America. They make a significant contribution to the economic growth of the United States and Canada, both as investors in their economies and as employers. Life and health insurance companies invest their assets in other businesses and industries, as well as in mortgage loans. These investments help provide the funds that other businesses need to operate and grow and that individuals need to purchase homes. (See Figure 1-2, which illustrates how insurance companies invest their assets.) The life and health insurance industry is also a major employer in the United States and Canada, employing several million people.

The financial services industry has undergone profound changes in the past few decades. Historically, financial services were provided by various types of financial intermediaries, and the activities of each type of financial intermediary were distinct. In fact, legal restrictions separated the activities of financial intermediaries. Banks, as well as U.S. savings and loan institutions and Canadian trust companies, accepted customer deposits and made consumer loans. Investment products were offered by investment companies. Insurance companies provided insurance products.

Today, however, the distinctions between these financial institutions have blurred. In both Canada and the United States, laws have been changed so that each type of financial intermediary can now offer a wider variety of products. Banks now can sell investment products and insurance products, in addition to the usual checking and savings accounts. Insurance companies have begun to offer a wider variety

> **FAST FACT**
>
> In 1997, the insurance business in the United States employed 2.2 million persons. Over 100,000 people are employed by life and health insurers in Canada.[4]

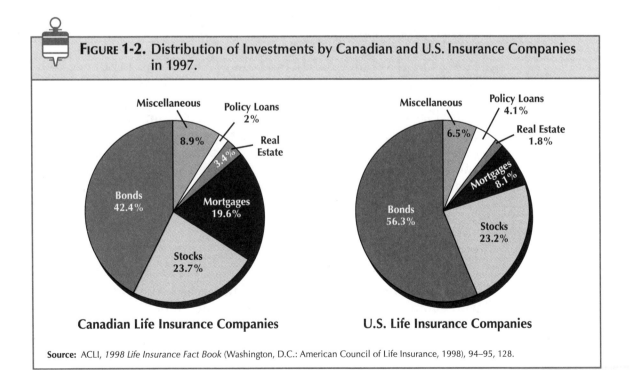

FIGURE 1-2. Distribution of Investments by Canadian and U.S. Insurance Companies in 1997.

Canadian Life Insurance Companies

Miscellaneous 8.9%
Policy Loans 2%
Real Estate 3.4%
Bonds 42.4%
Mortgages 19.6%
Stocks 23.7%

U.S. Life Insurance Companies

Miscellaneous 6.5%
Policy Loans 4.1%
Real Estate 1.8%
Mortgages 8.1%
Bonds 56.3%
Stocks 23.2%

Source: ACLI, *1998 Life Insurance Fact Book* (Washington, D.C.: American Council of Life Insurance, 1998), 94–95, 128.

of insurance and noninsurance products, such as savings plans, mortgage loans, and mutual funds. In short, financial intermediaries are competing with one another to provide a wide range of financial services to today's sophisticated consumers.

Overview of Life and Health Insurance Products

Life and health insurance companies market a variety of insurance and investment-type products. Throughout this text, we'll describe many of these products in detail. In this section, we give you a brief overview of life and health insurance products so that you can begin to understand how those products differ.

Individual and Group Insurance

Life and health insurance companies market insurance products to both individuals and groups. An ***individual insurance policy*** is an insurance policy that is issued to insure the life or health of a named person. Some individual policies also insure the person's immediate family or a second named person. We'll describe how individuals and businesses can both benefit from the purchase of individual life and health insurance.

A ***group insurance policy*** is a policy issued by an insurance company to a party that is purchasing insurance coverage for a specific group of people. For example, a group insurance policy is usually purchased by an employer to provide life or health insurance coverage to its employees and, sometimes, to the dependents of covered employees. Life and health insurance companies provide group insurance to various types of groups in addition to employer-employee groups. In Part 2 of this text, we describe the types of group insurance products that life and health companies market.

Life Insurance

A ***life insurance policy*** is a policy under which the insurance company promises to pay a benefit upon the death of the person who is insured. Life insurance is provided on both an individual and a group basis and is available under a variety of types of policies. We describe the following three major types of life insurance policies.

ZIGGY © 1984 ZIGGY AND FRIENDS, INC. Dist. by UNIVERSAL PRESS SYNDICATE.
Reprinted with permission. All rights reserved.

- **Term life insurance** provides a death benefit if the insured dies during a specified period. We describe individual term life insurance in Chapter 7.

- **Permanent life insurance** provides life insurance coverage throughout the insured's lifetime and also provides a savings element. As premiums are paid for these policies, an accumulated savings amount—known as the policy's *cash value*—gradually builds. A policy's cash value is a valuable asset that the policyowner can use in a number of ways. We describe permanent life insurance, including its savings element, in more detail in Chapters 8 and 11.

- **Endowment insurance** provides a policy benefit that is paid either when the insured dies or on a stated date if the insured lives until then. Endowment insurance has some characteristics of both term life insurance and permanent life insurance. Like term insurance, endowment insurance provides life insurance coverage for only a stated period of time. And like permanent life insurance, endowment insurance provides a savings element. We describe endowment insurance in Chapter 8.

In each case, the policy benefit is paid only if the policy is in force when a covered loss occurs. A policy remains *in force* and, thus, provides the specified insurance coverage as long as the required premiums are paid when due. In addition, each of these three types of life insurance products is available in a variety of forms.

Annuities and Investment Products

In addition to providing life insurance coverages, life insurance companies market various products that are designed to provide consumers with a way to provide themselves with periodic income benefits, especially retirement income benefits. An *annuity* is a series of periodic payments. For example, when the insured of a life insurance policy dies, a relatively large sum of money is often payable. Life insurance policy proceeds can be paid in the form of an annuity, over a period of time, rather than in a lump sum. An *annuity* can also be a contract under which an insurance company promises to make a series of periodic payments to a named individual in exchange for a premium or a series of premiums.

In addition to annuities, many insurance companies market various investment products to individuals and to groups. In Chapter 16, we describe individual annuities and investment products. We describe group retirement and pension plans in Chapter 17.

Health Insurance

A *health insurance policy* is a policy that provides protection against the risk of financial loss resulting from the insured person's sickness, accidental injury, or disability. The two major forms of health insurance coverage are as follows:

1. *Medical expense coverage* provides benefits to pay for the treatment of an insured's illnesses and injuries. In the United States, medical expense coverage is provided by various types of policies, which are identified and described in Figure 1-3. Canadian residents receive their medical expense coverage under governmental plans, and some people have supplemental coverages provided by commercial insurers.

2. *Disability income coverage* provides income replacement benefits to an insured who is unable to work because of sickness or injury.

Health insurance coverage is available to both individuals and groups and is provided by a variety of organizations and governmental programs in addition to being provided by commercial life and health

---

FIGURE 1-3. Types of Medical Expense Insurance Coverages Available in the United States.

Basic medical expense coverage provides separate benefits for each of the following specific types of covered medical care expenses:

- **Hospital expense coverage** provides benefits for specified hospital expenses such as room and board, medications, laboratory services, and other fees associated with a hospital stay.
- **Surgical expense coverage** provides benefits for the costs of inpatient and outpatient surgical procedures.
- **Physicians' expense coverage** provides benefits for charges associated with physicians' visits both in and out of the hospital.

Major medical insurance coverage provides substantial benefits for hospital and surgical expenses and physicians' fees.

The following types of **specified expense coverages** are also available to provide benefits for the costs of treating specified illnesses or for specified medical care expenses:

- **Long-term care coverage** provides medical and other services to insureds who, because of their advanced age or the effects of a serious illness or injury, need constant care in their own homes or in nursing homes.
- **Dental expense coverage** provides benefits for routine dental examinations, preventive work, and dental procedures needed to treat tooth decay and diseases of the teeth and jaw.
- **Prescription drug coverage** provides benefits for the purchase of drugs and medicines that are prescribed by a physician and are not available over-the-counter.
- **Vision care coverage** provides benefits for expenses incurred in obtaining eye examinations and corrective lenses.
- **Dread disease coverage** provides benefits for medical expenses incurred by an insured who has contracted a specified disease.
- **Critical illness coverage** provides benefits for medical expenses incurred by an insured who is suffering a critical illness that is specified in the policy.
- **Social insurance supplement coverage** provides benefits for medical care costs that are not covered under specified government health insurance programs, such as Medicare.

---

insurance companies. We'll describe individual and group health insurance in Part 2 of this text.

Other Providers of Life and Health Insurance

Most of our discussions in this text will relate to commercial life and health insurance companies. By that we mean corporations that are organized as stock or mutual insurance companies to provide life and/or health insurance coverages. But, in addition to insurance companies, an array of other organizations—public and private—provide life and health insurance.

Fraternal Benefit Societies

A *fraternal benefit society* is an organization formed to provide social, as well as insurance, benefits to its members. The members of such societies often share a common ethnic, religious, or vocational background, although membership in some societies is open to the general public. One of the legal requirements of being a fraternal benefit society is that the fraternal must have a representative form of government—the members must elect the officers of the fraternal society. Additionally, fraternals must operate through a lodge system whereby only lodge members and their families are permitted to own the fraternal society's insurance. In fact, applicants for insurance often become members of the society automatically once the society issues them a policy. Today, fraternal insurers in the United States and Canada hold more than $200 billion of in-force life insurance. (See Figure 1-1 for a graphic depiction of the amount of business fraternal benefit societies do compared to stock and mutual insurers.)

Banks

Most people in the United States do not think of banks as being providers of insurance. In certain instances, however, banks in the United States can sell insurance products. For example, U.S. banks have traditionally marketed mortgage or loan protection insurance to their loan customers. In addition, federal laws allow national banks to sell life insurance from branches located in towns of fewer than 5,000 people. Finally, in a few states, savings banks are permitted to sell what is known as *savings bank life insurance (SBLI)* and annuities to individuals and groups. These insurance products are generally sold over the counter by bank employees who are licensed to sell insurance. The maximum amount of SBLI that may be purchased by one person is defined by the laws of each state, and only people who live or work in one of these states are eligible to purchase SBLI.

> **FAST FACT**
>
> In 1997, savings banks had $46 billion of life insurance in force.[5]

Banks in Canada may own insurance companies, and banks are permitted to sell insurance subject to specific restrictions. Banks are permitted, for example, to sell credit life insurance from branch banks. (We describe credit life insurance in Chapter 7.) Branch bank employees, however, are not permitted to sell other types of life insurance unless they are members of a sales force that is separate from the bank's traditional sales force *and* they sell only insurance.

Governments

Federal, state, and provincial programs provide various health insurance and retirement income coverages to residents of the United States and Canada. We describe these government-sponsored programs in more detail later in the text. For now, you should know that in Canada most medical expense insurance is provided by government-sponsored programs, although many individuals are also covered under private plans that supplement the government programs. In the United States, although most health insurance coverage is provided by private health insurance plans, governmental programs provide health insurance coverages to eligible individuals.

Medical Care Plans

Various types of medical care plans provide health care benefits to individuals or groups either by (1) assuming coverage for insureds in exchange for a premium or (2) providing health care services on a prepaid basis. For example, *Blue Cross and Blue Shield plans* provide various medical expense coverages in exchange for the payment of premiums. A *health maintenance organization (HMO)* is an example of a health care organization that provides prepaid medical care services to its members. Later in the text, we describe the benefits provided by these and other health care organizations. Finally, a substantial number of employers in the United States and Canada serve as health insurance providers through their use of self-insured employee benefit plans.

Key Terms

profit	individual insurance policy
sole proprietorship	group insurance policy
partnership	life insurance policy
corporation	term life insurance
stock insurance company	permanent life insurance
mutual insurance company	endowment insurance
home office	annuity
regional office	health insurance policy
field office	medical expense coverage
financial intermediary	disability income coverage
financial services industry	fraternal benefit society

Other Important Terms

business
partners
stock
stockholders
stockholder dividends
policy dividends
mutualization
demutualization
head office

branch office
agency office
cash value
in-force policy
savings bank life insurance
    (SBLI)
Blue Cross and Blue Shield plans
health maintenance
    organization (HMO)

Endnotes

1. ACLI, *1998 Life Insurance Fact Book* (Washington, D.C.: American Council of Life Insurance, 1998), 9, 128.

2. HIAA, *Source Book of Health Insurance Data* (Washington, D.C.: Health Insurance Association of America, 1998), 10.

3. ACLI, 91, 128.

4. ACLI, 58; CLHIA, *Canadian Life and Health Insurance Facts* (Toronto: Canadian Life and Health Insurance Association Inc., 1998), 25.

5. ACLI, 58.

CHAPTER 2

Regulation of the Insurance Industry

After reading this chapter, you should be able to

- Identify the primary goals of insurance regulation in the United States and Canada and describe the insurance regulatory systems in both countries

- Define the purpose of the National Association of Insurance Commissioners (NAIC)

- Identify the purpose of the Canadian Life and Health Insurance Association (CLHIA) and define its role in regulating insurance in Canada

Every business that operates in the United States and Canada must comply with a host of applicable laws. For example, life and health insurance companies employ large numbers of people. As employers, insurance companies must comply with dozens of federal, state, and provincial laws that govern all aspects of the workplace, from employment and hiring practices to workplace safety. Like other businesses, insurance companies may be required to pay federal and local taxes and to comply with local laws, such as zoning ordinances. Dozens of other types of laws apply to all businesses, including life and health insurance companies.

In addition to employing many people, insurance companies protect millions of individuals against economic loss and offer them opportunities to save and invest money. Because the financial health of insurance providers is of such importance to so many people, insurers occupy a special position of public trust. As a result, the insurance industry is subject to regulation designed specifically to safeguard the public interest in insurance companies. In both Canada and the United States, the primary goals of insurance regulation are to ensure that insurance companies

- Remain *solvent*—that they are able to meet their debts and to pay policy benefits when they come due

- Conduct their businesses fairly and ethically

The two countries, however, have developed somewhat different regulatory systems to achieve these goals. The different regulatory systems emerged because of differences in how the United States and Canada have divided powers between the federal government and the state or provincial governments.

Insurance Regulation in the United States

In the United States, constitutional authority to regulate insurance belongs to the federal government, under its authority to regulate interstate commerce. However, the state governments have primary authority to regulate the insurance industry. In enacting the federal *McCarran-Ferguson Act,* or *Public Law 15,* the U.S. Congress agreed to leave insurance regulation to the states as long as Congress considered state regulation to be adequate. Congress retained the right to enact insurance legislation if it decides that state regulation is inadequate or not in the public interest, and a number of federal laws regulate various aspects of insurance.

Because each state has the power to regulate the operation of insurance companies within the state, regulation varies from state to state. This lack of uniformity has led many to argue that the industry should be subject to federal regulation, which would ensure uniform regulation across the country. Many others argue that state regulation functions well and that moving responsibility to the federal government would not improve the regulation of insurance. For now, this power remains with the states, except in the few situations that we describe later in the chapter.

State Regulation

Each state has enacted a variety of laws to regulate insurance companies and the products they sell. In addition, each state has established an administrative agency, typically known as the *state insurance department,* that is under the direction of an *insurance commissioner* or a *state superintendent of insurance.* The state insurance department is charged with ensuring that insurers operating within the state comply with all state insurance laws and regulations.

In most respects, the various state insurance laws are similar because they are based on model laws developed by the ***National Association of Insurance Commissioners (NAIC).*** The NAIC is a nongovernmental organization consisting of the insurance commissioners or superintendents of the various state insurance departments. The NAIC's primary function is to promote uniformity of state regulation by developing model bills and regulations that each state is encouraged to pass. A ***model bill*** is a sample law that state insurance regulators are encouraged to use as a basis for state insurance laws. We describe some specific model bills throughout this text.

As we noted in Chapter 1, insurance companies are required by law to operate as corporations. In the United States, a business becomes a corporation by complying with the incorporation laws of one state. When the company's organizers meet the requirements for incorporation, the state issues a *certificate of incorporation* or *corporate charter* by which the business gains its legal existence as a corporation. Thereafter, the corporation must govern itself and operate in accordance with that state's laws. State laws impose requirements on matters such as the minimum number of directors a corporation must have, the duties of directors and officers, and the rights of shareholders.

Before an insurance company begins conducting business and selling insurance products within a given state, the company must obtain from the state insurance department a *certificate of authority* or *license* that grants the insurer the right to conduct an insurance business in that state. The states impose a variety of licensing requirements that are designed primarily to ensure that insurance companies are financially able to meet their obligations to pay policy benefits.

Solvency Regulation

Each state has enacted laws designed to ensure that insurance companies operating within the state are solvent. To achieve that goal, the states impose minimum limits on the amount of the insurer's assets, liabilities, capital, and surplus. These amounts represent components in the company's basic accounting equation under which the company's assets must equal its liabilities and owners' equity.

Let's look at an insurance company's basic accounting equation.

Basic accounting equation:

Assets = Liabilities + Owners' equity

- *Assets* are all things of value owned by the company. Examples of assets include cash and investments. The states regulate the types of investments insurance companies can make to assure that those investments are conservative and prudent. The states also impose requirements on how insurers must determine the value of their assets.

- *Liabilities* are the company's debts and future obligations. A large portion of an insurance company's liabilities consists of the company's *policy reserves,* which represent the amount the insurer estimates it will need to pay policy benefits as they come due. The states impose requirements on the methods that insurers use to calculate the amount of their policy reserves. (Reserves are described in more detail in Chapter 6.)

- *Owners' equity* is the difference between the amount of the company's assets and the amount of its liabilities, and it represents the owners' financial interest in the company. Owners' equity in a stock insurance company consists of the company's capital and surplus. In this context, *capital* is the amount of money invested in the company by its owners. *Surplus* is the amount by which the company's assets exceed its liabilities and capital. Because a mutual insurer does not issue stock, it has no capital, and, therefore, owners' equity in a mutual company consists only of its surplus.

The states oversee the financial condition of insurance companies by reviewing an accounting report, known as the *Annual Statement,* which each insurer prepares each calendar year and files with the insurance department in each state in which it operates. The NAIC has developed an Annual Statement form that is accepted by all states so that an insurer can file the same form in all the states in which it operates.

In addition, state regulators conduct an on-site examination of each insurance company every three to five years. In such a periodic examination, state regulators physically check the insurer's business records. The NAIC has developed an organized system of on-site examinations to coordinate this function between the states so as to avoid duplication of effort by the various states.

Relatively few insurance companies become financially unsound. When such a situation does occur, the state insurance commissioners have the authority to take certain actions. If a **domestic insurer**—an insurer incorporated by the state—becomes financially unsound, the insurance commissioner can take steps to either rehabilitate or liquidate the company. In other words, if the company's finances can be turned around, the commissioner will try to rehabilitate it. If the company is too financially unsound, the commissioner may declare the company insolvent and act to liquidate—dissolve—the corporation. When a **foreign insurer**—an insurer incorporated under the laws of another state—becomes financially unsound, the insurance commissioner has authority to revoke or suspend the insurer's license to operate in the state.

Finally, all states have taken steps to protect policyowners and beneficiaries of life and health insurance companies that become financially unsound. Each state has established a guaranty association composed of the life and health insurance companies operating within the state. A **life and health guaranty association** is an organization that operates under the supervision of the state insurance commissioner to protect policyowners, insureds, beneficiaries, and specified others against losses that result from the financial impairment or insolvency of a life or health insurer that operates in the state. The financial obligations that guaranty associations cover for insolvent insurers vary from state to state. Typically, a guaranty association provides funds to guarantee payment for certain policies up to stated dollar limits, such as those described in Insight 2-1. In some cases, a policyowner may have the option to obtain a replacement policy. To pay these obligations, the guaranty association requires all life and health insurers operating in the state to pay money into a guaranty fund.

Regulation of Market Conduct

Each state has enacted **market conduct laws** that regulate how insurance companies conduct their business within the state. State insurance regulators perform periodic market conduct examinations

Insight 2-1. Oregon's Life and Health Insurance Guaranty Association.

The Oregon Life and Health Insurance Guaranty Association is typical of state guaranty funds. When a life or health insurer authorized to conduct business in Oregon becomes insolvent—unable to pay the costs of doing business—and is liquidated by a court order, the guaranty fund pays the claims of Oregon residents according to the terms of their in-force policies issued by the insolvent insurer. The coverage limits provided by Oregon's life and health guaranty fund are as follows:

Type of Insurance	Limits of Coverage
Death benefits	$300,000
Life insurance cash value	$100,000
Present value of annuity benefits	$100,000
Health and disability benefits	$100,000
Maximum per individual per insolvency	$300,000

Source: Oregon Department of Insurance website at http://www.cbs.state.or.us/external/ins/docs/choosing.htm#insolvent.

of insurers similar to the financial examinations described in the last section. In this section, we briefly describe how the states regulate (1) the marketing of insurance products and (2) policy forms.

Marketing of Insurance Products. We mentioned previously that insurance companies must be licensed by each state in which they operate. Every state also requires that before an individual begins to sell life or health insurance within the state, he[3] must be licensed by the state. The licensing process helps ensure that sales agents are reputable and knowledgeable about the insurance products they sell. (See Appendix A, which is an example of a state insurance license application developed by the NAIC.) In order to obtain an agent's license, a prospective agent must

- Be sponsored for licensing by a licensed insurance company

- Complete approved educational course work and/or pass a written examination

- Provide assurance that he is of reputable character

Agents' licenses typically must be renewed each year, and many states require agents to periodically participate in continuing education courses in order to renew their licenses. Continuing education is intended to improve the professionalism of agents and help them keep pace with a rapidly changing industry. A state may revoke or suspend an agent's license if she engages in certain unethical practices that violate the state's insurance laws. In general, most such unethical practices involve some form of misrepresentation in which the agent deliberately makes false or misleading statements to induce a customer to purchase insurance.

Most states prohibit insurers from engaging in a variety of other practices that are considered to be unfair trade practices. For example, state laws regulate the form and content of insurance advertisements to ensure that consumers are not misled about the features or limitations in advertised insurance policies.

Policy Forms. A *policy form* is a standardized contract form that shows the terms, conditions, benefits, and ownership rights of a particular insurance product. Each state regulates the policy forms that insurers may use within the state. An insurance company, therefore, usually must file with the state insurance department a copy of each policy form it plans to use and must receive the state insurance department's approval before using the form in the state. The insurance department reviews the policy form to ensure that it contains all required policy provisions and is not unfair or deceptive in any way. (We describe these required policy provisions in Chapter 10.)

Many states also impose readability requirements on insurance policies in order to reduce the amount of technical jargon and legal language included in those policies. When insurers simplify the language used in their insurance policies, consumers are better able to understand those policies. (See Figure 2-1 for an example of the "before" and "after" versions of a life insurance policy that was simplified to improve its readability.) A policy form that does not meet a state's readability requirements will not be approved for use in that state.

Federal Regulation

Although the states conduct most insurance company regulation, insurance companies also are subject to certain federal laws. One of the foremost areas in which federal regulation applies to insurance companies concerns the sale of investment-type insurance products. Businesses and individuals that sell securities must comply with federal securities laws, which are enforced by the federal *Securities and Exchange Commission (SEC)*. A *security* is a document or certificate representing either an ownership interest in a business (for example, a share of stock), or an obligation of indebtedness owed by a business, government, or agency (a bond, for example). The SEC has determined that some insurance products—notably variable life insurance and

FIGURE 2-1. "Before" and "After" Versions of a Life Insurance Policy to Improve Its Readability.

Compare the wording in the following clauses selected from an older policy and the same policy revised for readability.

Example Clause #1:

Before Revision	Revised for Readability

Before Revision

GRACE PERIOD: A grace period of 31 days will be granted for the payment of each premium falling due after the first premium, during which grace period the policy shall continue in force.

Revised for Readability

What Happens if Premiums Are Paid Late? — This policy stays in effect for 31 days after a premium is due and unpaid. These 31 days are called the grace period.

What Happens if a Premium is Not Paid? — If a premium is not paid by the end of the grace period, the policy terminates.

Example Clause #2:

Before Revision

REINSTATEMENT: If any renewal premium be not paid within the time granted the Insured for payment, a subsequent acceptance of premium by the Company or by any agent duly authorized by the Company to accept such premium, without requiring in connection therewith an application for reinstatement, shall reinstate the policy; provided, however, that if the Company or such agent requires an application for reinstatement and issues a conditional receipt for the premium tendered, the policy will be reinstated upon approval of such application by the Company or, lacking such approval, upon the 45th day following the date of such conditional receipt unless the Company has previously notified the Insured in writing of its disapproval of such application. The reinstated policy shall cover only loss resulting from such accidental injury as may be sustained after the date of reinstatement and loss due to such sickness as may begin more than 10 days after such date. In all other respects the Insured and Company shall have the same rights thereunder as they had under the policy immediately before the due date of the defaulted premium, subject to any provisions endorsed hereon or attached hereto in connection with the reinstatement.

Revised for Readability

Reinstating the Policy — We may allow you to reinstate a policy that has terminated for nonpayment of premiums. Your policy may be reinstated in one of the following ways:

- You may offer to pay the overdue premiums and the next premium due. If we (or one of our agents) accept your payment without asking for a reinstatement application, your policy is reinstated.

- If we (or one of our agents) ask for an application, you will be given a conditional receipt for your payment. Your policy will then be reinstated if and when we approve the application. If we do not act on the application, your policy will be reinstated 45 days after you submit the application and payment.

When Coverage Resumes — Coverage for accidental injuries resumes immediately upon reinstatement. We will provide benefits for treatment of sickness that begins more than 10 days after reinstatement.

Rights After Reinstatement — Our and your rights after reinstatement will be the same as before the due date of the unpaid premium. This is subject to any provisions we endorse on or attach to the policy.

Source: Information adapted with permission of Liberty Life Insurance Company.

variable annuities—are investment products as well as life insurance products and, thus, are subject to federal regulation. Thus, insurers that issue these variable products must comply with both federal securities laws and state insurance laws. Before selling these investment-type insurance products, a sales agent must be registered with the *National Association of Securities Dealers (NASD)* as a registered representative in accordance with federal securities laws; these sales agents must also be licensed by the state as insurance agents. To be a *registered representative,* an individual must complete a course of study and pass an examination. We describe variable life insurance and variable annuities later in the text.

The federal government has also enacted numerous laws that regulate employee benefit plans. As a result, group insurance plans that certain employers provide for their employees must comply with the provisions of these laws. For example, employee benefit plans must comply with the terms of the Employee Retirement Income Security Act (ERISA). We describe these federal laws in later chapters.

Insurance Regulation in Canada

Unlike a U.S. insurance company, a Canadian insurance company may be incorporated under the authority of either the federal government or one of the provincial governments.[4] Most Canadian companies are federally incorporated. However, because both levels of government are authorized to incorporate insurance companies, both levels have the corresponding authority to regulate the financial soundness of insurance companies. In addition, each provincial government regulates how insurers conduct business within the province.

Federal Regulation

The **Insurance Companies Act** is the primary federal law that governs specified insurance companies operating in Canada. The companies that must comply with the Insurance Companies Act are (1) federally incorporated insurers, (2) insurers incorporated in countries other than Canada—known as **foreign insurers,** and (3) specified provincially incorporated insurers.[5] The Act includes a number of provisions designed to ensure that all companies governed by the Act are solvent. Each insurer must maintain adequate capital and must maintain adequate assets from which to pay policy benefits. In addition, the Act states the types of investments that federally regulated insurance companies may make.

The Act also governs how a federally incorporated insurance company must operate. For example, the Act contains provisions that regulate the duties and obligations of the corporation's directors. Note that only federally incorporated insurers must comply with these sections of the Act. Foreign companies and provincially incorporated insurers must comply with similar laws enacted by the jurisdictions in which they were incorporated.

A federal agency, the *Office of the Superintendent of Financial Institutions (OSFI)*, under the direction of the *superintendent of financial institutions*, is responsible for overseeing all financial institutions in Canada, including life and health insurance companies. Every insurance company that is subject to federal regulation must file an ***Annual Return*** with the OSFI; this document provides the same general types of information about the filing company as does the Annual Statement filed by companies in the United States. The Insurance Companies Act requires the OSFI to examine the financial condition of each federally regulated insurer periodically; an examination is required at least every three years but can be more often if the superintendent believes an earlier examination is necessary.

The Insurance Companies Act contains additional provisions that describe how the superintendent may take control of an insurance company if the company appears to be financially unsound or has endangered policyowners' rights. If necessary, the superintendent may manage the company's business to ensure that policyowners are protected. If rehabilitating an insurer is not possible, the superintendent may declare the company insolvent and obtain a court order to liquidate the insurer.

The Canadian life and health insurance industry has implemented a plan to protect Canadian consumers against loss of benefits in the event a life or health insurance company becomes insolvent. Protection is provided by the ***Canadian Life and Health Insurance Compensation Corporation (CompCorp),*** which is a federally incorporated, nonprofit company established by the ***Canadian Life and Health Insurance Association (CLHIA).*** The CLHIA is an industry association of life and health insurance companies operating in Canada. Membership in CompCorp is open to all insurers licensed to sell life or health insurance in Canada, and most provinces require life and health insurers to become members of CompCorp in order to be licensed to do business within the province. If an insurer that is a member of CompCorp is declared insolvent, CompCorp guarantees payment under covered policies up to certain specified limits. CompCorp collects money from all its member companies to fund these guaranteed payments. Policyowners of an insolvent insurer also have the option of obtaining replacement policies within stated limits through CompCorp.

Provincial Regulation

Each province and territory has enacted laws to regulate insurance businesses conducted within the province or territory. In most respects, these laws are similar throughout Canada, but some differences do exist, especially between the laws of Quebec and the laws of the other provinces and territories. Many of these differences result from the different legal systems on which provincial laws are based. Quebec law is based on a *civil law system*; all other jurisdictions' laws are based on a *common law system.*[6] Throughout this text, we point out the significant differences that exist between Quebec insurance laws and the laws in the common law jurisdictions of Canada.

Each province has established an administrative agency to enforce the province's insurance laws and regulations. Typically, this agency is known as the **Office of the Superintendent of Insurance** and operates under the direction of an individual known as the *superintendent of insurance.*

The various provincial superintendents of insurance have voluntarily formed a collective body known as the **Canadian Council of Insurance Regulators (CCIR).** One purpose of the CCIR is to discuss insurance issues and to recommend uniform insurance legislation to the provinces. As we describe in a later chapter, provincial regulation of life and health insurance policies is fairly uniform because most provinces have enacted laws based on model legislation recommended by the CCIR. In addition, the CCIR has adopted **Superintendents' Guidelines,** a series of recommendations that concern a variety of matters. These guidelines were developed in cooperation with the insurance industry, working through its industry association, the CLHIA. In addition, the CLHIA from time to time issues **CLHIA Guidelines** concerning various matters. As members of the CLHIA, insurers are expected to abide by all Superintendents' Guidelines and CLHIA Guidelines, even though Guidelines do not have the force of law.

As we've noted, provincial regulation of insurance focuses on (1) overseeing the solvency of provincially incorporated insurance companies and (2) regulating how all insurance companies carry on business within the province. In the next section, we briefly describe both of these aspects of provincial insurance regulation.

Solvency Regulation

Each province has enacted legislation designed to safeguard the solvency of insurers. Among other things, these laws require the Office of the Superintendent of Insurance to supervise companies that were incorporated by the province and to examine those companies periodically. In addition, in order to operate within a province, an insurance company must first obtain a license from the province. Most of the licensing requirements seek to ensure that insurance companies are financially able to provide the benefits they promise to pay when they issue insurance policies.

To avoid duplication of solvency regulation, the provinces have agreed that provincially incorporated companies generally will be supervised by the province in which the insurer was incorporated. Furthermore, the provinces typically rely on the federal government to oversee the solvency of federally incorporated companies and foreign companies. The federal government has also agreed to supervise companies incorporated by some of the smaller provinces that do not have the resources to supervise insurers adequately. Each province, however, retains the right to supervise the operations of any insurer that operates within that province.

Regulation of Market Conduct

Each of the Canadian provinces regulates the operations of insurance companies within its borders to protect policyowners and ensure that companies operate fairly. This provincial regulation is very similar to state regulation of insurance company operations in the United States.

Provincial laws govern many aspects of the insurance policy forms that are issued within each province. Policies, for example, must contain certain provisions. Unlike requirements in the United States, however, the provinces do not require that all policy forms be filed with provincial regulators before being issued. Insurers are required to file policy forms in only two situations: (1) as a condition of obtaining a license to conduct an insurance business within the province and (2) before marketing a variable life insurance contract in the province. In actual practice, most insurers regularly file all their policy forms with the provincial superintendent of insurance.

The provinces also regulate many of the marketing activities of insurance companies. For example, many provinces have enacted laws to prohibit insurers from engaging in unfair trade practices, such as the use of false or misleading advertisements. In addition, every individual who plans to sell life and health insurance products in a province must first be licensed as an agent by that province. Agents' licensing requirements are similar to requirements in the United States and are designed to ensure that agents are knowledgeable about the products they sell and are of reputable character. The province may revoke or suspend an agent's license if the agent engages in unethical conduct in violation of provincial laws and regulations.

Key Terms

solvent
McCarran-Ferguson Act
state insurance department
National Association of
  Insurance Commissioners
  (NAIC)
model bill
assets
liabilities
policy reserves
owners' equity
capital
surplus
Annual Statement
domestic insurer
foreign insurer
life and health guaranty
  association

market conduct laws
policy form
Insurance Companies Act
foreign insurer
Annual Return
Canadian Life and Health
  Insurance Compensation
  Corporation (CompCorp)
Canadian Life and Health
  Insurance Association
  (CLHIA)
Office of the Superintendent of
  Insurance
Canadian Council of Insurance
  Regulators (CCIR)
Superintendents' Guidelines
CLHIA Guidelines

Other Important Terms

Public Law 15
insurance commissioner
state superintendent of
  insurance
certificate of incorporation
corporate charter
certificate of authority
license
Securities and Exchange
  Commission (SEC)
security

National Association of
  Securities Dealers (NASD)
registered representative
Office of the Superintendent of
  Financial Institutions (OSFI)
superintendent of financial
  institutions
civil law system
common law system
superintendent of insurance

Endnotes

1. ACLI, *1997 Life Insurance Fact Book* (Washington, D.C.: American Council of Life Insurance, 1997), 118.
2. Ibid., 120, 122.

3. Rather than using both the male and female pronouns (he or she, him or her, his or hers), we will alternate using male pronoun forms and female pronoun forms throughout this text.

4. Throughout this text, the term "province" refers also to the two Canadian territories.

5. Five insurers incorporated under the laws of the province of Nova Scotia are subject to federal regulation.

6. A *civil law system* is a legal system in which the laws have been codified into a relatively comprehensive civil code. A *common law system* is a legal system based on the common law of England. For a description of the differences between a common law system and a civil law system, see Harriett E. Jones, *Canadian Life and Health Insurance Law* (Atlanta: LOMA, 1992), 8–9.

CHAPTER 3

Introduction to Risk and Insurance

After reading this chapter, you should be able to

- Distinguish between speculative risk and pure risk

- List several ways to manage financial risk

- Identify the five characteristics of insurable risk

- Define insurable interest and determine in a given situation whether the insurable interest requirement is met

- Define antiselection

All insurance provides protection against some of the economic consequences of loss. Thus, insurance meets part of individuals' and businesses' need for economic security. The insurance industry constantly designs, alters, and updates insurance products to meet various aspects of this need. Despite these product changes, the underlying purpose of insurance products remains the same: to provide protection against the risk of financial loss. In order to understand insurance and how it works, you need to understand the concept of risk and which types of risks are insurable.

The Concept of Risk

Risk exists when there is uncertainty about the future. Both individuals and businesses experience two kinds of risk—speculative risk and pure risk. *Speculative risk* involves three possible outcomes: loss, gain, or no change. For example, when you purchase shares of stock, you are speculating that the value of the stock will rise and that you will earn a profit on your investment. At the same time, you know that the value of the stock could fall and that you could lose some or all of the money you invested. Finally, you know that the value of the stock could remain the same—you might not lose money, but you might not make a profit.

Pure risk involves no possibility of gain; either a loss occurs or no loss occurs. An example of pure risk is the possibility that you may become disabled. If you are unable to work, you will experience a financial loss. If, on the other hand, you never become disabled, then you will incur no loss from that risk. This possibility of financial loss without the possibility of gain—pure risk—is the only kind of risk that can be insured. The purpose of insurance is to compensate for financial loss, not to provide an opportunity for financial gain.

| EXAMPLE | Marie and Joseph Patterson are both employed full time. They have used $10,000 of their savings to purchase stock |

in a growing software company. They believe that the software company is strong and that their investment will soon be worth a lot more than $10,000.

| ANALYSIS | The Pattersons' investment in a software company is an example of speculative risk. As a result of their investment, the Pattersons may gain financially or they may lose part or all of their investment. The Pattersons are also faced with the pure risk that one or both of them could die and their family would lose the income that they now earn. |

Risk Management

We are surrounded by risks. We take risks when we travel, when we engage in recreational activities, even when we breathe. Some risks are significant; others are not. When we decide to leave an umbrella at home, we take the risk that we might get wet in a rain shower. Such a risk is insignificant. But what about the risks in the following situations?

- Ryan McGill is a 23-year-old single man who is working his way through college with part-time jobs. What if he becomes ill and requires a long hospital stay and expensive medical treatment?

- Danielle and John Peret are working parents of two school-aged children. What if either Danielle or John becomes disabled and cannot work to support the family?

- Jack and Jean Grayson own and manage a convenience store. What if a fire damages their building?

- The Widget Software Development Company's product development process depends on the genius of two employees who are computer "whizzes." What happens to the company if one or both of them dies?

- Catherine Walker is an artist who supports herself by selling her artwork. What happens when she retires and her income is no longer sufficient to meet her economic needs?

In each situation, the individual, family, or business can use risk management to control the level of financial risk it faces. Risk management involves identifying and assessing the financial risks we face.[1] In order to eliminate or reduce our exposure to a specific financial risk, we can choose any of at least four options: (1) avoid the risk, (2) control the risk, (3) accept the risk, and (4) transfer the risk.

Avoiding Risk

The first, and perhaps most obvious, method of managing risk is simply to avoid risk altogether. We can avoid the risk of personal injury that may result from an airplane crash by not riding in an airplane, and we can avoid the risk of financial loss in the stock market by not investing in it. Sometimes, however, avoiding risk is not effective or practical.

Controlling Risk

We can try to control risk by taking steps to prevent or reduce losses. For instance, Jack and Jean Grayson in one of our earlier examples could reduce the likelihood of a fire in their convenience store by banning smoking in their building and not storing boxes or papers near the building. In addition, the Graysons could install smoke detectors and a sprinkler system in their building to lessen the extent of damage likely to result from a fire. In these ways, the Graysons are attempting to control risk by reducing the likelihood of a loss and lessening the severity of a potential loss.

Accepting Risk

A third method of managing risk is to accept, or retain, risk. Simply stated, to accept a risk is to assume all financial responsibility for that risk. Sometimes, as in the case of an insignificant risk—losing an umbrella—the financial loss is not great enough to warrant much concern. We assume the cost of replacing the umbrella ourselves. Some people consciously choose to accept more significant risks. For instance, a couple like Danielle and John Peret from one of the previous examples may decide not to purchase disability income insurance because they believe they can just reduce their standard of living if one of them becomes disabled.

Individuals and businesses sometimes decide to accept total responsibility for a given financial risk rather than purchasing insurance to cover the risk. In this situation, the person or business is said to self-insure against the risk. *Self-insurance* is a risk-management technique by which a person or business accepts financial responsibility for losses associated with specific risks. For example, many employers provide medical expense benefits to their employees. An employer can self-insure such a benefit plan by either setting aside money to pay employees' medical expenses or paying those expenses out of its current income.

Another option is that individuals and businesses can accept only part of a risk. For instance, an employer can partially self-insure a medical expense benefit plan by paying its employees' medical expenses up to a stated amount and buying insurance to cover all expenses in excess of that stated amount. Many employers now use self-insurance to fund their employees' health insurance plans. We describe self-insurance more fully when we describe group health insurance in Part 2 of this text.

Transferring Risk

Transferring risk is a fourth method of risk management. When you transfer risk to another party, you are shifting the financial responsibility for that risk to the other party, generally in exchange for a fee. The most common way for individuals, families, and businesses to transfer risk is to purchase insurance coverage.

When an insurance company agrees to provide a person or a business with insurance coverage, the insurer issues an insurance policy. The **policy** is a written document that contains the terms of the agreement between the insurance company and the owner of the policy. The agreement is a legally enforceable contract under which the insurance company agrees to pay a certain amount of money—known as the **policy benefit,** or the *policy proceeds*—when a specific loss occurs provided that the insurer has received a specified amount of money, called the **premium.**

In general, individuals and businesses can purchase insurance policies to cover three types of risk—property damage risk, liability risk, and personal risk:

- *Property damage risk* includes the risk of economic loss to your automobile, home, or personal belongings due to accident, theft, fire, or natural disaster. *Property insurance* provides a benefit if insured items are damaged or lost because of various specified perils, such as fire, theft, or accident.

- *Liability risk* includes the risk of economic loss resulting from your being held responsible for harming others or their property. For example, you can be held liable for damage you cause to another person's vehicle in an automobile accident. A business can be held liable for injury to an individual who slips and falls while walking through the business establishment. *Liability insurance* provides a benefit payable on behalf of a covered party who is legally responsible for unintentionally harming others or their property. Property insurance and liability insurance (also referred to as *property and casualty insurance*) are commonly marketed together in one policy. Insurers that sell insurance policies to provide financial security from property damage risk and liability risk are known as *property and casualty insurers* or *property and liability insurers.*

- **Personal risk** includes the risk of economic loss associated with death, poor health, and outliving one's savings. Life and health insurers sell insurance policies to provide financial security from personal risk; in this book we will address the transfer of personal risk to life and health insurers. Both individuals and businesses purchase life and health insurance policies to obtain the financial security provided by these products.

Managing Personal Risks Through Insurance

You may wonder how an insurance company can afford to be financially responsible for the economic risks of its insureds. Insurers use a concept known as risk pooling. With risk pooling, individuals who face the uncertainty of a particular economic loss—for example, the loss of income because of a disability—transfer this risk to an insurance company. Insurance companies know that not everyone who is issued a policy to cover the risk of economic loss caused by disability will suffer a disability. In reality, only a small percentage of the individuals who purchase this type of insurance will actually become disabled at some time during the period of insurance coverage. By collecting premiums from all individuals and businesses that wish to transfer the financial risk of disability, insurers spread the cost of the few losses that are expected to occur among all the insured persons. Insurance, then, provides protection against the risk of economic loss by applying a simple principle:

> If the economic losses that actually result from a given peril, such as disability, can be shared by large numbers of people who are all subject to the risk of such losses *and* the probability of loss is relatively small for each person, then the cost to each person will be relatively small.

Characteristics of Insurable Risks

Insurance products are designed in accordance with some basic principles that define which risks are insurable. In order for a risk—a potential loss—to be considered insurable, it must have certain characteristics:

1. The loss must occur by chance.

2. The loss must be definite.

3. The loss must be significant.

4. The loss rate must be predictable.

5. The loss must not be catastrophic to the insurer.

These five basic characteristics define an insurable risk and form the foundation of the business of insurance. A potential loss that does not have these characteristics generally is not considered to be an insurable risk.

The Loss Must Occur by Chance

In order for a potential loss to be insurable, the element of chance must be present. The loss should be caused either by an unexpected event or by an event that is not intentionally caused by the person covered by the insurance. For example, people cannot generally control whether they will become seriously ill; as a result, insurers can offer health insurance policies to provide economic protection against financial losses caused by the chance event that an insured person will become ill and incur medical expenses.

When this principle of loss is applied in its strictest sense to life insurance, an apparent problem arises: death is certain to occur. The timing of an individual's death, however, is usually out of the individual's control. Therefore, although the event being insured against—death—is a certain event rather than a chance event, the timing of that event usually occurs by chance.

The Loss Must Be Definite

For most types of insurance, an insurable loss must be definite in terms of *time* and *amount*. In other words, the insurer must be able to determine *when* to pay policy benefits and *how much* those benefits should be. Death, illness, disability, and old age are generally identifiable conditions. The amount of economic loss resulting from these conditions, however, can be subject to interpretation.

One of the important terms of the contractual agreement between the insurance company and the owner of an insurance policy is the amount of policy benefit that will be payable if a covered loss occurs while the policy is in force. Depending on the way in which a policy states the amount of the policy benefit, every insurance policy can be classified as being either a contract of indemnity or a valued contract.

A *contract of indemnity* is an insurance policy under which the amount of the policy benefit payable for a covered loss is based on the actual amount of financial loss that results from the loss, as determined at the time of loss. The policy states that the amount of the benefit is equal to the amount of the covered financial loss or a maximum amount stated in the contract, whichever is *less*. When the owner of such a contract submits a *claim*—a request for payment under the terms of the policy—the benefit paid by the insurance company will not be greater than the actual amount of the financial loss.

Many types of health insurance policies pay a benefit based on the actual cost of a person's covered medical expenses and, as such, are contracts of indemnity. For example, assume that Bailey Smythe is insured by a health insurance policy which states the maximum amount payable to cover Bailey's medical expenses while he is hospitalized. If Bailey is hospitalized and his actual hospital expenses are less than that maximum amount, the insurer will *not* pay the stated maximum; instead, the insurer will pay a sum that is based on the actual amount of Bailey's hospital bill. Property and liability insurance policies are also contracts of indemnity.

A *valued contract* specifies the amount of the benefit that will be payable when a covered loss occurs, regardless of the actual amount of the loss that was incurred. Most life insurance policies state the amount of the policy benefit that will be payable if the insured person dies while the policy is in force. For example, if a woman buys a $50,000 insurance policy on her life, the $50,000 death benefit is listed in the policy. The amount of the death benefit is called the policy's *face amount* or *face value* because this amount is generally listed on the face, or first, page of the policy. Some life insurance policies provide that the amount of the death benefit may change over the life of the policy. These policies are still considered valued contracts because changes in the amount of the death benefit are based on factors that are not directly related to the amount of the actual loss that will result from the insured's death.

The Loss Must Be Significant

As described earlier, insignificant losses, like the loss of an umbrella, are not normally insured. The administrative expense of paying benefits when a very small loss occurs would drive the cost for such insurance protection so high in relation to the amount of the potential loss that most people would find the protection unaffordable.

On the other hand, some losses would cause financial hardship to most people and are considered to be insurable. For example, a person injured in an accident may lose a significant amount of income if he is unable to work. Insurance coverage is available to protect against such a potential loss.

The Loss Rate Must Be Predictable

In order to provide a specific type of insurance coverage, an insurer must be able to predict the probable rate of loss—the *loss rate*—that the people insured by the coverage will experience. To predict the loss rate for a given group of insureds, the insurer must predict the number and timing of covered losses that will occur in that group of insureds. An insurer predicts the loss rate for a group of insureds so that it can determine the proper premium amount to charge the owner of each policy.

No one can predict the losses that a specific person will experience. We do not know when a specific person will die, become disabled, or need hospitalization. However, insurers can predict with a fairly high degree of accuracy the number of people in a given large group who will die or become disabled or need hospitalization during a given period of time.

These predictions of future losses are based on the concept that, even though individual events—such as the death of a particular person—occur randomly, we can use observations of past events to determine the likelihood—or *probability*—that a given event will occur in the future. An important concept that helps assure us of the accuracy of our predictions about the probability of an event occurring is the law of large numbers.

> The *law of large numbers* states that, typically, the more times we observe a particular event, the more likely it is that our observed results will approximate the "true" probability that the event will occur.

For example, if you toss an ordinary coin, there is a 50-50 probability that it will land with the heads side up; this is a calculable probability. Four, or even a dozen, tosses might not give the result of an equal or approximately equal number of heads and tails. If you tossed the coin 1,000 times, though, you could expect a result of approximately 50 percent heads and 50 percent tails to occur. The more often you toss the coin, the more likely it is that you will observe an approximately equal proportion of heads and tails, and thus, the more likely it is that your findings will approximate the "true" probability.

Insurance companies rely on the law of large numbers when they make predictions about the covered losses that a given group of insureds is likely to experience during a given time period. Insurance companies collect specific information about large numbers of people in order to identify the pattern of losses that those people experienced. For many years, for example, U.S. and Canadian life insurance companies have recorded the number of insureds who have died and how old they were when they died. Insurance companies then compare this information with the general population records of the United States and Canada, noting the ages at which people in the general population had died.

Using these statistical records, insurance companies have been able to develop charts—called **mortality tables**—that indicate with great accuracy the number of people in a large group (of 100,000 or more) who are likely to die at each age. Mortality tables display the *rates of mortality*, or incidence of death, by age, among a given group of people. Insurance companies have developed similar charts, called **morbidity tables,** which display the *rates of morbidity*, or incidence of sickness and accidents, by age, occurring among a given group of people. By using accurate mortality and morbidity tables, life and health insurers can predict the probable loss rates for given groups of insureds; insurers use those predicted loss rates to establish premium rates that will be adequate to pay claims. You'll see an example of a mortality table in Chapter 6, where we describe how insurers price life insurance.

The Loss Must Not Be Catastrophic to the Insurer

A potential loss is not considered insurable if a single occurrence is likely to cause or contribute to catastrophic financial damage to the insurer. Such a loss is not insurable because the insurer could not responsibly promise to pay benefits for the loss. To prevent the possibility of catastrophic loss and ensure that losses occur independently of each other, insurers spread the risks they choose to insure. For example, a property insurer would be unwise to issue policies covering all homes within a 50-mile radius of an active volcano because one eruption of the volcano could result in more claims at one time than the insurer could pay. Instead, the insurer would also issue policies covering homes in areas not threatened by the volcano.

Alternatively, an insurer can reduce the possibility that it will suffer catastrophic losses by transferring risks to another insurer. An insurer transfers risks to another insurer by reinsuring those risks. **Reinsurance** is insurance that one insurance company—known as the **ceding company**—purchases from another insurance company—known as the **reinsurer**—in order to transfer risks on insurance policies that the ceding company issued. To **cede** insurance business is to obtain reinsurance on that business by transferring all or part of the risk to a reinsurer. A life insurance company typically sets a maximum amount of insurance—known as its **retention limit**—that the insurer is willing to carry at its own risk on any one life without transferring some of the risk to a reinsurer.

Through reinsurance, risks are redistributed among several insurance companies. Some insurance companies act only as reinsurers.

Other companies issue insurance policies to individuals and businesses *and* also act as reinsurers. A reinsurer also sometimes cedes risks to another reinsurer in a transaction known as a **retrocession.** The reinsurance company that reinsures risks ceded by another reinsurance company in a retrocession is known as a *retrocessionaire.*

An example will help illustrate a reinsurance transaction. Note, however, that there are many different types of reinsurance transactions, and this is only one example.

EXAMPLE   The Alpha Insurance Company established a retention limit of $750,000. Alpha has entered into a reinsurance agreement with the Celtic Reinsurance Company. Under the terms of the reinsurance agreement, when Alpha issues a policy with a face amount that exceeds its retention limit, the amount in excess of the retention limit is automatically ceded to Celtic. Alpha recently issued a $1,250,000 policy on the life of Norma Olson.

ANALYSIS   As a result of the reinsurance agreement, $500,000 of the coverage Alpha issued Norma will be ceded to Celtic. Alpha will retain liability to provide Norma with life insurance coverage of $1,250,000, but Celtic will reimburse Alpha for $500,000 of the death benefit payable if Norma dies while the policy is in force.

By setting a retention limit and entering into a reinsurance agreement, an insurer can issue policies that have relatively large face amounts without exposing itself to an excessive amount of risk. The owners of policies that have been reinsured generally are not aware of the reinsurance agreement between the insurer and the reinsurer. The insurance company that issued the policy collects the premiums and pays the policy benefits to the proper recipient when due. (See Figure 3-1, which illustrates a reinsurance relationship.)

Insurability of Specific Risks

The five characteristics we just described are useful in identifying the general kinds of losses that are insurable and provide a helpful framework for the study of insurance principles and products. But, as you will learn, insurance is sold on a case-by-case basis, and insurers consider a number of factors in order to determine whether a proposed risk is an insurable risk. Before we describe some of these factors, you need to understand the terminology we will use throughout the text to describe the people who are involved in the creation and operation of an insurance policy.

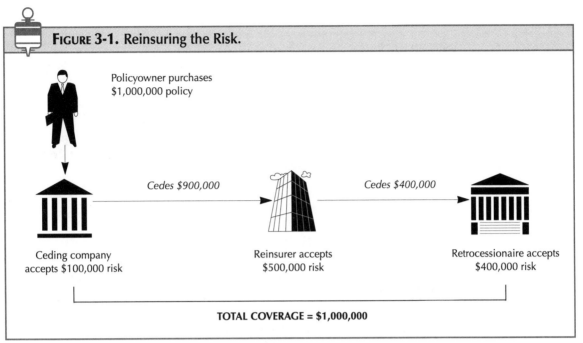

FIGURE 3-1. Reinsuring the Risk.

Policyowner purchases
$1,000,000 policy

Cedes $900,000

Cedes $400,000

Ceding company
accepts $100,000 risk

Reinsurer accepts
$500,000 risk

Retrocessionaire accepts
$400,000 risk

TOTAL COVERAGE = $1,000,000

The **applicant** is the person or business that applies for an insurance policy. When a policy is issued, the person or business that owns the insurance policy is known as the **policyowner.** In most cases, the applicant is also the policyowner.

The **insured** is the person whose life or health is insured under the policy. This is the commonly accepted definition of "insured" in the United States and in the province of Quebec. In all other jurisdictions in Canada, the person who is insured by a life insurance policy is referred to as the **life insured.** To eliminate confusion in this text, we'll use the term *insured* to mean the person whose life or health is insured by a policy. The policyowner and the insured may be, and often are, the same person. If, for example, you apply for and are issued an insurance policy on your life, then you are both the policyowner and the insured and may be known as the *policyowner-insured.* If, however, your mother applies for and is issued a policy on your life, then she is the policyowner and you are the insured. When one person purchases insurance on the life of another person, the policy is known as a **third-party policy.**

If the event insured against occurs while the insurance policy is in force, the insurer pays the policy benefit. Life insurance policy proceeds are usually paid to the policy's **beneficiary**—the person or party the policyowner named to receive the policy benefit. Health insurance policy benefits are usually paid either to the insured person or to the hospital, doctor, or medical care provider that provided the covered medical care services to the insured.

Assessing the Degree of Risk

When an insurance company receives an application for insurance, the company must assess the degree of risk it will take on if it agrees to issue the policy. An insurance company cannot afford to presume that each proposed risk represents an average likelihood of loss. Not all individuals of the same sex and age have an equal likelihood of suffering a loss. Further, those individuals who believe they have a greater-than-average likelihood of loss tend to seek insurance protection to a greater extent than do those who believe they have an average or a less-than-average likelihood of loss. This tendency, which is called **antiselection,** *adverse selection,* or *selection against the insurer,* is a primary reason that insurers need to carefully review each application to assess properly the degree of risk the company will be assuming if it issues the requested policy. As we discuss more fully later in this text, the premium rates that an insurance company establishes are based in large part on the amount of risk the company is assuming for the policies it issues. If the insurer consistently underestimates the risks that it assumes, its premium rates will be inadequate to provide the promised benefits.

The process of identifying and classifying the degree of risk represented by a proposed insured is called **underwriting** or *selection of risks,* and the insurance company employees who are responsible for evaluating proposed risks are called *underwriters.* Underwriting consists of two primary stages: (1) identifying the risks that a proposed insured presents and (2) classifying the degree of risk that a proposed insured represents.

Identifying Risks. As we noted earlier, insurers cannot predict when a specific individual will die, become injured, or suffer from an illness. Insurers, however, have identified a number of factors than can increase or decrease the likelihood that an individual will suffer a loss. The most important of these factors are physical hazards and moral hazards. A **physical hazard** is a physical characteristic that may increase the likelihood of loss. For example, a person with a history of heart attacks possesses a physical hazard that will increase the likelihood that the person will die sooner than will a person of the same age and sex who does not have a similar medical history. A person who is overweight has a physical characteristic that is known to contribute to health problems, and those health problems may result in the economic loss associated with higher-than-average medical expenses. Underwriters must carefully evaluate proposed insureds to detect the presence of such physical hazards.

Underwriters also must consider the effects of moral hazards on the degree of risk represented by a proposed insured. **Moral hazard** is the likelihood that a person may act dishonestly in the insurance

"You'd think an underwriter would know what 'risk' is!"

Reprinted with permission of Phil Interlandi and Bituminous Casualty Corporation.

transaction. For example, an individual with a confirmed record of illegal behavior is more likely to defraud an insurer than is a person with no such record, and an insurer must carefully consider that fact when evaluating such an individual's application for insurance. The individual may be seeking insurance for a dishonest reason. Underwriters also evaluate the moral hazards presented by individuals who provide false information on their applications for insurance. In these cases, the applicants may be trying to obtain insurance coverage that they might not otherwise be able to obtain. When underwriters evaluate applications for insurance, they take a variety of steps to identify proposed insureds who present these moral hazards.

Classifying Risks. After identifying the risks presented by a proposed insured, the underwriter can classify the proposed insured into an appropriate risk category. The purpose of classifying risks into categories is to enable the insurer to determine the equitable premium rate to charge for the requested coverage. People in different risk categories are charged different premium rates. Without these premium rate variations, some policyowners would be charged too much for their coverage, while others would be paying less than the actual cost of their coverage. Insight 3-1 describes the relationship between underwriters and *actuaries* who are trained in the mathematics of insurance and are responsible for calculating premium rates. (We describe pricing in detail in Chapter 6.)

In order to classify proposed insureds, underwriters apply general rules of risk selection, known as **underwriting guidelines,** established by the insurer. Underwriting guidelines generally identify at least three risk categories for proposed insureds: standard risks, substandard risks, and declined risks. Many insurance companies' underwriting guidelines include a fourth risk category: preferred risks.

- Proposed insureds who have a likelihood of loss that is not significantly greater than average are classified as **standard risks,** and the premium rates they are charged are called **standard premium rates.** Traditionally, most individual life and health insurance policies have been issued at standard premium rates.

- Those proposed insureds who have a significantly greater-than-average likelihood of loss but are still found to be insurable are classified as **substandard risks** or *special class risks.* Insurance companies use several methods to compensate for the additional risk presented by insureds who are classified as substandard risks. In individual life insurance, insurers typically charge substandard risks a higher-than-standard premium rate, called a **substandard premium rate** or *special class rate.* In individual health insurance, insurers may either charge a substandard

Insight 3-1. Trees in the Forest: Underwriters' Relationship with Actuaries.

What is pricing? Pricing a product is matching premium to risk. The underwriter and the actuary handle different aspects of pricing. Using standard, overall industry experience and assumptions about insurance products, the actuary develops the premium to be charged for the insurance coverage. The underwriter decides whether a particular proposed insured fits those assumptions. If the person proposed for insurance does not fit the standard assumptions, then the underwriter applies a rating to

the policy to charge more for the coverage, or, in extreme cases, denies the requested coverage.

The actuary's role is to find standard assumptions to be applied to average proposed insureds, while the underwriter's role is to determine the specific rating to be applied to a specific proposed insured. Perhaps the analogy about seeing the forest and seeing the trees is applicable. Actuaries look at each *forest* and make assumptions about the average health of all the trees in the forest. The

underwriter looks at the individual *trees* and tries to place them in the correct forests.

Actuaries cannot forget the individual trees when they develop average assumptions, or no trees may really fit the forest. Underwriters, on the other hand, cannot forget that the more trees they put into the wrong forest, the less predictable the forest's mortality becomes. Neither the actuary nor the underwriter should lose sight of the forest or the trees. ●

Source: Leroy H. Christenson and Doug Ingle, "The Underwriting Role," *On the Risk,* 12, no. 4 (October–December 1996): 95–99. Adapted with permission of the publisher.

premium rate or modify the policy in some way to compensate for the greater risk. (We'll discuss these modifications to health insurance policies in Part 2 of the text.)

- The **declined risk** category consists of those proposed insureds who are considered to present a risk that is too great for the insurer to cover. Applicants for disability income insurance coverage are also placed into the declined risk category if the insurer believes that the coverage is not needed to cover any income loss that would result from a disability.

- Many life insurers classify proposed insureds who present a significantly less-than-average likelihood of loss as **preferred risks** and charge these preferred risks a lower-than-standard premium rate. Some life insurers also have established a *super-preferred risk* classification that includes people who present an even lower level of risk than those who are classified as preferred risks. Insurance company practices vary widely as to what qualifies a proposed insured as a preferred risk or a super-preferred risk. As one example, some insurers categorize their standard risks into two risk classifications based on their smoking habits. Insureds who otherwise present a standard risk and are nonsmokers are classified as preferred risks and are charged less-than-standard premium rates; insureds who otherwise present a standard risk but who smoke are classified as standard risks and are charged standard premium rates.

> ### FAST FACT
>
> Liberalization of underwriting in life insurance is a continuing trend in the United States as insurers conduct research into the effects of various health and occupational hazards on life insurance and mortality. Most companies now insure fully recovered victims of cancer at standard rates; previously, such people were underwritten at substandard rates, if at all. Skin divers, in former years placed in the substandard risk classification, can now usually be insured at standard rates.[2]

Insurable Interest Requirement

We noted in the beginning of this chapter that only pure risks are insurable; insurance is intended to compensate an individual or a business for a financial loss, not to provide an opportunity for gain. At one time, people used insurance policies as a means of making wagers. For example, they purchased insurance policies on the lives of people who were completely unrelated to them and, in that way, created a possibility of financial gain for themselves if the insured people died.

The practice of purchasing insurance as a wager is now considered to be against public policy. As a result, laws in all states and provinces require that, when an insurance policy is issued, the policyowner must have an **insurable interest** in the risk that is insured—the policyowner must be likely to suffer a genuine loss or detriment should the event insured against occur. For example, a property insurer would not sell a fire insurance policy on a particular building to a person who does not own the building because that person would not suffer an economic loss if the building were destroyed by fire. In property insurance, ownership of property is one way in which an insurable interest in the property is established.

The Insurable Interest Requirement in Life Insurance. The presence of insurable interest must be established for every life insurance policy to ensure that the insurance contract is not formed as an illegal wagering agreement. If the insurable interest requirement is not met *when a policy is issued*, the policy is not valid. The presence of an insurable interest for life insurance usually can be found by applying the following general rule:

> An insurable interest exists when the policyowner is likely to benefit if the insured continues to live and is likely to suffer some loss or detriment if the insured dies.

Underwriters screen every application for life insurance to make sure that the insurable interest requirement imposed by law in the applicable jurisdiction will be met when the policy is issued. In other words, the insurer must determine whether the person who will be the owner of the life insurance policy—typically, the applicant for insurance—has an insurable interest in the proposed insured. If the insurer determines that the proposed policyowner does not meet the insurable interest requirement, then the insurer will not issue the policy.

In addition, each insurance company screens all applications to ensure they meet the company's own underwriting guidelines, which frequently include insurable interest requirements that go beyond the requirements imposed by law. Thus, even if the insurable interest requirement imposed by the applicable jurisdiction is met, an insurer can refuse to issue the policy if its own, more stringent insurable interest requirements are not met.

To understand how insurable interest requirements are met, we need to consider two possible situations: (1) an individual purchases insurance on her own life and (2) an individual purchases insurance on another's life. In both cases, the applicant for life insurance must name a beneficiary. Let's look at each of these situations.

All persons are considered to have an insurable interest in their own lives. A person is always considered to have more to gain by living than by dying. Therefore, an insurable interest between the policyowner and the insured is presumed when a person seeks to purchase insurance on her own life. For such a policy, insurable interest laws do not require that the named beneficiary have an insurable interest in the policyowner-insured's life. In other words, the laws allow a policyowner-insured to name anyone as beneficiary.

Most insurance company underwriting guidelines also require that the beneficiary have an insurable interest in the life of the policyowner-insured when a policy is issued. As a result, life insurers typically inquire into the named beneficiary's relationship to the proposed policyowner-insured and may refuse to issue the coverage if the beneficiary does not possess an insurable interest in the policyowner-insured's life. An exception exists in the state of California, where laws now permit a person to purchase insurance on his own life and to name anyone he wants as beneficiary, even if the beneficiary has no insurable interest in the policyowner-insured's life. As a result, insurers that issue policies subject to California law are prohibited from declining to issue a life insurance policy solely because the named beneficiary has no insurable interest in the proposed policyowner-insured's life.

In the case of a third-party policy, laws throughout Canada and in most U.S. jurisdictions require only that the policyowner have an insurable interest in the insured's life when the policy is issued. Most insurance company underwriting guidelines and the laws in some U.S. jurisdictions, however, require both the policyowner and the beneficiary of a third-party policy to have an insurable interest in the insured's life when the policy is issued.

Certain family relationships are assumed by law to create an insurable interest between an insured and a policyowner or beneficiary. The natural bonds of affection and financial dependence that generally exist between certain family members make this a reasonable assumption. In these cases, even if the policyowner or beneficiary has no financial interest in the insured's life, the bonds of love and affection alone are sufficient to create an insurable interest. According to laws in most jurisdictions, the insured's spouse, mother, father, child, grandparent, grandchild, brother, and sister are deemed to have an insurable interest in the life of the insured. (See Figure 3-2, which illustrates the family relationships that create an insurable interest.)

An insurable interest is *not* presumed when the policyowner or beneficiary is more distantly related to the insured than the relatives described above or when the parties are not related by blood or marriage. In these cases, a financial interest in the continued life of the insured must be demonstrated in order to satisfy the insurable interest requirement. For instance, if Mary Mulhouse obtains a $50,000 personal loan from the Lone Star Bank of Vermont, the bank would have a financial interest and, consequently, an insurable interest in Mary's life. If Mary should die before repaying the loan, the bank could lose some or all of the money it lent her. Similar examples of financial interest can be found in other business relationships.

The insurable interest requirement must be met before a life insurance policy will be issued. After the life insurance policy is in force, the presence or absence of insurable interest is no longer relevant.

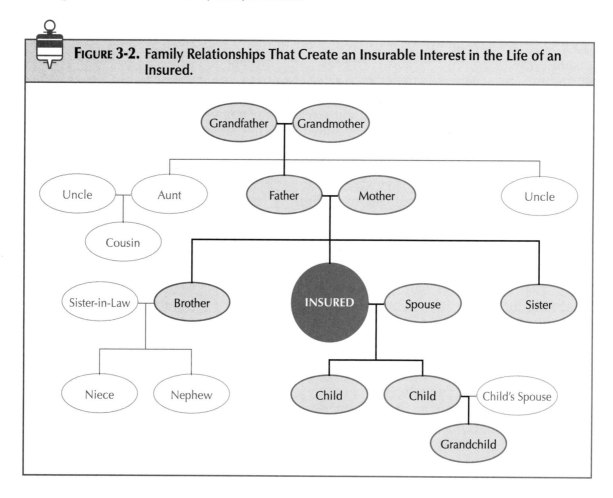

FIGURE 3-2. Family Relationships That Create an Insurable Interest in the Life of an Insured.

Therefore, a beneficiary need not provide evidence of insurable interest in order to receive the benefits of a life insurance policy.

The Insurable Interest Requirement in Health Insurance. The insurable interest requirement also must be met when a health insurance policy is issued. For health insurance purposes, the insurable interest requirement is met if the applicant can demonstrate a genuine risk of economic loss should the proposed insured require medical care or become disabled. Because of the nature of health insurance, applicants rarely seek health insurance on someone in whom they have no insurable interest. Typically, people seek health insurance for themselves and for their dependents. As a contract of indemnity, a health insurance policy provides coverage to pay for medical expenses that the insured has incurred or to replace a disabled insured's lost income. Applicants are generally considered to have an insurable interest in their own health. Additionally, for disability income insurance purposes, businesses have an insurable interest in the health of their key employees.

EXAMPLE | Image, Inc., is a small company that contracts with other companies to conduct seminars for their management staffs. Sarah Smithers works for Image, Inc., as their primary seminar leader. Because Sarah's expertise and teaching skills are essential to the success of the business, Image, Inc., has applied for disability income coverage on Sarah.

ANALYSIS | Image, Inc., would be unable to meet its scheduled seminar commitments if Sarah were ill or injured and, thus, unable to conduct seminars. As a result, Image, Inc., has a financial interest in Sarah's continued good health. This financial interest creates the necessary insurable interest for Image, Inc., to purchase disability income coverage on Sarah.

Key Terms

speculative risk
pure risk
self-insurance
policy
policy benefit
premium
personal risk
contract of indemnity
claim
valued contract
face amount
probability
law of large numbers
mortality tables
morbidity tables
reinsurance
ceding company
reinsurer
cede
retention limit

retrocession
applicant
policyowner
insured
life insured
third-party policy
beneficiary
antiselection
underwriting
physical hazard
moral hazard
underwriting guidelines
standard risk
standard premium rates
substandard risk
substandard premium rates
declined risk
preferred risk
insurable interest

Other Important Terms

policy proceeds
property damage risk
property insurance

liability risk
liability insurance
property and casualty insurance

Other Important Terms (continued)

property and casualty insurer	adverse selection
property and liability insurer	selection against the insurer
face value	selection of risks
loss rate	underwriters
rates of mortality	actuaries
rates of morbidity	special class risks
retrocessionaire	special class rate
policyowner-insured	super-preferred risk

Endnotes

1. For a complete discussion of risk management, see C. Arthur Williams Jr., Michael L. Smith, and Peter C. Young, *Risk Management and Insurance*, 7th ed. (New York: McGraw-Hill, 1995).

2. ACLI, *1998 Life Insurance Fact Book* (Washington, D.C.: American Council of Life Insurance, 1998), 16.

CHAPTER 4

Meeting Needs for Life Insurance

After reading this chapter, you should be able to

⊕ Identify the personal needs that life insurance can meet

⊕ Identify the reasons that businesses purchase life insurance products

⊕ Recognize situations in which individual life insurance can be used to fund a business continuation plan

⊕ Recognize the characteristics of split-dollar insurance plans and deferred compensation plans that are funded by life insurance

Although the basic need for financial security is common to most people, this need varies from person to person. In addition, people's financial needs tend to change over time. Insurance is one method people can use to provide for their financial security. Some people are very much aware of their need for financial security and actively seek to purchase insurance of all types to help them provide that security. Other people recognize the need for some types of insurance but not for other types. Still other people do not recognize the need for insurance at all. In fact, many people purchase life, health, and annuity products only after an insurance agent shows them how these insurance products can provide financial security. An **insurance agent,** or *sales agent,* is a person who is authorized by an insurance company to represent that insurance company in its dealings with applicants for insurance.

Insurance companies have adapted their marketing styles to accommodate consumers' varying levels of recognition of their insurance needs. Some companies make insurance available to customers in a department store setting where the customer initiates the purchase. Some companies make insurance available to customers of banks. Some companies market insurance through the mail; some market their products through newspaper, magazine, and Internet advertisements. But probably the oldest method of marketing insurance, and one that is still widely used today, is through personal contact initiated by an insurance agent.

Insurance can meet the needs of individuals, as well as the needs of businesses. In this chapter, we describe some of the general types of personal and business needs that life insurance can meet. Life insurance products are described in later chapters, and we will describe how the features of those products can meet different needs people have for financial security.

Personal Needs Met by Life Insurance Products

All life insurance products provide a monetary benefit if the insured person dies while the policy is in force. In addition, some types of life insurance policies provide an accumulated savings value while the insured person is still alive. People's needs for life insurance benefits are as varied as their needs for any other sum of money. Common needs

"Now, which of your nine lives did you want to insure?"

that life insurance benefits can meet include funds to cover final expenses, dependents' support, education costs, and retirement income.

Final Expenses and Estate Planning

When a person dies in the United States or Canada, an executor or administrator is typically appointed to settle the deceased person's estate. The estate consists of all things of value—the *assets*—owned by the person when he died. These assets include cash, bank and investment accounts, real estate, and ownership interests in a business. To settle the estate, the executor or administrator is responsible for identifying and collecting the deceased's property, filing any required tax forms, collecting all debts owed to the deceased, and paying all outstanding debts owed by the deceased. The executor or administrator then distributes the remaining property to the deceased person's heirs. An individual who wants to ensure that his estate will be settled in accordance with his wishes will develop a plan—called an *estate plan*—that considers the amount of assets and debts that he is likely to have when he dies and how best to preserve those assets so that they can pass to his heirs as he desires. Life insurance is often an important component of an estate plan.

When any person dies, certain bills may become payable. These bills include debts such as mortgage loans, personal loans, charge accounts, and automobile loans. In addition, some expense may be related to the death itself, such as doctor and hospital bills that are not covered by insurance, as well as funeral expenses. Many of these expenses must be paid regardless of whether the deceased worked or had any dependents. Various taxes may be imposed on a deceased person's estate, also. In the United States, for example, the federal government imposes an estate tax on estates that exceed a specified value. The executor or administrator may have to sell assets belonging to the deceased in order to raise cash to pay the deceased's debts. Such a forced sale of assets can result in the assets being sold for much less than if they could be sold in a more leisurely manner. As an alternative to a forced sale of assets to raise cash, individuals can purchase insurance on their lives to provide the cash needed to pay these expenses. As shown in Figure 4-1, death benefits paid in 1996 make up a sizable portion of total benefits paid to life insurance and annuity owners and beneficiaries.

> **FAST FACT**
>
> During 1997, U.S. life insurance companies paid $43.9 billion to beneficiaries of policyholders who died. Canadian life insurers paid over $2 billion in death benefits.[2]

EXAMPLE Kyle Larson is a 45-year-old widower who owns and operates a large farm. He has two sons who work with him. Kyle has recently obtained a large loan to finance an expansion of the business. He wants to ensure that if he should die, his sons will inherit the farm and will have enough cash on hand to pay the business loan and his other outstanding debts and estate taxes.

ANALYSIS As part of an estate plan, Kyle could consider purchasing insurance on his life and naming his sons as the beneficiaries. In deciding what face amount of insurance to purchase, Kyle should try to determine the amount of cash that his sons might need to pay his debts and estate taxes and to continue operating the farm.

Dependents' Support

A major selling point for life insurance is that people have a need to provide financial support for their dependents. If a person who supports or helps support a family dies, the surviving dependents may face serious problems in the months immediately following the person's death. Household expenses go on—rent or mortgage payments must be

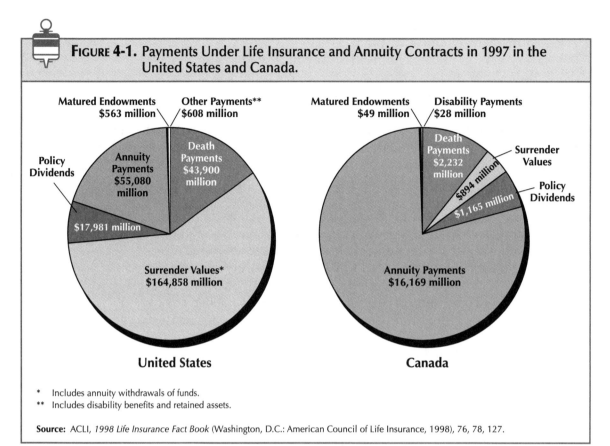

FIGURE 4-1. Payments Under Life Insurance and Annuity Contracts in 1997 in the United States and Canada.

* Includes annuity withdrawals of funds.
** Includes disability benefits and retained assets.

Source: ACLI, *1998 Life Insurance Fact Book* (Washington, D.C.: American Council of Life Insurance, 1998), 76, 78, 127.

made; utility bills must be paid; food and clothing must be purchased. The death may create additional expenses, such as the need to provide child care and daily household upkeep—all while family members try to cope with the emotional effects of the loss of a loved one.

Relatively few people have sufficient funds to pay their usual expenses for several months if the regular family income ceases or is substantially reduced. Life insurance can provide funds to support the family members until they obtain new methods of support or until they adjust to a lower income. In addition, the proceeds of a life insurance policy can be used to supplement the family's income. For example, the policy proceeds can be used to fund an annuity, which will provide periodic benefit payments to the insured's surviving dependents.

As a general rule, when the proceeds of a life insurance policy are paid in a lump sum to a named beneficiary following the death of the insured, those proceeds are not considered taxable income to the beneficiary. In other words, a policy beneficiary who receives policy death benefits is not required to pay income taxes on the policy proceeds. This favorable income tax treatment given to life insurance is designed to encourage people to provide for their dependents' financial needs.

Education Costs

One of the prime objectives of many parents is to be financially able to send their children to a university or college or to provide their children with technical training. Because the death of a working father or mother could mean that tuition would be beyond the family's reduced resources, parents can purchase term life insurance to help ensure that funds will be available when needed to provide for their children's educations. Parents can also use permanent life insurance to provide educational funds even if the parents are still living during the child's college years. Permanent life insurance can be used to accumulate savings that are available for just such future needs.

> ### FAST FACT
>
> During 1997, U.S. life insurance companies paid $184 billion to policyholders. This amount represented 77% of total life insurance benefit payments that year.[3]

EXAMPLE　Jane Echols is a single parent with a four-year-old son, Mark. She wants to make sure that if she should die before Mark is grown, he will be supported until he can finish his education and support himself.

ANALYSIS　Jane can purchase a term life insurance policy with a benefit amount sufficient to cover Mark's living expenses and college tuition until he has finished his schooling. If Jane has sufficient funds, she might consider purchasing permanent life insurance, which would provide life insurance coverage throughout her lifetime, as well as accumulating a cash value against which she could borrow to obtain money for Mark's college education.

Retirement Income

In the United States and Canada, various government programs are designed to provide individuals with retirement income. This income, however, is often insufficient to support a retiree fully and must be supplemented with either employer-sponsored retirement plans or individual savings plans, or both. Life insurance policies that accumulate savings can be used as vehicles for personal savings. Over a period of time, the accumulated savings in a permanent life insurance policy can grow to a substantial sum and, while growing, will still provide the insured with life insurance coverage.

Although the interest rate payable on a life insurance policy's accumulated savings may be lower than the interest rate available on many types of investments, using life insurance as a savings vehicle has some advantages. Many permanent life insurance policies, for example, guarantee that the policy's accumulated savings will not be reduced if the insurance company's investments lose money; these policies also guarantee that the policyowner will earn at least a specified interest rate on those funds. In addition, life insurance policies provide income tax advantages that typically are not available from investments. As long as a policy meets the applicable tax code's definition of "life insurance," the policyowner usually is not required to pay income taxes each year on the interest earned on the policy's accumulated savings. In contrast, taxpayers must pay income taxes each year on interest they earned that year from most types of investments. This favorable tax treatment of life insurance policies effectively increases the policyowner's investment return because that return is not reduced by the payment of income taxes each year the policy is in force. Note, however, that once a policyowner actually receives the policy values—by cancelling the policy and receiving its cash surrender value, for example—he may owe income taxes if he receives more from the policy than he paid for it.

The savings that accumulate in a permanent life insurance policy can be used to purchase an annuity when the owner of the policy approaches retirement. An annuity will guarantee a series of payments—usually on a monthly or an annual basis—either for a limited period or for life. For the policyowner, the permanent life insurance policy will have served the original purpose of providing insurance protection while it was needed during her working years. Later in the policyowner's life, the policy's accumulated savings can be used to fund another benefit—retirement income. Of course, the accumulated savings may also be used to meet other retirement needs, such as paying off a mortgage or buying a retirement residence.

EXAMPLE Bud and Mary Pasternak are approaching retirement age. Their house is paid for, but Bud and Mary are concerned that their Social Security and Bud's pension benefits will not be sufficient to support them after they both retire. When he was 25 years old, Bud purchased a permanent life insurance policy that has accumulated a considerable cash value.

ANALYSIS If Bud no longer needs life insurance coverage, he can use the cash value of his life insurance policy to purchase a single-premium annuity, which will provide a monthly or an annual income throughout the remainder of his and Mary's lifetimes.

Other Personal Needs for Life Insurance

Some individuals purchase life insurance policies so that they can donate the proceeds of the policy to a charitable organization, such as a church or an educational institution. In both the United States and Canada, if certain conditions are met, the premiums a taxpayer pays for an insurance policy that is payable to a charity are deductible for federal income tax purposes. In most other cases, life insurance premiums are not deductible by individual taxpayers. In general, needs for life insurance products depend on a person's circumstances and goals, and these needs change throughout the person's life.

Business Needs Met by Life Insurance Products

A business—or an individual who owns a business—generally purchases life insurance products for one of two reasons:

- An individual life insurance policy can provide funds to ensure that the business continues in the event of the death of an owner, partner, or key person.

- A business can purchase life insurance to provide benefits for its employees.

Business Continuation Insurance

A *business continuation insurance plan* is an insurance plan designed to enable a business owner (or owners) to provide for the business' continued operation if the owner or a key person dies. A *key person* is any person or employee whose continued participation in the business is necessary to the success of the business and whose death would cause the business a significant financial loss.

Any closely held business may need to establish a business continuation insurance plan in order to ensure that the business will continue if an owner or key employee dies. A *closely held business* is a sole proprietorship, a partnership, or a corporation that is owned by only a few individuals. A large corporation is not typically faced with this need for business continuation life insurance because it has the financial resources to ensure that its business continues beyond the death of any individual.

In this section, we first describe business continuation insurance plans that closely held businesses can use to fund the purchase of a deceased owner's or partner's share in the business. Then we describe business continuation insurance plans that protect a business against the death of a key person.

Buy-Sell Agreements

Ideally, the owners of any closely held business should consider what will happen to the business if the owner, a partner, or a shareholder dies. As we noted earlier, an individual's estate includes any ownership interest she had in a business. Thus, if one of the owners of a closely held business dies, the deceased owner's share of the business becomes part of her estate. For example, when the owner of a sole proprietorship dies, all of her assets—including the assets of the business—pass to her estate, and all of her liabilities—including the liabilities of the business—must be paid by the estate. Often the executor or administrator of the deceased's estate is forced to liquidate the business in order to provide funds to pay these liabilities. *Liquidation* is the process of selling off for cash a business' assets, such as its building, inventory, and equipment, and using that cash to pay the business' debts; any funds remaining are then distributed to the owners of the business. A forced liquidation places the surviving heirs in the position of having to take whatever price they can get for these assets at the time of the sale. The heirs often receive far less than if they had been able to wait for more acceptable offers.

A buy-sell agreement prepared in advance can alleviate many problems associated with the untimely death of a business owner. A *buy-sell agreement* is an agreement in which (1) one party agrees to purchase the financial interest that a second party has in a business following the second party's death and (2) the second party agrees to direct his estate to sell his interest in the business to the purchasing party. Buy-sell agreements vary somewhat depending on the form of the business organization—depending on whether it is a sole proprietorship, partnership, or closely held corporation. We'll give a few examples of how buy-sell agreements can be structured and how life insurance can be used to fund the purchase of a deceased owner's interest in a business.

Sole Proprietorship Buy-Sell Agreement. The owner of a sole proprietorship can ensure the continuation of her business following her death by entering into a buy-sell agreement with an individual who agrees to purchase the business from the owner's estate. The owner, for example, may be able to identify a current employee who has both the ability and the drive to take over the business. In the buy-sell agreement, the employee agrees to purchase the owner's interest in the business for either a stated price or for a price to be determined at the time of the purchase. In addition, the owner agrees to authorize her estate to sell the business to the employee according to the terms of the buy-sell agreement.

The employee, however, often does not have sufficient personal assets to fund the purchase of the business. In that case, individual life insurance is perhaps the easiest and most common way to fund the buy-sell agreement. The employee purchases an insurance policy on the life of the sole proprietor. The employee owns the policy, pays the premiums, and is the named beneficiary. The policy may be either a term insurance plan or a form of permanent life insurance. In any case, the face amount of the life insurance policy is believed to be sufficient to allow the employee to purchase the business according to the terms of the buy-sell agreement.

EXAMPLE Lisa Marceau owns a florist shop and is planning to retire in ten years. Her only child, Suzanne, is not interested in owning the shop. Lisa's only employee, Celeste Cellino, has agreed to purchase the florist shop when Lisa retires. Celeste, however, will not have enough cash to purchase the shop from Lisa's estate if Lisa should die within the next 10 years before her retirement.

ANALYSIS Celeste can purchase a term insurance policy on Lisa's life and name herself as the policy beneficiary. Celeste should purchase a policy with a face amount that is high enough to allow her to purchase the business from Lisa's estate if Lisa should die within the 10-year period before her retirement.

Partnership Buy-Sell Agreement. Although a partnership usually dissolves upon the death of a partner, the surviving partner (or partners) may create a new business. Partners often plan for the continuation of the business after the death of a partner by entering into a buy-sell agreement that sets out the terms under which a deceased partner's interest in the partnership will be purchased. The purchase of a deceased partner's share can be accomplished by one of two methods—the cross-purchase method or the entity method.

When the *cross-purchase method* is used, each partner agrees to purchase a proportionate share of a deceased partner's interest in the partnership. Each partner funds the buy-sell agreement by purchasing an insurance policy on the life of each of the other partners. Thus, each partner owns, pays the premiums on, and is the named beneficiary of a policy on the life of each of the other partners. If one partner dies, each surviving partner will receive the proceeds of a life insurance policy and can use those proceeds to purchase a proportionate share of the deceased partner's ownership interest in the partnership.

EXAMPLE John Sweet, Shelly Turner, and Ned Bailey formed a partnership known as Home Care. They have entered into a cross-purchase buy-sell agreement under which each partner agrees that if one of the partners dies, then each surviving partner will purchase one-half of the de-ceased's interest in Home Care. They have determined that the total value of the partnership is $150,000 and have agreed to purchase life insurance policies to fund the buy-sell agreement. What amount of life insurance should they each purchase on the lives of the other two partners?

ANALYSIS Let's evaluate this example by considering one partner's situation. John has agreed that if Shelly or Ned dies, he will purchase one-half of the deceased partner's interest in the partnership. Each partner's interest is valued at $50,000 ($150,000 total value divided among three partners = $50,000 interest per partner). If Shelly or Ned dies, John will pay $25,000 (one-half of $50,000) for his portion of the deceased partner's ownership interest. Thus, John needs to purchase a $25,000 insurance policy on Shelly's life and a $25,000 insurance policy on Ned's life.

Notice that in the preceding example the partners had to purchase a total of six individual life insurance policies in order to fund their buy-sell agreement—each of the three partners bought two policies. And each partner was individually responsible for paying the premiums for the coverage.

Under the *entity method* of buy-sell agreements, the partnership—rather than the individual partners—agrees to purchase the share of any partner who dies; the partnership also agrees to distribute a pro-portionate share of that ownership interest to each of the surviving partners. The partnership purchases an insurance policy on the life of each of the partners, pays the premiums, and is the named beneficiary of each policy. If a partner dies, the partnership uses the life insur-ance policy proceeds to purchase the deceased partner's share in the business from the deceased's estate.

EXAMPLE The partners of Home Care have entered into a buy-sell agreement with Home Care. Under the agreement, Home Care agrees to purchase the share of any deceased partner and to divide that share proportionately among the surviving partners.

ANALYSIS In the preceding example, we determined that the value of each partner's interest in Home Care was $50,000. In order to fund the buy-sell agreement, Home Care will purchase three life insurance policies—a $50,000 insurance policy on the life of each of the three partners. Home Care will also designate itself as the beneficiary of each policy. Thus, if a partner dies, Home Care can use the policy proceeds to purchase the deceased partner's share of the business from the deceased's estate.

Notice that under the entity method, only three life insurance policies are required to fund the buy-sell agreement. Also, under the entity method, the partnership itself becomes a party to the buy-sell agreement; under the cross-purchase method, only the individual partners are parties to the buy-sell agreement.

Closely Held Corporation Buy-Sell Agreement. The owners of a closely held corporation often enter into a buy-sell agreement, which is similar to the partnership buy-sell agreement just described. The owners may each agree to purchase insurance on the lives of each of the other owners—the cross-purchase method—or the corporation may purchase a policy on each of the owners' lives—the entity method.

Key Person Life Insurance

Another form of business continuation insurance is key person life insurance. *Key person life insurance*—or *key employee life insurance*—is insurance that a business purchases on the life of a person whose continued participation in the business is necessary to its success and whose death would cause financial loss to the business. As we described earlier in the chapter, a key person could be an owner, a partner, or an employee of the business. When a business purchases key person life insurance, the business owns, pays the premiums on, and is the beneficiary of the insurance policy. If the key person dies, the policy proceeds are paid to the business. Depending on the needs of the specific situation, a business might purchase either term or permanent insurance on the life of a key person.

Many businesses depend on the continued participation of certain valuable people. The loss of a key person's expertise and services may seriously affect the firm's earnings. For example, a top salesperson or a person with important business contacts may be responsible for a large portion of the firm's income. In addition to the potential loss of a key person's services, the business must also consider the cost of training or finding a replacement for the key person. A business can provide itself with an extra layer of financial security by purchasing an insurance policy on the life of the key person. The policy proceeds can supplement the firm's earnings while it searches for and trains a replacement for the deceased employee.

Another benefit the firm can gain through the purchase of key person insurance is the enhancement of its credit position. During the period following the death of a key person, the business is likely to need additional cash flow. Sales may drop off; productivity may decline; banks, creditors, and suppliers may become uneasy and withdraw or reduce the firm's credit privileges. If, however, the firm's banks, creditors, and suppliers know that the business has protected itself by insuring the lives of its key people, they may agree to continue their business relationships with the firm on the same terms as before a key person's death.

Life Insurance as an Employee Benefit

Businesses often use insurance products to provide benefits for their employees. Employers pay for all or part of these employee benefits as part of the total package under which they compensate their employees. As we describe in later chapters, the most common way in which employers provide these employee benefits is by establishing group life and health insurance plans. Many employers also provide a group retirement plan for their employees. We describe these group insurance and retirement plans in Part 2.

Individual insurance products are also used in certain instances to provide employee benefits for selected classes of employees. Employers sometimes offer these individual benefit plans to certain employees in addition to the employee benefits that all other employees receive. By offering these additional benefits to especially valuable employees, the business can more readily attract and retain those employees. We'll describe two types of individual life insurance benefit plans—split-dollar life insurance plans and deferred compensation plans.

Split-Dollar Life Insurance Plans

A *split-dollar life insurance plan* is an agreement under which a business provides individual life insurance policies for certain selected employees, who share in paying the cost of the policies. These selected employees are generally owners, officers, executives, or other key employees. Under the terms of a split-dollar agreement, the employer and employee agree to share the cost of an individual insurance policy on the life of the employee. The policy is usually a form of permanent life insurance and may be owned by either the employer or the employee. In either case, the employee is given the right to name the policy beneficiary.

Typically, the employer agrees to pay the portion of each annual premium that is equal to the amount by which the policy's cash value will increase that year. As a result, the total amount the employer has contributed in premiums at any given time is equal to the policy's cash value. As part of the split-dollar agreement, the employee agrees to pay the remainder of each annual premium.

In most cases, the employer is entitled to receive from the policy values an amount that is at least equal to what it paid in premiums for the policy. Thus, if the employee dies while the policy is in force, the employer will receive an amount equal to what it paid for the policy; the beneficiary named by the employee will receive the remainder of the policy proceeds. If the employee retires or leaves the firm, the employee is typically given ownership of the policy but must reimburse the employer for the premiums it paid on the employee's behalf.

Deferred Compensation Plans

An individual life insurance policy can also be used to fund a deferred compensation plan. A *deferred compensation plan* is a plan established by an employer to provide income benefits to an employee at a later date, such as after the employee's retirement, if the employee does not voluntarily terminate employment before that date. To fund a deferred compensation plan, the employee usually agrees to defer a portion of her salary or current compensation—such as a percentage of her regular pay, the amount of an annual salary increase, or the amount of a bonus—until some future date. The employer uses this deferred compensation to purchase an insurance policy on the employee's life. Thus, the employer owns, pays the premiums for, and is the named beneficiary of the policy insuring the employee's life. The insurance policy is not a part of the deferred compensation agreement between the employer and the employee. It is simply the funding instrument for the agreement.

The insurance policy is generally one that builds a cash value. As part of the agreement, the employer agrees that at the time of the employee's retirement, the policy's cash value will be used to fund an annuity, which will provide the employee with a retirement income. The employer also usually agrees that if the employee dies before reaching retirement, the policy proceeds will fund an annuity that will provide income benefits to the employee's spouse and family. Most deferred compensation agreements state that if the employee voluntarily terminates employment with the business before the date specified in the agreement, then she is entitled to receive only the total amount of compensation that she has deferred to date. Thus, the deferred compensation plan serves as an incentive for the employee to remain with the firm.

Key Terms

insurance agent

estate plan

business continuation
insurance plan

key person

closely held business

liquidation

buy-sell agreement

cross-purchase method

entity method

key person life insurance

split-dollar life insurance plan

deferred compensation plan

Other Important Terms

sales agent

assets

key employee life insurance

Endnotes

1. Robert M. Baranoff, "Estate Planning: The Market and the Competition Are Growing," LIMRA's *MarketFacts* (July/August 1995): 46–48.

2. ACLI, *1998 Life Insurance Fact Book* (Washington, D.C.: American Council of Life Insurance, 1998), 76, 127.

3. Ibid., 47.

CHAPTER 5

The Insurance Policy

After reading this chapter, you should be able to

- Distinguish between a formal and an informal contract, between a bilateral and a unilateral contract, between a commutative and an aleatory contract, and between a contract of adhesion and a bargaining contract, and identify which of these types of contracts an insurance contract represents

- Define valid contract, void contract, and voidable contract, and identify the legal effect of each type of contract

- Identify the four requirements for the creation of a valid informal contract and how each of these requirements can be met in the formation of an insurance contract

- Identify the property rights that a policyowner has in the insurance policy he owns

An insurance policy is the physical evidence that an individual or organization has purchased some type of insurance coverage. In this chapter, we describe several aspects of the insurance policy. First, we describe the policy as a contract and the requirements that the parties must meet in order to enter into a valid insurance contract. Then, we describe the policy as a type of property in which the policyowner gains valuable ownership rights.

Fundamentals of Contract Law

Whenever an individual purchases life or health insurance, the individual and the insurance company must first reach an agreement—the individual must agree to buy the insurance coverage from the company, and the company must agree to issue that coverage. The individual and the insurance company must also agree on the price that the individual will pay for the coverage and the benefits that will be payable by the insurer. The policy describes the terms of their agreement.

An insurance policy represents a special kind of agreement known as a contract. A **contract** is a legally enforceable agreement between two or more parties. The two parties to an individual life or health insurance contract are the insurance company that issued the policy and the individual who purchased the policy.

The fact that a contract is legally enforceable means that the parties are bound to carry out the promises they made when entering into the contract. If a party does not carry out its promise, then that party has breached the contract. Laws provide an innocent party with remedies for losses resulting from a breach of contract. A huge body of contract law has developed over the years to define which promises are legally enforceable and what remedies are available to enforce those promises.

In Chapter 1, we described contracts of indemnity and valued contracts. As we noted, health insurance policies are typically contracts of indemnity and life insurance policies are valued contracts. Contracts may be described in several other ways, and we describe various types of contracts in this section. We also describe the requirements imposed by law on the formation of contracts.

Types of Contracts

In order to understand how life and health insurance policies function as contracts, we will discuss each of the following pairs of terms that are used to categorize and describe contracts:

- Formal contracts and informal contracts

- Bilateral contracts and unilateral contracts

- Commutative contracts and aleatory contracts

- Bargaining contracts and contracts of adhesion

We will also identify which descriptive term in each pair applies to life and health insurance policies and why that term is appropriate.

Formal and Informal Contracts

Contracts are either formal or informal. A *formal contract* is one that is enforceable because the parties to the contract met certain formalities concerning the form of the agreement. These formalities generally require that the contract be in writing and that the written document contain some form of seal in order to be enforceable. Property deeds, for example, are formal contracts.

In contrast, life and health insurance contracts are informal contracts. An *informal contract* is a contract that is enforceable because the parties to the contract met requirements concerning the substance of the agreement rather than requirements concerning the form of the agreement. An informal contract may be expressed in either an oral or a written fashion. Writing an agreement merely provides evidence of the contract, and oral informal contracts are usually enforceable. For example, suppose you have agreed to pay your neighbor $35 if he will wash your windows. If your neighbor finishes the job, you will become legally obligated to pay him the $35 whether or not you signed a written agreement. If the agreement was not written, then you would have made an oral contract.

In theory, life and health insurance contracts, as informal contracts, could be made in either written or oral form. In Canada, however, provincial laws require insurance contracts to be in writing, and some states impose such a requirement. Life and health insurance contracts typically are expressed in written form—whether required by law or not—for two practical reasons:

- Putting the contract in writing helps prevent misunderstandings between the parties as to the terms of their agreement. Life and health insurance policies must contain a number of provisions that set forth the conditions of the contract and enable the insurance company to carry out the wishes of the policyowner. Without a written policy, legal problems are likely to arise as a result of disputes between the parties as to the terms of the agreement.

- A written contract provides a permanent record of the agreement. Life and health insurance policies are often in effect for many years. The memory of someone's oral promises made many years in the past may not be reliable, even under the best circumstances.

Some insurers are beginning to market life insurance on the Internet and allowing people to apply for insurance electronically rather than in written form. Insight 5-1 examines some legal issues that arise when a life insurance policy is issued electronically over the Internet rather than as a written document.

Bilateral and Unilateral Contracts

As we stated previously, life and health insurance contracts typically are agreements entered into by two parties—the insurance company

Insight 5-1. Potential Pitfalls of Internet Insurance Contracts.

Can a person enter into a valid life insurance contract on the Internet? "From a practical standpoint, the answer is probably yes," says Marybeth Stevens, counsel for the American Council of Life Insurance (ACLI). "But there are some serious issues involved."

In some states, statutes say that an insurance policy must be in writing. If you sell a policy over the Internet, is the electronic document "in writing"? Not necessarily. Insurers have to pre-file applications and policies with state insurance departments. Does that imply that there have to be written, non-electronic copies of the application and policy? Yes, says David Leifer, also counsel for the ACLI.

According to Leifer, under the existing body of law, in order to rescind a policy on the basis of misrepresentation, the policy, the application, and any other documents pertinent to the underwriting decision must be attached to the paperwork sent to the court. Case law even exists to the effect that paperwork physically has to be attached with a staple. "That creates a very important problem in the courts for life insurers doing electronic transactions, and I don't know how it will be resolved," Leifer says. "There will probably have to be some common law developed to handle electronic policies and applications."

Unfortunately, use of imaging technology is not yet a solution to the legal ambiguities surrounding electronic documents. Right now the courts are specific, saying the insured must receive a hard copy of his policy with the application attached to it. The validity of imaged documents as "originals" is still being shaped by emerging law. There is legislation in some states, particularly in Utah and California, stating that imaged documents are considered originals, but such laws are only a beginning. They focus mostly on the abilities of state government agencies to present things as evidence—for example, facsimile signatures for pleadings in court. Insurance policies are dramatically different from these other types of documents, and the existing legislation that allows an imaged document to be an "original" might well be interpreted differently if a case involves an insurance contract. •

Source: Debra Bailey Helwig, "Legal Issues and the Internet," *Resource* (November 1997): 18. Adapted with permission of the publisher.

and the individual or organization that purchased the coverage. A contract between two parties may either be unilateral or bilateral. If both parties make legally enforceable promises when they enter into a contract, the contract is **bilateral.** If only one of the parties makes legally enforceable promises when the parties enter into the contract, the contract is **unilateral.**

Suppose, for example, you contract with the Backyard Aquatics Company to have the company build a swimming pool on your property for a mutually agreed-upon price. The contractor has promised to complete the construction for that price, and you have promised to pay that amount. This contract is bilateral—both you and the contractor have made legally enforceable promises.

Life and health insurance policies, on the other hand, are unilateral contracts. The insurer promises to provide coverage in return for a stated premium. As long as premiums are paid, the insurer is legally bound by its contractual promises. The purchaser of the policy, on the other hand, does not promise to pay the premiums and cannot be compelled by law to pay the premiums. A policyowner has the right to stop paying premiums and cancel the policy at any time. Because only the insurer can be legally held to its promises, life and health insurance contracts are unilateral contracts.

Commutative and Aleatory Contracts

Contracts may also be classified as either commutative or aleatory. A **commutative contract** is an agreement under which the parties specify in advance the values that they will exchange; moreover, the parties generally exchange items or services that they think are of relatively equal value. In our earlier example, your contract with the Backyard Aquatics Company is a commutative contract. When the contract was made, you and the contractor specified the service to be provided and the price to be exchanged for that service. In essence, you agreed that the swimming pool and the price you paid for the pool were of equal value. Most contracts fall into this like-for-like exchange category and can be classified as commutative.

In an **aleatory contract,** one party provides something of value to another party in exchange for a conditional promise. A **conditional promise** is a promise to perform a stated act *if* a specified, uncertain event occurs. If the event occurs, then the promise must be performed; if the event does not occur, the promise will not be performed. Also, under an aleatory contract, if the specified event occurs, one party may then receive something of greater value than that party gave.

Life and health insurance policies are aleatory contracts. A life insurance policy is an aleatory contract because the performance of the insurer's promise to pay the policy proceeds is contingent on the death of the insured while the policy is in force, and no one can say with

---

FAST FACT

In 1997, the average amount of life insurance coverage per insured U.S. household was about $165,800.[1]

certainty when the person whose life is insured will die. In fact, if a policy is allowed to terminate prior to the death of the insured, the insurer's promise to pay the policy proceeds will never be performed, even if a number of premiums have been paid. Conversely, death may occur soon after a life insurance policy is issued, and the death benefit then becomes payable. The beneficiary would, in such a case, receive substantially more money than had been paid in premiums. Similarly, a health insurance policy is an aleatory contract under which the insurer may be liable to pay a much larger sum in benefits than it received as premiums for the policy. The insurer does not know if or when it will be liable to pay health insurance policy benefits.

Bargaining Contracts and Contracts of Adhesion

Contracts may be further classified as either bargaining contracts or contracts of adhesion. Suppose that when you made the contract with the Backyard Aquatics Company, you and the contractor held several discussions about the contents of the contract. You asked him to specify his time schedule, the materials he would use, and the way the actual construction would be accomplished. In turn, he quoted a price for each of your requirements. You and the contractor then bargained with one another to arrive at a contract agreeable to both of you. This is an example of a ***bargaining contract,*** one in which both parties, as equals, set the terms and conditions of the contract.

In contrast, individual life and health insurance policies are contracts of adhesion. A ***contract of adhesion*** is a contract that one party prepares and that the other party must accept or reject as a whole, without any bargaining between the parties to the agreement. While the applicant for individual life or health insurance has choices as to some of the contract provisions, generally the applicant must accept or reject the contract as the insurance company has written it. As a result, if any policy provision is ambiguous, the courts usually interpret that provision in whatever manner would be most favorable to the policyowner or beneficiary. In other words, the terms of the contract are construed against the insurance company that drafted the contract. (See Figure 5-1, which lists the types of contracts and identifies which types apply to insurance contracts.)

FAST FACT
By year end 1997, Canadians owned over $870 billion of individual life insurance. The average amount owned per insured individual was $107,900.[2]

General Requirements for a Contract

The principles of contract law determine the legal status of a contract. In other words, these principles dictate whether a contract is legally enforceable and who has the right to enforce a contract. In describing the legal status of a contract, the words *valid*, *void*, and *voidable* are often used. Each of these contract terms is explained below.

FIGURE 5-1. Types of Contracts.

Type of Contract	Applies to an Insurance Contract
Formal Contract	
Informal Contract	✔
Bilateral Contract	
Unilateral Contract	✔
Commutative Contract	
Aleatory Contract	✔
Bargaining Contract	
Contract of Adhesion	✔

- **Valid.** A *valid contract* is one that is enforceable at law.

- **Void.** The term *void* is used in law to describe something that was never valid. A *void contract* is one that was never enforceable at law.

- **Voidable.** At times, one of the parties to an otherwise enforceable contract may have grounds to reject, or *avoid*, it. A *voidable contract* is one in which a party has the right to avoid her obligations under the contract without incurring legal liability.

The formation of a valid informal contract, such as a life or health insurance policy, involves four general requirements:

1. The parties to the contract must manifest their mutual assent to the terms of the contract.

2. The parties to the contract must have contractual capacity.

3. The parties to the contract must exchange legally adequate consideration.

4. The contract must be for a lawful purpose.

Note that these requirements must be met when life or health insurance policies are formed because they are informal contracts.

Mutual Assent

Whether a contract is made when the parties sign a written agreement or shake hands, the parties involved have agreed to something. The requirement of ***mutual assent*** is met when the parties reach a meeting of the minds about the terms of their agreement. For life and health insurance policies, as well as for other contracts, the parties reach this meeting of the minds through a process of *offer and acceptance* in which one party makes an offer to contract and the other party accepts that offer. In order for the parties to mutually assent to a contract, they must all intend to be bound by the terms of the contract. In addition, each party must clearly manifest his intent to be bound by making some outward expression of that intent.

Contractual Capacity

In order for an insurance contract to be binding on all parties, the parties must have ***contractual capacity***—they each must have the legal capacity to make a contract. Thus, the insurance company must have the legal capacity to issue the policy and the applicant must have the legal capacity to purchase the policy.

Contractual Capacity of Individuals. Every individual is presumed to have the legal capacity to enter into a valid contract. Some people, however, do not have full contractual capacity, and therefore, most of the contracts they enter into are void or voidable. In most jurisdictions, the majority of people who have limited contractual capacity either (1) are minors or (2) lack mental capacity.

Generally, contracts entered into by a minor are voidable by the minor. A ***minor*** is a person who has not attained the age of majority. Although the age of majority in Canada and in most states in the United States is 18, in many jurisdictions the age of majority for the purpose of making life insurance contracts has been modified by law. These modifications of the age of majority permit people at ages 16, 15, or even younger to purchase life and health insurance and to exercise some of a policy's ownership rights as though they were adults. In most such situations, however, the beneficiary of such a life insurance policy must be a member of the minor's immediate family.

Laws altering the age of majority for the purpose of entering into life and health insurance contracts protect insurance companies from the possibility that minors will later use their lack of legal capacity to avoid the contract. If an insurance company were to sell an insurance policy to a person who is younger than the permissible age to purchase insurance, then the company would have to provide the promised insurance protection. The minor, however, could sue to avoid the policy, and the insurance company would have to return the premiums the minor had paid on that policy.

A person's lack of mental capacity may affect her contractual capacity in two situations. In one situation, a court declares the person to be insane or mentally incompetent. A contract entered into by a person who has been declared insane or incompetent is usually *void*.

In the second situation, the person's mental competence is impaired, but he has not been declared insane or mentally incompetent by a court. For example, the person can be mentally impaired as a result of being drunk, drugged, or insane. Contracts entered into by someone whose mental competence is impaired are generally *voidable* by the mentally impaired person. If the person later regains mental competence, he may either reject the contract *or* require that it be carried out. The other party to the contract does not have the right to reject the contract and must carry out its terms if required to do so.

Contractual Capacity of Organizations. As we stated previously, an applicant for insurance may either be an individual or an organization that is purchasing coverage for an individual or a group. Organizations are generally presumed to have the contractual capacity of a mentally competent adult. So, an organization that has been created in accordance with the laws of the applicable jurisdiction is presumed to have contractual capacity to purchase insurance.

An insurer acquires its legal capacity to enter into an insurance contract by being licensed or authorized to do business by the proper regulatory authority of the applicable state or province. A company that is not licensed or authorized as an insurance company does not have the legal capacity to make an insurance contract. Should an unauthorized insurer issue a policy to a person who is unaware of the insurer's lack of legal capacity, the policy may be enforceable against the insurer. The legal effect of such a contract depends on the laws of the particular jurisdiction. In some jurisdictions, the contract is *void;* in other jurisdictions, the contract is *voidable* by the policyowner.

Legally Adequate Consideration

In order for an informal contract to be valid, the parties to the contract must exchange **consideration;** each must give or promise something that will be of value to the other party. In addition, the consideration exchanged must be *legally adequate.* A complete description of what is considered to be legally adequate is beyond the scope of this text. In general, the courts will not concern themselves with whether the parties exchanged equal consideration; the question the courts usually focus on in such cases is whether the parties exchanged consideration that has some value to them.

The application and the **initial premium**—the first premium paid for an insurance policy—are given by the policyowner as consideration

> **FAST FACT**
>
> In the United States, the average size of a newly purchased individual life insurance policy increased from $59,981 in 1987 to $97,358 in 1997.[3]

for a life or health insurance contract. This consideration is given in return for the insurer's promise to pay the benefit if the conditions stated in the policy occur. If the initial premium is not paid, then no contract has been formed because the applicant has not provided the required consideration. ***Renewal premiums,*** which are premiums payable after the initial premium, are a condition for continuance of the policy and are *not* consideration for the policy.

Lawful Purpose

No contract can be made for a purpose that is illegal or against the public interest—a contract must be made for a lawful purpose. The courts will not enforce an agreement in which one person promises to perform an illegal act, and any such contract is void. For example, unless there are statutes to the contrary, gambling agreements are not enforceable at law. Also, one person cannot make a legally enforceable agreement that requires another person to do something that is in conflict with an existing law. An agreement that requires one person to kill or defraud another would not be legally enforceable.

The requirement of lawful purpose in the making of an individual life or health insurance contract is fulfilled by the presence of *insurable interest.* The primary purpose of all insurance is to protect against financial loss, not to provide a means of possible financial gain. In Chapter 3, we discussed insurable interest and its importance in insurance. The requirement that insurable interest be present at the time of application provides assurance that a life or health insurance contract is being made for the lawful purpose of providing protection against financial loss, rather than for an unlawful purpose, such as speculating on a life or profiting from ill health. The lawful purpose requirement must be met as a condition for the *formation* of a contract. As a result, if the insurable interest requirement is not met, a valid contract was never formed and the agreement is void. Recall, however, that if the insurable interest requirement is met and the parties enter into a valid insurance contract, a continuing insurable interest is not required for the contract to remain valid.

> **FAST FACT**
>
> During 1997, Canadians purchased over $110 billion in individual life insurance. The average size of individual policies purchased was $123,700.[4]

EXAMPLE When Ann Saul died, she was insured under a life insurance policy. In evaluating the death claim, the insurer discovered that the insurable interest requirement had not been met when the policy was issued.

ANALYSIS The contract is void and the insurer is not required to pay the policy death benefit. The insurer will likely refund all the premiums that were paid for the policy.

| EXAMPLE | When Juan Gomez purchased an insurance policy on his life, he named his wife Lois as the beneficiary. Juan and Lois divorced several years later, but Juan did not change the policy beneficiary designation. After Juan's death, Lois filed a claim for the policy proceeds. |

| ANALYSIS | The insurable interest requirement was met when Juan purchased the policy because the named beneficiary was his wife, who had an insurable interest in Juan's life at that time. As a result, the contract is valid. Lois was no longer required to have an insurable interest in Juan's life in order to receive the policy proceeds following his death. |

The Policy as Property

In addition to being governed by contract law, insurance policies are a type of property and, thus, are also subject to the principles of property law. In legal terminology, **property** is defined as a bundle of rights a person has with respect to something. In most jurisdictions in the United States and Canada, **real property** is land and whatever is growing on or affixed to the land. All property other than real property is characterized as **personal property** and includes tangible goods such as clothing, furniture, and automobiles, as well as intangible property such as contractual rights. An insurance policy is *intangible personal property*—it represents intangible legal rights that have value and that can be enforced by the courts. The owner of an insurance policy—rather than the insured or the beneficiary—holds these ownership rights in an insurance policy.

Ownership of property is the sum of all the legal rights that exist in that property. The legal rights an owner has in property include the right to use and enjoy the property and the right to dispose of the property.

Right to Use and Enjoy Property

The right to use and enjoy property that one owns is an inherent feature of property ownership. The owner of an insurance policy has the right to deal with the policy in a number of ways. For example, the owner of a life insurance policy has the right to name the policy beneficiary. The policyowner also usually has the right to change the beneficiary designation at any time while the policy is in force. In some cases, however, the policyowner may give up the right to change the beneficiary designation by making the designation irrevocable. We describe naming and changing the beneficiary in Chapter 11.

Right to Dispose of Property

The owner of property generally has the right to dispose of the property. For example, if you own an automobile, you have the right to give it away or sell it. Similarly, the owner of an insurance policy can dispose of it. The policyowner may transfer ownership of the policy by making a gift of the policy to someone else. We describe some of these aspects of policy ownership in later chapters. For now, just remember that as property, an insurance policy consists of a bundle of ownership rights.

Key Terms

contract
formal contract
informal contract
bilateral contract
unilateral contract
commutative contract
aleatory contract
conditional promise
bargaining contract
contract of adhesion
valid contract
void contract

voidable contract
mutual assent
contractual capacity
minor
consideration
initial premium
renewal premiums
property
real property
personal property
ownership of property

Other Important Terms

offer and acceptance
legally adequate consideration

insurable interest
intangible personal property

Endnotes

1. ACLI, *1998 Life Insurance Fact Book* (Washington, D.C.: American Council of Life Insurance, 1998), 12.

2. CLHIA, *Canadian Life and Health Insurance Facts* (Toronto: Canadian Life and Health Insurance Association Inc., 1998), 6.

3. ACLI, 1.

4. CLHIA, 8.

CHAPTER 6

Pricing Life Insurance

After reading this chapter, you should be able to

- Identify three methods that organizations have used over the years to fund life insurance and distinguish among those methods

- Identify the three factors insurance companies use to calculate life insurance premiums under the legal reserve system and recognize how each factor affects premium rate calculations

- Recognize the features of the level premium pricing system

- Identify two methods an insurer might use to change the price of a life insurance policy after it has been issued

- Define policy reserves and contingency reserves

- Calculate the insurer's net amount at risk for a given life insurance policy

I n order for an insurer to have enough money available to pay policy benefits when they become due, the insurer determines the premium the company must charge for the specific insurance coverage provided. Establishing premium rates is one function of an actuary. Insurance companies employ actuaries to develop the mathematical bases and calculations needed to price insurance products.

In this chapter, we describe the methods that have evolved over the years for determining life insurance premiums. We describe health insurance pricing and the pricing of annuities in Part 2 when we describe those products.

Methods of Funding Life Insurance

The first insurers were individuals who were willing to assume someone else's risk of economic loss in return for a mutually agreed-upon price. The insurer usually issued a contract or policy that was signed at the bottom to show that the risk had been accepted. This signature under the terms of the contract is the origin of the insurance term *underwriter*. The insurer had underwritten, or accepted, the risk by placing his signature on the contract. These insurers were known as individual underwriters.

Issuing insurance at that time was a very speculative business venture. Individual underwriters had no way to predict accurately the losses they were likely to incur. Further, the underwriter had to pay all claims from his own funds. If he incurred losses that far exceeded the premiums he had received, it was possible that he might not be able to pay all claims. When organizations began to issue life insurance, they first experimented with two funding systems—the mutual benefit method and the assessment method.

Mutual Benefit Method

Organizations known as mutual benefit societies developed an early method of obtaining money to pay death claims; they collected money *after* the death of the person who was insured. This funding method became known as the **mutual benefit method** or the *post-death assessment method*. Each member of a mutual benefit society agreed to pay an equal, specific amount of money when any other member died. Usually, the person or persons doing the administrative work for the society would receive a fee, often a small percentage of the money collected, and the rest would be paid to the insured's beneficiary. For example, upon the death of a member, a society with 500 members might require a $10 payment from each surviving participant. The total amount collected—$4,990—minus administrative fees was paid to the insured member's beneficiary.

Three major problems were associated with the mutual benefit method:

1. Mutual benefit societies often had problems collecting the money to pay death benefits. A society could not force its members to pay their shares and, thus, could not guarantee the amount of death benefit that would be paid when a member died.

2. Unless a society constantly recruited new members, the size of the group became smaller and smaller as members died or resigned from the society. As a society's membership declined, the society either had to reduce the amount of the death benefit paid or increase the amount each surviving member was required to pay for each death.

3. As the members of a society grew older, the number of deaths increased each year. The more deaths that occurred in a given year, the more death benefits the society paid; thus, each member's cost increased each year. As the cost of membership in a society increased, attracting new members became more difficult for the society. In addition, many members in good health dropped out of the society as their membership costs increased. Thus, the contributions required of the remaining members soared.

In order to cope with these problems, organizations developed a new form of funding life insurance benefits. This method, commonly referred to as the *assessment method*, funded life insurance benefits using pre-death assessments.

Assessment Method

Under the ***assessment method*** for funding life insurance benefits, the organization that offered insurance coverage estimated its operating costs for a given period, usually one year. These operating costs included anticipated death claims and the organization's administrative expenses. The organization then divided the total amount of money needed to pay operating costs for the period equally among the participants in the plan.

| **EXAMPLE** | At the beginning of a given year, a society with 500 members anticipated that 3 members would die in that year |

and that the society would incur $500 in administrative expenses. The society had agreed to pay a $5,000 death benefit to each member's beneficiary.

| **ANALYSIS** | At the beginning of the year, each member would be assessed $31. That amount is calculated as follows: |

$ 15,000	Expected death benefits payable ($5,000 × 3 deaths)
+ 500	Plus: Administrative expenses
$ 15,500	Equals: Total amount needed to pay death benefits and expenses
÷ 500	Divided by: Number of members
$ 31	Equals: $31/member

If the total actual cost of operations during a period was less than expected, then each participant received a refund. Alternatively, if the total operating cost was higher than expected, then the organization levied an additional assessment on each member.

Although prepayment of assessments solved the major collection problem that mutual benefit societies had faced, collection of any additional assessments was still difficult. In addition, the assessment method did not solve the problems caused by the aging of the group of insureds. As time passed, the number of deaths occurring in the group increased, and the size of each assessment then had to be increased. This higher cost deterred new members from joining, and consequently, the costs of paying death benefits had to be spread among fewer and fewer members. Finally, the assessment became so large that it was no longer affordable.

In an attempt to make an assessment plan more attractive to younger people, some organizations did charge somewhat higher assessments for older members. This approach, however, succeeded only in discouraging the healthier, older participants from continuing in the plan, and many of those participants dropped out.

Legal Reserve System

The modern system used to price life insurance evolved from these early funding methods. Today's pricing system, known as the *legal reserve system,* is based on several premises:

- The amount of the death benefit payable under a life insurance policy should be specified or calculable in advance of the insured's death.

- The money needed to pay death benefits should be collected in advance so that the insurer will have funds available to pay claims and expenses as they occur.

- The premium an individual pays for an insurance policy should be directly related to the amount of risk the insurance company assumes for that policy.

The legal reserve system is based on laws requiring that insurance companies establish policy reserves. In Chapter 2, we noted that U.S. and Canadian insurers are required to establish *policy reserves,* which are *liabilities* that represent the amount the insurer estimates it needs to pay policy benefits as they come due. Because these reserves are required by law, they are sometimes referred to as *legal reserves* or *statutory reserves.*

Remember that in order to keep its basic accounting equation in balance, the insurer's assets must equal its liabilities and owners' equity. If the amount of the insurer's liabilities—which includes its policy reserves—increases, then the insurer must also make a corresponding increase in the amount of its assets. The insurance company is required by law to maintain assets that are at least equal to the amount of its policy reserve liabilities. We discuss reserves in more detail later in this chapter.

Premium Rate Calculations

Insurance companies employ specialists, known as *actuaries,* who are responsible for calculating the premium rates the company will charge for its products. Actuaries are trained in the mathematics of insurance and are responsible for performing all of the calculations needed to ensure that a company's products are mathematically sound. Thus, in addition to calculating premium rates, actuaries also calculate the amounts of a company's policy reserves and of its policy dividends.

Insurance company actuaries consider many factors as they perform the calculations necessary to establish premium rates that are adequate and equitable. Premium rates must be *adequate* for the company to have enough money to pay policy benefits. Premium rates must be *equitable* so that each policyowner is charged premiums that reflect the degree of risk the insurer assumes in providing the coverage. The following factors are included in the calculation of life insurance premium rates:

- **Rate of mortality.** The rate at which the people whose lives are insured are expected to die

- **Investment earnings.** The money that an insurance company earns from its investment of premium dollars

- **Expenses.** All the costs involved in issuing insurance policies and operating an insurance company

We devote much of this chapter to discussing these factors and how they are used in determining premium rates for individual life insurance.

Rate of Mortality

As we noted in Chapter 3, an insurer must be able to estimate accurately the number and timing of claims in order to determine how much money will be needed to pay future claims. To price life insurance products, then, an insurer must be able to predict the approximate number of deaths that will occur each year among a given group of insureds.

Keep in mind that the actuaries in an insurance company are concerned with estimating the number of deaths that will occur in a given group of insureds, called a *block of insureds,* and not with predicting which individual insureds will die. Therefore, when we mention a single life insurance policy in this text, you can assume that all calculations relating to that policy are based on calculations for a *block of policies* that are like that individual policy. A ***block of policies*** is a group of policies issued to insureds who are all the same age, the same sex, and in the same risk classification. Each insurance company decides which policies are included in a block of policies when calculating premium rates. For example, an insurance company may classify into one block all term insurance policies issued to males age 35 who are nonsmokers and have no significant medical history.

In most cases, insurers calculate premium rates for a block of policies based on a $1,000 life insurance coverage amount. Consequently, the premium rate is often expressed as the rate per thousand.

EXAMPLE	The annual premium rate for a $50,000 life insurance policy might be expressed as $3.50 per thousand.

ANALYSIS	The annual premium amount for that policy would be $175. That amount is calculated as follows:

$ 3.50   Price per unit ($1000 of coverage)
× 50   **Times:** Number of units (50,000 ÷ 1,000)
$ 175   **Equals:** Annual premium

In the early days of the insurance industry, few statistics were available for insurers to use to predict mortality rates. What little information insurers were able to gather included figures for the entire population, even for people who were in such poor health that they would have been considered uninsurable. Once insurers began issuing policies and paying claims, however, they began to collect data regarding insured lives. These figures were more accurate for the purpose of developing insurance mortality statistics because they related only to people who insurers considered to be acceptable risks.

Mortality Tables and How They Are Used

Today, some insurers that issue life insurance accumulate and share statistical information so that figures on the insurance industry's overall mortality experience may be used by all insurance companies. This information has been organized into charts showing the mortality rates that are expected to occur at each age. The term ***expected mortality,*** or *tabular mortality,* is used to mean the number of deaths that have been predicted to occur in a group of people at a given age according to the mortality table. The number of deaths that actually occur in a given year among a given group of insureds is referred to as the group's ***mortality experience.***

Mortality tables, therefore, are charts that show the death rates an insurer may reasonably anticipate among a particular group of insured lives at certain ages—that is, how many people in each age group may be expected to die in a particular year. Although the rates of mortality that actually occur may fluctuate from group to group, the fluctuations will tend to offset one another, being higher than expected for one group and lower than expected for another.

An example of a mortality table is shown in Figure 6-1. The table is based on the 1980 Commissioners Standard Ordinary Mortality Table (1980 CSO Table), which is widely used by insurance department regulators to monitor the adequacy of each insurer's life insurance policy reserves. The table has two sides, labeled male and female. Each side of the table (male and female) is divided into four columns that give the following information:

- Column 1: shows the ages of all people in the group

- Column 2: shows the number of people alive at each age at the beginning of the year

- Column 3: shows the number of people expected to die at each age during the year

- Column 4: shows how many people out of each thousand are expected to die at each age during the year

To illustrate how mortality tables are designed, we'll look at the section of this table that contains mortality statistics for males. It begins with a group of 10 million newborn males. By using extensive statistics about the rate of mortality, insurance companies have been able to estimate that 41,800 of the original 10 million males may be expected to die before they reach their first birthday. Using this information, we can then determine that 4.18 out of every 1,000 males will die between birth and age 1.

If you go down to the next row of numbers, you will see that 9,958,200 males from this group are assumed to be alive at age 1. This number is found by subtracting the 41,800 deaths from the original 10 million males (10,000,000 – 41,800 = 9,958,200). Of the number of males living at age 1, 10,655 are expected to die before reaching age 2, indicating that 1.07 out of every 1,000 males who have reached age 1 will die before they are 2 years old. Thus, you can follow the progression of the mortality table from age 0 to age 99 by which age the last males in the original group of 10 million can be expected to die. Life insurers realize that some people live beyond the age of 99, but the number of people living beyond that age is so statistically insignificant that insurers end their tables at a very high age, such as age 99 or age 100. Although this table ends at age 99, other mortality tables may end at a lower or higher age.

For a more graphic representation of the rate of mortality, look at Figure 6-2. This figure shows mortality rates of males and females based on the 1980 CSO Table. As a group, females live longer than males, and the mortality rate of females at any given age—up to age 99—is lower than that for males. Mortality rates of both males and females start high at birth and then decrease dramatically at age 1. They both then steadily decrease until about age 10, at which point they begin increasing slightly. Mortality rates of females continue this steady increase, while those of males begin to climb sharply

FIGURE 6-1. The 1980 Commissioners Standard Ordinary Mortality Table (1980 CSO Table).

	Male			Female			
Age	Number Living	Number Dying	Mortality Rate per 1,000	Number Living	Number Dying	Mortality Rate per 1,000	Age
0	10 000 000	41 800	4.18	10 000 000	28 900	2.89	0
1	9 958 200	10 655	1.07	9 971 100	8 675	.87	1
2	9 947 545	9 848	.99	9 962 425	8 070	.81	2
3	9 937 697	9 739	.98	9 954 355	7 864	.79	3
4	9 927 958	9 432	.95	9 946 491	7 659	.77	4
5	9 918 526	8 927	.90	9 938 832	7 554	.76	5
6	9 909 599	8 522	.86	9 931 278	7 250	.73	6
7	9 901 077	7 921	.80	9 924 028	7 145	.72	7
8	9 893 156	7 519	.76	9 916 883	6 942	.70	8
9	9 885 637	7 315	.74	9 909 941	6 838	.69	9
10	9 878 322	7 211	.73	9 903 103	6 734	.68	10
11	9 871 111	7 601	.77	9 896 369	6 828	.69	11
12	9 863 510	8 384	.85	9 889 541	7 120	.72	12
13	9 855 126	9 757	.99	9 882 421	7 412	.75	13
14	9 845 369	11 322	1.15	9 875 009	7 900	.80	14
15	9 834 047	13 079	1.33	9 867 109	8 387	.85	15
16	9 820 968	14 830	1.51	9 858 722	8 873	.90	16
17	9 806 138	16 376	1.67	9 849 849	9 357	.95	17
18	9 789 762	17 426	1.78	9 840 492	9 644	.98	18
19	9 772 336	18 177	1.86	9 830 848	10 027	1.02	19
20	9 754 159	18 533	1.90	9 820 821	10 312	1.05	20
21	9 735 626	18 595	1.91	9 810 509	10 497	1.07	21
22	9 717 031	18 365	1.89	9 800 012	10 682	1.09	22
23	9 698 666	18 040	1.86	9 789 330	10 866	1.11	23
24	9 680 626	17 619	1.82	9 778 464	11 147	1.14	24
25	9 663 007	17 104	1.77	9 767 317	11 330	1.16	25
26	9 645 903	16 687	1.73	9 755 987	11 610	1.19	26
27	9 629 216	16 466	1.71	9 744 377	11 888	1.22	27
28	9 612 750	16 342	1.70	9 732 489	12 263	1.26	28
29	9 596 408	16 410	1.71	9 720 226	12 636	1.30	29
30	9 579 998	16 573	1.73	9 707 590	13 105	1.35	30
31	9 563 425	17 023	1.78	9 694 485	13 572	1.40	31
32	9 546 402	17 470	1.83	9 680 913	14 037	1.45	32
33	9 528 932	18 200	1.91	9 666 876	14 500	1.50	33
34	9 510 732	19 021	2.00	9 652 376	15 251	1.58	34
35	9 491 711	20 028	2.11	9 637 125	15 901	1.65	35
36	9 471 683	21 217	2.24	9 621 224	16 933	1.76	36
37	9 450 466	22 681	2.40	9 604 291	18 152	1.89	37
38	9 427 785	24 324	2.58	9 586 139	19 556	2.04	38
39	9 403 461	26 236	2.79	9 566 583	21 238	2.22	39
40	9 377 225	28 319	3.02	9 545 345	23 100	2.42	40
41	9 348 906	30 758	3.29	9 522 245	25 139	2.64	41
42	9 318 148	33 173	3.56	9 497 106	27 257	2.87	42
43	9 284 975	35 933	3.87	9 469 849	29 262	3.09	43
44	9 249 042	38 753	4.19	9 440 587	31 343	3.32	44
45	9 210 289	41 907	4.55	9 409 244	33 497	3.56	45
46	9 168 382	45 108	4.92	9 375 747	35 628	3.80	46
47	9 123 274	48 536	5.32	9 340 119	37 827	4.05	47
48	9 074 738	52 089	5.74	9 302 292	40 279	4.33	48
49	9 022 649	56 031	6.21	9 262 013	42 883	4.63	49
50	8 966 618	60 166	6.71	9 219 130	45 727	4.96	50
51	8 906 452	65 017	7.30	9 173 403	48 711	5.31	51
52	8 841 435	70 378	7.96	9 124 692	52 011	5.70	52
53	8 771 057	76 396	8.71	9 072 681	55 797	6.15	53
54	8 694 661	83 121	9.56	9 016 884	59 602	6.61	54
55	8 611 540	90 163	10.47	8 957 282	63 507	7.09	55
56	8 521 377	97 655	11.46	8 893 775	67 326	7.57	56
57	8 423 722	105 212	12.49	8 826 449	70 876	8.03	57
58	8 318 510	113 049	13.59	8 755 573	74 160	8.47	58
59	8 205 461	121 195	14.77	8 681 413	77 612	8.94	59
60	8 084 266	129 995	16.08	8 603 801	81 478	9.47	60
61	7 954 271	139 518	17.54	8 522 323	86 331	10.13	61
62	7 814 753	149 965	19.19	8 435 992	92 458	10.96	62
63	7 664 788	161 420	21.06	8 343 534	100 289	12.02	63
64	7 503 368	173 628	23.14	8 243 245	109 223	13.25	64
65	7 329 740	186 322	25.42	8 134 022	118 675	14.59	65
66	7 143 418	198 944	27.85	8 015 347	128 246	16.00	66
67	6 944 474	211 390	30.44	7 887 101	137 472	17.43	67
68	6 733 084	223 471	33.19	7 749 629	146 003	18.84	68
69	6 509 613	235 453	36.17	7 603 626	154 810	20.36	69
70	6 274 160	247 892	39.51	7 448 816	164 693	22.11	70
71	6 026 268	260 937	43.30	7 284 123	176 494	24.23	71
72	5 765 331	274 718	47.65	7 107 629	190 982	26.87	72
73	5 490 613	289 026	52.64	6 916 647	208 260	30.11	73
74	5 201 587	302 680	58.19	6 708 387	227 616	33.93	74
75	4 898 907	314 461	64.19	6 480 771	247 825	38.24	75
76	4 584 446	323 341	70.53	6 232 946	267 830	42.97	76
77	4 261 105	328 616	77.12	5 965 116	286 564	48.04	77
78	3 932 489	329 936	83.90	5 678 552	303 519	53.45	78
79	3 602 553	328 012	91.05	5 375 033	319 008	59.35	79
80	3 274 541	323 656	98.84	5 056 025	333 647	65.99	80
81	2 950 885	317 161	107.48	4 722 378	347 567	73.60	81
82	2 633 724	308 804	117.25	4 374 811	360 484	82.40	82
83	2 324 920	298 194	128.26	4 014 327	371 446	92.53	83
84	2 026 726	284 248	140.25	3 642 881	378 167	103.81	84
85	1 742 478	266 512	152.95	3 264 714	379 033	116.10	85
86	1 475 966	245 143	166.09	2 885 681	373 090	129.29	86
87	1 230 823	220 994	179.55	2 512 591	360 105	143.32	87
88	1 009 829	195 170	193.27	2 152 486	340 480	158.18	88
89	814 659	168 871	207.29	1 812 006	315 180	173.94	89
90	645 788	143 216	221.77	1 496 826	285 520	190.75	90
91	502 572	119 100	236.98	1 211 306	253 005	208.87	91
92	383 472	97 191	253.45	958 301	219 269	228.81	92
93	286 281	77 900	272.11	739 032	185 874	251.51	93
94	208 381	61 660	295.90	553 158	154 503	279.31	94
95	146 721	48 412	329.96	398 655	126 501	317.32	95
96	98 309	37 805	384.55	272 154	102 259	375.74	96
97	60 504	29 054	480.20	169 895	80 695	474.97	97
98	31 450	20 693	657.98	89 200	58 502	655.85	98
99	10 757	10 757	1000.00	30 698	30 698	1000.00	99

Source: "Report of the Special Committee to Recommend New Mortality Tables for Valuation," *Transactions of the Society of Actuaries XXXIII* (1981): 617–54.

FIGURE 6-2. Comparison of Male and Female Mortality Curves.

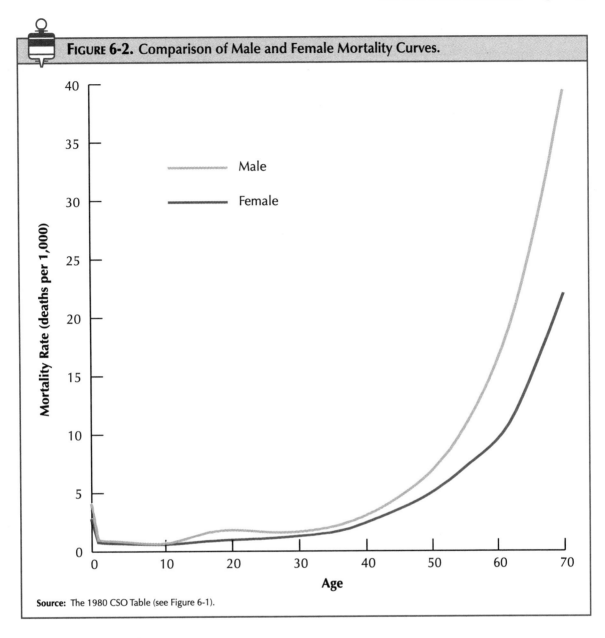

Source: The 1980 CSO Table (see Figure 6-1).

during the teenage years, then drop again in the mid-twenties, and begin to rise again in the early thirties. Finally, the mortality rates of both males and females age 65 or over accelerate sharply with each passing year. Note that, according to the 1980 CSO Table, the mortality rates of males and females are the same at age 99.

Life insurers use mortality tables as a first step in determining the price of a block of life insurance policies—the price of all life policies issued to a specific group of insureds. Throughout the remainder of this discussion, we'll use the 1980 CSO Table to illustrate the discussion so that you can refer to the mortality table included in

Figure 6-1. In practice, though, insurance companies do not use this mortality table for premium rate calculations because the 1980 CSO Table shows higher mortality rates than insured groups actually experience. Insurers, therefore, use mortality tables that more accurately reflect the mortality experience of their insureds. Further, the mortality tables that insurers use in premium rate calculations break down the information about each sex into two additional categories—smokers and nonsmokers. In other words, mortality tables often show mortality rates for four categories of people—male nonsmokers, male smokers, female nonsmokers, and female smokers. Smoking has such a dramatic effect on mortality rates that insurance companies routinely account for that factor in the mortality tables they use to calculate life insurance premium rates.

In general, the higher the mortality rate is for a group of insureds, the higher the premium rate will be for the block of life insurance policies issued to that group. For example, assume a life insurer based premium rates on the mortality rates shown in Figure 6-1. The insurer would charge a lower premium rate for policies issued to males age 25, who have an expected mortality rate of 1.77 per thousand, than the insurer would charge for comparable policies issued to males age 35, who have an expected mortality rate of 2.11 per thousand. Similarly, the insurer would charge much lower premium rates for policies issued to females age 35, who have an expected mortality rate of 1.65 per thousand, than would be charged for comparable policies issued to females age 60, whose expected mortality rate is 9.47 per thousand.

The mortality table that we have used as an example shows the expected mortality rates for the insured population as a whole. The mortality rates of some groups of people, however, do not follow this pattern of standard mortality rates and are not represented in that table. For example, factors such as being overweight or underweight, engaging in certain occupations or hobbies, and having various illnesses have all been studied, and results have been compiled to show how such factors affect the death rate at each age. When these results indicate that a particular factor increases the insured's mortality risk, an insurer may decide to charge a higher premium rate for people who possess such a risk factor. As noted in Chapter 3, people who are charged a higher than standard premium rate because they possess such risk factors are called *substandard risks,* and the premium rate charged to these people is called a *substandard premium rate.*

As we have seen, mortality tables show that, on average, women live longer than men. Recognizing this difference in expected life spans, most insurers price equivalent life insurance policies at a lower rate for women than for men of the same age. However, the state of Montana now requires companies to charge men and women the same premium rate based on unisex mortality tables; charging

---

FAST FACT

Although older applicants generally represent higher mortality risks, insurers are interested in providing products to older people because seniors are the fastest growing portion of the population. By the year 2040, more than 1 in every 5 people in the United States will be over age 65.[2]

men and women different premium rates is considered, in this state, to be a form of sexual discrimination.

Investment Earnings

The second factor that insurance companies consider when establishing life insurance premium rates is their investment earnings—the money that insurers earn by investing premium dollars. Remember that premium dollars are the primary source of funds used to pay life insurance claims. Because most policies are in force for some time before claims become payable, the premium dollars are available for the insurer to invest. The earnings from these investments provide additional funds that allow insurance companies to charge lower premium rates than they could if they relied on the premium amounts alone. For example, 28 percent of the total income of U.S. life insurance companies in 1997 resulted from investment earnings.[3]

Insurance companies invest premium dollars in many different ways—in government and corporate bonds, mortgages, real estate, and corporate stock. In fact, insurance companies can place money in any safe investment that is likely to provide good earnings and is not prohibited by government regulation.

How Investments Create Earnings

Interest is basically money that is paid for the use of money. The amount of interest that is charged for the use of money is expressed in terms of a percentage, such as 10 percent. A 10 percent interest rate indicates that a borrower must pay the lender the amount originally borrowed, plus an additional 10 percent of that amount. For example, if you were to lend your brother $1,000 for one year at an annual interest rate of 10 percent, he would owe you $1,100 at the end of the year—the $1,000 you loaned him plus $100 ($1,000 × 0.10 = $100). This example illustrates the payment of **simple interest,** which is interest paid on the original sum only.

When interest has been *earned* on money, but not paid, interest can accrue, or accumulate, on that unpaid interest. Paying interest on both an original principal sum and on accrued interest is called *compounding,* and the interest paid under these conditions is known as **compound interest.** For example, if you let your brother keep the $1,000 loan for an additional year without paying you the $100 of interest for the previous year, you would actually be making a second loan of $1,100 (the amount due you at the end of the first year). At a 10 percent rate of interest, you'll earn $110 interest during the second year ($1,100 × 0.10 = $110). Therefore, at the end of the second year, your brother will owe you a total of $1,210 ($1,100 + $110). The interest in this example was compounded annually. Interest can be compounded, however, during any selected period—a half-year, a month, or a day, for example.

Over a long period of time, compound interest has a dramatic effect on the amount of principal that has accumulated at interest. For example, if you were to save $1,000 per year for 25 years at no interest, you would have $25,000 at the end of the 25-year period. If you saved the same $1,000 per year and invested it at an interest rate of 8 percent, compounded annually, you would have over $73,000 at the end of 25 years. (See Figure 6-3, which illustrates this example.)

For the sake of simplicity, we illustrated investment earnings in terms of an interest rate earned on loans. Any investment earnings, however, can be expressed in terms of the rate of return that the investor has earned. For example, insurance companies invest money by buying stock in other companies. While it owns stock, an insurance company will probably earn dividends on that stock. In addition, the insurer might be able to sell the stock for more than it paid

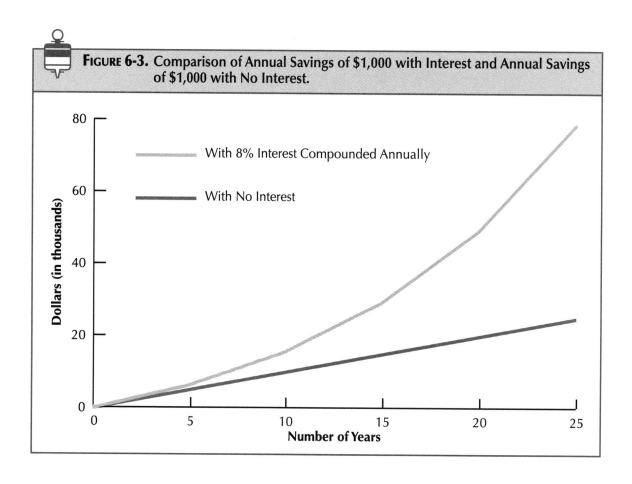

Figure 6-3. Comparison of Annual Savings of $1,000 with Interest and Annual Savings of $1,000 with No Interest.

for the stock. The insurer's total earnings on the stock can be expressed in terms of a percentage rate of return.

Many factors enter into the insurance company's calculations concerning the rate of return expected to be earned on its investments, and we will not go into greater detail here regarding those calculations. Students should be aware, however, that investments such as stocks, real estate, and other business ventures produce a significant part of an insurance company's investment earnings.

How Investment Earnings Affect Pricing

The effect of investment earnings on insurance companies and their policyowners becomes especially important in premium rate calculations. An insurer's investment earnings enable it to charge lower premium rates than would be possible if the insurer considered only the mortality risk factor. The longer a policy is in force, the greater the effect investment earnings will have on premium rate calculations. The effect of investment earnings on the cost of insurance policies that are in force for only one year is slight; by contrast, investment earnings have a substantial effect on the cost of policies that are in force for long terms or for the insured's entire lifetime.

To illustrate, assume that 1,000 men age 35 purchase insurance policies. Each policy has a face amount of $10,000, and each policy will terminate when the insured dies or reaches age 60, whichever occurs first. Because this type of policy is designed to terminate at the end of a specified term, it is a form of term insurance. The company uses a mortality table to find the number of people in this group who can be expected to die each year during the next 25 years and the number of people who will be left alive to pay premiums each year. If the company used the 1980 CSO Table (Male) to estimate the number of deaths each year, the insurance company would find that approximately 148 of the insured people will die during the next 25 years. Therefore, the company would need a total of $1,480,000 just to provide enough money to pay for all expected claims. Using calculations that take into account both the number of people who are expected to die each year and the number of people who are expected to stay alive, the insurer can determine that if each person purchasing a policy pays a premium of approximately $62 each year, then the insurer will have enough money to pay benefits as the insureds die.

Calculating the premium this way, however, assumes that the life insurance company will take the money paid as premiums, put it in a vault or some other safe place, and do nothing with it until it is needed to pay claims.

Insurance companies, however, do not treat premium dollars in this manner. Instead, companies invest the premium payments they receive. Therefore, if the insurance company in the previous example

> **FAST FACT**
>
> During 1997, U.S. life insurance companies earned $170.7 billion of investment income.[4]

projects that it can invest the money paid as premiums to earn a 5 percent rate of return each year for 25 years, then the company can reduce the annual premium charged each policyowner to about $49, yet still have enough money to pay the estimated $1,480,000 in expected claims. In this example, investment income is responsible for approximately a 21 percent reduction in the premium the insurer will charge for each policy. If the insurance company knew that it could earn a higher rate of return on investments, then the insurance company could reduce the premium amount even further.

Expenses

A policy's **net premium** is the amount of money the insurer needs in order to provide benefits for the policy. In order to calculate net premium rates, life insurers must make assumptions as to mortality rates, investment earnings, and lapse rates. The term *lapse rate* refers to the rate at which policyowners decide to drop their coverage or allow it to lapse (expire) for nonpayment of premium before the end of the premium-payment period specified in their policies. In many such situations, the insurer will not have collected enough in premiums to cover the costs of underwriting and issuing the coverage. Therefore, an insurer must add an amount to the net premium that will compensate for the costs incurred to issue policies that will be dropped or lapse.

When pricing insurance, insurers must also consider their operating costs, such as sales and commission costs, taxes, personnel salaries, and the cost of establishing and maintaining a home office, regional offices (if any), and sales offices. In addition, recordkeeping costs, including operating both manual and computer systems, are a major operating expense for insurance companies. (See Figure 6-4, which shows the portion of insurance company expenditures that is attributable to operating costs and the portion that is attributable to paying policy benefits.)

The insurance company must add an amount to the net premium to cover all of these operating costs and to provide itself with some profit. The total amount added to the net premium to cover all of the insurer's costs of doing business is called the **loading**. The net premium with the loading added is called the **gross premium**, which is the premium amount the insurer charges the policyowner to keep the policy in force.

> **Net premium + Loading = Gross premium**

We have now discussed three factors that insurers must consider in calculating the premium rate for a life insurance policy: mortality rates, investment earnings, and expenses. The premium charged for a

FIGURE 6-4. Portion of Each Dollar of Insurance Company Expenditures Attributable to Expenses in 1997.

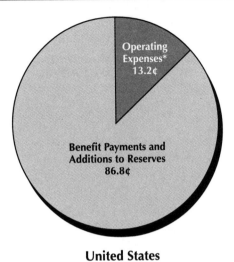

Operating Expenses*
13.2¢

Benefit Payments and
Additions to Reserves
86.8¢

United States

* Includes taxes and stockholder dividends.

Source: ACLI, *1998 Life Insurance Fact Book* (Washington, D.C.: American Council of Life Insurance, 1998), 75–76.

life insurance policy must include these factors, though the manner in which insurers express a policy's cost varies depending on the type of policy. Some insurance policies, such as universal life policies, state the amount of money that the insurer needs to cover mortality and expenses and the rate of return on investments that the insurer will use to calculate the amount of the policy's premiums. We describe these policies in detail in Chapter 8. Other policies, such as term insurance and whole life insurance policies, state only the gross premium that the insurer will charge for the policy.

The Level Premium Pricing System

The *level premium system* is a life insurance pricing system that allows the purchaser to pay the same premium amount each year the policy is in force. It is used to price whole life insurance, term insurance that provides coverage for more than one year, and endowment insurance. As we have seen, because mortality rates increase with age, the cost of providing life insurance must also increase. Unfortunately, many people cannot afford the cost of insurance in their later years when mortality rates are greater. In order to provide life insurance coverage for periods of more than one year at a premium rate that does *not* increase each year with the insured's age, the life insurance industry developed the level premium pricing system.

The leveling of premiums is possible because premium rates charged for level premium policies are higher than needed to pay claims and expenses that occur during the early years of those policies. In the early years, the excess premium dollars collected—those premium dollars not needed to pay claims and expenses that occur during the early years—are invested by the insurance company. As people in a group insured under a block of level premium policies grow older, the insurance company expects an increasing number of death claims from the group each year. Under the level premium system, these claims can be paid in large part with the excess premium dollars, plus investment earnings, that were collected during the early policy years. Thus, the premium rate on any one of these policies can remain level throughout the duration of the policy.

To demonstrate the relationship between the premium rate for a level premium policy and the premium rates for a series of 1-year policies, we can return to a previous example. Just a few pages back, we described the net premium calculation for a block of $10,000 life insurance policies issued to 1,000 males age 35. The net premium for each policy was $49, payable each year during the policy's 25-year term. If each of the same 1,000 males age 35 buys a $10,000 life insurance policy that provides coverage for 1 year, instead of 25 years, the net premium charged that first year would be about $20.

This $20 net premium is less than half the $49 net premium for the level premium policy because in calculating the $20 net premium, the insurer considers the mortality rate of the group of 35-year-olds for only 1 year. If a policyowner repurchases the $10,000 policy each succeeding year, the net premium for the 1-year policy would increase each year, reaching about $43 by the time the insured reaches age 45. This amount is still less than the net premium for the level premium policy, but the price has more than doubled in the 10 years since the insureds were age 35 because the group's mortality rate increases each year. By the time the men in the insured group reach age 55, the net premium for the 1-year term policy would increase to $100, over double the net premium for the level premium policy, and by the time the insureds reach age 60, the net premium would reach $153. (See Figure 6-5, which shows the difference between the level premium amount and the premium amounts for the 1-year term policies.)

Because at the time of purchase a one-year term insurance policy is less expensive than a similar level premium, long-term policy, a one-year policy can provide relatively inexpensive, short-term protection. As an insured's age increases, however, so does the premium rate for a one-year policy. The premium rate for a level premium policy, on the other hand, does not increase after the policy has been

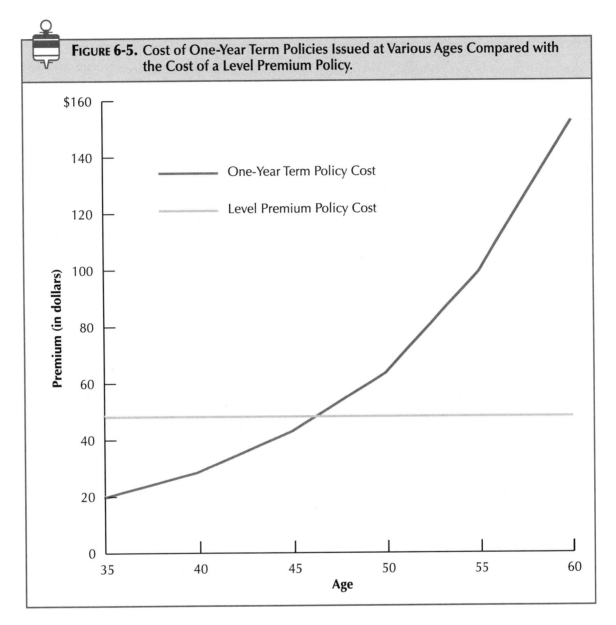

FIGURE 6-5. Cost of One-Year Term Policies Issued at Various Ages Compared with the Cost of a Level Premium Policy.

issued. Thus, the level premium system allows people to buy long-term life insurance policies that protect them at a steady cost even while their risk of death is increasing over the duration of the policy.

Policies with Nonguaranteed Elements

We have described the elements that insurance companies must consider when pricing life insurance policies and some of the methods that insurers use to make projections regarding future experience with each pricing element. In our discussion, however, we have assumed that once each pricing element is assigned a value and the premium is set for a particular policy, the pricing process is finished. That is not always the case.

Several types of life insurance policies provide that the policy's price can change after the policy is issued. Insurance companies primarily use two methods of changing the price of a policy after it has been issued:

- The first method is to reduce the price by returning to policy-owners a portion of the premium that was paid for the coverage. This premium refund is called a *policy dividend.*

- The second method consists of changing the values of the pricing factors while the policy is in force and, consequently, changing the amount charged to the policyowner for the coverage.

Policy Dividends

Life insurance policies can be issued on either a participating or nonparticipating basis. A **participating policy,** sometimes referred to as a *par policy,* is one under which the policyowner shares in the insurance company's divisible surplus. A **nonparticipating policy,** also known as a *nonpar policy,* is one in which the policyowner does not share in the insurer's surplus. As we noted in Chapter 2, *surplus* is the amount by which a company's assets exceed its liabilities and capital. Surplus results from a company's profitable operations. The amount of surplus available for distribution to owners of participating policies is called the **divisible surplus,** and a policyowner's share of this divisible surplus is called a **policy dividend.** Policy dividends are considered premium refunds, and, unlike dividends earned on shares of stock, they usually are not considered taxable income to the policyowner.

The most important concern of insurers is to ensure that enough money will be available to pay anticipated claims and expenses, as well as any additional, unexpected claims and expenses. Therefore, insurers are generally cautious when making assumptions about mortality, investment earnings, expenses, and contingencies. Actual experience in these areas is often better than anticipated. By issuing participating policies, insurance companies can return money to policyowners in the form of dividends when conditions are favorable, yet establish premium rates that will be sufficient to pay promised benefits when conditions are unfavorable. Nevertheless, the insurance company must be careful that it isn't too conservative in its pricing;

the company wants to establish premium rates that are competitive with the rates charged by other insurance companies.

Each cost element involved in setting premium rates is a potential source of surplus. If the people insured by a company experience a more favorable mortality rate than the company expected, fewer claims will be paid. If a company earns a higher rate of return on investments than anticipated, the investment income will be greater than needed to maintain the reserves at the required levels. And if a company spends less money on administrative expense than was planned, additional funds will be available from the loading. An insurer that issues participating policies can distribute a portion of this surplus to the owners of those participating policies in the form of policy dividends.

A participating policy contains a policy dividend provision that gives the policyowner several choices in the way policy dividends can be used. These choices are known as *dividend options* and will be discussed in Chapter 12.

Generally, the premium rates for nonparticipating policies are lower than the premium rates for equivalent participating policies because insurers issuing nonparticipating policies often use less cautious assumptions regarding mortality, investment earnings, expenses, and contingencies than do insurers issuing participating policies. However, determining in advance which type of policy—participating or nonparticipating—will ultimately be less expensive is difficult because policy dividends received by the owner of a participating policy reduce the amount of the policy's actual cost. Policy dividend amounts are not known in advance, and the policyowner is not guaranteed that policy dividends will be paid.

Laws in the United States and Canada do *not* require insurance companies to declare regular policy dividends. In both countries, however, policies must state whether they are participating or nonparticipating policies, and participating policies must indicate that when the insurer declares policy dividends, they will be paid yearly on the policy anniversary date.

Changes in Pricing Factors

Earlier we mentioned that some insurance policies specify each cost element of the policy, while others specify only the gross premium amount. Policies that list the cost elements separately usually guarantee a maximum or a minimum value for each cost element. Such a policy, for example, might guarantee that the policy's savings element will accumulate at a minimum annual interest rate of at least 4 percent; the insurer, however, also promises to pay a higher interest rate if market conditions permit it to earn a higher than predicted rate of return on its investments. When the insurer pays interest at a rate that is higher than the guaranteed interest rate, the cost of the policy is reduced. Likewise, such policies also specify the maximum mortality charges that the insurer will assess but provide that the insurer will assess lower mortality charges if the insurance company's actual mortality experience is more favorable than was expected. The more favorable mortality charges are not guaranteed, but if applied, they reduce the policy's cost.

In most situations, policies with variable pricing factors are issued on a nonparticipating basis because their pricing structure makes declaring policy dividends unnecessary. (Remember that policy dividends are essentially premium refunds.) As with participating policies, cost comparisons among policies with varying pricing elements are difficult to make because projected favorable values are not guaranteed or known in advance. In Chapter 1, we mentioned that an organization that sells life insurance may be established as a stock insurance company or as a mutual insurance company. Stock companies can offer both participating and nonparticipating policies. In the past, mutual companies tended to offer only participating policies. Today, however, many mutuals offer both participating and nonparticipating policies. In many cases, mutual companies that want to offer nonparticipating policies (such as policies with variable pricing factors) do so by establishing a subsidiary that is organized as a stock company and offering the nonparticipating policies through that subsidiary.

Life Insurance Reserves

Of all the terms used in the insurance industry, *reserves* is one of the most important and also one of the most easily misunderstood. In our everyday lives, we use the term *reserves* to mean something extra, something that is available in addition to our usual supply. For example, in a broad financial sense, people use the term *reserves* to refer to a fund of additional money that is available in case of some special need. In the insurance industry, however, reserves are not typically a source of money. Rather, reserves are liabilities representing the amounts of money an insurer estimates it will need to pay its future obligations.

Insurance laws impose a variety of reserve requirements on insurance companies. A discussion of all those requirements is beyond the scope of this text. Nevertheless, you should know that insurers establish a number of different types of reserve liabilities; some reserves are required by law, and others are established voluntarily by insurance companies. In the next section, we describe policy reserves and contingency reserves to give you an idea of some types of reserve liabilities that insurance companies establish.

Policy Reserves

As noted earlier, policy reserves represent the amount an insurer estimates it will need to pay policy benefits as they come due. Insurance companies must maintain assets that exceed their policy reserve liabilities so that they will have the funds to pay claims when they come due. In addition, policy reserves must be adequate to pay claims and the funds backing those reserves must be safely invested.

Much of the regulation of the life insurance industry by governmental agencies has to do with policy reserves. To calculate the amount needed for policy reserves, for example, regulators require insurance companies to use a conservative mortality table, such as the 1980 CSO Mortality Table. A **conservative mortality table** is one that shows *higher* mortality rates than the company anticipates for a particular block of policies. By using a conservative mortality table, the company is required to set aside more assets than it will probably need to pay future claims. To guarantee the safety of the assets backing policy reserves, regulators require insurers to place the funds in safe investments. Laws regarding minimum reserve amounts and investment safety are designed to protect the interests of the policyowners and beneficiaries who rely on the long-term solvency of life insurance companies.

Let's look at an example of a whole life insurance policy to illustrate the operation of the policy reserve. Under the level premium system, the insurer receives more in premiums for a block of whole life insurance policies in the early years than it needs to pay claims. The insurer must invest those excess premiums and build assets that are sufficient to back the policy reserve it has established for the block of policies. Note that the insurer must calculate policy reserves for each block of policies it has issued. Once it has established the amount of the policy reserve for a block of policies, the insurer can assign a proportionate share of that total amount to each policy.

The difference between the face amount of a policy—the amount that will be paid as a death benefit—and the policy reserve at the end of any given policy year is known as the insurance company's **net amount at risk** for the policy.

> **Net amount at risk = Face amount − Policy reserve**
>
> As the amount of the policy reserve *increases,* the policy's net amount at risk *decreases.*

For example, if a $10,000 whole life insurance policy has a reserve of $3,000, then the insurance company's net amount at risk for that policy is $7,000. If a claim should become payable on that policy, the insurer would pay $3,000 of the death benefit from the assets that back the reserve on that particular policy, and it would pay $7,000—the net amount at risk—from other funds it holds. Figure 6-6 shows how a reserve for a whole life insurance policy can build up while the policy is in force. As the reserve *increases,* the net amount at risk *decreases.* In the early years of a policy, the net amount at risk is large, but by the policy's final years, the reserve can grow large enough to pay for all or almost all of the death benefit.

Insurers must also establish reserves for policies with far shorter durations, such as one-year term insurance policies. For purposes of establishing policy reserves for one-year term policies, the insurer assumes that it receives the total amount of premiums owed for the policies at the beginning of the year. The insurer can invest those funds until they are needed to pay claims, and thus must establish a policy reserve liability. During the policy year, the insurer pays any death claims that are incurred and thus reduces the amount of its policy

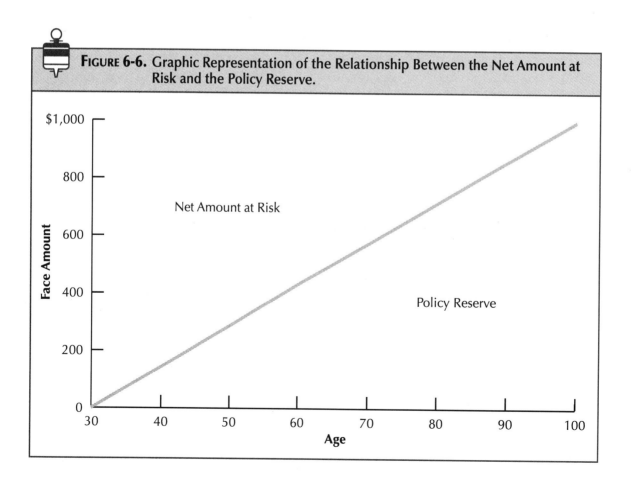

FIGURE 6-6. Graphic Representation of the Relationship Between the Net Amount at Risk and the Policy Reserve.

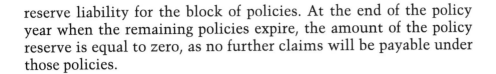

reserve liability for the block of policies. At the end of the policy year when the remaining policies expire, the amount of the policy reserve is equal to zero, as no further claims will be payable under those policies.

Contingency Reserves

An insurance company must be able to pay death claims even if conditions occur that are less favorable than those expected when it calculated premium rates. Although mortality statistics show the overall rates of mortality that can be expected, fluctuations can occur in special instances—for example, in the case of an epidemic. Such unexpected occurrences could have an adverse effect on the mortality rates experienced by those who are insured. Insurers also have limited control over the rates of return they earn on their investments, and a company may not be able to earn the rate of investment return it anticipated when it calculated premium rates. Additionally, operating expenses may rise faster than an insurer expected when it set premium rates.

The loading added to the net premium sometimes includes a small amount to cover such unusual occurrences. Companies use these extra amounts to set up *contingency reserves,* which are reserves against unusual conditions that may occur. Contingency reserves provide a safety margin in case actual experience in any area—mortality, investment earnings, or expenses—is worse than the insurer expected. Although some insurers establish contingency reserves for life insurance policies, insurers typically establish contingency reserves for health insurance policies.

Key Terms

mutual benefit method
assessment method
legal reserve system
policy reserves
actuaries
block of policies
expected mortality
mortality experience
mortality tables
interest
simple interest
compound interest

net premium
loading
gross premium
level premium system
participating policy
nonparticipating policy
divisible surplus
policy dividend
conservative mortality table
net amount at risk
contingency reserves

Other Important Terms

underwriter
post-death assessment method
liabilities
legal reserves
statutory reserves
adequate premium rates
equitable premium rates
block of insureds
tabular mortality

substandard risks
substandard premium rate
compounding
lapse rate
par policy
nonpar policy
surplus
dividend options

Endnotes

1. ACLI, *1998 Life Insurance Fact Book* (Washington, D.C.: American Council of Life Insurance, 1998), 63, 127.

2. Tom McWilliams, "Older Age Underwriting," *On the Risk* (January–March 1996): 91–97.

3. ACLI, 61.

4. Ibid., 64.

5. ACLI, 6; CLHIA, *Canadian Life and Health Insurance Facts* (Toronto: Canadian Life and Health Insurance Association Inc., 1998), 7.

CHAPTER 7

Term Life Insurance

After reading this chapter, you should be able to

- Describe the coverage provided by term life insurance policies and determine when the premium charged for term life insurance coverage may increase

- Identify three different plans of term life insurance coverage and give an example of each

- Distinguish between renewable term life insurance and convertible term life insurance

All life insurance policies provide for the payment of a benefit upon the death of the insured while the policy is in force. Beyond that, however, the features of life insurance policies vary depending on the type of policy. We describe three major types of life insurance policies in this text. This chapter describes *term life insurance,* which provides a death benefit if the insured dies during a specified period. We describe the other two types of life insurance policies—permanent life insurance and endowment insurance—in the next chapter.

Characteristics of Term Life Insurance Products

By definition, all term insurance products provide coverage for a specified period of time, called the *policy term.* The policy benefit is payable *only* if (1) the insured dies during the specified term *and* (2) the policy is in force when the insured dies. If the insured lives until the end of the specified term, the policy may give the policyowner the right to continue life insurance coverage. If the policyowner does not continue the coverage, then the policy expires and the insurer has no liability to provide further insurance coverage.

The length of the term varies considerably from policy to policy. The term may be as short as the time required to complete an airplane trip or as long as 40 years or more. Generally speaking, though, insurers seldom sell term life insurance to cover periods of less than 1 year. The term may be described as a specified number of years—1 year, 5 years, 10 years, 20 years—or it may be defined by specifying the age of the insured at the end of the term. For example, a term insurance policy that covers an insured until age 65 is referred to as *term to age 65,* and the policy's coverage expires on the policy anniversary that falls either closest to, or immediately after, the insured person's 65th birthday. The *policy anniversary* generally is the anniversary of the date on which coverage under the policy became effective. Both the expiration date and the policy anniversary date are usually stated on the face page of the policy.

Term life insurance protection is usually provided by an insurance policy, but it can also be provided by a rider added to a policy. A *policy rider,* which is also called an *endorsement,* is an amendment to an insurance policy that becomes a part of the insurance contract and that either expands or limits the benefits payable under the contract. A policy rider is as legally effective as any other part of the insurance contract. Riders are commonly used to provide some type of supplementary benefit or to increase the amount of the death benefit provided by a policy, although riders may also be used to limit or modify a policy's coverage. Some of the supplementary benefits—including some term insurance benefits—that are commonly provided through riders attached to life insurance policies are described in Chapter 9.

Plans of Term Life Insurance Coverage

The amount of the benefit payable under a term life insurance policy or rider usually remains level throughout the term of the policy. Term life insurance, however, may also be purchased to provide either a benefit that *decreases* over the policy's term or a benefit that *increases* over the policy's term.

Level Term Life Insurance

By far, the most common plan of term insurance is **level term life insurance,** which provides a death benefit that remains the same amount over the term of the policy. For example, under a five-year level term policy that provides $100,000 of coverage, the insurer agrees to pay $100,000 if the insured dies at any time during the five-year period that the policy is in force. The amount of each renewal premium payable for a level term life insurance policy usually remains the same throughout the stated term of coverage.

Decreasing Term Life Insurance

Decreasing term life insurance provides a death benefit that decreases in amount over the term of coverage. The policy's death benefit begins as a set face amount and then decreases over the term of coverage according to some stated method that is described in the policy. For example, assume that the benefit during the first year of coverage of a five-year decreasing term policy is $50,000 and then decreases by $10,000 on each policy anniversary. The coverage is $40,000 for the second policy year, $30,000 for the third year, $20,000 for the fourth year, and $10,000 for the last year. At the end of the fifth policy year, the coverage expires. The amount of each renewal premium payable

Reprinted with special permission of King Features Syndicate.

for a decreasing term insurance policy usually remains level throughout the term of coverage.

Insurance companies offer several plans of decreasing term insurance, including (1) mortgage redemption insurance, (2) credit life insurance, and (3) family income insurance. We describe how each of these plans provides benefits to meet a specific need for insurance.

Mortgage Redemption Insurance

Mortgage redemption insurance is a plan of decreasing term insurance designed to provide a death benefit amount that corresponds to the decreasing amount owed on a mortgage loan. If you have ever bought a home, you are probably aware that each payment a borrower makes on a mortgage loan consists of both principal and interest on the loan. The amount of the outstanding principal balance owed on the mortgage loan gradually decreases over the term of the mortgage, although initially the decrease is fairly slow. (See Figure 7-1 for a graphic illustration of mortgage redemption insurance.) If the borrower purchases mortgage redemption insurance, the amount of the policy benefit payable at any given time generally equals the amount the borrower then owes on the mortgage loan.

The term of a mortgage redemption policy is based on the length of the mortgage, which is usually 15 or 30 years. Renewal premiums payable for mortgage redemption insurance are generally level throughout the term. Often, the beneficiary of a mortgage redemption policy uses the policy benefit to pay off the mortgage. The beneficiary, however, typically is not required to do that. In most instances, the life insurance policy is independent of the mortgage—the institution

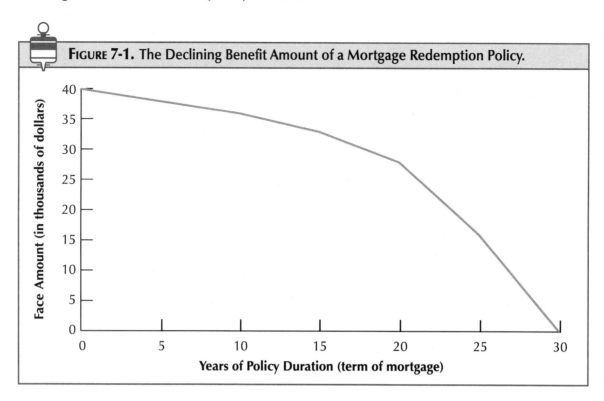

FIGURE 7-1. The Declining Benefit Amount of a Mortgage Redemption Policy.

granting the mortgage is not a party to the insurance contract—and the beneficiary is not required to use the proceeds of the policy to repay the mortgage. The following example describes this situation.

EXAMPLE Bill Marley and his wife, Allyson, purchased a new home and obtained a 30-year mortgage from the New Home Mortgage Company. Bill decided to purchase a mortgage redemption life insurance policy from the Star Life Insurance Company. He wanted to ensure that Allyson had funds to supplement her income so that she could afford to stay in the home if he should die before the mortgage loan was repaid. So, he named Allyson as the beneficiary. Three years later, Bill died in an accident, and Star Life paid Allyson a death benefit of $72,150—the loan amount remaining on the mortgage. Allyson invested the policy proceeds in a mutual fund and continued to make monthly mortgage payments.

ANALYSIS Because the contract for insurance was between Star Life and Bill Marley, Allyson was under no obligation to use the proceeds to pay the balance due on the mortgage.

A mortgage lender sometimes requires a borrower, as a condition for obtaining a mortgage loan, to purchase mortgage redemption insurance and to name the lender as beneficiary. In this case, the borrower who purchases mortgage redemption coverage from an insurance company is the owner of the policy, and the terms of his mortgage loan require him to maintain that coverage payable to the lender in the event of his death during the term of the mortgage. The insurance company is not a party to the mortgage loan contract, however, and its only obligation is to carry out its obligations under the mortgage redemption insurance policy.

A variation of mortgage redemption insurance is joint mortgage redemption insurance. *Joint mortgage redemption insurance* provides the same benefit as a mortgage redemption policy except the joint policy insures the lives of two people. If both insureds survive until the end of the stated term, the joint mortgage policy expires. But if one of the insureds dies while the policy is in force, the insurer will pay the death benefit to the beneficiary, who is typically the surviving insured. Note that the beneficiary is not required to use the policy benefit to pay off the mortgage. Joint mortgage redemption insurance can meet the needs of two people who own a home together and who both must work in order to have enough income to make their monthly mortgage payments.

Credit Life Insurance

Credit life insurance is a type of term life insurance designed to pay the balance due on a loan if the borrower dies before the loan is repaid. Like mortgage redemption insurance, credit life insurance is usually decreasing term insurance. Unlike mortgage redemption insurance policies, credit life insurance policies always provide that the policy benefit is payable directly to the lender, or creditor, if the insured borrower dies during the policy's term. Generally, the loan must be of a type that can be repaid in ten years or less. Although credit life insurance is available on an individual insurance basis, most credit life insurance is sold to lending institutions as group insurance to cover the lives of the borrowers of that lender. We describe group creditor life insurance in Chapter 15.

Credit life insurance is available for automobile loans, furniture loans, and other personal loans. In addition, many credit card holders are covered by credit life insurance for the amounts they owe on their accounts; in such cases, the amount of life insurance coverage in force at any given time depends on the amount of the outstanding debt. Credit life insurance guarantees the lender that the insured's outstanding debt will be paid if the insured borrower dies before the loan is repaid. Credit life insurance also protects the insured's estate from having to pay these outstanding debts.

As with mortgage redemption insurance, the amount of benefit payable under a credit life insurance policy is usually equal to the amount of the unpaid debt. Thus, as the amount of the loan decreases, the face amount of credit life insurance provided decreases. Premiums may be level over the duration of the loan or, in cases in which the amount of the loan varies, may increase or decrease as the amount of the outstanding loan balance—and the corresponding policy benefit—increases or decreases. Premiums for credit life insurance may be paid to the insurance company by the lender or by the insured borrower. In most cases, however, the borrower pays the credit life insurance premium to the lender, which then remits the premium to the insurer.

Family Income Coverage

Family income coverage is a plan of decreasing term insurance that provides a stated monthly income benefit amount to the insured's surviving spouse if the insured dies during the term of coverage. Monthly income benefits continue until the end of the term specified when the coverage was purchased. Family income coverage is a form of decreasing term insurance because the longer the insured remains alive during the term of coverage, the shorter the length of time over which the insurer may be required to pay monthly income benefits; the shorter the length of the benefit payment period, the smaller the total amount of benefits the insurer will pay out.

Under some family income coverages, the insurer promises to pay the income benefit amount for at least a stated minimum number of years if the insured dies during the policy's term. For example, Arnold Aceelo has purchased 10-year family income coverage that provides for a $1,000 monthly income benefit. His coverage specifies that the income benefit will be paid for at least 3 years if he dies during the 10-year term of coverage. If Arnold dies 2 years after buying the family income coverage, the insurer will pay a total of $96,000 in monthly income benefits ($1,000 × 12 months × 8 years) to Arnold's wife. If he dies 6 years after buying the coverage, the monthly income benefit will be paid for 4 years; thus, the insurer will pay Arnold's wife a total of $48,000 ($1,000 × 12 months × 4 years). If, however, Arnold dies 9 years after purchasing the coverage, then the income benefit will continue for the specified 3-year minimum, for a total of $36,000 ($1,000 × 12 months × 3 years). If he dies 11 years after purchasing the coverage, no monthly income benefit would be paid because the decreasing term insurance coverage expired 1 year before his death.

Family income coverage is most commonly purchased as a rider to a permanent life insurance policy, which we describe in the next chapter. Insurance companies sometimes also include family income coverage as a feature of a whole life policy, in which case the policy is usually called a *family income policy.* The death benefit from the whole life insurance portion of the family income policy is usually paid in a lump sum following the insured's death, and the insurer then begins paying the monthly income benefits. Some family income policies, however, provide that the insurance company will pay the lump-sum death benefit to the beneficiary after it has paid all the monthly income benefits. Interest on the policy proceeds that the insurer holds until the end of the monthly income benefit period may either be added to the amount of each installment payment or paid with the proceeds at the end of the installment period.

Increasing Term Life Insurance

Increasing term life insurance provides a death benefit that starts at one amount and increases by some specified amount or percentage at stated intervals over the policy term. For example, an insurance company may offer coverage that starts at $100,000 and then increases by 5 percent on each policy anniversary date throughout the term of the policy. Alternatively, the face amount may increase according to increases in the cost of living, as measured by a standard index such as the Consumer Price Index (CPI).[3] The premium for increasing term insurance generally increases as the amount of coverage increases. The policyowner is usually granted the option of freezing at any time the amount of coverage provided by the increasing term life insurance. This coverage may be provided by an increasing term life insurance policy or, more commonly, as a policy rider.

Features of Term Life Insurance Policies

Term life insurance provides only temporary protection—at the end of the stated term, the policy expires. In some cases, however, a policyowner may wish either to continue the insurance coverage for an additional term or to change the coverage to a plan of permanent insurance. Term life insurance policies often contain features that allow the policyowner to continue the life insurance coverage beyond the end of the original term. If the policy gives the policyowner the option to continue the policy's coverage for an additional policy term, then the policy is known as a *renewable term insurance policy.* If the policy gives the policyowner the right to convert the term policy to a permanent plan of insurance, then the policy is referred to as a ***convertible term insurance policy.*** Some policies, known as *renewable/convertible term insurance policies,* contain both of these features.

Renewable Term Life Insurance

Renewable term life insurance policies include a ***renewal provision*** that gives the policyowner the right, within specified limits, to renew the insurance coverage at the end of the specified term without submitting ***evidence of insurability***—proof that the insured person continues to be an insurable risk. In other words, the insured is not required to undergo a medical examination or to provide the insurer with an updated health history. Often, all the policyowner must do in order to renew the policy is pay the renewal premium.

According to the provisions of nearly all renewable term insurance policies, the policyowner has the right to renew the coverage for the same term and face amount that were originally provided by the policy. For example, a 10-year, $100,000 renewable term policy usually can be renewed for another 10-year period and for $100,000 in coverage. One-year term policies and riders are usually renewable. Such coverage is called ***yearly renewable term (YRT) insurance*** or *annually renewable term (ART) insurance.* Most insurers also allow the policyowner to renew the policy for a *smaller* face amount and/ or a *shorter* period than provided by the original contract, but not for a larger face amount and/or a longer period.

In many cases, the renewal provision places some limit on the policyowner's right to renew. The most common limitations are that (1) the coverage may be renewed only until the insured attains a stated age or (2) the coverage may be renewed only a stated maximum number of times. For example, the renewal provision of a policy may specify that the coverage is not renewable after the insured has reached the age of 75. Another policy may specify that the coverage is renewable no more than three times. Such restrictions exist in order to minimize antiselection.

When a term life insurance policy is renewed, the policy's premium rate increases. The renewal premium rate is based on the insured person's ***attained age***—the age the insured has reached (attained) on the renewal date. As we described in an earlier chapter, mortality rates generally increase as people grow older. Because the insured's mortality risk has increased over the initial term of coverage, the renewal premium rate must also be increased. The renewal premium rate remains level throughout the new term of coverage. The renewal feature can lead to some antiselection; insureds in poor health will be more likely to renew their policies because they may not be able to obtain other life insurance. Because of this risk of antiselection, the premium for a renewable term life insurance policy is usually slightly higher than the premium for a comparable nonrenewable term life insurance policy. The following example illustrates how the renewal feature works.

> Allen Padred, age 30, just purchased a $100,000, three-year term life insurance policy on his own life. The policy's annual premium is $126. During the three-year policy term, Allen will pay $126 each year for his coverage. The policy contains a *renewal provision* that gives Allen the option to renew his policy without having to submit evidence of his insurability. Thus, on the *policy anniversary* at the end of the three-year term, Allen has the right to renew his coverage. The coverage will be for the same $100,000 face amount as the original policy and for the same three-year term. The new premium amount, however, will be $145 per year to reflect Allen's *attained age* at the time of renewal. Allen will pay this higher premium each year during the three-year renewal period. At the end of the second three-year period, Allen will again have the option to renew the policy at a premium rate based on his attained age. The policy allows Allen to continue to renew his coverage until the policy anniversary date nearest his 65th birthday.

Convertible Term Life Insurance

Convertible term insurance policies contain a **conversion privilege** that allows the policyowner to change—convert—the term insurance policy to a permanent plan of insurance *without* providing evidence that the insured is an insurable risk. Even if the health of the person insured by a convertible term policy has deteriorated to the point that she would otherwise be uninsurable, the policyowner can obtain permanent insurance coverage on the insured because evidence of insurability is not required at the time of conversion. The premium that the policyowner is charged for the permanent coverage cannot be based on any increase in the insured's mortality risk, except with regard to an increase in the insured's age.

As in the case of the renewal provision, the conversion privilege can lead to some antiselection; insureds in poor health are more likely to convert their coverage because they may not be able to obtain other life insurance. As a result, insurers usually charge a higher premium rate for a convertible term policy than they charge for a comparable nonconvertible term policy. In addition, insurers usually limit the conversion privilege in some way. For instance, some policies do not permit conversion after the insured has attained a specific age, such as 55 or 65, or after the term policy has been in force for a specified time. For example, a ten-year term policy may permit conversion only during the first seven or eight years of the term. Conversion also may be limited to an amount that is only a percentage of the original face amount. For example, a ten-year term policy may permit conversion of 100 percent of the face amount only within the first five years of the term, and a smaller percentage, such as 50 percent of the face amount, if the policy is converted during the last five years of the ten-year term.

As we noted in Chapter 1, permanent life insurance policies build a cash value. In order to provide a cash value, the premium charged for a permanent insurance policy is higher than the premium charged for a comparable term insurance policy. Therefore, when a term insurance policy is converted to permanent insurance, the new premium rate is higher than the premium rate the policyowner paid for the term insurance policy. The specific amount of the premium charged for the permanent insurance coverage that is provided following conversion depends on the effective date of the permanent insurance policy. The effective date of the permanent coverage is either the date the term policy is converted to a permanent plan of insurance—known as an *attained age conversion*—or the date the convertible term policy was issued—known as an *original age conversion*.

When term coverage is converted to permanent insurance under an **attained age conversion,** the renewal premium rate is based on the insured's age when the coverage is converted. For example, suppose John Matthews was 35 years old when he bought a five-year convertible term policy on his life. Four years later, John decided to convert the term insurance policy to a whole life policy. The effective date of his permanent coverage is the date the conversion takes place. Consequently, the premium rate that John is charged for the whole life policy will be the rate charged insureds who are age 39, his attained age at the time of conversion.

Some convertible term life insurance policies permit the policyowner to convert to permanent coverage by means of an **original age conversion.** When a policyowner converts to permanent coverage under this type of policy, the effective date of the permanent coverage is considered to be the date on which the policyowner purchased the original term policy. As a result, the premium rate for the permanent coverage is based on the insured's age at the time the policyowner purchased the original term policy.

The renewal premium rate charged for the permanent insurance is lower under an original age conversion than under an attained age conversion because the premium rate is based on a younger age. If, in our earlier example, John Matthews had chosen an original age conversion, the renewal premium rate for the permanent insurance would be the premium rate charged for a 35-year-old male, even though John was actually 39 years old when the coverage was converted. In many cases, an insurance company will not allow an original age conversion if more than a stated number of years—such as more than five years—have elapsed since the original policy was purchased.

Under an original age conversion, the permanent insurance coverage is treated as if it had been in effect since the effective date of the convertible term policy. As noted, a permanent life insurance policy also builds a cash value, and the insurer must establish a policy reserve liability that gradually builds over the life of the policy. When a term life insurance policy is converted on an original age basis, the insurance company must establish a policy reserve equal to the reserve that would have accumulated if the coverage had originally been issued as permanent insurance. In order to provide the insurer with the funds to establish this reserve, the converting policyowner is required to pay all, or part, of the difference between the premiums already paid for the term insurance policy and the premiums that would have been payable had the coverage been issued as permanent insurance. This payment will often represent a sizable outlay of money. Attained age conversion is much more common than original age conversion because it does not require the policyowner to make a large cash outlay at the time of conversion.

The renewal and conversion privileges are of obvious potential value to the policyowner, but they are also of value to the insurance company. Most policyowners renew or convert their term policies, not because they are in poor health, but because they want to continue their insurance protection. Therefore, insurance companies are able to keep such insurance in force without the expense of initiating new sales. Other cost savings for such coverages arise because relatively few term insurance policies result in death claims—term insurance is normally purchased to cover periods when the mortality rates for insureds are low. Usually, a term life insurance policy will (1) expire before the insured dies, (2) be converted to permanent insurance, or (3) terminate because renewal premiums have not been paid.

Key Terms

term life insurance
policy term
policy anniversary
policy rider
level term life insurance
decreasing term life insurance
mortgage redemption insurance
joint mortgage redemption
   insurance

credit life insurance
family income coverage
family income policy
increasing term life insurance
renewable term insurance policy
convertible term insurance
   policy
renewal provision
evidence of insurability

Key Terms (continued)

yearly renewable term (YRT)
   insurance
attained age

conversion privilege
attained age conversion
original age conversion

Other Important Terms

term to age 65
endorsement
renewable/convertible term
   insurance policy

annually renewable term (ART)
   insurance

Endnotes

1. ACLI, *1998 Life Insurance Fact Book* (Washington, D.C.: American Council of Life Insurance, 1998), 5.

2. ACLI, *1997 Life Insurance Fact Book* (Washington, D.C.: American Council of Life Insurance, 1997), 14.

3. An *index* provides a mathematical measure that indicates the relative changes in a specific factor—such as costs, production, or prices—at a given point in time as compared to a specific time in the past. The *Consumer Price Index (CPI)* measures the change in the price of a fixed basket of goods bought by a typical consumer. The goods included in the CPI include food, transportation, housing, utilities, clothing, and medical care.

4. ACLI, *1998 Life Insurance Fact Book*, 5.

5. CLHIA, *Canadian Life and Health Insurance Facts* (Toronto: Canadian Life and Health Insurance Association Inc., 1998), 6.

CHAPTER 8

Permanent Life Insurance and Endowment Insurance

After reading this chapter, you should be able to

- Identify the features of whole life insurance, modified whole life insurance, and joint whole life insurance and recognize how these plans of insurance differ from one another

- Distinguish home service life insurance products from other life insurance products

- Identify which characteristics of universal life insurance are similar to characteristics of other permanent life insurance and which characteristics are unique to universal life insurance

- Distinguish between universal life, variable life, and variable universal life insurance

- Identify the characteristics of indeterminate premium life insurance and interest-sensitive whole life insurance

- Describe the characteristics of endowment insurance

As we have noted, all ***permanent life insurance*** provides insurance coverage throughout the insured's lifetime, as long as any necessary renewal premiums are paid. All forms of permanent life insurance also include a cash value. Nevertheless, permanent life insurance is available in a wide range of products that contain unique features. In this chapter, we describe a variety of permanent life insurance products, ranging from traditional whole life insurance to newer insurance products such as universal life and variable life insurance.

We also describe endowment insurance. Sales of endowment insurance in the United States and Canada have fallen steadily in recent years, primarily because of the unfavorable income tax treatment afforded it. Endowment insurance, however, remains a popular product in insurance markets in many other countries where tax laws treat it in a more favorable light.

Permanent Life Insurance

Two primary characteristics distinguish permanent life insurance products from term life insurance products:

- **Permanent life insurance products offer lifetime coverage.** Term life insurance provides protection for a certain period of time and provides no benefits after that period ends. In contrast, permanent life insurance provides protection for the *entire* lifetime of the insured, so long as the policy remains in force.

- **Permanent life insurance products provide insurance coverage and contain a savings element.** Term life insurance usually provides only insurance protection. In contrast, permanent life insurance not only provides insurance protection, it also builds a cash value that functions as a savings element.

Sales of some types of permanent insurance date back almost a hundred years; other permanent products have been introduced in more recent years. Although both traditional whole life insurance products and the newer plans of permanent insurance share characteristics that distinguish them from term life insurance products, the features and benefits of the various plans of permanent life insurance differ widely.

You may have noticed that the terminology used to describe insurance products is not consistent throughout the insurance industry. You may see two or more different terms used to identify the same product, and sometimes one term can be used in several contexts. The term *whole life* is perhaps the best example of an insurance term that is employed in several contexts. In one context, *whole life* refers to the broad classification of insurance products that are considered to be permanent insurance; thus, in this context, some of the newer products such as universal life insurance, variable life insurance, and adjustable life insurance are forms of whole life insurance. *Whole life* is also used to refer to a specific type of permanent insurance product, and this text will use the term *whole life* in this last sense to refer to a specific type of permanent insurance product.

Traditional Whole Life Insurance

Whole life insurance provides lifetime insurance coverage at a level premium rate that does not increase as the insured ages. As we noted in Chapter 6, insurers use the level premium system to price life insurance so that the premium rates do not increase as the insureds' mortality rates increase. The insurance company invests the excess premium dollars it collects in the early years under the level premium system and accumulates assets that are at least equal to the amount of the policy reserve liability the insurer has established for those policies. (The CD-ROM included in the back cover contains a sample whole life insurance policy.)

As we have described, a permanent life insurance policy contains a savings element that is known as the policy's **cash value.** A whole life insurance policy includes a chart that illustrates how the cash value will grow over time. If for some reason the policy does not remain in force until the insured's death, the insurer agrees to refund the cash value to the policyowner—less any surrender charges and outstanding policy loans. Because the policyowner generally has the right to surrender a permanent life insurance policy for its cash value during the insured's lifetime, the amount of the cash value that a policyowner is entitled to receive upon policy surrender is referred to as the **cash surrender value** or the *surrender value.* We describe the cash surrender value in detail in Chapter 10.

The size of a policy's cash value at any given time depends on a number of factors, such as the face amount of the policy, the length of time the policy has been in force, and the length of the policy's premium payment period. The reserve and the cash value of a whole life policy will increase throughout the life of the policy and will eventually equal the face amount of the policy. The cash value, however, does not equal the face amount until the time the insured reaches the age at the end of the mortality table used to calculate premiums for that policy, usually age 99 or 100. At that point, the insurer typically pays the face amount of the policy to the policyowner, even if the insured is still living.

A policy's cash value represents the policyowner's ownership interest in the policy. Therefore, any permanent insurance policy that has accumulated a cash value may be used as security for a loan. The policyowner may receive a loan, known as a **policy loan**, from the insurance company itself, or the policyowner may use the cash value of the policy as collateral for a loan from another financial institution. If the insured dies before a policy loan is repaid, however, the unpaid amount of the loan—plus any interest outstanding—is subtracted from the policy benefit. Policy loans are discussed in more detail in Chapter 10.

Premium Payment Periods

Whole life policies can be classified on the basis of the length of the policy's premium payment period. Most whole life policies are classified as either (1) continuous-premium policies or (2) limited-payment policies. The length of a policy's premium payment period directly affects both the amount of the periodic premium required for the policy and the pace at which the policy's cash value builds.

Continuous-Premium Policies. Under a **continuous-premium whole life policy** (sometimes referred to as a *straight life insurance policy* or an *ordinary life insurance policy*), premiums are payable until the death of the insured. Because premiums are payable over the life of the policy, the amount of each premium payment required for a continuous-premium whole life policy is lower than the premium amount required under any other premium payment schedule.

Limited-Payment Policies. A **limited-payment whole life policy** is a whole life policy for which premiums are payable only until some stated period expires or until the insured's death, whichever occurs first. The policy may describe the stated period over which premiums are payable in one of two ways:

1. Premiums may be payable for a specific number of years. For example, a 20-payment whole life insurance policy is a policy for which premiums are payable for 20 years.

2. Premiums may be payable until the insured reaches a specified age. For example, a paid-up-at-age-65 whole life insurance policy provides that premiums are payable until the insured reaches the policy anniversary closest to or immediately following her

65th birthday, at which time the premium payments cease but the coverage continues. A policy that requires no further premium payments but continues to provide coverage is said to be a *paid-up policy.*

In either case, if the insured dies before the end of the specified premium payment period, the insurer will pay the death benefit to the named beneficiary and no further premiums are payable.

Limited-payment policies are designed to meet a policyowner's need for permanent life insurance protection that is funded over a limited time period. The policyowner, for example, may expect that his income will drop considerably when he retires, and yet he anticipates that he will still need life insurance coverage after retirement.

EXAMPLE Arabella Simpson, who has just turned 42, plans to retire at age 62, at which time her income will be reduced considerably. Arabella wishes to obtain permanent life insurance, but she is concerned that she will not be able to pay the premiums from her retirement income. She has, therefore, purchased a 20-payment whole life policy.

ANALYSIS Arabella will make her last premium payment at age 61, at which time she will have a paid-up policy that will require no further premium payments but will provide life insurance coverage for the rest of her life.

The insurer establishes the premium amounts required for a limited-payment policy so that, at the end of the premium payment period, sufficient premiums have been paid to keep the policy in force for the rest of the insured's lifetime. Because fewer annual premium payments are expected to be made for a limited-payment policy than for a comparable continuous-premium policy, the annual premium for the limited-payment policy is larger than the annual premium for an equivalent continuous-premium policy.

Likewise, cash values generally build more rapidly under limited-payment policies than they do under continuous-premium policies. Under a limited-payment policy, a cash value is often available at the end of the first policy year, whereas a cash value under a continuous-premium policy may not be available until the end of the third policy year.

Single-Premium Policies. A *single-premium whole life policy* is a type of limited-payment policy that requires only one premium payment. The insurer uses a large part of that single premium to set up the policy's reserve. And because the cash value available on any whole life policy is related to the amount of the policy reserve—although often somewhat lower than the reserve—a sizable cash value is available immediately on any single-premium policy.

Figure 8-1 shows how the length of the premium payment period affects the build-up in a policy's reserve. The shorter the premium payment period, the more quickly the reserve builds. Note that the reserve on every whole life policy eventually equals the face amount of the policy. Because Figure 8-1 is based on a mortality table that ends at age 100, the reserve equals the policy's face amount when the insured reaches age 100.

Modified Whole Life Insurance

The traditional whole life insurance products described so far provide a constant face amount of life insurance coverage in exchange for a single premium or a series of level premiums. Some insurance companies issue whole life insurance policies under which either (1) the

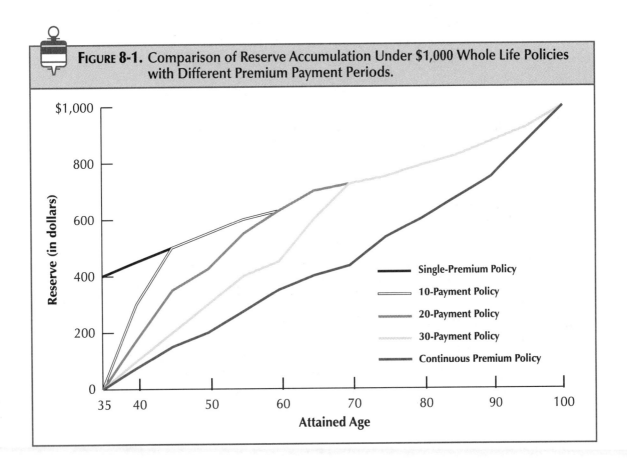

FIGURE 8-1. Comparison of Reserve Accumulation Under $1,000 Whole Life Policies with Different Premium Payment Periods.

amount of the premium payments required changes at some point in the life of the policy or (2) the face amount of coverage changes during the life of the policy.

Modified Premiums

A *modified-premium whole life policy* functions in the same manner as a traditional whole life policy except that the policy's annual premium changes after a specified initial period, such as 5, 10, 15, or 20 years. The initial annual premium for a modified premium whole life policy is less than the initial annual premium for a similar whole life policy issued on a level-premium basis. After the specified period, the annual premium for a modified-premium policy increases to a stated amount that is somewhat higher than the usual (nonmodified) premium would have been. This new increased annual premium is then payable as long as the policy remains in force.

The face amount of a modified-premium whole life policy remains level throughout the life of the policy. For example, a $50,000 continuous-premium whole life policy issued on the life of a 25-year-old man might call for an annual premium of $400. The annual premium for a modified-premium whole life policy for the same face amount could be $310 for the first 10 years, with the premium increasing to $600 per year thereafter for the rest of the life of the policy. (See Figure 8-2, which illustrates this example.)

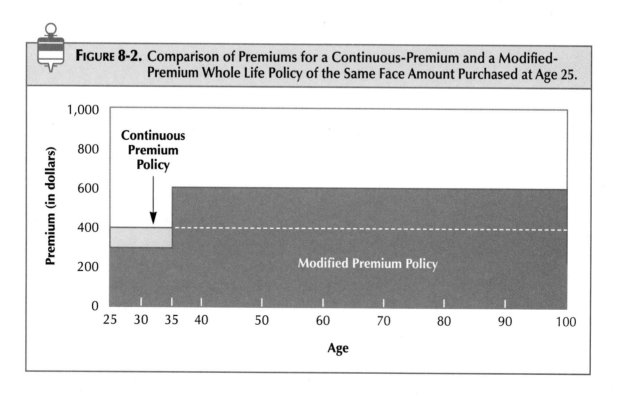

FIGURE 8-2. Comparison of Premiums for a Continuous-Premium and a Modified-Premium Whole Life Policy of the Same Face Amount Purchased at Age 25.

The chief advantage to the policyowner of buying a modified-premium whole life policy is that he is able to purchase a larger face amount of whole life insurance than he would otherwise be able to afford. The chief disadvantage of a modified-premium whole life policy is that the cash value builds more slowly under a modified-premium policy than under a traditional whole life policy.

Some insurers issue whole life policies for which premium payments are modified even more frequently. Generally known as *graded-premium policies,* these policies call for three or more levels of annual premium payment amounts, increasing at specified points in time—such as every three years—until reaching the amount to be paid as a level premium for the rest of the life of the policy. As in all modified-premium plans, the face amount of insurance remains level throughout the life of the policy.

Modified Coverage

The second method of modifying traditional whole life insurance policies is based on the assumption that the need for large amounts of life insurance is likely to diminish as the insured grows older. For example, as a policyowner-insured grows older, she may pay off debts and mortgages, her children may leave home, and her financial obligations may decrease. If the policyowner has accumulated savings and other assets over the years, the need for life insurance may become less important. A *modified coverage policy* provides that the amount of insurance will decrease by specific percentages or amounts either when the insured reaches certain stated ages or at the end of stated time periods. For example, the face amount of a modified coverage whole life policy may begin at $100,000, decrease to $75,000 when the insured reaches age 60, decrease further to $50,000 at age 70, and then remain level for the rest of the insured's lifetime.

In anticipation of such reduced coverage at the older ages, an insurer is able, from the time of policy issue, to provide the $100,000 modified whole life policy for a lower annual premium than if the insurer were liable for the full $100,000 of coverage through the entire expected lifetime of the insured. The reason is that during the period of greatest risk of death—the period when the insured is at an advanced age—the face amount of the policy will be at its lowest level.

Joint Whole Life Insurance

Joint whole life insurance has the same features and benefits as individual whole life insurance, except that it insures two lives under the same policy. Joint whole life insurance is often referred to as *first-to-die life insurance* because, upon the death of one of the insureds, the policy death benefit is paid to the surviving insured and the policy coverage ends.

Because coverage under a joint whole life policy ends once the policy death benefit is paid, the surviving insured may be left uninsured. To give the surviving insured the ability to obtain life insurance coverage, joint whole life policies usually provide a specified period—frequently 60 or 90 days—following the first insured's death within which the surviving insured may purchase an individual whole life policy of the same face amount without providing evidence of insurability. Some joint whole life policies provide the surviving insured with temporary term insurance coverage during this specified period.

Last Survivor Life Insurance

Last survivor life insurance—also known as *second-to-die life insurance*—is a variation of joint whole life insurance under which the policy benefit is paid only after both people insured by the policy have died. Premiums for last survivor life insurance coverage may be payable only until the first insured dies, or premiums may be payable until the death of both insureds. In either case, a couple can obtain insurance on both of their lives for an annual premium that is usually less than the cost of either (1) two individual whole life insurance policies or (2) a joint whole life insurance policy.

Last survivor life insurance was designed primarily to insure married couples who want to provide funds to pay estate taxes that may be levied after their deaths. We noted in Chapter 4 that in the United States, federal estate taxes are payable on estates that exceed a stated amount.

Family Policies

Some insurers market a *family policy,* which is a whole life insurance policy that includes term life insurance coverage on the insured's spouse and children. The amount of term insurance coverage provided on the insured's spouse and children is a fraction—generally one-fourth or one-fifth—of the amount of the insured's whole life insurance coverage. For example, a family with three children might purchase a family policy that provides $50,000 of whole life insurance coverage on the primary insured, $12,500 of term insurance coverage on the insured's spouse (one-fourth of the amount of the coverage on the primary insured), and $10,000 of term insurance coverage for each child (one-fifth of the amount of coverage on the primary insured). Thus, a total of $92,500 of life insurance would be provided by one family policy. Typically, the applicant for a family policy must provide evidence that all family members are insurable. Once the policy is issued, however, each child born to or adopted by the family thereafter is automatically covered by the policy, although the coverage is often not effective until the child reaches age 15 days and an additional premium may be payable for the additional coverage. Because mortality rates are low for children older than 15 days, family policies often provide automatic coverage for additional children without imposing an additional premium charge for that coverage.

Monthly Debit Ordinary

A *monthly debit ordinary (MDO) policy* is a whole life insurance policy that is marketed under the home service distribution system and is paid for by monthly premium payments. The *home service distribution system* is a method of selling and servicing insurance policies through commissioned sales agents, known as *home service agents,* who sell a range of products and provide specified policyowner services, including the collection of renewal premiums, within a specified geographic area. A home service agent's assigned territory is referred to as a *debit, agency,* or *account.* MDO policies have many of the same characteristics as traditional whole life insurance, but MDO policies tend to be sold in smaller face amounts than other whole life insurance policies.

Pre-Need Funeral Insurance

Pre-need funeral insurance, or *pre-need insurance,* is whole life insurance that provides funds to pay for the insured's funeral and burial. An individual who purchases a pre-need insurance policy typically has made the arrangements for his funeral and burial and purchases the policy to pay for those final expenses. In many cases, the policyowner-insured names the funeral home as the policy beneficiary. Because funeral and burial arrangements are made while the insured is living, the insured's survivors are spared from having to make these arrangements following the insured's death. Pre-need funeral insurance tends to be sold in relatively small face amounts. Some insurers market pre-need funeral insurance through funeral home employees who are licensed as insurance agents.

A Newer Generation of Permanent Products

During the 1970s and 1980s, the North American economy changed to such a degree that insurers, like many other financial institutions, were forced to take a long look at the products they offered. Inflation hit record highs; interest rates on savings accounts and consumer loans soared. Consumers realized that the cash values of their whole life policies were earning investment returns at rates that were much lower than the rates that savings accounts and other investment vehicles could earn. Insurers realized that much of their invested assets were earning a lower return than could be obtained through newer investments.

To address the need for insurance products that were more responsive to the changing economy, insurers began marketing a new generation of insurance products. These plans are able to reflect current conditions in the financial marketplace. These new generation products include universal life, adjustable life, variable life, variable universal life, interest-sensitive whole life, and indeterminate premium products.

Universal Life Insurance

Universal life insurance is a form of permanent life insurance that is characterized by its flexible premiums, its flexible face amounts and death benefit amounts, and its unbundling of the pricing factors. All of the policies that we have described until now—both term insurance policies and whole life insurance policies—state the gross premium that the policyowner must pay in order to keep the policy in force. As we noted in Chapter 6, however, some policies—most notably universal life insurance policies—list each of the three pricing factors (mortality, interest, and expenses) separately. In addition, the policyowner can determine, within certain limits, the amount of the premium she wants to pay for the coverage. The larger the premium that the policyowner pays, the larger the amount of coverage that will be provided and the greater the policy's cash value will be.

In the following sections, we describe the distinguishing characteristics of universal life policies. In particular, we describe its flexibility—both in terms of death benefit amounts and premium amounts—and how its unbundled pricing works. We also show how a typical universal life policy operates and describe some other characteristics of the policy. Because the unbundling of the pricing structure is at the core of the operation of a universal life policy, we begin with that aspect of the policy.

Unbundled Pricing Factors

Each of the three factors that the insurer will apply to price a universal life policy is listed separately in the policy. Thus, each universal life policy specifies (1) the mortality charges that the insurer will apply, (2) the interest rate that the insurer will credit to the policy's cash value, and (3) the expense charges that the insurer will apply.

Mortality Charges. The insurer periodically deducts a mortality charge from the universal life policy's cash value. This mortality charge is the amount needed to cover the mortality risk the insurer has assumed by issuing the universal life policy. In other words, the mortality charge pays the cost of the life insurance coverage.

The amount of the mortality charge is based on the insured's risk classification, and the charge typically increases each year as the insured ages. Universal life policies guarantee that the mortality charge will never exceed a stated maximum amount. In addition, these policies usually provide that the mortality charge will be less than the specified maximum if the insurance company's mortality experience is more favorable than expected.

Universal life policies express the mortality charge as a charge per thousand dollars of net amount at risk. Although policies define *net amount at risk* in various ways, in general, a life insurance policy's net amount at risk at any given time is equal to the difference between (1) the amount of the policy death benefit and (2) the amount of the policy's cash value. In other words, the net amount at risk is the amount of the insurer's funds that would be required at any given time to pay the policy death benefit.

FAST FACT

During 1997, sales of universal life insurance in the United States totaled $194.4 billion, increasing total universal life insurance in force to about $2.2 trillion.[3]

Interest. A universal life insurance policy guarantees that the insurer will pay at least a stated minimum interest rate on the policy's cash value each year. The policy also provides that the insurer will pay a higher interest rate if economic and competitive conditions warrant. For example, some policies state that the interest rate paid will reflect current interest rates in the economy. Some policies state that the interest rate to be paid on the cash value will be tied to the rate paid on a standard investment, such as a specified category of United States Government Treasury Bills. According to the terms of some universal life policies, the guaranteed interest rate is paid on cash values up to a stated amount, such as $1,000; the insurer credits any cash values greater than the stated amount with the higher current interest rate. Finally, most universal life policies provide that any portion of the cash value that is being used as security for a policy loan will earn interest at a rate that is lower than the current rate. This reduced interest rate, however, will not fall below the guaranteed minimum interest rate.

Expenses. Each universal life insurance policy lists the expense charges that the insurance company will impose to cover the costs it incurs to administer the policy. The following expense charges may be imposed:

- A flat charge the first policy year to cover sales and policy issue costs

- A percentage of each annual premium (such as 5 percent) to cover expenses

- A monthly administration fee

- Specific service charges for coverage changes, cash withdrawals, and policy surrenders

Flexibility Features

A universal life insurance policy gives the policyowner a great deal of flexibility, both when he purchases the policy and over the life of the policy. When he purchases the policy, the policyowner decides, within certain limits, what the policy's face amount will be, the amount of the death benefit payable, and the amount of premiums he'll pay for that coverage. The policyowner can change these choices during the life of the policy, but the insurance company must approve certain types of changes.

Face Amount and Amount of the Death Benefit. At the time of purchasing a universal life policy, the policyowner specifies the policy's face amount and decides whether the amount of the death benefit payable will be level or will vary with changes in the policy's cash value. Under an **Option A plan** (also known as an *Option 1 plan*), the amount of the death benefit is level; the death benefit payable is always equal to the policy's face amount. Under an **Option B plan** (also known as an *Option 2 plan*), the amount of the death benefit at any given time is equal to the policy's face amount *plus* the amount of the policy's cash value. Note that the net amount at risk for an Option A plan decreases as the amount of the cash value increases. The net amount at risk for an Option B plan, however, is always equal to the policy's face amount. (See Figure 8-3, which illustrates the operation of these two plans.)

After the policy has been in force for a specified minimum time—often one year—the policyowner can request an increase or decrease in the policy's face amount. The insurer typically requires the policyowner to provide evidence of the insured's continued insurability when a proposed increase in the policy's face amount would also significantly increase the policy's net amount at risk.

Before approving a decrease in a policy's face amount, the insurer must ensure that the decrease would not cause the policy to lose its status as an insurance contract and instead be classified as an investment contract. Later in this section, we describe the regulatory requirements that a policy must meet in order to be classified as an insurance product rather than an investment product.

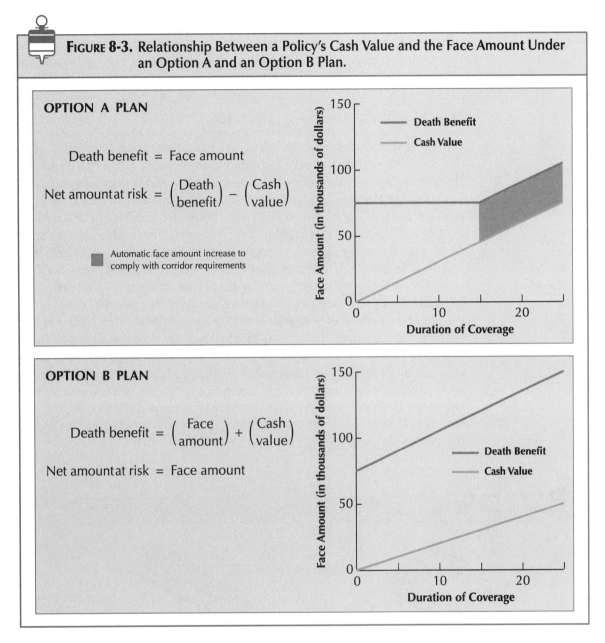

Figure 8-3. Relationship Between a Policy's Cash Value and the Face Amount Under an Option A and an Option B Plan.

Flexible Premiums. The owner of a universal life policy can determine, within certain limits, how much to pay both for the initial premium and for each subsequent renewal premium. The policyowner also has great flexibility to decide when to pay renewal premiums. The insurance company imposes maximum limits on the amounts of the initial and renewal premiums in order to ensure that the policy will maintain its status as an insurance product. In addition, the insurance company requires payment of at least a stated minimum initial premium. As long as the policy's cash value is large enough to pay the periodic mortality and expense charges the insurer imposes, the policy will remain in force even if the policyowner does not pay renewal premiums. If, however, the policy's cash value is insufficient to cover the periodic charges, the policy will lapse unless the policyowner pays an adequate renewal premium.

How a Universal Life Policy Operates

When an insurer receives a universal life premium payment, it first deducts the amount of any applicable expense charges. The insurer then credits the remainder of the premium to the policy's cash value. Each month the policy remains in force, the insurer deducts the periodic mortality charges from the cash value and credits the remainder of the cash value with interest. From time to time, the insurer may deduct additional expense charges from the policy's cash value. (See Figure 8-4, which illustrates how a universal life policy operates.)

The more a policyowner pays in premiums above the amount needed to pay the policy's costs, the greater the policy's cash value will be. Regardless of when or if renewal premiums are paid, the insurer periodically deducts the mortality and expense charges from the policy's cash value and credits the cash value with interest earnings. At any time, if the cash value is not sufficient to pay those periodic charges, the insurer gives the policyowner a stated amount of time—at least 60 days—in which to pay a premium to cover those charges. If the policyowner does not make the premium payment, the policy will lapse.

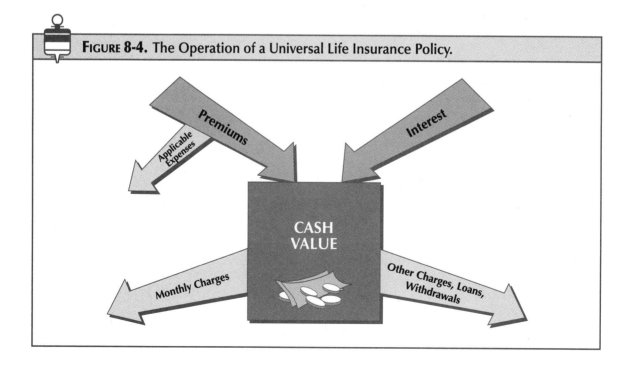

FIGURE 8-4. The Operation of a Universal Life Insurance Policy.

The cash value of a universal life insurance policy may be used as collateral for a policy loan in much the same way that the cash value of a traditional whole life policy may be used. In addition, the universal life policyowner has the right to withdraw funds from the policy's cash value. When a policyowner withdraws funds from the cash value of a universal life policy, the cash value is reduced by the amount withdrawn plus any applicable withdrawal fees. In such cases, the policy remains in force as long as the remaining cash value is sufficient to fund the applicable mortality and expense charges. Some universal life policies also provide that the face amount of the policy will be reduced by the amount of a cash value withdrawal. We describe the policy withdrawal provision in Chapter 10.

Effects of Regulation on Universal Life Policies

Because the operation of a universal life policy gives the policyowner the ability to pay much more in premiums than is needed to fund the cost of insurance, the amount of the policy's cash value can be much greater in relation to the face amount of the policy than is possible with a whole life insurance policy. The larger the cash value is in relation to the policy's face amount, the more a policy seems to be an investment product rather than an insurance product. Recall that U.S. federal tax laws treat life insurance products favorably. In order to assure that this favorable tax treatment is available only to life insurance products, federal tax laws establish limits on the size of a life insurance policy's cash value in relation to its face amount. If the cash value exceeds the regulatory limits, then the policy is treated for tax purposes as an investment product rather than an insurance policy. In the United States, the difference between a policy's face amount and the policy's cash value required to qualify as a life insurance policy rather than an investment product is often referred to as the **Section 7702 corridor** because Internal Revenue Code Section 7702 is the section that establishes the limits on the amount of a policy's cash value. In Canada, requirements concerning the cash values and face amounts of universal life policies are much stricter than the requirements are in the United States; consequently, universal life policies are rarely sold in Canada.

Insurance companies do not allow a policyowner to pay a premium amount that would result in the cash value's exceeding the legislatively defined percentage of the face amount. In addition, most universal life policies provide that if the cash value exceeds the specified percentage of the face amount, then the face amount of the policy automatically is increased to an amount that will meet the legislative requirements.

Another aspect of regulation affecting some forms of universal life concerns the terminology used to refer to a policy's cash value. In some forms of universal life policies, the cash value amount is reduced by significant expense charges, called **surrender charges,** if the policyowner chooses to surrender the policy. For these types of universal life policies, state regulators may require that the insurance company use another term, such as *reserve value* or *accumulation value*, to describe the cash value that accumulates in the policy, and a second term, either *net cash value* or *cash surrender value*, to describe the amount available to policyowners. For simplicity's sake, in this text we will continue to use the term *cash value* in connection with universal life policies.

Periodic Reports

Because so many aspects of a universal life insurance policy change over the course of a year, insurers send each policyowner an annual, semiannual, or quarterly report giving the policy's current values and benefits. (See Figure 8-5, which shows a sample universal life policy report.) Generally, this report includes the following types of information:

- The amount of the death benefit payable

- The amount of the policy's cash value

- The amount of the cash surrender value, if different from the cash value

- The amount of interest earned on the cash value

- The amount of the mortality charges deducted

- The amount of the expense charges deducted

- The amount of premiums paid during the reporting period

- The amount of policy loans outstanding

- The amount of any cash value withdrawals

Adjustable Life Insurance

Adjustable life insurance is designed to allow policyowners to vary the type of coverage provided by their policies as their insurance needs change. The applicant usually specifies the face amount of the adjustable life policy and the premium amount she wishes to pay for

FIGURE 8-5. Sample Annual Report for a Universal Life Insurance Policy.

ABC Life Insurance Company
Universal Life
Policy Number 000-000-00

ANNUAL NOTICE OF YOUR POLICY'S STATUS FOR YEAR ENDING JANUARY 19, 1999
INSURED: James E. Doe
200 Spring Street
Anytown, Anystate 10000

Date	Payments/ (Withdrawals)	Expense Charges	Cost of Insurance	Interest Credited	Unpaid Loans	Ending Cash Value
01/19/98						826.66
02/19/98	100.00	11.50	11.91	—	—	903.25
03/19/98	100.00	11.50	11.90	4.68	—	984.53
04/19/98	100.00	11.50	11.90	5.15	—	1,066.28
05/19/98	100.00	11.50	11.89	5.58	—	1,148.47
06/19/98	100.00	11.50	11.88	6.04	—	1,231.13
07/19/98	100.00	11.50	11.87	6.48	—	1,314.24
08/19/98	100.00	11.50	11.86	6.95	—	1,397.83
09/19/98	100.00	11.50	11.85	7.40	—	1,481.88
10/19/98	100.00	11.50	11.85	7.85	—	1,566.38
11/19/98	100.00	11.50	11.84	8.32	—	1,651.36
12/19/98	100.00	11.50	11.83	8.78	—	1,736.81
01/19/99	100.00	11.50	11.82	9.58	—	1,823.07
Totals	1,200.00	138.00	142.40	76.81	0	

Death Benefit as of February 6, 1999	100,296.00
Cash Value Balance as of January 19, 1999	1,823.07
Interest to be earned February 6, 1999	+ 10.07
Total Cash Value, February 6, 1999	1,833.14
Surrender Value as of February 6, 1999	1,731.98*

The cash value currently earns 7% except the cash value equal to any policy loan earns 6%. From February 6, 1998, to December 5, 1998, the current interest rate was 6.75%. The interest rates are effective annual interest rates.

* The total cash value has been reduced by the surrender charge of $101.16 to arrive at the surrender value.

Continued planned payments of $100 each month will provide coverage until February 6, 2051, based on guaranteed rates.

If no further payments are made, your policy will provide coverage until January 6, 2011, based on current rates; and until January 6, 2006, based on guaranteed rates.

the coverage. The insurance company then determines the specific plan of insurance it can provide based on the requested face amount and premium. The plan of insurance for an adjustable life policy can range from a term insurance policy of short duration to a limited-payment whole life policy.

As the policyowner's needs change, the insurer and policyowner may agree to change the policy's face amount and/or premium amount within limits specified in the policy. Any *increase in premium* or *decrease in face amount* will change the plan of insurance to either lengthen the term of the policy or shorten the premium payment period, depending on the terms of the policy. For example, if the policy is a permanent form of life insurance, the length of the policy term cannot be extended, and, thus, the length of the premium payment period will be shortened. Conversely, any decrease in premium or increase in face amount will either shorten the term of the policy or lengthen the premium payment period, depending on the terms of the policy. Any adjustments, however, must result in a plan, premium, and face amount that fall within the minimums and maximums specified in the adjustable life policy. Policyowners usually must provide evidence of the insurability of the insured in order to increase the face amount of an adjustable life policy, but they do not have to provide such evidence to change the policy's premium or plan.

Indeterminate Premium Life Insurance

An **indeterminate premium life insurance policy** is a type of nonparticipating whole life policy that specifies two premium rates—both a maximum guaranteed premium rate and a lower premium rate. The insurer charges the lower premium rate when the policy is purchased and guarantees that rate for at least a stated period of time, such as one year, two years, five years, or ten years. After that period, the insurer uses its actual mortality, interest, and expense experience to establish a new premium rate that may be higher or lower than the previous premium rate. In no case, though, will the new premium rate exceed the maximum rate guaranteed in the policy. This premium modification process continues periodically throughout the life of the policy. In general, the maximum premium rate charged is slightly higher than the rate for an equivalent nonparticipating whole life policy.

In all other respects, the indeterminate premium policy functions in the same manner as a traditional nonparticipating whole life policy. It enables insurers that issue nonparticipating policies to be more flexible in their pricing because they can change their premium rates to reflect changes in their current mortality, interest, and expense experience. Note that, in order to change the premium rate for an indeterminate premium policy, an insurer must change the premium rate for an entire class of policies based on the insurer's experience for that class of policies. An indeterminate premium policy is also known as a *nonguaranteed premium life insurance policy* and a *variable-premium life insurance policy.*

Interest-Sensitive Whole Life Insurance

Interest-sensitive whole life insurance, which is also called *current assumption whole life insurance,* takes the concept of indeterminate premium policies one step further. In addition to varying the premium rate to reflect changing assumptions regarding the mortality, investment, and expense factors, these policies also provide that the cash value can be greater than that guaranteed if changing assumptions warrant such an increase. Each policyowner usually decides whether he wants favorable changes in pricing assumptions to result in a lower premium or in a higher cash value for the policy. The policyowner can also change this decision after the policy is in force. Most interest-sensitive whole life policies state that if the policyowner does not elect an option, then the cash value increase option will apply. On the other hand, a few of these policies state that changes in pricing assumptions will result in a higher face amount rather than in a lower premium or higher cash value.

If changes in the insurer's pricing assumptions result in a higher premium than the insurer charged when the policy was purchased, then the policyowner may choose to (1) lower the policy's face amount and maintain the previous level of premiums or (2) pay the higher premium and maintain the original face amount. As with an indeterminate premium policy, an interest-sensitive whole life policy guarantees that the premium rate for the coverage cannot increase above the rate guaranteed in the policy.

Variable Life Insurance

Recall that the face amount of a traditional whole life insurance policy remains level throughout the life of the policy and that the policy's cash value grows as periodic premiums are paid and earn interest at a specified rate. Assets that back the policy reserves of traditional whole life policies are considered part of the insurer's general investment account and are placed in a varied group of secure investments. A ***general investment account*** is an account in which a life insurer maintains funds from the guaranteed insurance products the insurer has issued. The insurer can anticipate a steady rate of return on the assets in its general investment account.

By contrast, assets representing the policy reserves for variable life insurance policies are placed in investment accounts that the insurer keeps separate from its general investment account. *Variable life insurance* is a form of whole life insurance under which the death benefit and the cash value of the policy fluctuate according to the investment performance of a special investment account. In the United States, this special account is usually called a *separate account;* in Canada, it is usually called a *segregated account.*

Most variable life policies permit the policyowner to select from among several separate accounts and to change this selection at least annually. The insurer follows a different investment strategy for each separate account. For example, some accounts concentrate on investing in high-growth stocks, while other accounts may concentrate on investing in bonds. The amount of both the policy's death benefit and cash value depend on how well the separate account investments perform. If the separate account investments perform well, then the death benefit and the cash value of the policy will increase. If the investment performance is poor, then the death benefit and cash value will decline. Most variable life policies guarantee that the face amount will not fall below the amount that was initially purchased, regardless of the separate account's performance. Variable life policies, however, do not guarantee either investment earnings or a minimum cash value.

Note that the policyowner, not the insurer, assumes the investment risk of a variable life insurance policy. As a result, the U.S. Securities and Exchange Commission (SEC) has determined that variable life insurance policies are securities and, thus, are subject to federal securities regulation. Insurers that market variable life products in the United States must comply with a range of regulatory regulatory requirements in addition to complying with applicable state insurance regulatory requirements. For example, before issuing a variable life insurance product, an insurer must register the product with the SEC. Also, sales agents must be licensed as registered representatives in accordance with federal securities laws before they sell variable insurance products. According to federal securities laws, any communication—written or oral—that offers a security for sale is a *prospectus* that must contain specified information. At or before the initial sales call, a sales agent is required to present the potential buyer of a variable life insurance policy with a written *policy prospectus* that complies with federal securities laws. The prospectus contains detailed information about the proposed policy, such as explanations of (1) the expense charges, (2) the investment options, and (3) the investment objectives of each option. The policy prospectus also contains an analysis of the past performance of the various investment options and describes policy benefit provisions, policyowner rights, and the manner in which surrender charges will be applied if necessary.

Variable Universal Life Insurance

Variable universal life insurance, which is also called *universal life II* and *flexible-premium variable life insurance,* combines the premium and death benefit flexibility of universal life insurance with the investment flexibility and risk of variable life insurance. Like a universal life policy, a variable universal life policy allows the policyowner to choose the premium amount and face amount. Like a variable life policy, the cash value of a variable universal life policy is placed in a separate investment account. The policyowner chooses from among several investment accounts and may change the chosen option at least annually. The investment returns that the insurer credits to the policy's cash value reflect the investment earnings of the separate accounts. Most insurers allow the policyowner to choose whether the policy's death benefit will remain level (an Option A account) or will vary along with changes in the investment earnings of the separate account (an Option B account). Like variable life policies, variable universal policies do not guarantee investment earnings or cash values. In the United States, variable universal life products are considered securities and, thus, must comply with the federal securities laws described earlier.

> **FAST FACT**
>
> Almost $839 billion of variable universal life insurance was in force in the United States at the end of 1997.[5]

Endowment Insurance

Endowment insurance provides a specified benefit amount whether the insured lives to the end of the term of coverage or dies during that term. Each endowment policy specifies a **maturity date,** which is the date on which the insurer will pay the policy's face amount to the policyowner if the insured is still living. The maturity date is reached either (1) at the end of a stated term or (2) when the insured reaches a specified age. For example, the maturity date of a 20-year endowment policy is 20 years following the policy's effective date; the maturity date of an endowment at age 65 policy is when the insured reaches age 65. If the insured dies before the maturity date, then the insurer pays the policy's face amount to the designated beneficiary. Thus, an endowment insurance policy pays a fixed benefit whether the insured *survives* to the policy's maturity date or *dies* before that maturity date.

Endowment policies share many of the features of permanent life insurance policies. For example, premiums usually are level throughout the term of an endowment policy, although a policyowner can purchase an endowment policy with a single premium or with a series of premiums over a limited period of time. Like permanent life insurance policies, endowment policies steadily build cash values.

Recall that the reserve and the cash value of a whole life policy eventually equal the policy's face amount—but not until the insured reaches the age at the end of the mortality table used to calculate premiums for that policy, usually age 99 or 100. In contrast, the reserve and cash value of an endowment policy will usually equal the policy's face amount on the policy's maturity date, which is typically much sooner than when the insured reaches age 99 or 100. As a result, an endowment policy's cash value builds much more rapidly than does the cash value of a comparable whole life insurance policy.

Because endowment policies build cash values rapidly and because the cash value of an endowment policy is quite large in relationship to the face amount of the policy, endowment policies generally do not maintain the required corridor (the Section 7702 corridor) between the amount of the cash value and the face amount described earlier in connection with universal life policies. As a result, endowment policies do not receive the same favorable federal income tax treatment in the United States and Canada as do life insurance policies.

Key Terms

permanent life insurance
whole life insurance
cash value
cash surrender value
policy loan
continuous-premium whole life
  policy
limited-payment whole life
  policy
paid-up policy
single-premium whole life
  policy
modified-premium whole life
  policy
graded-premium policy
modified coverage policy
joint whole life insurance
last survivor life insurance
family policy
monthly debit ordinary (MDO)
  policy
home service distribution
  system

home service agent
pre-need funeral insurance
universal life insurance
Option A plan
Option B plan
Section 7702 corridor
surrender charges
adjustable life insurance
indeterminate premium life
  insurance policy
interest-sensitive whole life
  insurance
general investment account
variable life insurance
separate account
segregated account
prospectus
policy prospectus
variable universal life insurance
endowment insurance
maturity date

Other Important Terms

surrender value
straight life insurance policy
ordinary life insurance policy
first-to-die life insurance
second-to-die life insurance
debit
agency
account
pre-need insurance
net amount at risk
Option 1 plan
Option 2 plan

reserve value
accumulation value
net cash value
nonguaranteed premium life
 insurance policy
variable-premium life insurance
 policy
current assumption whole life
 insurance
universal life II
flexible-premium variable life
 insurance

Endnotes

1. ACLI, *1998 Life Insurance Fact Book* (Washington, D.C.: American Council of Life Insurance, 1998), 5.

2. CLHIA, *Canadian Life and Health Insurance Facts* (Toronto: Canadian Life and Health Insurance Association, 1998), 8.

3. ACLI, 10.

4. Ibid., 9.

5. Ibid., 10.

6. Ibid., 79, 127.

CHAPTER 9

Supplementary Benefits

After reading this chapter, you should be able to

- Identify three types of disability benefits that life insurance policies may provide

- Describe the characteristics of an accidental death benefit rider

- Identify three types of accelerated death benefit riders and recognize the differences between those riders

- Explain how a life insurance policy's coverage can be expanded to insure more than one individual

- Identify the two types of insurability benefit riders

I n previous chapters, we have described the basic coverages that different types of individual life insurance products provide. Although their features vary, each type of life insurance policy we have described provides a benefit payable upon the death of the insured. We have also noted that term insurance can be provided by a policy or by adding a term insurance rider to another policy, such as a whole life policy. A number of other benefits can also be added to the various forms of life insurance policies. These additional benefits are usually provided by adding riders to the life insurance policy, although in some situations the benefits are provided through standard policy provisions.

Policy riders benefit both the policyowner and the insurer because they give both parties flexibility. When an insurance company issues a policy, it can include riders in order to customize a basic plan of insurance for the policyowner. If the policyowner later wants to adapt the policy to better meet his needs, the insurer can drop or add riders. Thus, the insured and the insurer need not enter into a new contract when the insured desires customized or additional coverage.

The insurance company usually charges an additional premium amount for each supplementary benefit that is added to a policy. These additional premiums, however, do not affect the cash value, if any, of the basic policy. This additional premium charge typically ends when the supplementary benefit expires or is cancelled.

Although a variety of supplementary benefits are available, several types of supplementary benefits are fairly standard in the industry. We describe the most common supplementary benefits in this chapter.

Supplemental Disability Benefits

Disability benefits are generally classified as a type of health insurance coverage because such benefits are paid to cover financial losses that result from a sickness or injury rather than those that result from the insured's death. Some disability benefits, however, can be added to the coverage provided by a life insurance policy. In this section, we describe three types of disability benefits that a life insurance policy or policy rider may provide. These benefits are the waiver of premium for disability benefit, the waiver of premium for payor benefit, and the disability income benefit.

Waiver of Premium for Disability Benefit

One of the most common supplementary benefits that may be added by rider to nearly all individual life insurance policies is the **waiver of premium for disability (WP) benefit.** Under a WP benefit rider, the insurer promises to give up—to *waive*—its right to collect renewal premiums that become due while the insured is totally disabled. In the case of a universal life insurance policy, the WP benefit rider typically specifies that the insurer will waive any mortality and expense charges that become due while the insured is totally disabled. In contrast, the WP benefit provided by some universal life insurance policies specifies that the insurer will waive the amount of the target premium while the insured is totally disabled. The *target premium* is the amount of premium that, if paid on a regular basis, will maintain the policy in force.

Premiums that are waived under a WP benefit are actually paid by the insurance company. Therefore, if the policy is one that builds a cash value, the cash value will continue to increase just as if the policyowner paid the premiums. In the case of a participating policy, the insurance company continues to pay policy dividends as if the policyowner were paying premiums.

In order to receive benefits under a WP rider, the policyowner must notify the insurance company in writing of a claim and must provide proof that the insured is totally disabled as defined by the WP benefit rider. Most WP riders define **total disability** as the insured's inability to perform the essential acts of her own occupation or any other occupation for which she is reasonably suited by education, training, or experience. The insurance company usually reserves the right to require periodic submission of proof that the insured continues to be

"Now then—suppose somebody were to hit you with a great big rock ..."

Reprinted with permission of Rex F. May (Baloo).

totally disabled. Premiums are waived throughout the life of the policy as long as the insured remains totally disabled.

The WP benefit usually contains some limitations. First, most WP riders contain a three- to six-month waiting period after the insured becomes disabled before the insurer will waive the payment of renewal premiums. Thus, if the WP rider calls for a six-month waiting period, the policyowner must continue to pay any renewal premiums that come due during the first six months of the insured's disability. Some WP benefit riders provide that, if the insured is still disabled when the waiting period ends, then the waiver will be retroactive to the beginning of the disability and the insurer will refund to the policyowner any premiums that he paid during the waiting period.

A second limitation is that the WP benefit is usually available to cover only disabilities that begin during a specified age span. For example, the waiver may become effective only if the insured is between the ages of 15 and 65. This limitation is included because the chance of disability increases significantly with age, and, consequently, the cost of providing the WP benefit would be quite high if this benefit were to cover disabilities that begin after the insured reaches age 65.

A third limitation included in most WP riders is that once a disability begins, the interval at which premium payments are due cannot be changed. This limitation prevents a policyowner from changing to a more frequent premium payment schedule. For example, if renewal premiums are payable annually, the policyowner may not change to a monthly premium payment mode. Doing so could result in some of the premiums being waived even if the disability were to end before the annual premium became due.

Finally, WP riders typically exclude some risks from the rider's coverage. For example, disabilities resulting from the following causes are typically excluded from coverage:

- Intentionally self-inflicted injuries

- Injuries the insured suffered while committing a crime

- Pre-existing conditions

- Injuries resulting from any act of war while the insured is in military service

As noted earlier, the WP benefit rider may be added to almost all types of life insurance policies, including renewable and convertible term insurance policies. If a renewable term policy's premium is being waived on a renewal date, the insurer generally renews the policy automatically in accordance with the policy's renewal provision. The insurer will continue to waive renewal premiums until either the insured is no longer totally disabled or the policy is no longer renewable.

> **FAST FACT**
>
> During 1997, U.S. consumers purchased $1.97 trillion of new life insurance coverage. Canadians purchased more than $215 billion of life insurance.[1]

If a convertible term insurance policy's premiums are being waived when the policy becomes convertible to whole life insurance, the policyowner is usually allowed to convert to a whole life policy, in accordance with the policy's conversion provision; the WP rider, however, may or may not be included in the new whole life policy. If the rider is included, renewal premiums continue to be waived as long as the insured is totally disabled. If the rider is not included, the policyowner must resume paying renewal premiums in order to keep the new whole life policy in force. Some WP riders provide that the convertible term insurance policy is automatically converted to a whole life policy if the insured is totally disabled at the conversion date. These policies usually state that the insurer will continue to waive premiums until the recovery or death of the insured.

Waiver of Premium for Payor Benefit

Note that the WP benefit provides a waiver of premium if the *insured* becomes totally disabled. Most individual life insurance policies are issued to a policyowner who is also the policy's insured, and the WP benefit was designed for such policies. By contrast, the waiver of premium for payor benefit was designed for third-party policies, such as juvenile insurance policies. A ***juvenile insurance policy*** is a policy that is issued on the life of a child but is owned and paid for by an adult, usually the child's parent or legal guardian. The ***waiver of premium for payor benefit*** provides that the insurance company will waive its right to collect a policy's renewal premiums if the *policyowner*—the person responsible for paying premiums—dies or becomes totally disabled. Waiver of premium for payor benefit riders generally include a two-part definition of *total disability*. During the first two years of disability, the policyowner is considered totally disabled if he is unable to perform the essential acts of his own occupation, and after that two-year period, the policyowner is considered totally disabled if he is unable to perform the essential acts of any occupation for which he is reasonably suited by education, training, or experience.

Because the disability or death of the policyowner triggers the waiver of premium for payor benefit, the policyowner generally must provide satisfactory evidence of his own insurability—in addition to providing evidence of the insurability of the insured—before the insurer will add this benefit to a life insurance policy. When the benefit is added to a juvenile life insurance policy, the policy or rider usually states that the insurance company will waive the premium payments only until the insured reaches a specified age, such as 18 or 21, when ownership and control of the policy typically passes to the insured.

Disability Income Benefit

Another benefit that may be added to a life insurance policy is the *disability income benefit,* which provides a monthly income benefit to the policyowner-insured if she becomes totally disabled while the policy is in force. Like WP benefit riders, disability income benefit riders typically define *total disability* as the insured's inability to perform the essential acts of her own occupation or any occupation for which she is reasonably suited by education, training, or experience.

Typically, the amount of the monthly disability income benefit is a stated dollar amount—such as $10—per $1,000 of life coverage. Life insurance coverage provided by the policy continues, and, if the insured dies before recovering from the disability, the insurer pays the policy's death benefit to the named beneficiary. The disability income benefit rider also usually includes a three- to six-month waiting period before disability income benefits will begin.

EXAMPLE Paxton Haymes was the policyowner-insured of a $150,000 life insurance policy that included a disability income benefit rider. The rider stated that, if Paxton became totally disabled, then the insurance company would pay him a monthly benefit of $10 per $1,000 of life insurance coverage during the period of disability; the income benefit would begin three months after the onset of a disability. While the policy was in force, Paxton became disabled as defined in the disability income benefit rider. Two years later, he died as a result of his disability.

ANALYSIS Three months after he became disabled, Paxton became eligible to receive a disability income benefit of $1,500 per month.

$ 10	Monthly benefit per unit	
× 150	Times: Number of units ($150,000 ÷ $1,000)	
$1,500	Equals: Monthly disability income	

This monthly disability income benefit was payable as long as Paxton remained disabled. Upon Paxton's death, the policy's death benefit became payable to the named beneficiary.

Policies issued with a disability income benefit generally include a WP benefit as well. In such a case, both the renewal premiums charged for the life policy and the additional premiums charged for the disability income benefit are waived during the total disability of the insured.

Accident Benefits

Accident benefits may be added to any type of life insurance policy. The two most commonly offered accident benefits are accidental death benefits and dismemberment benefits.

Accidental Death Benefit

A policy rider that provides an *accidental death benefit* specifies that if the insured dies as a result of an accident, the insurer will pay the named beneficiary an amount of money in addition to the basic death benefit provided by the life insurance policy. This additional sum is often equal to the policy's face amount. When the amount of the accidental death benefit is equal to the face amount of the life insurance policy, the benefit is often referred to as a *double indemnity benefit* because the total death benefit payable if the insured dies in an accident is double the policy's face amount. The additional sum payable if the insured dies accidentally may also be some other multiple of the policy's face amount—such as three times the face amount—or it may be an amount that is unrelated to the policy's face amount. Most accidental death benefit riders expire when the insured reaches age 65 or 70.

Generally, in order for the accidental death benefit to be payable, the insured person's death must have been caused, directly and independently of all other causes, by an accidental bodily injury. Determining the precise cause of an insured's death, however, can sometimes be quite difficult.

EXAMPLE An insured with a history of heart problems died in an automobile accident. Her policy provides a $50,000 death benefit and includes an accidental death benefit rider that provides an accidental death benefit of $50,000.

ANALYSIS The accident itself may have caused the insured's death. In that case, the accidental death benefit is payable in addition to the policy's basic death benefit. On the other hand, she may have died from a heart attack while driving her automobile. If so, then the death did not result from an accident, and only the policy's basic death benefit is payable to the named beneficiary.

Accidental death benefit provisions usually contain several exclusions and limitations. For example, the provision typically states that the insurance company will not be required to pay the accidental death benefit if the insured's death results from certain stated causes, including

- Self-inflicted injuries (suicide)

- War-related accidents

- Accidents resulting from aviation activities if, during the flight, the insured acted in any capacity other than as a passenger

- Accidents resulting from the insured's engaging in an illegal activity

Laws in some jurisdictions, however, prohibit insurers from excluding some of these causes from their accidental death benefit provisions.

Some accidental death benefit provisions contain a limitation that relates to the time span between the insured's death and the accident that caused the death. This time span is usually stated as 3 months or 90 days, though some provisions specify a longer period. The insured's death must occur within the stated time after the accident in order for the accidental death benefit to be payable. This limitation is included because of the difficulty that can arise in determining the cause of an insured's death. When the insured obviously died as the result of an accident, many insurance companies will disregard the stated time limit and pay the accidental death benefit. Now medical science often can prolong life functions almost indefinitely, sometimes extending the life of an accident victim who in the past would have died shortly after the accident. Further, some jurisdictions prohibit insurers from including a limitation concerning time span in accidental death benefit riders.

Keep in mind that these exclusions and limitations relate only to the accidental death benefit. With few exceptions, which will be described later in this text, the basic death benefit provided by the life insurance policy is payable regardless of the cause of the insured's death.

> **FAST FACT**
>
> Life insurance coverage in the United States totaled $13.2 trillion by the end of 1997.[2]

Dismemberment Benefit

An accidental death benefit rider also may provide an additional benefit for dismemberment, in which case the rider is called an *accidental death and dismemberment (AD&D) rider.* These riders generally specify that the insurer will pay a stated benefit amount if an accident causes the insured to lose any two limbs or sight in both eyes. The amount of the dismemberment benefit is usually equal to the amount of the accidental death benefit. In many cases, however, a smaller amount—such as one-half the amount of the accidental death benefit—will be payable if the insured loses one limb or sight in one eye as the result of an accident. The loss of a limb may be defined either as the actual physical loss of the limb or as the loss of the use of the limb. Usually, AD&D riders state that the insurer will not pay both accidental death benefits and dismemberment benefits for injuries suffered in the same accident.

Accelerated Death Benefits

During the late 1980s, a new type of life insurance policy benefit became available. *Accelerated death benefit riders,* also known as *living benefit riders,* provide that a policyowner may elect to receive all or part of the policy's death benefit before the insured's death if certain conditions are met. The payment of an accelerated death benefit reduces the death benefit that will be paid to the beneficiary at the insured's death by the amount of the living benefit that was paid to the policyowner. These benefits continue to gain popularity for several reasons. First, the segment of the population comprised of the elderly is growing. These individuals frequently suffer from illnesses that require medical care. Second, the cost of health care continues to increase. And third, medical advances tend to postpone death and prolong the need for medical care.

In an effort to keep administrative costs down, life insurers generally offer accelerated death benefit coverage only on policies with large face amounts, such as $100,000 or $250,000. Some insurers also require that before they pay any accelerated death benefit, the beneficiary must sign a release acknowledging that the policy's death benefit will be reduced by the amount paid to the policyowner under the accelerated death benefit provision. Also, if the policyowner has assigned the policy, then the assignee must sign such a release. (We describe assignments in Chapter 12.)

The specific amount of accelerated death benefits that are payable under a policy, and the circumstances that trigger such payments, depend on the wording of the benefit rider. In this section, we describe three commonly offered types of accelerated death benefits—the terminal illness benefit, the dread disease benefit, and the long-term care benefit.

Terminal Illness Benefit

The most common of the accelerated death benefits is the terminal illness benefit. The ***terminal illness (TI) benefit*** is a benefit under which the insurer pays a portion of the policy's death benefit to a policyowner if the insured suffers from a terminal illness and has a physician-certified life expectancy of 12 months or less. A statement by an attending physician establishes evidence of the terminal condition and certifies that the insured is likely to die within the time period specified in the rider. Insight 9-1 describes how a few individuals used the funds they received in the form of TI benefits.

Unlike other supplementary benefits, the terminal illness benefit is typically paid for by an administrative charge that the insurer assesses when a policyowner elects to exercise the TI benefit. By contrast, when they issue a policy that provides other supplementary benefits, insurers typically impose an additional premium charge for each supplementary benefit that the policy provides.

The amount of the TI benefit that is payable varies from insurer to insurer. Some policies permit payment of the full face amount prior to the insured's death. Generally, however, the maximum TI benefit payable is a stated percentage—usually between 25 and 75 percent—of the policy's face amount up to a specified maximum dollar limit such as $250,000. The benefit is usually paid in a lump sum to the policyowner. The remainder of the death benefit is paid to the beneficiary at the insured's death.

Insight 9-1.   Using Accelerated Death Benefits.

Insureds who take advantage of an accelerated death benefit provision may use the early payout for more than just medical expenses. Quoted in an article that appeared in *Best's Review,* Jim Longo, of Prudential, told of a policyowner in Virginia who had to travel to Nebraska for treatment of a brain tumor. An early payout of her life insurance policy benefits allowed her husband, who stayed in Virginia to care for their children, to fly to her bedside frequently during her final days. An AIDS patient in Canada used part of his benefits to buy a washer and dryer so he could do his laundry at home.[3] A man dying of stomach cancer in Chicago used his accelerated benefits to pay off his mortgage, automobile, and credit card debts and to arrange his funeral. "It gave him great peace of mind," said Longo. "When you're terminally ill, little debts suddenly seem tremendous. [Policyowners who receive accelerated death benefits] are all grateful that they've got this insurance. Rather than feel powerless, they feel they've got some control over their lives."[4] •

Dread Disease Benefit

One of the earliest forms of accelerated death benefit coverage offered by insurers is the **dread disease (DD) benefit** under which the insurer agrees to pay a portion of the policy's face amount to a policyowner if the insured suffers from one of a number of specified diseases. The remainder of the death benefit is paid to the beneficiary at the insured's death. (Another form of dread disease coverage can be purchased as a stand-alone health insurance policy. We discuss that form in Part 2 of the text.)

An insured becomes eligible for DD benefits when he has certain diseases or undergoes certain medical procedures specified in the rider. These specified diseases or medical procedures are known as the *insurable events* and usually include

- Life-threatening cancer

- AIDS

- End-stage renal (kidney) failure

- Myocardial infarction (heart attack)

- Stroke

- Coronary bypass surgery

Some DD benefit riders also include vital organ transplants and Alzheimer's disease as insurable events.

Although the accelerated death benefit is usually paid in a lump sum, some insurers pay the benefit in monthly installments over a period of 6 to 12 months. Most insurers provide DD coverage only to insureds who are under the age of 70 and only to insureds who are standard risks, and some insurers do not make payments for multiple or recurring events.

The DD benefit may offer a premium waiver option under which the insurer agrees to waive all renewal premiums payable after the accelerated death benefit payment. Sometimes the premium waiver option applies only to premiums payable while the insured is disabled; if the insured recovers, then subsequent renewal premiums are no longer waived.

Long-Term Care Benefit

A **long-term care (LTC) benefit** is payable as a monthly benefit to a policyowner if the insured requires constant care for a medical condition. For example, an insured who has severe arthritis or advanced Alzheimer's disease may need some form of constant care. The types of care that an LTC benefit rider covers are specified in the rider. For example, the rider may provide benefits for an insured to be cared for either in an approved nursing facility or in the insured's home by a licensed home health agency.

The specific requirements that an insured must meet in order to qualify for LTC benefits depend on the terms of the LTC benefit rider. The LTC rider may, for example, require that the care be medically necessary. Determining when care is medically necessary is often difficult, however, and LTC riders take various approaches to making such a determination. For example, some LTC riders require that an insured must be hospitalized for at least three days to establish the need for home health care or nursing home care. A few riders specify only that the insured's physician approve the care. However, the latter approach is not used frequently because of the difficulty of making sure that all physicians use the same criteria for approving the care.

Perhaps the most common approach to determining if an insured is eligible for LTC benefits is to require that the insured be unable to perform a certain number of activities of daily living (ADLs) in order to demonstrate the need for long-term care. *Activities of daily living* include activities such as eating, bathing, dressing, going to the bathroom, getting in and out of bed or a wheelchair, and mobility (walking indoors). Some LTC riders state that an insured must demonstrate her inability to perform a greater number of ADLs in order to receive benefits for nursing home care than the number of ADLs needed to receive benefits for home health care. In order to assess ADLs, insurers can (1) rely on physician certification, (2) contract with a firm that specializes in such assessments, or (3) develop their own assessment tools.

The amount of each monthly LTC benefit payment is generally equal to some stated percentage of the policy's death benefit. For example, the rider may state that 2 percent of the policy's death benefit will be paid each month if the insured requires nursing home care and 1 percent of the death benefit will be paid each month if the insured requires home health care. The insurer usually continues to pay monthly benefits until a specified percentage of the policy's basic death benefit has been paid out. This percentage typically falls between 50 and 100 percent of the policy's face amount. Any remaining death benefit is paid to the beneficiary after the insured's death.

Most LTC benefit riders impose a 90-day waiting period before accelerated death benefits are payable; no benefits are payable until 90 days following the date on which the insured becomes eligible for benefits. According to the terms of some LTC benefit riders, however, coverage must be in force for a given period of time, usually one year or more, before the insured will qualify for LTC benefits. Premiums are generally waived on both the long-term care rider and the basic life insurance policy during the period that the insured receives LTC benefits.

Benefits for Additional Insureds

Term insurance riders can be added to most permanent life insurance policies in order to increase the amount of the benefit payable if the insured dies while the coverage is in force. In addition, various riders can be added to life insurance policies to provide benefits if someone other than the policy's insured dies. These riders take several forms, but the most common are the spouse and children's insurance rider, the children's insurance rider, and the second insured rider.

Spouse and Children's Insurance Rider

In the last chapter, we described the family insurance policy, which is a whole life insurance policy that provides coverage on the insured's entire family. A *spouse and children's insurance rider* added to a permanent life insurance policy provides coverage similar to that provided by a family insurance policy. The coverage provided by such a rider, however, is typically sold on the basis of coverage units. In contrast, the coverage provided on the insured's family under a family insurance policy is typically a percentage of the face amount provided on the life of the primary insured.

Usually, each coverage unit of a spouse and children's insurance rider provides $5,000 of term insurance coverage on the spouse and $1,000 of term insurance coverage on each child. Thus, if a person purchases three coverage units, then the amount of coverage provided by the rider would be $15,000 on the spouse and $3,000 on each child. Most insurance companies do not offer more than five or ten coverage units.

The premium for the children's coverage is a specified, flat amount that does not change with the number of children in the family. Therefore, the insurer charges the same premium for a family with one child as it charges for a family with six children. For this reason, the insurer does not have to revise the premium for a spouse and children's insurance rider if additional children are born or adopted into the family after the coverage is purchased. Those additional children are covered automatically at no extra premium charge, although the coverage does not typically take effect until the child reaches age 15 days.

The term insurance coverage on each child expires when that child reaches a stated age, typically 21 or 25. Such riders, however, usually include a conversion privilege that allows the child to convert his term insurance coverage to an individual life insurance policy. For example, the rider may permit each child to convert up to five times the amount of his term insurance coverage to an individual permanent insurance policy without providing evidence of his insurability.

Children's Insurance Rider

Partly in recognition of the growing number of single-parent households, most insurance companies offer a ***children's insurance rider.*** This rider operates in the same fashion as does a spouse and children's insurance rider, except that no spousal coverage is included. The premium charged for each coverage unit is a stated amount, regardless of the number of children covered, the ages of those children, or the age and sex of the insured parent. For example, a single mother of three children could purchase a children's insurance rider for the same amount that would be charged to a single father of two children.

Second Insured Rider

A ***second insured rider,*** also called an *optional insured rider* or an *additional insured rider,* provides term insurance coverage on the life of an individual other than the policy's insured. The individual insured under the rider is known as the *second insured* and may be the spouse of the insured, another relative, or an unrelated person. For example, the second insured may be a business partner of the person insured by the policy. The amount of coverage a second insured rider provides is not usually related to the amount of coverage the basic policy provides. The premium rate required for the second insured rider is based on the risk characteristics of the second insured, not on the risk characteristics of the person insured under the basic policy.

Insurability Benefits

Two types of insurability benefits are offered as riders to life insurance policies. These benefits are the guaranteed insurability benefit and the paid-up additions option benefit.

Guaranteed Insurability Benefit

The ***guaranteed insurability (GI) benefit***—sometimes referred to as a *guaranteed insurability option (GIO)*—is usually provided by a rider that gives the policyowner the right to purchase additional insurance of the same type as the life insurance policy to which the GI rider is attached. The policyowner has the right to purchase additional insurance—for an additional premium amount—on specified option dates during the life of the policy without supplying evidence of the insured's insurability. Thus, the GI rider guarantees that the policyowner will be able to purchase additional life insurance even though the insured may no longer be in good health.

Typically, the amount of coverage the policyowner may purchase on an option date is limited to the policy's face amount or to an amount specified in the GI rider, whichever is smaller. For example, a GI rider attached to a $50,000 traditional whole life policy may give the owner the right to purchase an additional $10,000 of whole life insurance coverage on each of certain stated dates. The GI rider may also permit the purchase of additional life insurance coverage when certain events occur, such as when the insured marries or at the birth of a child. Most GI riders, however, limit the benefit by permitting the policyowner to exercise the GI option only until the insured reaches age 40.

Although the right to purchase the additional coverage is automatic, the actual purchase is not. A policyowner who desires the extra coverage must take positive action to purchase the new coverage. Most GI riders specify that if the policyowner does not exercise the option on one of the specified dates, that option is lost forever, though the policyowner can still exercise the next option when it comes due.

Some GI riders provide automatic temporary term insurance coverage for the period during which the policyowner has the right to exercise her option to purchase additional insurance coverage. This term insurance coverage usually lasts 60 to 90 days and is designed to protect the beneficiary in cases in which the policyowner is delayed in taking the necessary action to exercise an option.

If the life insurance policy also includes a WP rider and the insured is disabled at the time an option to purchase additional insurance goes into effect, then the insurance company automatically issues the additional life insurance coverage. The insurance company also waives the payment of renewal premiums for all of a policy's coverages to which the WP rider applies until the recovery or death of the insured.

Paid-Up Additions Option Benefit

The *paid-up additions option benefit* allows the owner of a whole life insurance policy to purchase single-premium paid-up additions to the policy on stated dates in the future and thus to increase the amount of coverage provided under the basic policy. For example, many paid-up additions option riders allow the policyowner to purchase paid-up additional whole life insurance on each policy anniversary. Because the additions are whole life insurance, the paid-up additions also have their own cash values.

Premiums for the paid-up additions are based on the net single premium rate for the coverage at the insured's age at the time the paid-up additions were purchased. Typically, the premium that a policyowner can apply to purchase the paid-up additions must fall between the minimums and maximums established in the rider. Most riders state that if the policyowner does not exercise the purchase option for a stated number of years, then the rider will terminate. At that time, the paid-up additions already purchased remain in force, but the policyowner can no longer exercise the option to purchase new paid-up additions.

As we will discuss in Chapter 12, a paid-up additions option is typically one of the dividend options provided in a participating policy. The owner of a participating policy can select the paid-up additions dividend option at any time. In contrast, a policyowner must provide evidence of the insured's insurability in order to add a paid-up additions option rider to an in-force policy. Once the rider is in force, however, no additional evidence of insurability is required to purchase each paid-up addition.

Key Terms

waiver of premium for disability (WP) benefit
total disability
juvenile insurance policy
waiver of premium for payor benefit
disability income benefit
accidental death benefit
double indemnity benefit
accidental death and dismemberment (AD&D) rider
accelerated death benefit rider

terminal illness (TI) benefit
dread disease (DD) benefit
long-term care (LTC) benefit
activities of daily living (ADLs)
spouse and children's insurance rider
children's insurance rider
second insured rider
guaranteed insurability (GI) benefit
paid-up additions option benefit

Other Important Terms

waive
target premium
living benefit riders

insurable events
optional insured rider
additional insured rider

Other Important Terms (continued)

second insured
guaranteed insurability option (GIO)

Endnotes

1. ACLI, *1998 Life Insurance Fact Book* (Washington, D.C.: American Council of Life Insurance, 1998), 1; CLHIA, *Canadian Life and Health Insurance Facts* (Toronto: Canadian Life and Health Insurance Association, 1998), 4.

2. ACLI, 1.

3. Sean Armstrong, "AIDS and the Trusted Adviser," *Best's Review*, Life/Health edition (September 1994), 39.

4. Ibid.

5. CLHIA, 4.

CHAPTER 10

Life Insurance Policy Provisions

After reading this chapter, you should be able to

◉ Identify the documents that make up the entire contract between the owner of a life insurance policy and the insurer

◉ Recognize situations in which an insurer has the right to avoid a life insurance contract

◉ Apply the terms of the standard grace period provision to determine in a given situation whether a life insurance policy has lapsed for nonpayment of premium

◉ Identify the types of policies that contain a policy loan provision and the types that contain a policy withdrawal provision

◉ Identify situations in which a life insurance policy can be reinstated and the conditions the policyowner must meet in order to reinstate the policy

◉ Determine the action an insurer likely will take if it discovers a misstatement of the age or sex of the person insured by a life insurance policy

◉ Identify the exclusions that insurers sometimes include in individual life insurance policies

As we described in Chapter 3, an insurance policy is a written document that describes the agreement between the contracting parties—the insurance company and the owner of the policy—and sets forth the rights and obligations of the parties. In this chapter, we describe some of the provisions that are typically included in individual life insurance policies. We begin our discussion with an overview of how the state and provincial governments regulate the content of individual life insurance policies.

Regulation of Policy Provisions

As we noted in Chapter 2, the provincial governments in Canada and the state governments in the United States have all enacted laws designed to protect the rights of life insurance policyowners and beneficiaries. These laws contain various requirements concerning the provisions that are included in policies. In the United States, state laws typically require individual life insurance policies to include specified provisions that spell out the rights of policyowners and beneficiaries. Other provisions may be included at the insurer's option. In addition, most states require insurance companies to file each policy form with—and receive approval from—the state insurance department before issuing the policy form in the state. By reviewing each policy form, the state insurance department can assure that policy forms comply with applicable regulatory requirements.

In Canada, the common law provinces and territories have all enacted insurance laws patterned, with minor variations, on the Uniform Life Insurance Act (Uniform Act). The *Uniform Life Insurance Act* is a model law adopted by the Canadian Council of Insurance Regulators (CCIR) to regulate life insurance policies. Although it has not adopted the Uniform Act, the province of Quebec has enacted laws that govern life insurance policies and that are very similar to the Uniform Act. These provincial insurance laws require insurers to include certain provisions in life insurance policies. Provincial insurance laws also directly grant certain rights to policyowners and beneficiaries and impose certain obligations on insurers. These statutory rights and obligations are enforceable without regard to the terms of the insurance policy. Although Canadian insurance laws do not require policies to include provisions spelling out these statutory rights and obligations, insurers routinely include such provisions in their life insurance policies. With only a few exceptions, the provinces do not require insurers to file policy forms with provincial regulators.

Despite these regulatory differences, life insurance policies issued throughout Canada and the United States generally contain the same basic provisions. When the applicable insurance laws require a policy provision—or provide a statutory right—the insurer is free to include a provision that is more favorable to the policyowner or beneficiary than that required. Insurers often provide policy terms that are more favorable than those required by law.

Standard Policy Provisions

Although the specific wording varies from policy to policy and from insurer to insurer, individual life insurance policies generally contain the following standard provisions:

- A free-look provision

- An entire contract provision

- An incontestability provision

- A grace period provision

- A reinstatement provision

- A misstatement of age or sex provision

- A settlement options provision

In addition, participating life insurance policies include a policy dividends provision, and permanent life insurance policies that build a cash value generally must include a nonforfeiture provision and a policy loan provision. In this section, we describe each of these standard policy provisions.

Free-Look Provision

Individual life insurance policies generally include a ***free-look provision*** or *free-examination provision* that gives the policyowner a stated period of time—usually ten days—after the policy is delivered in which to examine the policy. During the free-look period, the policyowner has the right to cancel the policy and receive a full refund of the initial premium payment. Insurance coverage is in effect throughout the free-look period, or until the policyowner rejects the policy, if sooner.

EXAMPLE | Yoko Matsuto applied for an individual insurance policy on her life and paid the initial premium. The insurer issued the policy, which the sales agent delivered to Yoko. The sales agent reviewed the policy with Yoko and pointed out the policy's ten-day free-look period. Two days later, Yoko changed her mind about purchasing the policy. Before she could contact her sales agent to cancel the policy, Yoko was killed.

ANALYSIS | During the ten-day free-look period, Yoko had the right to cancel the policy and receive a full premium refund. However, because the policy was in force when Yoko died, the insurer is obligated to pay the policy death benefit to the named beneficiary.

Entire Contract Provision

The *entire contract provision* defines the documents that constitute the contract between the insurance company and the owner of the insurance policy. By limiting the terms of the contract to the specified written documents, the entire contract provision prevents oral statements from affecting the terms of the policy and prevents controversies from developing regarding the terms of the contractual agreement.

The specific wording of the entire contract provision varies depending on whether the policy is a closed contract or an open contract. A *closed contract* is a contract for which only those terms and conditions that are printed in—or attached to—the contract are considered to be part of the contract. The entire contract provision in these policies states that the entire contract consists of the policy, any attached riders, and the attached copy of the application for insurance. The provision assures that policyowners have access to all of the terms of the contractual agreement. With the exception of policies issued by fraternal insurers, all individual life insurance policies issued in the United States and Canada are closed contracts.

An *open contract* is a contract that identifies the documents that constitute the contract between the parties, but the enumerated documents are not all attached to the contract. Fraternal insurers in the United States and Canada typically issue life insurance policies as open contracts which state that the entire contract consists of the policy and any attached riders; the fraternal society's charter, constitution, and bylaws; the attached policyowner's application for membership in the society; and the attached declaration of insurability, if any, signed by the applicant. When a fraternal insurer issues a policy, it does not attach a copy of the fraternal's charter, constitution, and bylaws to the policy. Fraternal insurers are permitted to use open contracts because membership in the fraternal society is a requirement for purchasing insurance through the society. When a person becomes a member of a fraternal society, he receives a copy of the society's charter, constitution, and bylaws, and, thus, has the opportunity to examine these documents.

In addition to defining the documents that make up the contract, the entire contract provision usually states that (1) only specified individuals—such as certain officers of the insurer—can change the contract, (2) no change is effective unless made in writing, and (3) no change will be made unless the policyowner agrees to it in writing.

Incontestability Provision

As noted in Chapter 5, when a contract is voidable, one party to the contract has the right to avoid his obligations under the contract without incurring legal liability to the other party. In other words, the party has the right to avoid, or reject, an otherwise enforceable contract. The rules of contract law give an insurer the right to avoid an otherwise enforceable insurance contract if the applicant misrepresented material facts in the application for insurance. State and provincial insurance laws, however, limit the time within which an insurer has such a right. As a result, life insurance policies contain an *incontestability provision* that describes the time limit within which the insurer has the right to avoid the contract on the ground of material misrepresentation in the application. In this section, we describe material misrepresentations and the operation of the incontestability provision.

Material Misrepresentation

Applications for life insurance policies contain questions designed to provide the insurance company with relevant information so that it can decide whether the proposed insured is an insurable risk. According to the rules of contract law, statements made by the parties when they enter into a contract can be classified as either warranties or representations. A *warranty* is a statement made by a contracting party that will invalidate the contract if the statement is not literally true. In contrast, a **representation** is a statement made by a contracting party that will invalidate the contract if the statement is not substantially true. Statements made in an application for insurance are considered to be representations rather than warranties.

EXAMPLE	Dominique Ravel purchased an insurance policy on her life, stating on her application that she had visited the doctor for an infected toe on her left foot. In fact, she had visited the doctor for an infected toe on her right foot.

ANALYSIS	The statement in Dominique's application is not literally true. However, statements made in an application for life insurance are representations, not warranties. As a result, even though the statement is not literally true, it does not automatically invalidate the contract as long as it is substantially true.

A false or misleading statement in an application for insurance is known as a **misrepresentation.** Some statements contained in the application are more important to the insurer's decision to issue a policy than are other statements. A misrepresentation that would affect the insurance company's evaluation of the proposed insured is called a **material misrepresentation.** A misrepresentation is considered material when, if the truth had been known, the insurer would not have issued the policy or would have issued the policy on a different basis, such as for a higher premium or for a lower face amount. A misrepresentation in an application for life insurance gives the insurer grounds to avoid the contract only if it was a material misrepresentation. Some examples will help to illustrate the types of misrepresentations that are considered to be material misrepresentations.

EXAMPLE	Indira Patel's application for life insurance contained the statement that she had visited a doctor on July 10, when the actual date of the visit was July 9.

ANALYSIS	The insurer's decision as to whether Indira is an insurable risk will not change based on the misstatement as to the date of the doctor visit. This misrepresentation, therefore, is not a material misrepresentation and cannot be used by the insurance company to avoid the contract.

EXAMPLE | Anthony Abernathy's application for life insurance contained the statement that he had visited a doctor on July 10 for a regular physical examination when, in fact, the reason for the visit was that he was being treated for heart disease.

ANALYSIS | The purpose of a proposed insured's visit with a doctor may be very relevant to the insurance company's evaluation of the application for insurance. In order to evaluate his application properly, the insurance company needed to know that Anthony suffered from heart disease. As a result, the misrepresentation about the purpose of the doctor visit is a material misrepresentation if the insurance company would have made a different decision about issuing the life insurance policy had it known the truth.

Operation of Incontestability Provision

If an insurer discovers a material misrepresentation in an application for life insurance when it is evaluating the application, the insurer probably will decide not to issue the policy. What happens if the insurance company issues a life insurance policy and later discovers a material misrepresentation in the application? In such a case, the terms of the policy's incontestability provision govern whether the insurance company can avoid the contract. Because the insurance laws regarding the contestability of a life insurance policy are somewhat different in the United States and Canada, we describe the incontestability provision typically used in each country.

United States. A typical incontestability provision included in life insurance policies issued in the United States reads as follows:

> **Incontestability.** We will not contest this policy after it has been in force during the lifetime of the insured for two years from the date of issue.

The provision limits the period during which the insurer has the right to avoid the contract to two years from the date the policy was issued. This two-year contestable period is the maximum period permitted by law in most states. A period shorter than two years is permitted because that would be more favorable to the policyowner, and some policies do include a one-year contestable period.

It is important for the insurer to include the phrase *during the lifetime of the insured* because, in effect, this phrase makes the policy contestable forever if the person whose life is insured dies during the stated contestable period. As a result, the insurance company will have the opportunity to investigate for material misrepresentation when a death claim arises within the contestable period of a life insurance policy. If the phrase *during the lifetime of the insured* were not included and the insured died during the contestable period, the beneficiary could possibly delay making a death claim until after the contestable period expired. The insurer might then be prevented from contesting the policy and, thus, would be required to pay the death claim even if the application contained a material misrepresentation.

In the United States, an insurer has the right to use a material misrepresentation in the application as the basis for avoiding a life insurance contract only if a copy of the application for insurance was attached to the policy the insurer issued and delivered to the applicant. In other words, the application for insurance is not considered a part of the contract unless it is attached to the policy when the policy is issued. Fraternal insurers meet the requirement that the application be attached by attaching to the policy a copy of the policyowner's application for membership in the fraternal society and the declaration of insurability, if any, signed by the applicant for insurance.

The purpose of the incontestability provision is to assure policyowners and beneficiaries that after the contestable period has passed, the insurer cannot avoid the policy on the basis of a material misrepresentation in the application for insurance. The provision allows the beneficiary to know with certainty that if all required premiums are paid and the policy has been in force for at least the stated period, the insurer will pay the policy proceeds following the insured's death.

EXAMPLE In the previous example, Anthony Abernathy did not disclose the true reason for his visit to the doctor. Anthony died five years after the policy was issued. In evaluating the death claim, the insurer discovered this material misrepresentation.

ANALYSIS Because the policy's contestable period had expired by the time the insurer discovered the misrepresentation, the insurer does not have the right to contest the validity of the contract. As a result, the insurer must pay the policy proceeds to the named beneficiary.

Canada. A typical incontestability provision included in life insurance policies issued in Canada reads as follows:

> **Incontestability.** In the absence of fraud, we will not contest this policy after it has been in force during the lifetime of the insured for two years from when the policy takes effect or two years from the date it has been reinstated, if later.

As in the United States, provincial insurance laws limit to a maximum period of two years after the policy becomes effective the time during which the insurer may avoid a life insurance contract on the ground of material misrepresentation. The provincial insurance laws, however, contain an exception—an insurer may contest a policy at any time if the application contained a fraudulent misrepresentation. A *fraudulent misrepresentation* is a misrepresentation that was made with the intent to induce the other party to enter into a contract and that did induce the innocent party to enter into the contract. In reality, insurance companies seldom exercise their right to avoid a life insurance contract on the basis of a fraudulent misrepresentation because they are usually unable to obtain sufficient evidence to prove the misrepresentation was fraudulent.

EXAMPLE | Assume that Anthony Abernathy, mentioned in the two previous examples, lived in Canada and purchased his life insurance policy from a Canadian insurer. Anthony died after the expiration of the two-year contestable period. The insurer determined that Anthony deliberately included incorrect information on his application for insurance, knowing that the insurer would not issue him a policy if he disclosed his heart disease.

ANALYSIS | The insurer has the right to avoid Anthony's policy if it can prove the misrepresentation in the application was a fraudulent misrepresentation, even though the discovery of the misrepresentation was made after the two-year contestable period had expired.

Provincial insurance laws state that the application for insurance is a part of the contract. As a result, even if a copy of the application is not attached to the policy when it is issued, the insurer has the right to contest the contract's validity based on material misrepresentations contained in that application.

The two incontestability provisions we have included here contain another difference—the provision typically used in Canada states that the insurance company may contest the validity of a life insurance policy within two years after the policy was reinstated. Although the sample U.S. policy provision does not contain this statement, insurance companies in the United States also have the right to contest the validity of a life insurance policy within a stated time after the policy was reinstated. We describe the contestability of reinstated policies later in the chapter when we describe the reinstatement provision.

Grace Period Provision

Insurance laws in the United States and Canada require every individual life insurance policy to state the period of grace within which a required renewal premium may be paid. The **grace period** is a specified length of time within which a renewal premium that is due may be paid without penalty. Notice that a grace period is available only with respect to the payment of renewal premiums; no grace period is provided for the payment of a policy's initial premium because the policy does not become effective until the initial premium is paid. A typical grace period provision follows.

> **Grace period.** We allow 31 days from the due date for payment of a premium. All insurance continues during this grace period.

In most jurisdictions in the United States and Canada, the minimum grace period required is 30 or 31 days. An insurance company can, and some companies do, provide a longer grace period. The policy remains in force throughout the grace period. If the insured dies during the grace period, then the insurer will pay the policy proceeds to the named beneficiary. The insurer, however, usually deducts the amount of any unpaid renewal premium from the amount of the policy proceeds.

If a renewal premium is not paid by the end of the grace period, the policy is said to **lapse.** Some insurers, however, do not consider a policy as having lapsed if that policy has a cash value; the owner of a policy that provides a cash value has the right to continue the coverage under a nonforfeiture option. We describe nonforfeiture benefits later in the chapter. This text, in keeping with general usage, will use the terms *lapse* or *lapsed* in connection with any policy on which a renewal premium has not been paid by the end of the grace period.

FAST FACT

According to studies by LIMRA International, traditional whole life insurance policies have the lowest lapse rate of any type of individual life insurance policy. The types of policies that policy-owners most often allow to lapse during the first two policy years are interest-sensitive policies and annually renewable term policies.[1]

EXAMPLE Michael Etheridge was the policyowner-insured of a $100,000 term life insurance policy. The policy's annual renewal premium was due on March 21 of each year. His policy contained a typical grace period provision. Michael died on April 10, 1998, without having paid the renewal premium then due.

ANALYSIS Because Michael died during his policy's 31-day grace period, the insurer was liable to pay the policy proceeds to the named beneficiary, but it may deduct the amount of the unpaid renewal premium from those proceeds.

EXAMPLE   Assume that Michael Etheridge died on June 15, 1998, without having paid the renewal premium due on March 21, 1998.

ANALYSIS   The insurer would not be obligated to pay the policy benefit to the named beneficiary because the policy lapsed for nonpayment of premium on April 21, 1998—following the expiration of the policy's grace period.

Some life insurance policies, such as universal life insurance policies, do not require scheduled premium payments. The grace period provision contained in a universal life policy is applied when the cash value is insufficient to meet the policy's monthly mortality and expense charges. Depending on the wording of the grace period provision, the grace period for such a policy will begin on either (1) the date on which the cash value is insufficient to cover the policy's entire monthly mortality and expense charges, in which case the grace period will continue for 61 or 62 days after that date, or (2) the date on which the cash value is zero, in which case the grace period will continue for 30 or 31 days after that date. The grace period provision in these life insurance policies also states that at least 30 or 31 days before the coverage expires, the insurance company will notify the policyowner that the cash value is insufficient to meet the policy charges and that the coverage will terminate if the policyowner does not make a premium payment that is large enough to cover those charges. If the person whose life is insured dies during the policy's grace period, then the insurer will pay the policy death benefit, but it will deduct from those proceeds the amount required to pay the overdue mortality and expense charges.

EXAMPLE   Felicia Wagner is the policyowner-insured of a universal life insurance policy. Felicia has not made a premium payment in several years, during which time the insurer has used the policy's cash value to pay the monthly mortality and expense charges. Currently, the policy's remaining cash value is insufficient to cover the mortality and expense charges that are payable.

ANALYSIS   The insurer will send Felicia a notice that her policy will continue under the grace period provision for 61 days, by which time she must make a premium payment sufficient to cover the overdue mortality and expense charges in order to keep the policy from lapsing. If Felicia should die during the 61-day grace period, the insurer will pay the policy death benefit, less the amount of any overdue mortality and expense charges, to the named beneficiary.

Policy Loans and Policy Withdrawals

Life insurance policies that accumulate a cash value typically grant the policyowner the right to borrow money from the insurer by using the cash value of the policy as security for the loan. The **policy loan provision** grants the owner of a life insurance policy the right to take out a loan for an amount that does not exceed the policy's net cash value less one year's interest on the loan. A policy loan is actually an advance payment of part of the amount that the insurer eventually must pay out under the policy.

A policy loan differs from a commercial loan in two respects. First, the policyowner is not legally obligated to repay a policy loan. The policyowner, however, may repay any part or all of the loan at any time. If a policy loan has not been repaid when the insured dies, the insurer deducts the amount of the unpaid loan from the policy benefit that is payable. In contrast, a commercial loan creates a debtor-creditor relationship between the borrower and the lender. The borrower is legally obligated to repay a commercial loan.

EXAMPLE At the time of his death, Joseph Mangano was insured by a $50,000 whole life insurance policy. The policy had an unpaid policy loan in the amount of $2,000.

ANALYSIS The insurance company will deduct the amount of the unpaid policy loan from the policy proceeds. As a result, the named beneficiary will receive $48,000 ($50,000 – $2,000).

A policy loan also differs from a commercial loan in that the insurance company does not perform a credit check on a policyowner who requests a policy loan. The policyowner's request is evaluated only in terms of the amount of the net cash value available. The laws in most states and provinces permit companies to defer granting policy loans, except for loans made for the purpose of paying premiums, for a specified period, usually up to six months. This deferral option, which insurers rarely enforce, is intended to protect insurers from suffering significant financial losses if large numbers of policyowners request policy loans.

Insurers charge interest on each policy loan, and interest usually is charged annually. Although policy loan interest may be paid at any time, the policyowner is not required to pay the interest. Any interest charges that are unpaid become part of the policy loan. Therefore, when we speak of the amount of the policy loan outstanding, that amount includes any unpaid interest that has accrued on the loan. If the amount of a policy loan plus unpaid interest increases to the point at which the total indebtedness is greater than the amount of the policy's cash value, then the policy terminates without further value. The insurer must notify the policyowner at least 30 days in advance of such a policy termination.

In the past, the interest rate that insurers charged on policy loans was guaranteed in each policy. Currently, however, most U.S. and Canadian jurisdictions permit insurers to specify in their policies that the policy loan interest rate will vary—that is, the interest rate that is charged may change from year to year according to current economic conditions. Many policies that include a varying loan interest rate specify that the rate charged will not exceed a stated maximum rate.

Universal life insurance policies typically include a policy withdrawal provision and a policy loan provision. A **policy withdrawal provision,** which is often called a *partial surrender provision,* permits the policyowner to reduce the amount in the policy's cash value by withdrawing up to the amount of the cash value in cash. Insurers do not charge interest on policy withdrawals; the amount in the cash value is simply reduced by the amount of the withdrawal. Many policies impose a charge for each withdrawal and limit the number of withdrawals allowed within each one-year period.

Reinstatement Provision

Individual life insurance policies typically include a **reinstatement provision** which describes the conditions that the policyowner must meet in order to reinstate a policy. **Reinstatement** is the process by which a life insurance company puts back into force a life insurance policy that has either (1) been terminated because of nonpayment of renewal premiums or (2) been continued under the extended term or reduced paid-up insurance nonforfeiture option. (We describe these nonforfeiture options later in the chapter.) Most insurers do not permit reinstatement if the policyowner has surrendered the policy for its cash surrender value. When an insurer reinstates a policy, the original policy is again in effect; the insurer does not issue a new policy.

In the United States, about one-half of the states require individual life insurance policies to include a reinstatement provision. Laws in these states require policies to provide at least a three-year period during which the policyowner has the right to reinstate a policy that has lapsed. Most insurers in the United States include a reinstatement provision in all individual life insurance policies as a matter of practice. And some insurers provide a reinstatement period that is longer than the required three-year period.

Laws in all Canadian provinces and territories also require individual life insurance policies to include a reinstatement provision. Canadian laws specify a minimum reinstatement period of two years. Insurers are permitted to extend this period if they wish, and five-year time periods are not uncommon.

In order to reinstate a life insurance policy, a policyowner must fulfill certain conditions. Most reinstatement provisions require that the following conditions be met in order to reinstate an insurance policy:

- The policyowner must complete a reinstatement application within the time frame stated in the reinstatement provision. (See Figure 10-1, which shows a sample reinstatement application.)

- The policyowner must present to the insurance company satisfactory evidence of the insured's continued insurability.

- The policyowner must pay a specified amount of money; the amount required depends on the type of policy being reinstated. We describe this amount later in this section of the chapter.

- The policyowner may be required to either pay any outstanding policy loan or have the policy loan reinstated with the policy.

Perhaps the most significant of these conditions concerns the required evidence of insurability. This condition is necessary to help prevent antiselection. If no evidence of insurability were required, those people who were unable to obtain insurance elsewhere because of poor health or other factors would be more likely to apply for reinstatement than would those who were in good health.

How much and what kind of evidence of insurability is necessary depends upon the circumstances of each individual policy and upon the practices of each insurer. If a policy has been out of force for a very short time and the insurer has no reason to suspect a problem, it may accept a simple statement from the insured certifying that he is in good health. In fact, if reinstatement is requested and if overdue premiums are paid only a month or so after the expiration of the grace period, many insurers will reinstate the policy without requiring evidence of insurability. Insurance companies, however, may require a medical examination or other evidence of insurability if (1) the grace period expired longer than a month before the reinstatement request,

FAST FACT

About 83% of all Canadian households are covered by some type of life insurance policy.[2]

FIGURE 10-1. Sample Reinstatement Application.

Application for Reinstatement of Life Insurance

ABC LIFE INSURANCE COMPANY
100 Ordinary Avenue, New York, New York 00000

Note: This form can be used only within the 6 months after the date in Section A.

SECTION A

The Insurer specified above is requested to reinstate Policy No. _____ 200 000 000 _____
including any loan agreement. The first unpaid premium was due on _____ April 1 _____,
19___9 and the total sum required (including any interest) to reinstate is $ _____ 116.32 _____.
(Please enclose your check for this amount.)

SECTION B

1. INSURED?

John	Doe
First Name	Middle Initial	Last Name

2. DATE OF BIRTH?   Mo. __7__ Day __1__ Yr. __58__

3. Since the date in Section A, has the insured or any other person who was covered under
the policy (in Section A):

	Yes	No
(a) been in a hospital or other medical facility or been unable to be actively at work or to attend school?	☐	☒
(b) consulted with, or intend to consult with, a physician for any illness or for symptoms of undiagnosed origin? (Do not include colds, minor virus infections, minor injuries, or normal pregnancy.) If "Yes" to either 3(a) or 3(b), this application may not be used. Contact your ABC agent or our local office for further assistance.	☐	☒

THOSE WHO SIGN THIS APPLICATION AGREE THAT:

1. Reinstatement will not take effect until (a) the Insurer approves the application, and (b) the sum
required by the Insurer with respect to this application is paid during the lifetime of all persons to
be covered under the reinstated policy.

2. All of the statements in this application are correctly recorded and are complete and true to the
best of the knowledge and belief of those who made them.

3. No agent has any right to accept risks, make or change contracts, or give up any of ABC's rights or
requirements.

Dated at _____ Any Town, Any State _____   Signature of
        (City or town, and state or province)   Insured _____ John Doe _____

on _____ July 1 _____, 19 99   Signature of Owner if other
                                                          than Insured _____

Countersigned by _____   Spouse or Other Required
        (Lic. resident agent, if required   Signature, if any _____
         by statute or regulation)

(2) the insurer has any reason to suspect that a health or other problem may be present, and/or (3) the face amount of the policy is large.

The specific amount of money required to reinstate a policy depends on the type of policy. For a fixed-premium policy, such as a whole life policy, the policyowner must pay all back premiums plus interest on those premiums. The insurer charges interest at the rate specified in the reinstatement provision. Payment of back premiums with interest is needed in order to bring the policy reserve to the same level as the reserve for a similar policy that has been kept in force without a lapse in premium payments.

For a flexible-premium policy, such as a universal life policy, the policyowner must pay an amount sufficient to cover the policy's mortality and expense charges for at least two months. In addition, some such policies require that the policyowner pay mortality and expense charges for the period between the date of lapse and the date of reinstatement.

Because reinstating a life insurance policy may require the policyowner to pay a sizable sum of money, each policyowner must decide whether reinstating the original policy or purchasing a new policy is more advantageous. One advantage to reinstating a fixed-premium policy is that the premium rate for the original policy is based on the insured's age at the time the policy was purchased. A comparable new policy usually calls for a higher premium rate because the new policy's premium rate is based on the age the insured has attained. Another advantage of reinstatement is that the original policy's cash value is also reinstated. A new policy may take two or three years to begin building a cash value. In addition, the original policy may contain certain provisions that are more liberal than the provisions in policies that the insurer is currently issuing. For example, the interest rate for a policy loan on the original policy may be lower than the interest rate that will be charged for a policy loan under a new policy.

Another important point about reinstatement is that in most jurisdictions in the United States and Canada, a new contestable period begins on the date on which the policy is reinstated. During this new contestable period, the company may avoid a reinstated policy only on the basis of material misrepresentations made in the application for reinstatement. The insurer may not avoid the policy on the basis of material misrepresentations made in the original application unless the original contestable period has not yet expired.

For term life insurance policies that have lapsed for nonpayment of premiums, some insurance companies have adopted a practice known as *redating.* Under this practice, the insurance company agrees to reinstate a term insurance policy that has lapsed and to redate the policy. In other words, the insurer changes the policy date to the date on which the policy is reinstated. As a result, the premium rate charged for the redated policy will be based on the insured's attained age and will be higher than the premium rate charged for the original policy. However, the policyowner is able to reinstate the policy without having to repay all back premiums and interest. The requirements for redating are that the policyowner request the reinstatement within the time frame stated in the policy's reinstatement provision and provide evidence of the insured's continued insurability.

Misstatement of Age or Sex Provision

An insurer or a policyowner may discover that the age or sex of the insured is incorrect as stated in the life insurance policy. Because the age and sex of the insured are significant factors in determining the amount of the premium charged for a policy, a misstatement of the insured's age or sex is a significant error. Most life insurance policies include a *misstatement of age or sex provision* that describes the action the insurer will take to adjust the amount of the policy benefit in the event that the age or sex of the insured is incorrectly stated. This provision in a life insurance policy states that if the age or sex of the insured is misstated and the misstatement resulted in an incorrect premium amount for the amount of insurance purchased, then the insurer will adjust the face amount of the policy to the amount the premium actually paid would have purchased if the insured's age or sex had been stated correctly.

Insurers follow the procedure we just described whenever the misstatement is discovered *after* the death of the insured. If the misstatement is discovered *before* the death of the insured, however, the insurer may grant the policyowner the option to pay—or receive as a refund—any premium amount difference caused by the misstatement instead of having the insurer adjust the policy's face amount.

Note that when an insurance company adjusts the amount of the benefit payable under a life insurance policy because of a misstatement of age or sex, the insurer is enforcing the misstatement of age or sex provision. Such an action by an insurance company is not a contest of the validity of the contract and, thus, is not prohibited by the policy's incontestability provision.

EXAMPLE   While processing a death claim, the insurance company discovered that when Lamar Corleone applied for insurance on his life, he mistakenly listed his age as 25, when in fact he was then age 30.

ANALYSIS   The insurer will reduce the policy's face amount to the amount that the premiums paid would have purchased for Lamar at age 30.

> **EXAMPLE** While processing a death claim, the insurance company discovered that when Leeanne Bouvier applied for insurance on her mother's life, she mistakenly stated that her mother was age 60, when in fact she was then 55 years old.

> **ANALYSIS** When it calculates the amount of policy proceeds payable, the insurer will increase the face amount of the policy to the amount that the premiums paid would have purchased for Leeanne's mother at age 55.

Settlement Options Provision

Another provision that insurers include as a standard practice in life insurance policies is the *settlement options provision*—or the *payout option provision.* Such provisions grant a policyowner or beneficiary the right to decide how the policy benefits will be paid. We describe life insurance policy settlement options in Chapter 12.

Policy Dividends Provision

Participating life insurance policies include a provision that describes the payment of policy dividends. This provision gives the policy-owner the right to choose from among several dividend payout options. Laws in most jurisdictions in the United States and Canada require participating policies to describe the dividend options that are available to the policyowner. We describe the *dividend options provision* in Chapter 12.

Nonforfeiture Benefits

Nonforfeiture benefits are benefits available to the owner of a life insurance policy that builds a cash value. As we described in earlier chapters, most term life insurance provides temporary insurance protection only and does not build a cash value. If the policyowner stops paying renewal premiums, then the policy lapses and the parties have no further liability to each other. In contrast, permanent life insurance provides insurance protection and builds a cash value. If the policyowner stops paying required renewal premiums on a permanent life insurance policy, the policy lapses for nonpayment of premiums, but the policyowner does not forfeit her interest in the policy's cash value. Instead, the policyowner has the right to exercise one of the nonforfeiture options contained in the policy. We describe each of the nonforfeiture benefit options in detail later in this section of the chapter.

State insurance laws require insurance companies to include nonforfeiture benefits in all individual life insurance policies that build a cash value. Although provincial insurance laws do not require insurance companies to include nonforfeiture benefits in policies that build a cash value, insurance companies throughout Canada usually include nonforfeiture benefit provisions in such policies. Most nonforfeiture benefit provisions give the policyowner the right to select from among several nonforfeiture options if a premium is unpaid when the grace period expires. These nonforfeiture options include cash surrender benefits and continued insurance coverage benefits, which may be in the form of reduced paid-up insurance or extended term insurance. In some states, the automatic premium loan benefit is considered a nonforfeiture benefit.

Cash Surrender Value

The *cash surrender value nonforfeiture option* states that a policyowner who discontinues premium payments can elect to surrender the policy and receive the policy's cash surrender value. Following the surrender of a policy, all coverage under the policy terminates.

Permanent policies include a chart that lists cash surrender values at various times, and these policies describe the method used to compute those values. Laws in most states in the United States require that these cash surrender values meet or exceed the amount that would be provided based on a formula stated in the laws. This formula takes into account the type and plan of insurance, the age of the policy, and the length of the policy's premium payment period. In most cases, applying this formula requires that the policy provide a cash surrender value by the end of the second or third policy year. Insurance companies often issue policies that provide a cash surrender value sooner than required by law and that provide a larger cash surrender value than that required by law. Although minimum cash surrender values are not mandated by law in Canada, insurers typically provide cash surrender values that are competitive with those provided by U.S. insurers.

The amount of cash value actually available to a policyowner upon surrender of a policy may not be the exact cash surrender value amount described in the policy. Paid-up additions, dividend accumulations, advance premium payments, and policy loans will result in additions to and subtractions from the cash surrender value. (We describe dividend accumulations and advance premium payments in Chapter 13.) The amount the policyowner will actually receive after such adjustments have been made is called the *net cash value.* Because paid-up additions also build cash values, the cash values of such additions are

---

FAST FACT

In the United States, about 85% of all married couples have life insurance coverage.[3]

also added to the amount the policyowner can collect upon surrender of the policy. Study the following example of a net cash value calculation:

$ 5,000	**Cash Value Amount Listed in Policy**	
+ 150	**Addition:** Cash value of paid-up additions	
− 550	**Deduction:** Policy loan outstanding	
$ 4,600	**Net Cash Value**	

When a policyowner withdraws the net cash value, the policy—and all coverage under the policy—terminates. At the time of the withdrawal, the policyowner usually surrenders the policy—that is, returns it to the insurer.

Laws throughout Canada and the United States allow an insurer to reserve the right to defer payment of any policy's cash surrender or accumulated value for a period of up to six months after the owner of the policy requests payment. A few jurisdictions, however, have shortened this maximum deferral period. The insurance company's right to defer payment is designed to protect the insurer's cash reserves should a rush of surrenders occur over a short period of time. Insurers have rarely enforced this right to defer payment.

Continued Insurance Coverage Nonforfeiture Options

Many policies that build a cash value provide the insured with the option of discontinuing premium payments and continuing insurance coverage as either reduced paid-up insurance or extended term insurance.

Reduced Paid-Up Insurance. Under the *reduced paid-up insurance nonforfeiture option,* the policy's net cash value is used as a net single premium to purchase paid-up life insurance of the same plan as the original policy. The premium charged for the paid-up insurance is based on the age the insured person has attained when the option goes into effect. The amount of paid-up insurance that can be purchased under this option is smaller than the face value of the original policy—thus the name *reduced* paid-up insurance.

Policies that include this option contain a chart listing the amount of reduced paid-up insurance that is available each year for the first 20 years the policy is in force. The amount of reduced paid-up insurance listed for each year is based on the cash value listed in the policy for that year. The actual amount of reduced paid-up insurance available might be higher or lower than the amount listed, depending on the size of the net cash value. If the net cash value is larger than the listed cash value amount, as might be the case if the policy includes paid-up additions, then the amount of reduced paid-up insurance available is greater than the reduced paid-up amount listed in the chart.

If a policy loan is outstanding, the net cash value is lower than that listed in the chart because the insurer subtracts the amount of the outstanding loan from the listed cash value; as a result, the amount of reduced paid-up insurance available is less than the amount listed in the policy. The policyowner, however, may ask the insurer to use the actual cash value without deducting the outstanding loan amount to purchase the reduced paid-up insurance. In that case, the policy loan remains in effect and the insurer continues to charge interest on the loan. If the loan is not repaid before the insured dies, the loan amount is deducted from the amount payable at the insured's death. By continuing the loan, however, the policyowner can purchase a larger amount of paid-up life insurance because the net cash value is not reduced by the amount of the policy loan.

The insurance purchased under the reduced paid-up insurance option has the same duration as the original policy. Thus, if the original policy was a whole life policy, then the reduced paid-up coverage remains in force throughout the insured's entire lifetime. If the original policy was an endowment at age 65 policy, then the coverage remains in force until the insured attains age 65.

Note that the premium amount charged by the insurer for this coverage is based on net premium rates; that is, the insurer does not add an amount to the net premium to cover expenses. As a result, buying insurance in this manner is usually less expensive than taking the policy's value in cash and purchasing another paid-up insurance policy. The coverage issued under this option continues to have and to build a cash value, and the policyowner continues to have the rights available to the owner of any life insurance policy, including the right to surrender the policy for its cash value and the right to receive dividends if the original policy was issued on a participating basis. Any supplemental benefits that were available on the original policy, such as accidental death benefits, are usually *not* available when the policy is continued as reduced paid-up insurance. (See Figure 10-2, which illustrates the amount of paid-up insurance that

FIGURE 10-2. Illustrative Reduced Paid-Up Insurance Amounts (Male, 40 Years of Age).

Type of Policy	Paid-Up Insurance per $1,000 of Face Amount at End of Policy Year		
	5	10	20
Continuous-premium whole life policy	$178	$368	$ 613
20-payment whole life policy	283	557	1,000

might be available to a male applicant 40 years of age under two traditional whole life policies.)

Extended Term Insurance. Under the ***extended term insurance nonforfeiture option***, the insurance company uses the policy's net cash value to purchase term insurance for the full coverage amount provided under the original policy for as long a term as the net cash value can provide. The length of the term depends upon the amount of the coverage, the amount of the net cash value, the sex of the insured, and the insured's attained age when the policyowner exercises the extended term option.

In order to calculate the amount and term of the extended term insurance, the insurer first determines the amount of the policy's net cash value that is available to pay the premium for the coverage. We described earlier in this section how a policy's net cash value is calculated. The insurer then calculates the amount of extended term insurance available under this option. Generally, the amount of extended term insurance available is the amount of insurance that would have been payable under the original policy. Recall, however, that amounts such as paid-up additions, dividend accumulations, and policy loans result in additions to and subtractions from the face amount of insurance provided by a policy. Because the amount payable under the policy would be reduced by the amount of any indebtedness, such as a policy loan, and would be increased by the face amount of any paid-up additions, these reductions and increases typically are also made when the insurer calculates the amount of coverage available under the extended term insurance option. Otherwise, the insurer would, in effect, be granting a greater or lesser amount of actual coverage than the amount that was in effect before the policyowner exercised the nonforfeiture option. The following example illustrates how the amount of extended term insurance available is typically calculated.

$10,000	**Face Value of Policy**
+ 200	**Addition:** Face value of paid-up additions
− 1,000	**Deduction:** Policy loan outstanding
$ 9,200	**Amount of Term Insurance Available**
$ 2,500	**Listed Cash Value**
+ 50	**Addition:** Cash value of paid-up additions
− 1,000	**Deduction:** Policy loan outstanding
$ 1,550	**Net Cash Value**

Thus, the insurer would use the $1,550 net cash value as a net single premium to purchase $9,200 of term life insurance for as long a period as that $1,550 would purchase.

By contrast, some insurers take a different approach to calculating the amount of extended term insurance available when a policy loan is outstanding. These insurers account for the existence of a policy loan by reducing the amount of the net cash value by the amount of the policy loan but do not reduce the face amount of coverage. The following example illustrates how these insurers would calculate the amount of extended term insurance available:

$10,000	**Face Value of Policy**
+ 200	**Addition:** Face value of paid-up additions
$10,200	**Amount of Term Insurance Available**
$ 2,500	**Listed Cash Value**
+ 50	**Addition:** Cash value of paid-up additions
− 1,000	**Deduction:** Policy loan outstanding
$ 1,550	**Net Cash Value**

Thus, the insurer would use the $1,550 net cash value as a net single premium to purchase $10,200 of term life insurance for as long a period as that $1,550 would purchase.

According to the terms of most policies, a policyowner who has elected the extended term nonforfeiture option can no longer exercise the policy loan privilege or receive policy dividends. The policyowner, however, does have the right to cancel the extended term insurance and surrender the policy for its remaining cash value. As with the reduced paid-up option, any supplementary benefits that were available under the original policy usually are not available when the policy is placed under the extended term insurance option.

A life insurance policy that includes the extended term insurance option contains a chart showing the length of time the original face value of the policy will be continued in force under the extended term option for each of the first 20 policy years. (Figure 10-3 shows a sample table of guaranteed values for a whole life policy, including the duration of extended term insurance available at the end of specified policy years.)

Because of the way in which they operate, universal life insurance policies typically do not include an extended term insurance nonforfeiture option. Recall that the insurer periodically deducts mortality and expense charges from the policy's cash value. Thus, even if the owner of a universal life policy pays no premium, the policy continues in force until the cash value is exhausted by the routine monthly deductions.

FIGURE 10-3. Sample Table of Guaranteed Nonforfeiture Values.

Table of Guaranteed Values*

Plan: Whole Life
Face Amount: $50,000
Age of Insured at Issue: 35

End of Policy Year	Cash Value	Alternatives to Cash Value				End of Policy Year
		Paid-Up Insurance	or	Extended Insurance		
				Years	Days	
1	—	—		—	—	1
2	—	—		—	—	2
3	$ 150	$ 750		0	336	3
4	600	2,750		3	101	4
5	1,050	4,600		5	55	5
6	1,550	6,550		6	311	6
7	2,000	8,100		8	23	7
8	2,550	9,950		9	132	8
9	3,050	11,450		10	85	9
10	3,600	13,000		11	9	10
11	4,200	14,600		11	270	11
12	5,050	16,900		12	305	12
13	5,900	19,050		13	257	13
14	6,800	21,150		14	169	14
15	7,700	23,150		15	13	15
16	8,650	25,050		15	192	16
17	9,550	26,700		15	296	17
18	10,550	28,500		16	51	18
19	11,500	30,000		16	113	19
20	12,500	31,550		16	170	20
Age 60	16,800	36,100		15	186	Age 60
Age 65	21,450	39,750		14	9	Age 65

* This table assumes premiums have been paid to the end of the policy year shown. These values do not include any dividend accumulations, paid-up additions, or policy loans.

Automatic Nonforfeiture Benefits

Most policies that build cash values typically provide an automatic nonforfeiture benefit. An **automatic nonforfeiture benefit** is a specific nonforfeiture benefit that becomes effective automatically when a renewal premium is not paid by the end of the grace period *and* the insured has not elected another nonforfeiture option. The most typical automatic nonforfeiture benefit is the extended term insurance benefit. The laws in a few jurisdictions, however, require that policies include an automatic premium loan provision and specify that the automatic nonforfeiture option is the automatic premium loan. An *automatic premium loan (APL) provision* states that the insurer will automatically pay an overdue premium for the policyowner by making a loan against the policy's cash value as long as the cash value equals or exceeds the amount of the premium due. The use of the automatic premium loan keeps the original policy in force for the full amount of coverage, including all supplemental benefits. The APL provision is also widely used in policies issued in jurisdictions where it is not required by law. Under such a policy, the policyowner must ask the insurer to apply the automatic premium loan provision in order for the insurer to act according to the terms of the provision.

Universal life insurance policies usually do not include the automatic premium loan provision because a similar benefit is already provided in these policies as part of their monthly cash value deduction mechanism.

Life Insurance Policy Exclusions

Life insurance policies sometimes contain *exclusions*—provisions that describe circumstances under which the insurer will not pay the policy proceeds following the death of the insured. State and provincial insurance laws permit, but do not require, insurance companies to include these provisions in life insurance policies.

During periods of war or threat of war, insurance companies have in the past included in life insurance policies a *war exclusion clause,* which stated that the insurer would not pay the policy proceeds if the insured's death was connected with war. Currently, insurers rarely include a war exclusion provision in policies they issue. Similarly, in the early years of air travel, life insurance policies often included an *aviation exclusion provision,* which stated that the insurer would not pay the policy proceeds if the insured's death resulted from aviation-related activities. Today, this type of policy exclusion is primarily applied only to activities connected with military or experimental aircraft. Some insurers, however, include an aviation exclusion in policies that insure pilots and crew members flying privately owned aircraft.

An exclusion still typically included in individual life insurance policies is the *suicide exclusion provision* that governs the payment of policy proceeds if the insured dies as a result of suicide. Insurance companies try to protect themselves against the possibility of anti-selection by excluding suicide as a covered risk for a specified period—usually two years—following the date the policy is issued. The general opinion is that this exclusion period is sufficient to protect against situations in which a person purchases insurance with the knowledge that the insured plans to commit suicide. A sample suicide exclusion provision follows.

> **Suicide exclusion.** Suicide of the insured, while sane or insane, within two years of the date of issue, is not covered by this policy. In that event, this policy will end and the only amount payable will be the premiums paid to us, less any loan.

Note that in the event the insured's death from suicide occurs during the two-year exclusion period, the insurance company is not liable to pay the policy's death benefit. The insurer, however, will return the premiums paid for the policy less the amount of any unpaid policy loan. The suicide exclusion provision in some policies states that the insurer will pay the larger of (1) the policy's cash value or (2) the premiums paid for the policy.

Key Terms

Uniform Life Insurance Act
free-look provision
entire contract provision
closed contract
open contract
incontestability provision
warranty
representation
misrepresentation
material misrepresentation
fraudulent misrepresentation
grace period
lapse
policy loan provision
policy withdrawal provision
reinstatement provision
reinstatement

redating
misstatement of age or sex
    provision
nonforfeiture benefits
cash surrender value
    nonforfeiture option
net cash value
reduced paid-up insurance
    nonforfeiture option
extended term insurance
    nonforfeiture option
automatic nonforfeiture benefit
automatic premium loan (APL)
    provision
exclusions
suicide exclusion provision

Other Important Terms

free-examination provision
partial surrender provision
settlement options provision
payout option provision

dividend options provision
war exclusion clause
aviation exclusion provision

Endnotes

1. ACLI, *1998 Life Insurance Fact Book* (Washington, D.C.: American Council of Life Insurance, 1998), 10.

2. CLHIA, *Canadian Life and Health Insurance Facts* (Toronto: Canadian Life and Health Insurance Association, 1998), 7.

3. ACLI, 1.

CHAPTER 11

Life Insurance Policy Beneficiaries

After reading this chapter, you should be able to

- Distinguish between primary and contingent beneficiaries

- Identify in a given situation the person who is entitled to receive the proceeds of a life insurance policy

- Identify the features of a preference beneficiary clause and a facility-of-payment clause

- Distinguish between a revocable beneficiary and an irrevocable beneficiary

- Recognize the effect of community-property laws on the policyowner's right to deal with a life insurance policy

- Distinguish between a preferred beneficiary and a beneficiary for value

- Identify situations in which a policyowner may designate a beneficiary in a will

One of the most valuable ownership rights that a policyowner has in a life insurance policy is the right to name the beneficiary who will receive the policy proceeds following the death of the insured. In this chapter, we describe the policy provisions and insurance company practices that govern the designation of a policy's beneficiary.

Naming the Beneficiary

The beneficiary of a life insurance policy may be a named individual, the executor of an estate, a trustee, a corporation, a charitable organization, or any other entity. A policyowner can also designate a group of persons as beneficiary. A beneficiary designation that identifies a certain group of persons, rather than naming each person, is called a *class designation.* The beneficiary designation "my children" is an example of a class designation. (See Figure 11-1, which illustrates the most common beneficiary-to-insured relationships for individual life insurance policies in the United States and Canada.)

In Chapter 3, we described the insurable interest requirement that helps prevent an insurance contract from being purchased as an illegal wagering agreement. Recall from that discussion that if the insurable interest requirement is not met at the creation of a life insurance contract, then the contract is void. Thus, insurance companies routinely review the beneficiary designations contained in applications for life insurance to determine whether the insurable interest requirement has been met. Insurance companies do not, however, review later changes in the beneficiary designation because the insurable interest requirement applies only at the time of policy issue.

Primary and Contingent Beneficiaries

The *primary beneficiary,* or *first beneficiary,* is the party designated to receive the policy proceeds following the death of the insured. If more than one party is named as primary beneficiary, the policyowner may indicate how the proceeds are to be divided among the parties. If the policyowner does not make such an indication, then the insurer divides the proceeds evenly among the primary beneficiaries who survived the insured. Note that, in order to receive policy proceeds, the primary beneficiary must survive the insured; the beneficiary's

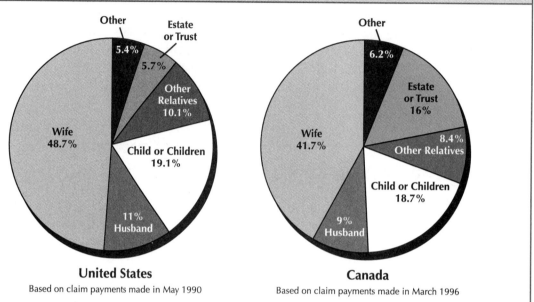

Figure 11-1. Relationship of Beneficiary to Insured, Based on Individual Life Insurance Policy Death Claims Received.

United States
Based on claim payments made in May 1990

Canada
Based on claim payments made in March 1996

Sources: ACLI, *1997 Life Insurance Fact Book* (Washington, D.C.: American Council of Life Insurance, 1997), 44; CLHIA, *Canadian Life and Health Insurance Facts* (Toronto: Canadian Life and Health Insurance Association, 1998), 16.

estate has no claim to the policy proceeds if the beneficiary dies before the insured.

EXAMPLE   At the time of her death, Val Lundy owned an insurance policy on her life. Val's three brothers were named as the policy beneficiaries, and all three brothers survived Val.

ANALYSIS   Unless Val had indicated otherwise, the policy proceeds will be divided equally among the three beneficiaries.

The policyowner also may designate a contingent beneficiary who will receive the policy proceeds if all primary beneficiaries should die before the insured. A ***contingent beneficiary,*** sometimes referred to as a *secondary beneficiary* or *successor beneficiary,* can receive the policy proceeds only if all designated primary beneficiaries have predeceased the insured. The policyowner can name any number of contingent beneficiaries and may decide how the proceeds are to be divided among the contingent beneficiaries. The designation of contingent beneficiaries can be especially important in cases in which the primary beneficiary dies and the policyowner is unable to designate a new beneficiary before the policy becomes payable. Review the following examples that illustrate the rights of primary and contingent beneficiaries to receive the policy proceeds.

EXAMPLE   Ira Shulman owned a $50,000 insurance policy on his life. He named his wife, Myrna, as primary beneficiary and his sons, Abe and Jacob, as equal contingent beneficiaries. Ira was survived by his wife and both sons.

ANALYSIS   The $50,000 policy proceeds are payable to the primary beneficiary, Myrna.

EXAMPLE   Ira Shulman named his wife, Myrna, as primary beneficiary and his sons, Abe and Jacob, as equal contingent beneficiaries. Both Myrna and Abe died several years before Ira died.

ANALYSIS   As the sole surviving contingent beneficiary, Jacob is entitled to receive the $50,000 policy proceeds.

EXAMPLE   Ira Shulman named his sons, Abe and Jacob, as equal primary beneficiaries and his wife, Myrna, as contingent beneficiary. Jacob died several years before Ira, who was survived by Abe and Myrna.

ANALYSIS   As the sole surviving primary beneficiary, Abe is entitled to receive the $50,000 policy proceeds.

An insurance company usually prefers that the policyowner name at least a primary and a contingent beneficiary, and most companies permit the designation of additional levels of contingent beneficiaries. Naming additional levels of contingent beneficiaries helps the policyowner to be certain that the proceeds will be paid to the desired party. Contingent beneficiaries at any given level typically have a right to the policy proceeds only if all beneficiaries in the preceding levels have predeceased the insured. Keep in mind, however, that the disposition of policy proceeds in any given case depends on the specific wording of the beneficiary designation.

No Surviving Beneficiary

If no beneficiary has been named or none of the named beneficiaries is living when the insured dies, then the policy proceeds are paid to the policyowner, if the policyowner is living. If the policyowner is deceased, then the proceeds are paid to the policyowner's estate.

EXAMPLE When Pearl Windsor died, she owned an insurance policy on her life. Pearl's husband was the primary beneficiary and her two children were contingent beneficiaries. No named beneficiary survived Pearl.

ANALYSIS Because no named beneficiary survived the insured, the policy proceeds are paid to the policyowner's—in this case, Pearl's—estate.

Alternatively, some policies contain a ***preference beneficiary clause,*** or *succession beneficiary clause,* which states that if the policyowner does not name a beneficiary, then the insurer will pay the policy proceeds in a stated order of preference. For example, a preference beneficiary clause might list the following order: the spouse of the insured, if living; then the children of the insured, if living; then the parents of the insured, if living. If no living recipients are available from that list, then the proceeds would be paid to the estate of the insured. The preference beneficiary clause is found more often in group and monthly debit ordinary insurance policies than in ordinary individual life insurance policies.

Facility-of-Payment Clause

Certain types of policies, generally those with small face amounts, allow the insurance company to pay some part of the proceeds to someone other than the named beneficiary. Group life, monthly debit ordinary life, and a few individual ordinary life insurance policies contain a ***facility-of-payment clause*** that permits the insurance company to make payment of all or part of the policy proceeds either to a relative of the insured or to anyone who has a valid claim to those proceeds. The amounts paid under this clause are usually small and are intended to reimburse an individual who has incurred funeral expenses or final medical expenses on behalf of the insured. This clause is very important in cases in which a party other than the named beneficiary has assumed these expenses on behalf of the insured and either (1) the named beneficiary is a minor or (2) the named beneficiary is dead and the policyowner's estate has become the beneficiary of the policy.

We discuss facility-of-payment clauses in more detail in Chapter 15.

EXAMPLE For several months before his death, Clyde Dozier was cared for by his brother, Dwayne, who paid some of Clyde's final medical expenses. Clyde was the policyowner-insured of a life insurance policy that contained a facility-of-payment clause. The policy proceeds were payable to Clyde's estate.

ANALYSIS In accordance with the terms of the facility-of-payment clause, the insurer will be able to pay some part of the policy proceeds to Dwayne as reimbursement for the medical expenses he incurred on Clyde's behalf. Any remaining policy proceeds will be paid to Clyde's estate.

Clarity of Designation

Making the beneficiary designation clear and distinct is of value to both the policyowner and the insurer. The policyowner's goal is to be sure that the insurance company distributes the policy proceeds according to his wishes. The insurance company's goal is to pay the proceeds in a simple and timely manner without any legal problems. Problems occur when the manner in which the designation was written leaves doubts as to how the policyowner wanted the proceeds to be distributed. For example, a designation such as "to my children: Maurice and Taylor" appears to be clear and uncomplicated. However, if Shanelle, a third child, were born after the designation was made and if she were never added to the beneficiary designation, a problem might arise. Should the insurance company divide the proceeds between Maurice and Taylor, or should the company divide the proceeds among Maurice, Taylor, and Shanelle?

A policyowner should review and update beneficiary designations when changes occur in family, marital, or financial situations. Such action is necessary in order for the policyowner to be sure that the proceeds will be paid to the desired parties. In the next section, we discuss changing the beneficiary designation.

Changing the Beneficiary

Life insurance policies issued in the United States and Canada usually give the policyowner the right to change the beneficiary designation as many times as she desires over the life of the policy. This right to change the beneficiary designation is known as the **right of revocation.** A beneficiary designation is said to be *revocable* if the policyowner has the unrestricted right to change the designation during the life of the insured. Most companies refer to any beneficiary so designated as a **revocable beneficiary.** If the policyowner has the right to change the beneficiary designation only after obtaining the beneficiary's consent, then the designation is said to be *irrevocable.* Insurers refer to any beneficiary so designated as an **irrevocable beneficiary.**

A beneficiary designation is considered to be revocable *unless* one of the following situations occurs:

- The policyowner voluntarily gives up the right to change the beneficiary

- Legislation limits the policyowner's right to change the designation

We will examine the rights of revocable and irrevocable beneficiaries and the most common legislative limitations on the policyowner's right to change the beneficiary designation.

Revocable Beneficiary

The vast majority of designated beneficiaries of life insurance policies are revocable beneficiaries. A revocable beneficiary generally has neither a legal interest in the proceeds nor any involvement with the policy until the insured person dies. During the insured's lifetime, the revocable beneficiary has no rights to any policy values and cannot prohibit the policyowner from exercising any policy ownership rights, including the right to change the beneficiary. Thus, during the insured's lifetime, a revocable beneficiary's interest in the life insurance policy is said to be a "mere expectancy" of receiving the policy proceeds.

Irrevocable Beneficiary

A policyowner may at any time designate a beneficiary as an irrevocable beneficiary. Upon making such a designation, the policyowner gives up the right to change the beneficiary designation unless the irrevocable beneficiary consents to such a change. An irrevocable

By permission of MELL LAZARUS and Creators Syndicate.

beneficiary has a vested interest in the proceeds of the life insurance policy even during the lifetime of the insured. A *vested interest* is a property right that has taken effect and cannot be altered or changed without the consent of the person who owns the right.

Because an irrevocable beneficiary has a vested interest in the policy proceeds, most insurers will not permit the policyowner who has designated an irrevocable beneficiary to exercise all of her ownership rights in the contract without that irrevocable beneficiary's consent. For example, the policyowner cannot obtain a policy loan, surrender the policy for cash, or assign ownership of the policy to another party without the consent of the irrevocable beneficiary. (Assignments will be discussed in Chapter 12.)

Irrevocable beneficiary designations are sometimes used in situations in which the protection of the beneficiary's rights is a primary concern. For example, a divorce settlement may require one party to maintain a life insurance policy on his life and to name his former spouse as the irrevocable beneficiary. As a result, if the insured dies, the surviving former spouse will receive the policy proceeds. In such a case, the irrevocable beneficiary designation ensures that neither the designation nor the policy's status will be changed unless the beneficiary approves the change.

Under certain circumstances, a policyowner may be able to name a new beneficiary, even if the original beneficiary designation is irrevocable. Commonly, if the policyowner wishes to make a change, the policyowner must obtain the irrevocable beneficiary's written consent to the change of beneficiary. In addition, most life insurance policies contain a provision stating that the rights of any beneficiary, including an irrevocable beneficiary, will terminate if the beneficiary should die before the insured dies. This provision prevents the automatic payment of the proceeds to the estate of the irrevocable beneficiary and permits the policyowner to designate a new beneficiary following the death of an irrevocable beneficiary.

| EXAMPLE | When Omar Mikulsky purchased an insurance policy on his life, he named his sister Shari as the irrevocable benefi- |

ciary. Several years later, Omar married and wanted to change the beneficiary designation to his wife. At that time, however, Shari was terminally ill and unable to provide a written consent to the beneficiary change.

| ANALYSIS | Without the consent of the irrevocable beneficiary—or a person who qualifies to represent her—Omar cannot change |

the policy's beneficiary designation. If Shari dies, Omar can then change the beneficiary designation.

Legislative Restrictions on Beneficiary Changes

In most U.S. and Canadian jurisdictions, the policyowner's right to change the policy's beneficiary designation is not restricted in any way by legislation. In some jurisdictions, however, legislation does limit a policyowner's right to change the beneficiary designation. In Quebec, for example, if the owner of a life insurance policy designates his spouse as the beneficiary, then that designation is considered by law to be an irrevocable designation *unless* the policyowner specifically reserves the right to change the beneficiary. Additional legislative restrictions on the policyowner's right to change the beneficiary are found in community-property states in the United States and in the common law jurisdictions of Canada.

United States: Community-Property States

In community-property states, a revocable beneficiary who is the policyowner's spouse may have certain rights to the policy proceeds. A *community-property state* is one in which, by law, each spouse is entitled to an equal share of the income earned by the other and, under most circumstances, to an equal share of the property acquired by the other during the period of their marriage. In the community-property states (Arizona, California, Idaho, Louisiana, Nevada, New Mexico, Texas, Washington, and Wisconsin), an insurance policy is property that may be classified as community property. As a result, a policyowner's spouse may acquire community property rights in a life insurance policy.

When a policyowner in a community-property state names his spouse as the revocable beneficiary of a policy, the spouse may be required to consent to a beneficiary change if the change would deprive the spouse of that part of the proceeds to which she otherwise would be entitled. If the policyowner were to change the beneficiary designation from his spouse to another party without the spouse's consent, then the courts may hold that the spouse had a community property right to the proceeds. Depending on the circumstances, the court in such a case would find that the new beneficiary has an interest in only half the proceeds or has no interest in the proceeds.

Canada: Common Law Jurisdictions

Beneficiaries of policies now being issued throughout Canada are designated as revocable or irrevocable in the manner described earlier in this section. That is, the policyowner may designate the beneficiary revocably or irrevocably. In the past, however, laws in the common law jurisdictions of Canada placed limitations on the policyowner's right to name and change the beneficiary, and other types of beneficiary designations were available. Some of these beneficiary designations remain in effect today, and the limitations continue to apply to those designations. These limitations concern two classes of beneficiaries—preferred beneficiaries and beneficiaries for value—that were established by pre-1962 legislation.

The *preferred beneficiary classification* consisted of the husband, wife, children, parents, and grandchildren of the insured. Members of this group belonged to a preferred class and were known as *preferred beneficiaries.* As a class, these beneficiaries had vested rights to policy proceeds. The policyowner had the right to change a preferred beneficiary, but only if the new beneficiary was also in the preferred class. If the preferred beneficiary consented, the policyowner could regain all rights of ownership, including the right to change the beneficiary to a person not included in the preferred class. In most cases, if the preferred beneficiary died before the insured died, all ownership rights were returned to the policyowner.

The class of beneficiaries known as *beneficiaries for value* was composed of persons who were named as policy beneficiaries in return for providing valuable consideration to a policyowner. For example, a policyowner might have named an individual as a beneficiary for value in exchange for a personal loan. A beneficiary for value had vested rights to the policy proceeds similar to the rights of a preferred beneficiary. The principal difference lay in the fact that the death of a beneficiary for value did not cancel the vested rights of the deceased beneficiary. Because consideration had been given, this vested interest in the policy proceeds passed on to the estate of the beneficiary for value.

The revised Uniform Life Insurance Act discontinued use of these two classes of beneficiaries in policies issued after June 30, 1962. Nevertheless, the rules that were in effect previously with regard to these beneficiaries continue to apply to policies issued while the prior legislation was in effect if, as of June 30, 1962, the beneficiary of such a policy was a member of the preferred class or was a beneficiary for value. Once the beneficiary of such a policy is changed to a beneficiary

FAST FACT

During 1997, Canadian insurance companies paid out $5.9 billion in life insurance policy benefits.[2]

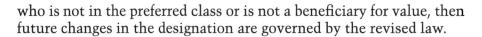

who is not in the preferred class or is not a beneficiary for value, then future changes in the designation are governed by the revised law.

EXAMPLE In 1960, Julius Poteet purchased an insurance policy, which was issued in a common law province, on his life. He named his friend Jamal McQueen as the beneficiary for value in exchange for Jamal's loaning him $2,500. When Jamal died in 1995, he was still the designated beneficiary of the policy.

ANALYSIS Because the policy was issued before July 1, 1962, Jamal's designation as a beneficiary for value remained in effect throughout his life. As a result, Jamal's vested interest in the policy proceeds passed to his estate, which will have a right to receive the policy proceeds if Julius dies while the policy is in force.

EXAMPLE In 1960, Lesley Crosby purchased an insurance policy on her life and named her husband Roman as the policy beneficiary. The policy, which was issued in a common law province, remained in force when Roman died in 1995, and he remained the designated beneficiary.

ANALYSIS Because the policy was issued before July 1, 1962, and Roman was the insured's husband, he was a preferred beneficiary. Throughout Roman's life, Lesley could change the beneficiary only if she named another person in the preferred class or if Roman consented to such a change. Following Roman's death, however, Lesley had the unrestricted right to name anyone she wishes as the policy's beneficiary.

Beneficiary Change Procedure

If a policyowner has retained the right to change the beneficiary, the procedure to make such a change is straightforward and relatively simple. Each life insurance policy specifies the change of beneficiary procedure required. A sample change of beneficiary provision follows.

> While the Insured is living, you can change a beneficiary in a notice you sign which gives us the facts that we need. When we record a change, it will take effect as of the date you signed the notice, subject to any payment we made or action we took before recording the change.

Note that a beneficiary change can be made only during the insured's lifetime. Once the insured dies, the named beneficiary has a vested interest in the policy proceeds, and the policyowner cannot deprive the beneficiary of that interest.

The most important procedural point in a change of beneficiary is a written notification to the insurer of the change. Most insurance companies require only that the policyowner notify the company in writing of the change of beneficiary in order for the change to be effective. This method of changing the beneficiary is called the **recording method.** Some insurers may also require that a change of beneficiary request be signed by disinterested witnesses or that the documents requesting the change be notarized. (See Figure 11-2, which shows a sample change of beneficiary form.)

A few policies contain a change of beneficiary procedure known as the endorsement method. An **endorsement** is a document that is attached to a policy and is a part of the policy contract. Under the *endorsement method,* the name of the new beneficiary must be added to the policy itself in order for the beneficiary change to be effective. The endorsement method is rarely used today, although it was a common procedure in the past.

Beneficiary Named in a Will

At times, a policyowner may wish to use a will to indicate the way in which the proceeds of a life insurance policy should be distributed following her death. In most states in the United States, beneficiary designations or changes in beneficiary designations by will are ineffective for most types of policies. One exception is that United States Government Life Insurance policies and National Service Life Insurance policies issued to veterans and persons in the armed forces specifically permit policyowners to use a will to dispose of their policy proceeds.

Throughout Canada, a will can be used to designate the beneficiary of a life insurance policy as long as the will clearly identifies both the insurance policy in question and the person designated to receive the policy benefit. In Canada, a declaration contained in a will is always treated as a revocable beneficiary designation. Also, a will can be used to change the beneficiary designation of a policy in Canada. In most cases in which a beneficiary is named or changed in a will, that designation or change of beneficiary remains effective only so long as the will remains valid and effective. Thus, if the will is revoked, then any designation or change of beneficiary contained in that will is also revoked. A will can be revoked in a variety of ways. For example, a person can revoke a will by executing a new will.

FIGURE **11-2.** Sample Change of Beneficiary Form.

Change of Beneficiary

(Read the provisions printed below before completing this form. Please print or type.)

ABC LIFE INSURANCE COMPANY is requested to make the following changes of beneficiary. Indicate how many policies to be changed _____.

Policy (or Policies) Numbered _____

on the life of _____ the Insured

First Name & Middle Initial   Last Name

Request for Change of Beneficiary

Change the beneficiary designation of the above numbered policy (or policies) to (give Full Name, Residence Address, and Relationship to Insured):

First Beneficiary _____

Second Beneficiary _____

Third Beneficiary _____

I understand and agree that:

1. The Provisions Relating to Beneficiary Designation printed below are made a part of the above beneficiary designation and a part of the above numbered policy (or policies).

2. When countersigned for ABC Life, this change of beneficiary will take effect as of the date this request was signed, subject to any payment made or other action taken by the Company before recording the change. When this change takes effect, it will terminate any existing settlement agreement or election of an optional method of payment, and any existing beneficiary designation.

3. Every beneficiary named above, including a spouse, is revocable unless this designation provides that such beneficiary is irrevocable.

_____   _____
              Secretary   President

Date _____, 19_____   _____

Signature(s) of person(s) with right to change beneficiary (and any other required signature)

FOR ABC LIFE USE ONLY: Recording of Beneficiary Change Request

Countersigned for ABC Life by _____ on _____, 19___

☐ Change(s) Recorded and Copy(ies) Returned to be Retained with Policy(ies)

☐ Change(s) Recorded and Copy(ies) Attached as Endorsement on Policy(ies)

Returned to: _____ By _____ on _____, 19___

Provisions Relating to Beneficiary Designation

Naming of Beneficiary and Death of Beneficiary: Unless otherwise provided in the policy, or in the beneficiary designation above, the following provisions shall apply:

1. Beneficiaries (or payees) may be classed as first, second, and so on. The stated shares of life insurance or death benefit proceeds will be paid to any first beneficiaries who survive the insured. If no first beneficiaries survive, payment will be made to any surviving second beneficiaries, and so on. Surviving beneficiaries in the same class will have an equal share in the proceeds, or in any periodic income payments payable from these proceeds, unless the shares are otherwise stated.

2. If no beneficiary for a stated share of any life insurance or death benefit proceeds survives the Insured, the right to those proceeds will pass to the Owner. If the Owner was the Insured, the right to those proceeds will pass to the Insured's estate. If any beneficiary dies at the same time as the insured or if the policy so provides, within 15 days after the Insured but before proof of the Insured's death is received by the Company, the proceeds will be paid as though that beneficiary died first.

Change of Beneficiary: Even if there is anything in the policy (or policies) that states otherwise, the person having the right to change a beneficiary can do so while the Insured is living by using this signed notice, furnishing the necessary information to the Company without submitting the policy to the Company for endorsement. A copy of this form will be returned to the Owner to be kept with the policy after the change has been recorded. When the Company records the change, it will take effect as of the date this notice was signed, subject to any payment made or other action taken by the Company before recording.

EXAMPLE Milo Forrester is a Canadian resident who owns an insurance policy on his life. In 1990, Milo executed a will in which he named his brother Puckett as the policy beneficiary. In 1995, Milo executed a new will that did not specifically mention the insurance policy's beneficiary designation.

ANALYSIS By executing a new will, Milo revoked the earlier will and thereby revoked the designation of Puckett as the policy beneficiary.

Key Terms

class designation
primary beneficiary
contingent beneficiary
preference beneficiary clause
facility-of-payment clause
right of revocation
revocable beneficiary
irrevocable beneficiary

vested interest
community-property state
preferred beneficiary
   classification
beneficiary for value
recording method
endorsement

Other Important Terms

first beneficiary
secondary beneficiary
successor beneficiary

succession beneficiary clause
preferred beneficiary
endorsement method

Endnotes

1. ACLI, *1998 Life Insurance Fact Book* (Washington, D.C.: American Council of Life Insurance, 1998), 75.

2. CLHIA, *Canadian Life and Health Insurance Facts* (Toronto: Canadian Life and Health Insurance Association, 1998), 5.

3. Ibid., 7.

CHAPTER 12

Additional Ownership Rights

After reading this chapter, you should be able to

- Recognize the premium payment modes that insurers typically offer on individual life insurance policies

- Identify the various methods by which a policyowner may pay life insurance policy premiums

- Identify the policy dividend options that are most commonly included in participating life insurance policies and recognize the characteristics of each option

- Identify the settlement options that are typically included in life insurance policies and describe the features of each option

- Distinguish between a collateral assignment and an absolute assignment

- Identify the two methods by which ownership of a life insurance policy may be transferred and recognize the requirements that must be met for the transfer to be valid

*I*n addition to the right to name the beneficiary who will receive the proceeds of an individual life insurance policy, the policyowner has a number of other valuable ownership rights in the policy. Most of these ownership rights are spelled out in the policy, and some ownership rights vary depending on the type of policy. In this chapter, we describe the policyowner's rights with respect to premium payments, policy dividends, and settlement options. We also describe how the owner of a policy can transfer her ownership rights to another party.

Premium Payments

Most individual life insurance policies grant the policyowner several rights concerning premium payments, including the right to choose the premium payment mode (frequency) and the right to choose from among several premium payment methods.

Mode of Premium Payment

When a policyowner is required to pay periodic renewal premiums in order to keep the policy's coverage in force, the policyowner and insurer must agree on how often those premiums will be paid. A policy's *premium payment mode* is the frequency at which renewal premiums are payable. Each insurance company determines which premium payment modes it will make available to its policyowners. Most insurers offer to accept renewal premiums for individual life insurance policies on an annual, semiannual, quarterly, or monthly basis. The applicant selects one of these premium payment modes when he completes the application for insurance. Typically, the policyowner may also change the mode of premium payment after the policy has taken effect. (See Figure 12-1, which illustrates the most commonly selected modes of paying premiums.)

Often, insurance companies seek to keep their administrative costs down by requiring scheduled renewal premium payments to be at least equal to a stated minimum amount. The policyowner may not select a premium payment mode that results in a premium less than that required minimum amount. For example, the insurance company may require that in order for a policyowner to choose a monthly premium payment mode, the monthly premium payment must be at

FIGURE 12-1. Most Commonly Selected Modes of Premium Payment (Based on Number of Policies) in 1997.

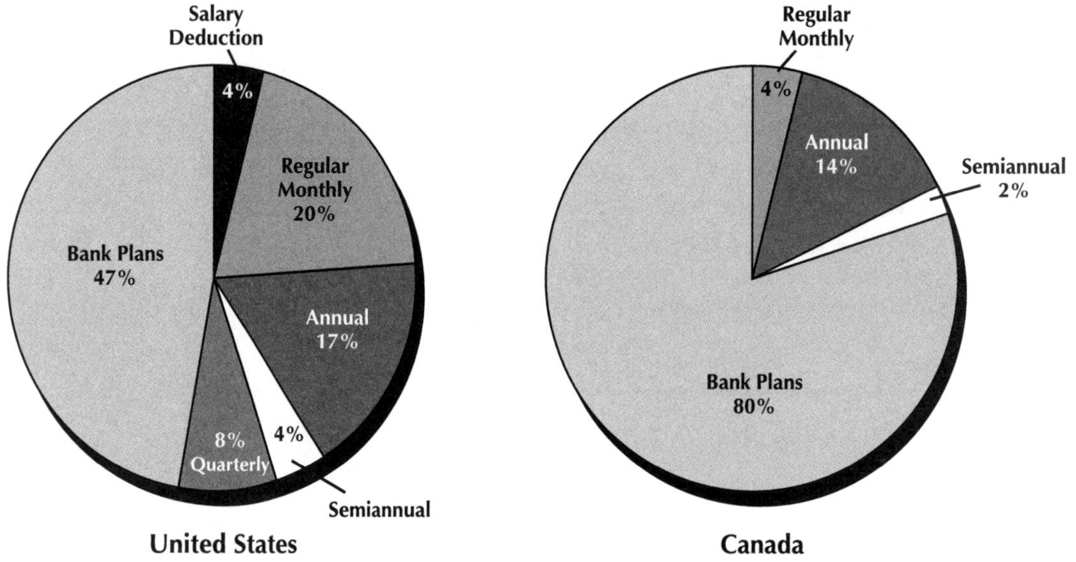

United States

Salary Deduction 4%
Regular Monthly 20%
Bank Plans 47%
Annual 17%
8% Quarterly
4%
Semiannual

Canada

Regular Monthly 4%
Annual 14%
Semiannual 2%
Bank Plans 80%

Sources: Nilufer R. Ahmed, Maria V. Dynia, and Kenneth N. Isenberg, *1997 U.S. Buyer Study* (Washington, D.C.: LIMRA International, 1998). Nilufer R. Ahmed, Maria V. Dynia, and Phyllis Van Gorder, *1997 Canadian Buyer Study* (Washington, D.C.: LIMRA International, 1998).

least $20. If the monthly premium amount were less than that minimum, then the policyowner would be required to choose a less frequent mode of payment, such as quarterly or semiannually.

Method of Premium Payment

Individual insurance policies usually state that renewal premiums are payable at the home office or at an authorized branch office of the insurance company. A policyowner, however, does not need to visit an insurance company office in order to pay each premium. Although renewal premiums for policies may be paid in person, policyowners usually pay premiums by mail, by automatic payment techniques, or through payroll deduction. In most cases, policyowners do not pay renewal premiums to a sales agent of the insurer because these agents generally are authorized to accept only initial premiums. One exception, as noted in Chapter 8, is that home service agents generally are authorized to accept renewal premium payments.

Payment by Mail

A policyowner who chooses to pay renewal premiums by mail receives a premium notice from the insurance company before each premium due date. In most cases, the policyowner returns a portion of the notice along with the premium payment.

A policyowner may pay the renewal premium in cash, by money order, or by check. A few insurers will also accept a charge against a policyowner's credit card as a means of paying the premium. If the premium is not paid in cash, however, the insurer's acceptance of the premium is contingent on its actual collection of the money. In other words, if a policyowner pays a premium by check and the check is not honored by the policyowner's bank because of insufficient funds, then the premium payment was not made. When a required renewal premium is paid by a check that is not honored, the policy will lapse if the policyowner does not pay the required premium within the policy's grace period.

EXAMPLE A quarterly premium payment was due on April 8 on Sidney Bullock's life insurance policy, which contained a 31-day grace period. Sidney mailed a check to the insurance company on May 4 for the full amount of the premium due. The insurer received the check on May 7. But Sidney's bank refused to honor the check because his bank account did not have enough funds to cover the amount of the check.

ANALYSIS Because the insurance company received the check on May 7, the premium was received within the policy's grace period. However, the check was not honored by Sidney's bank. As a result, the renewal premium was not paid within the policy's grace period, and the insurer has the right to lapse Sidney's policy.

Automatic Payment Techniques

Many policyowners choose to pay renewal premiums through an automatic payment technique. Policyowners who choose an automatic payment method do not receive renewal premium notices and do not regularly mail premium payments to the insurance company. Instead, these policyowners arrange to have renewal premiums paid automatically. The most common automatic premium payment techniques include the preauthorized check system, the electronic funds transfer method, and the payroll deduction method. The descriptions we give of these techniques are those that have traditionally been used. Note, however, that the terminology used throughout the insurance industry varies widely from company to company.

Under the ***preauthorized check (PAC) system,*** the policyowner authorizes the insurance company to generate checks against the policyowner's checking or savings account. The insurance company sends these checks directly to the policyowner's bank or savings institution for payment. The policyowner also authorizes the bank or savings institution to honor these checks and to deduct the funds directly from the policyowner's account. The policyowner usually receives a notification of each such transaction on her bank statement.

Most insurance companies today use the ***electronic funds transfer (EFT) method*** under which policyowners authorize their banks to pay premiums automatically on premium due dates. When this method is used, funds to pay premiums are automatically transferred from the bank to the insurer. No paper checks are generated, and notice of the transaction simply appears on the policyowner's bank statement.

The third automatic payment technique—the payroll deduction method—requires the cooperation of the policyowner's employer. Under the ***payroll deduction method,*** the employer deducts insurance premiums directly from an employee's paycheck. Generally, several employees must use the payroll deduction method and have policies with the same insurance company in order for the employer to institute such a system. The employer usually sends the insurer a single check for the total amount of premiums due on all such policies.

Automatic premium payment methods have produced two important results. They have (1) reduced insurance companies' administrative expenses for policies with monthly and quarterly premium payment modes and (2) reduced the instances in which policyowners forget to pay renewal premiums. Therefore, when policyowners choose one of these automatic payment methods, most insurance companies forgo or reduce the extra charges that would otherwise be added for semiannual, quarterly, or monthly premium payment modes. In addition, some companies offer monthly and quarterly premium payment modes only to those policyowners who have chosen an automatic payment technique.

Policy Dividend Options

We noted in Chapter 6 that a participating policy gives the policyowner the right to share in the insurer's divisible surplus through the receipt of policy dividends. Although dividends are not guaranteed, most insurers pay dividends on their participating life insurance policies that are expected to remain in force over a long term. Any policy dividend declared for a policy is payable on the policy's anniversary date, and the terms of many life insurance policies state that the policy must be in force for two years before any policy dividends will be payable.

The amount payable as policy dividends is determined annually by the insurance company's board of directors. In determining the amount of policy dividends payable, the insurer's board of directors must act in accordance with applicable statutory requirements. The amount of any policy dividend that is paid primarily reflects (1) the insurance company's actual mortality, interest, and expense experience during the year; (2) the plan of insurance; (3) the policy's premium amount; and (4) the length of time the policy has been in force. Generally, dividend amounts increase substantially with the age of the policy.

The owner of a participating life insurance policy may receive policy dividends in a number of different ways, called *dividend options.* Most jurisdictions in Canada and the United States require participating life insurance policies to include a provision that describes the available dividend options. Most insurance companies include five dividend options in their participating life insurance policies. We describe each of these five options in this chapter. (See Figure 12-2, which illustrates the percentage of dividends that are applied under each of the available options in the United States and Canada.)

The applicant for a participating policy usually selects a dividend option when she completes the policy application. Over the life of a participating policy, the policyowner may change the dividend option at any time, though a change to the additional term insurance option is subject to certain restrictions. Each participating life insurance policy also specifies an *automatic dividend option,* which is the

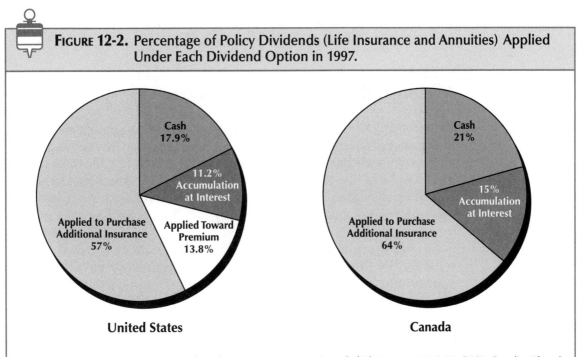

FIGURE 12-2. Percentage of Policy Dividends (Life Insurance and Annuities) Applied Under Each Dividend Option in 1997.

United States

- Cash 17.9%
- 11.2% Accumulation at Interest
- Applied Toward Premium 13.8%
- Applied to Purchase Additional Insurance 57%

Canada

- Cash 21%
- 15% Accumulation at Interest
- Applied to Purchase Additional Insurance 64%

Sources: ACLI, *1998 Life Insurance Fact Book* (Washington, D.C.: American Council of Life Insurance, 1998), 78; CLHIA, *Canadian Life and Health Insurance Facts* (Toronto: Canadian Life and Health Insurance Association, 1998), 18.

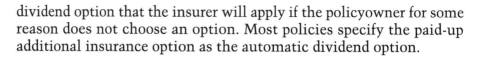

dividend option that the insurer will apply if the policyowner for some reason does not choose an option. Most policies specify the paid-up additional insurance option as the automatic dividend option.

Cash Dividend Option

Under the *cash dividend option,* the insurance company sends the owner of the policy a check in the amount of the policy dividend that was declared. Some policies also provide that if the policyowner does not cash the dividend check within a stated period, such as one year, then the insurer will apply the amount of the dividend under another option, such as the paid-up additions option.

Premium Reduction Option

Under the *premium reduction dividend option,* the insurer applies policy dividends toward the payment of renewal premiums. Unless a policy has been in force for many years, the annual policy dividend is usually not large enough to pay an entire annual renewal premium. If a policyowner is paying premiums more often than annually, the dividend may cover one or more of the installments. The insurer notifies the policyowner of the amount of the policy dividend and bills the policyowner for the difference, if any, between the premium amount due and the amount of the policy dividend.

Accumulation at Interest Option

Participating life insurance policies usually contain an *accumulation at interest dividend option* under which the policy dividends are left on deposit with the insurer to accumulate at interest. During the life of the policy, the policyowner typically has the right to withdraw part or all of these dividends and accumulated interest at any time. If the policyowner surrenders the policy, the insurer will pay the policyowner both the accumulated value of the policy dividends and the policy's cash surrender value. Any policy dividends that are on deposit with the insurer when the insured dies are usually payable to the named beneficiary rather than to the policyowner.

Paid-Up Additional Insurance Option

Under the *paid-up additional insurance dividend option,* the insurer uses any declared policy dividend as a net single premium to purchase paid-up additional insurance on the insured's life; the paid-up additional insurance is issued on the same plan as the basic policy and in whatever face amount the dividend can provide at the insured's attained age.

Many people consider the option to purchase paid-up additions to be one of the most valuable ownership rights available under a participating life insurance policy because the premium charged for paid-up additions does not include an amount to cover expenses. Consequently, the cost of paid-up additions is less than the cost of comparable coverage provided by a new life insurance policy. The paid-up additional insurance option is also considered valuable because the policyowner's right to purchase paid-up additions is not subject to the insurance company's evaluation of any evidence of insurability when the dividends are applied to purchase the additional coverage. As a result, a policyowner can use this dividend option to increase the amount of the insured's life insurance coverage, even if the insured has become uninsurable.

If the policy is one that builds cash values, then the paid-up additions purchased with policy dividends will also build cash values, and the policyowner has the right to surrender those additions for their cash value at any time while the policy is in force. Although the face amount of the paid-up additions purchased each year under this option may be relatively small, over the life of a policy, the total additional insurance available can be substantial.

Figure 12-3 illustrates how the paid-up additional insurance option increases the total death benefit payable under a policy. In this illustration, the insured was 40 years old when he purchased the $100,000 participating whole life insurance policy and selected the paid-up additional insurance option. After the policy had been in force for two

FIGURE 12-3. Illustration of Paid-Up Additional Insurance Option.

Insured's Age	Dividend Declared	Paid-Up Additions Current Year	Total Paid-Up Dividend Additions Purchased to Date	Total Death Benefit
40	$ 0	$ 0	$ 0	$100,000
42	5	16	16	100,016
43	21	65	81	100,081
—	—	—	—	—
50	229	598	1,905	101,905
—	—	—	—	—
60	1,664	3,342	22,280	122,280
—	—	—	—	—
65	2,771	5,042	49,357	149,357

years, the insurer declared a dividend of $5 for his policy. The insurer automatically applied the $5 dividend to purchase a paid-up whole life addition of $16, the amount of paid-up whole life insurance that the $5 net single premium would purchase at the insured's attained age. As a result, the total death benefit payable under the policy increased to $100,016. The next year, the insurer used the $21 policy dividend to purchase another paid-up whole life addition—this time for $65—and the total death benefit payable under the policy increased to $100,081. As you can see from the illustration in Figure 12-3, when the insured reached age 65, the total amount of paid-up additions purchased with policy dividends totaled $49,357, thus increasing the total death benefit payable under the policy to $149,357.

Additional Term Insurance Option

Under the ***additional term insurance dividend option,*** the insurer uses each policy dividend as a net single premium to purchase one-year term insurance on the insured's life. Often called the *fifth dividend option,* the additional term insurance option is not offered by as many insurance companies as are the other dividend options.

The policyowner's right to purchase one-year term insurance under this option is limited in some respects. First, the maximum amount of one-year term insurance that can be purchased each year is often limited to the amount of the policy's cash value. Second, in order for a policyowner to change from another dividend option to the additional term insurance option, insurers usually require evidence of the insured's insurability. This requirement is designed to prevent antiselection because a policyowner is more likely to change to this dividend option if the insured is in poor health rather than to apply dividends to purchase the more expensive paid-up additions. In contrast, insurers usually allow a policyowner to change to the paid-up additional insurance option without providing evidence of the insurability of the insured.

If the annual policy dividend is larger than the premium required to purchase the amount of one-year term insurance permitted—generally the cash value of the policy—then the insurer will apply the remaining amount under one of the other dividend options.

Figure 12-4 illustrates how the additional term insurance dividend option increases the amount of a policy's death benefit. Note that this is the same policy we illustrated in Figure 12-3. In this example, any dividends not needed to purchase additional term insurance are used to purchase paid-up additions. On the policy's anniversary date after the second policy year (insured age 42), the insurer paid a policy dividend of $5. The insurer used $3 of that amount to purchase one-year term insurance equal to the policy's cash value ($1,400). The $2 remaining of the policy dividend was used to purchase paid-up additions; in this case, the insurer was able to purchase additions of $9. As a result, the total death benefit available during the policy's third year was $101,409—the $100,000 face amount *plus* the $1,400 of one-year term insurance *plus* the $9 paid-up addition. The $1,400 in one-year term coverage expired at the end of the policy year, but the $9 paid-up addition remained in force. On the next policy anniversary, the insurer paid a policy dividend of $21, which it used to purchase one-year term insurance in the amount of the policy's cash value; any dividends remaining were used to purchase paid-up additions. As in our earlier illustration, the amount of paid-up insurance purchased with the excess dividends builds gradually; but it does not build as rapidly as it does when the total amount of the policy dividend each year is used to purchase paid-up additions.

Settlement Options

The proceeds of a life insurance policy are usually paid in a lump sum following the insured's death. Typically, the insurer pays the lump sum directly to the beneficiary in the form of a check. Alternatively,

FIGURE 12-4. Illustration of Additional Term Insurance Dividend Option.

(1)	(2)	(3)	(4)	(5) (Column 2 − Column 4)	(6)	(7) ($100,000 + Column 3 + Column 6)	(8) ($100,000 + Column 6)
Age of Insured	Dividend Declared	Amount of One-Year Term Available (Cash Value of Policy)	Cost of One-Year Term Insurance	Remaining Dividend	Total Amount of Paid-Up Additions Purchased to Date	Total Death Benefit (Beginning of Year)	Total Death Benefit (End of Year)
40	$ 0	$ 0	$ 0	$ 0	$ 0	$100,000	$100,000
42	5	1,400	3	2	9	101,409	100,009
43	21	2,829	5	16	81	102,910	100,081
—	—	—	—	—	—	—	—
50	229	13,100	35	194	1,539	114,639	101,539
—	—	—	—	—	—	—	—
60	1,664	32,800	218	1,446	18,903	151,703	118,903
—	—	—	—	—	—	—	—
65	2,771	42,800	479	2,292	36,138	178,938	136,138

many insurance companies deposit the policy proceeds into an *interest-bearing checking account* that the insurer establishes in the beneficiary's name. The insurer periodically pays interest at a specified rate on all funds that it holds in such an account. Interest is often paid monthly at current market rates. The insurer provides the beneficiary with checks that the beneficiary can use as he wishes to withdraw the account funds. For example, the beneficiary can withdraw the entire amount deposited into the account by writing one check, or he can write any number of checks. Once the beneficiary has withdrawn all of the funds, the insurer closes the account.

Both of the foregoing payment methods constitute lump-sum settlements because the beneficiary has immediate and complete access to the total amount of the policy proceeds. And many beneficiaries need the full policy proceeds. For example, the proceeds may be needed to pay debts, to buy partnership shares in a business, to pay estate taxes, or to be used in other ways that require a single sum of money.

On the other hand, some beneficiaries may not be capable of dealing satisfactorily with the sudden receipt of a large sum of money, either because of the emotional problems resulting from the death of a loved one or because the beneficiary is inexperienced in handling financial affairs. For such beneficiaries, placing the policy proceeds under a settlement option may be a good solution.

In addition to lump-sum settlements of policy proceeds, insurance companies also make available to the policyowner and the beneficiary several alternative methods of receiving the proceeds of a life insurance policy. These alternative methods are called **settlement options** or *optional modes of settlement*. Most jurisdictions require insurance companies to include a settlement options provision in their life insurance policies. The **settlement options provision** grants a policyowner or a beneficiary several choices as to how the insurance company will distribute the proceeds of a life insurance policy.

The policyowner may select one of the optional modes of settlement at the time of application or at any time while the policy is in force. The policyowner also has the right to change to another settlement option at any time during the insured's lifetime. When the policyowner selects an optional mode of settlement while the policy is in force, the terms of the settlement usually are incorporated into a **settlement agreement,** which is a contractual agreement that governs the rights and obligations of the parties after the insured's death.

The policyowner who selects a settlement option for the beneficiary may choose to make the settlement mode *irrevocable,* in which case the beneficiary will not be able to change to another option when the policy proceeds become payable. If the settlement agreement does not state that the settlement mode is irrevocable, then the mode is considered to be *revocable* and the beneficiary has the right to select another settlement option when the proceeds become payable. Further, if the policyowner has not chosen a settlement mode when the policy proceeds become payable, then the beneficiary has the right to choose a settlement option. When the beneficiary selects a settlement mode, the insurance company and the beneficiary usually enter into a settlement agreement; this type of settlement agreement between an insurer and a policy beneficiary is sometimes referred to as a *supplementary contract.*

The person or party who is to receive the policy proceeds in accordance with the terms of a settlement agreement is referred to as the *payee.* The person or party who elects an optional mode of settlement—either the policyowner or the beneficiary—also has the right to designate a *contingent payee,* or *successor payee,* who will receive any proceeds still payable at the time of the payee's death.

Insurers commonly offer four optional modes of settlement in their individual life insurance policies. These settlement options include the interest option, the fixed-period option, the fixed-amount option, and the life income option. We describe each optional mode of settlement separately.

Interest Option

The *interest option* is a settlement option under which the insurance company invests the policy proceeds and periodically pays interest on those proceeds to the payee. The policy usually guarantees that the insurer will pay at least a stated minimum interest rate, but the insurer may pay a higher rate if that rate is consistent with the company's investment earnings.

Generally, the insurance company pays interest on the proceeds annually, unless the payee requests more frequent payments. A payee may request a more frequent payment schedule only if the amount of the proceeds being held is large enough to generate interest installments of at least a specified amount during each selected period. For example, a policy's settlement provision may state that a payee can request monthly interest installments only if the policy proceeds would earn at least \$50 a month in interest. If the amount of each payment would fall below the specified minimum, then the administrative costs the insurer incurs in making monthly payments would be too high. Therefore, the insurer would require the payee to select a less frequent payment schedule—annually or quarterly, for example.

Occasionally, the payee prefers for the insurance company to invest the policy proceeds and to allow the interest earned to accumulate rather than to be paid to the payee. Insurance companies, however, generally will not allow the interest to be left on deposit indefinitely. If the payee is a minor, however, companies often agree to hold the accumulated interest until the minor reaches the age of majority.

An insurance company will not hold policy proceeds under the interest option indefinitely. The maximum length of time a company will hold policy proceeds at interest is usually the lifetime of the payee or 30 years, whichever is longer. If the payee dies before receiving payment and the 30-year period has expired, the insurer will pay the policy proceeds in a lump sum to the contingent payee. If the payee dies before the 30-year period has expired, then the contingent payee may have the insurance company continue to hold the policy proceeds under the interest option until the original 30-year period ends; at the end of the original 30-year period, the insurer will pay the policy proceeds to the contingent payee in a lump sum.

The beneficiary generally has the right to withdraw all or part of the policy proceeds at any time or to place all of the proceeds—including any interest that the insurer is holding—under another settlement option. Sometimes, however, the beneficiary's withdrawal privilege is limited. When the policyowner selects the interest option, he may choose to give the beneficiary a restricted or an unrestricted withdrawal privilege. A restricted withdrawal privilege usually limits the amount of the policy proceeds that the beneficiary may withdraw. Often, however, the policyowner specifies the interest option as the mode of settlement so that the beneficiary will have the time to make a rational decision on which method of settlement will be most suitable for him. In such cases, an unrestricted withdrawal privilege is usually included in the option, and the beneficiary may at any time choose to withdraw all the proceeds in a lump sum or to place all the proceeds under another settlement option.

Fixed-Period Option

The *fixed-period option* is a settlement option under which the insurance company agrees to pay policy proceeds in installments of equal amounts to the payee for a specified period of time. Each payment will consist partly of the policy proceeds being held by the company and partly of the interest earned on the proceeds. As with the interest option, the policy states the minimum guaranteed interest rate that will be earned on the proceeds and states that the rate may be higher if the company's investment returns are better than expected.

The amount of each installment paid under the fixed-period option depends primarily on the amount of the policy proceeds, the interest rate, and the length of the payment period that the policyowner or beneficiary chooses. Installments may be paid annually or more frequently—even monthly if the amount of each installment is large enough to meet the company's minimum requirements. Policies usually contain a chart that shows, for selected payment periods, the guaranteed amount of monthly payments that will be made per $1,000 of net policy proceeds.

EXAMPLE When she died, Jocelyn Schiller owned a $100,000 insurance policy on her life. She had named her son Randy as sole beneficiary and had selected the fixed-period settlement option. The policy stated that the insurer would pay interest of at least 4 percent and contained the following chart—based on a 4 percent interest rate—listing the amount of each installment payment that would be payable under the fixed-period option:

Fixed Period (Number of Years)	Minimum Monthly Payment per $1,000 of Proceeds
1	$85.12
2	43.39
3	29.49
4	22.55
5	18.38

Jocelyn specified that the insurer should make the benefit installment payments over a four-year period.

ANALYSIS According to the terms of the policy, the insurer guarantees that it will pay Randy $2,255 each month over the four-year period.

$ 22.55	Minimum monthly payment per unit
× 100	**Times:** Number of units ($100,000 ÷ $1,000)
$ 2,255	**Equals:** Minimum monthly benefit payment

The amount of the monthly payment may be larger than $2,255 if the insurance company earns a more profitable rate of return than that guaranteed by the policy.

If the policyowner has not designated the fixed-period option as irrevocable, many policies permit the payee to cancel the option at any time and to collect all of the remaining policy proceeds and unpaid interest in a lump sum. The payee, however, usually does not have the right to withdraw only a part of the funds during the payment period. Such a partial withdrawal would reduce the amount of the remaining funds and would require the insurer to recalculate the entire schedule of benefit payments.

The fixed-period option is designed to provide the payee with a temporary income for a specified period of time—for example, while children are dependent or while a payee is receiving education or training to become income producing. This option is also widely used to provide the payee with income until another anticipated income source, such as a pension, begins.

Fixed-Amount Option

The *fixed-amount option* is a settlement option under which the insurance company pays equal installments of a stated amount until the policy proceeds, plus the interest earned, are exhausted. As with the fixed-period option, the fixed-amount option states the minimum guaranteed interest rate that the insurer will pay on the policy proceeds it holds. The number of installments that the insurer will pay depends on the amount of the policy proceeds, the interest rate, and the fixed amount selected. The larger the amount of the proceeds, the longer the period for which the insurer will make installment payments of the fixed amount. If the payee dies before the proceeds plus interest are exhausted, the insurer will pay the total amount of remaining proceeds to the contingent payee.

The payee receiving the policy proceeds under the fixed-amount settlement option generally has the right to withdraw part or all of the remaining policy proceeds at any time. If the payee withdraws all of the remaining proceeds, then the supplementary contract ends. If the payee makes a partial withdrawal, then the insurer will continue making installment payments of the selected amount but will reduce the number of installments it pays. In many cases, the payee also has the right to increase or decrease the amount of each installment payment. Increasing the amount of each payment means that the proceeds will be exhausted more rapidly and fewer payments will be made. Alternatively, reducing the amount of each installment means that the proceeds will be paid over a longer time.

The fixed-amount option is useful when the policyowner or beneficiary wants to be sure that adequate income will be available, even if for only a short time. For instance, the beneficiary may have the capacity to earn an adequate income but may have reasons to postpone employment.

Life Income Option

The *life income option* is a settlement option under which the insurance company agrees to pay the policy proceeds in periodic installments over the payee's lifetime. As we have seen, both the fixed-amount and fixed-period options provide installment payments for only a limited time. Therefore, the policyowner or beneficiary who chooses one of those options must be certain that providing a temporary income is the best way to distribute the policy proceeds. If other sources of income are not likely to be available in the future, then the beneficiary may be better served by a permanent income provided through the life income option, even though this method of settlement typically results in smaller installment payments than would be available under the fixed-amount or fixed-period options.

Under the life income option, the insurance company agrees to use the policy proceeds as a net single premium to purchase a life annuity for the beneficiary. Recall that an *annuity* is a series of periodic payments. A **life annuity** is an annuity that provides periodic benefits payments for *at least* the lifetime of a named individual. In other words, the beneficiary is entitled to receive annuity benefit payments throughout his lifetime. As we describe in Chapter 16, insurance companies offer several types of life annuity policies. Therefore, insurance companies also give the policyowner or beneficiary who chooses the life income option the right to select from among several types of life annuities. The policy's settlement options provision most commonly includes the following life income options:

- The **straight life income option** under which the policy proceeds are used to purchase a *straight life annuity*

- The **life income with period certain option** under which the policy proceeds are used to purchase a *life income annuity with period certain*

- The **refund life income option** under which the policy proceeds are used to purchase a *life income with refund annuity*

- The **joint and survivorship life income option** under which the policy proceeds are used to purchase a *joint and survivor annuity*

The various types of life annuities we have mentioned are defined in Figure 12-5 and are described in more detail in Chapter 16.

The policy's settlement options provision also guarantees that the periodic annuity benefit payments will be at least as large as a stated amount. Policies typically contain charts that list the amount of the guaranteed minimum benefit payments that will be available under each of the life income options. If the insurer's annuity rates in effect at the time of settlement would result in larger payment amounts, then the insurer typically provides the larger amounts, rather than the guaranteed amounts.

Figure 12-5. Types of Life Annuities.

Straight life annuity. This type of life annuity guarantees only that periodic benefit payments will be made throughout the lifetime of the annuitant.

Life income annuity with period certain. This type of life annuity guarantees that annuity benefits will be paid throughout the annuitant's life *and* guarantees that the payments will be made for at least a certain period, even if the annuitant dies before the end of that period.

Life income with refund annuity. This type of life annuity provides annuity benefits throughout the lifetime of the annuitant *and* guarantees that at least the purchase price of the annuity will be paid in benefits.

Joint and survivor annuity. This type of life annuity provides a series of payments to two or more individuals and those payments continue until both or all of the individuals die.

Transfer of Policy Ownership

If the owner of a life insurance policy has contractual capacity, then she has the right to transfer ownership of some or all of her rights in the policy. An ownership transfer, however, is not accomplished by simply handing someone the policy. The two ways in which a policy-owner may transfer ownership rights are by assignment and by endorsement.

Transfer of Ownership by Assignment

An *assignment* is an agreement under which one party transfers some or all of his ownership rights in a particular property to another party. The property owner who makes an assignment is known as the *assignor;* the party to whom the property rights are transferred is known as the *assignee.*

The right to assign any property, including a life insurance policy, is subject to some restrictions. In order to make a valid assignment of an insurance policy, the policyowner must have contractual capacity. As a result, if the policyowner is a minor or, for some other reason, lacks contractual capacity, any attempt by the policyowner to assign the policy is invalid.

Another restriction is that the assignment of a life insurance policy may not infringe on the vested rights, if any, of a beneficiary. If the policy's beneficiary has been named irrevocably, or is a member of a preferred class in Canada, then the beneficiary has a vested right to the policy proceeds. An assignment made without such a beneficiary's consent is invalid. Note that when the beneficiary is a revocable beneficiary, the policyowner has an unlimited right to assign the policy.

The final restriction is that an assignment that is made for illegal purposes, such as speculating on a life or committing fraud, is invalid.

Assignment Provision

Because the right to assign any property is granted by law, insurers are not required to give the policyowner notice of his right to assign a life insurance policy. Most life insurance policies, however, do include an assignment provision. The **assignment provision** describes the roles of the insurer and the policyowner when the policy is assigned. An example of a life insurance policy's assignment provision follows.

> **Assignment.** While the Insured is living, you can assign this policy or any interest in it. As owner, you still have the rights of ownership that have not been assigned. We must have a copy of any assignment. We will not be responsible for the validity of an assignment. An assignment will be subject to any payment we make or other action we take before we record it.

The insurance company is not obligated to act in accordance with the terms of an assignment unless it has received written notice of the assignment. Because the assignee wants to protect her own interests, the assignee typically assumes responsibility for notifying the insurance company, in writing, of the assignment.

An assignment is an agreement between the assignee and the assignor. The insurance company is not a party to the agreement. Therefore, the policy's assignment provision states that the insurer is not responsible for the validity of any assignment. When an insurance company receives written notice of an assignment, the company presumes that the assignment is valid. The insurance company, however, has no control over the validity of the assignment and usually cannot be held liable for having acted in accordance with an assignment that is later determined to be invalid. However, if the insurer were aware of circumstances that should have made the insurer question the assignment's validity—for example, if the insurer were aware that the policyowner had been declared mentally incompetent—then the insurer may be held liable for acting in accordance with the assignment.

EXAMPLE Jim Pipcinski was the policyowner-insured of a life insurance policy issued by the Ace Life Insurance Company. When Jim died, Ace's policy records indicated that the policy had been assigned to the Cargill Bank. As a result, Ace paid the policy proceeds to Cargill. Later, a court determined that the assignment to Cargill was invalid.

ANALYSIS Whether Ace will be liable to pay the policy proceeds again will depend on whether Ace was aware of any facts that should have made it question the validity of the assignment. If Ace had no such knowledge, then it will not be required to pay the policy proceeds again.

Types of Assignment

An assignment may take one of two forms: an absolute assignment or a collateral assignment. Whether an assignment is absolute or collateral depends on whether the assignee has received complete ownership of the policy or only certain specified ownership rights in the policy.

Absolute Assignment. An *absolute assignment* of a life insurance policy is an assignment under which a policyowner transfers all of his policy ownership rights to the assignee. The policyowner-assignor has no further rights under the contract and the assignee becomes the policyowner. If a policyowner absolutely assigns a policy without receiving any payment in exchange, he is considered to have made a gift of the policy to the assignee. For example, parents who purchase insurance on their child's life often transfer ownership of the policy—as a gift—to the child when she reaches the age of majority. By contrast, if financial compensation is involved, the absolute assignment is considered to be the equivalent of a sale of the policy. For example, a business organization that owns an insurance policy on the life of a key person may sell the policy to the key person in exchange for the policy's cash value when that key person leaves employment. Such a transfer of the policy's ownership is typically accomplished by means of an absolute assignment.

In most situations, such as those mentioned above, an absolute assignment is made to the person insured by the policy. In most jurisdictions, however, a policy can be absolutely assigned to anyone, regardless of whether the assignee has an insurable interest in the life of the insured.

Collateral Assignment. A *collateral assignment* of a life insurance policy is a temporary assignment of the monetary value of a life insurance policy as collateral—or security—for a loan. For example, if a person takes out a personal loan from a bank, that person may collaterally assign a life insurance policy to the bank as security for the loan. A collateral assignment differs from an absolute assignment in three general respects.

1. **The collateral assignee's rights are limited to those ownership rights that directly concern the monetary value of the policy.** The policyowner retains all ownership rights that do not affect the policy's value. For example, the right to name the policy beneficiary and the right to select a dividend payment option remain with the policyowner. The policyowner-assignor, however, is not permitted to take out a policy loan or surrender the policy for its cash surrender value while a collateral assignment is in effect unless the assignee consents. This limitation is imposed to protect the assignee's right to the policy's value because a policy loan and a policy surrender both diminish that value.

2. **The collateral assignee has a vested right to the policy's monetary values, but that right is limited.** The assignee's rights to the policy's values are limited to the amount of the assignor's indebtedness to the assignee. Consequently, if the policy proceeds become payable, the assignee is entitled to receive only the amount of the indebtedness; any remaining amount must be paid to the policy's beneficiary. Note also that the assignee can receive this amount only in a lump sum and cannot select a settlement option.

3. **The collateral assignee's rights to the policy values are temporary.** If the assignor repays the amount owed to the collateral assignee, the assignment terminates, and all of the policy's ownership rights revert to the policyowner. Once the loan is repaid, the policyowner usually secures from the assignee a release of the assignee's claim to the policy proceeds. The policyowner then forwards that release to the insurance company in order to notify the company that the assignment is no longer in effect.

Problems Resulting from Assignment

Some problems may arise when a policyowner assigns his life insurance policy. The most common problem occurs when the insurer is not notified in writing of an assignment. An insurance company will pay the proceeds of a policy to the recipient who appears entitled to those proceeds according to the company's records. If the company were not notified of an assignment, then it would pay the proceeds to the person the policyowner named to receive those proceeds—the beneficiary of the life insurance policy or the payee of annuity benefits. The assignee might then attempt to collect the proceeds. If the insurer were not notified of the assignment before it paid the proceeds to the beneficiary, then the insurer would be protected from also having to pay the proceeds to the assignee.

E X A M P L E | Isabel Mahoney collaterally assigned the insurance policy she owned on her life as security for a loan. When Isabel died, the insurance company had not been notified of the assignment, and, thus, it paid the policy proceeds to the named beneficiary. The assignee later claimed the policy proceeds.

A N A L Y S I S | Because the insurer was not notified of the assignment before it paid the policy death benefit, it has no liability to pay the proceeds again to the assignee.

Transfer of Ownership by Endorsement

Many life insurance policies issued today in the United States specify a simple, direct method of transferring all the policy's ownership rights. Under this method, known as the ***endorsement method,*** policy ownership is completely transferred without requiring the policyowner to enter into a separate assignment agreement. The endorsement method is commonly used when a policy is given as a gift. For example, a parent may give a child ownership of a policy on the child's life when the child reaches age 21.

The right to change the policy's owner is generally spelled out in the policy. A typical change of ownership provision follows.

Change of Ownership. You can change the owner of this policy, from yourself to a new owner, in a notice you sign, which gives us the facts that we need. When this change takes effect, all rights of ownership in this policy will pass to the new owner.

When we record a change of owner or successor owner, these changes will take effect as of the date you signed the notice, subject to any payment we made or action we took before recording these changes. We may require that these changes be endorsed in the policy. Changing the owner or naming a new successor owner cancels any prior choice of successor owner, but does not change the beneficiary.

According to this policy provision, in order to change the ownership of the policy, the policyowner must notify the insurer, in writing, of the change. When the insurance company records the ownership change in its records, the change becomes effective as of the date the policyowner signed the written notification. For example, assume that on December 10, a policyowner signed and mailed to the insurer a written notice giving ownership of his life insurance policy to his daughter. The insurer received the written notice on December 14 and recorded the change in its records on that day. As a result, the ownership change will be considered effective on December 10.

Note, however, that the change of ownership provision gives the insurer the right to require that the ownership change be endorsed in the policy. In such a case, the policyowner must send the policy to the insurance company, and the insurer will add to the policy an endorsement that states the name of the new owner. In some situations, the policy cannot be submitted to the company in order for the ownership change to be endorsed in the policy. For example, after an unfriendly divorce, a spouse who is the revocable beneficiary may have the policy and refuse to give it to the policyowner. In such situations, the general rule of law is that if the policyowner has taken all reasonable steps to submit the policy and if the insurance company has received written notice to change the ownership of the policy, then the requested change of ownership will be effective.

The transfer of ownership provision usually states that the insurance company is not responsible for any payments it made to the owner of record before it received written notice of an ownership change and recorded that change. This provision protects the insurance company from the new owner's contesting the insurer's actions if a loan were granted or benefit payments were made between the date the policyowner signed the notification and the date the insurance company recorded the change.

Key Terms

premium payment mode
preauthorized check (PAC) system
electronic funds transfer (EFT) method
payroll deduction method
dividend options
automatic dividend option
cash dividend option

premium reduction dividend option
accumulation at interest dividend option
paid-up additional insurance dividend option
additional term insurance dividend option
settlement options

Key Terms (continued)

settlement options provision
settlement agreement
supplementary contract
payee
contingent payee
interest option
fixed-period option
fixed-amount option
life income option
life annuity
straight life income option
life income with period certain
    option

refund life income option
joint and survivorship life
    income option
assignment
assignor
assignee
assignment provision
absolute assignment
collateral assignment
endorsement method

Other Important Terms

fifth dividend option
interest-bearing checking
    account
optional modes of settlement
successor payee
annuity

straight life annuity
life income annuity with period
    certain
life income with refund annuity
joint and survivor annuity

Endnotes

1. ACLI, *1998 Life Insurance Fact Book* (Washington, D.C.: American Council of Life Insurance, 1998), 78, 127.

2. Ibid., 79.

3. Ibid., 77–78, 127.

CHAPTER 13

Paying Life Insurance Policy Proceeds

After reading this chapter, you should be able to

- Identify the steps that claim examiners follow to evaluate life insurance claims

- Recognize the general rule stated in U.S. and Canadian survivorship laws and explain how that rule is affected if a policy contains a common disaster (time) clause

- Identify the remedies provided by law in the United States and Canada to protect insurers that are faced with conflicting claimants to life insurance policy proceeds

- Calculate the proceeds payable under a given life insurance policy following the death of the insured

- State why an insurer may have difficulty paying life insurance policy proceeds to a beneficiary who lacks legal capacity

- Identify why an insurer may deny a death claim when the insured person has disappeared

- Recognize how laws in various jurisdictions define a *wrongful killing* that disqualifies the beneficiary of a life insurance policy from receiving the policy proceeds

ost people purchase life insurance because they think
the policy's death benefit will be needed when the insured person dies. In order to fulfill its responsibilities
to its life insurance policyowners and beneficiaries, the
insurer must take steps to ensure that policy proceeds are paid
promptly to the correct party. Additionally, in order to protect the
insurance industry and the public from abuses of the insurance
contract, insurance companies must guard against paying fraudulent
or mistaken claims.

In this chapter, we describe the procedures that insurers typically
follow to process routine life insurance policy claims. We also describe
some special claim situations insurers sometimes face in determining
who is entitled to receive life insurance policy proceeds.

Processing Life Insurance Claims

Each insurance company must establish standard procedures that its
employees follow when they process life insurance claims. These
standard procedures are designed to strike a balance between the beneficiary's right to prompt settlement of his claim and the insurance
company's need to examine each claim's validity. Not only does the
beneficiary have the right to expect prompt settlement, but the laws
of most jurisdictions require prompt settlement of claims. On the other
hand, the beneficiary may have, intentionally or unintentionally, submitted an invalid claim. Insurers must take reasonable steps to avoid
paying invalid claims; otherwise, the cost of insurance and, consequently, premium rates would rise dramatically. The insurance company also must be certain that it pays policy proceeds to the proper
beneficiary, or the insurer could be faced with a valid second claim to
those proceeds.

The claim examination process begins when the claimant to policy
proceeds notifies the insurance company that the insured has died.
Typically, the person who claims life insurance policy proceeds following the insured's death is the policy's primary beneficiary.

Claim Form

Upon being notified of the insured's death, the insurance company typically provides the claimant with a claim form on which the claimant

provides the information the insurer needs to begin processing the claim. Insurance laws in most states in the United States mandate that if the insurer requires the claimant to complete a claim form, then the insurer must provide a claim form to the claimant within 15 days of a request for a claim form. If the insurer fails to do so, the claimant is presumed to have submitted the completed form, and the insurer must process the claim without the form. Although insurers in Canada usually require claimants to complete a claim form, provincial insurance laws do not impose a requirement that insurers provide a claim form within a stated time. (See Figure 13-1, which shows a sample claim form.)

Proof of Loss

Along with completing the claim form, the claimant must furnish the insurer with proof of his claim. In other words, the claimant must provide the insurer with proof that the person insured by the policy has died. In the United States, the claimant for life insurance policy proceeds most commonly submits an official death certificate as proof of loss. In Canada, most insurance companies will accept an official death certificate, an Attending Physician's Statement (APS), a coroner's certificate of death, or a hospital's certificate of death as proof of an insured's death. When a claimant submits the claim form and proof of loss document, the insurer begins to evaluate the claim.

Claim Examination Process

The insurance company employee who is responsible for carrying out the claim examination process is generally known as a ***claim examiner,*** *claim approver, claim analyst,* or *claim specialist.* In processing and paying a claim, the claim examiner will (1) determine the status of the policy, (2) verify the identity of the insured, (3) verify that the loss insured against has occurred, (4) verify that the loss is covered by the policy, (5) determine who is entitled to receive the policy proceeds, and (6) determine the amount of the benefit that is payable. We describe each of these steps in the claim examination process.

Status of Policy

The claim examiner must check the status of the policy to ensure that it was in force when the insured died. For example, the claim examiner must verify that the policy had not lapsed for nonpayment of premium before the insured's death. In addition, the claim examiner must ensure that the policy did not terminate for any other reason

FIGURE 13-1. Sample Claim Form.

ABC Life Insurance Company
100 Ordinary Avenue, New York, N.Y. 00000

Please see proof of death requirements on reverse side before completing this form.

Policies under which claim is made by the undersigned:

Numbers	Numbers	Numbers
_____	_____	_____
_____	_____	_____
_____	_____	_____

1. a. Deceased's name in full _____

   b. Residence _____

   c. Occupation _____

2. Date of birth _____   Place of birth _____

3. a. Date of death _____   Place of death _____

   b. Cause of death _____

   c. Duration of illness _____

4. Names & Addresses of Attending Physicians

Name	Address
_____	_____
_____	_____

5. a. What is your relationship to the deceased? _____

   b. Do you claim this insurance as beneficiary? _____

   c. If you are not the beneficiary, in what capacity are you making this claim? _____

NOTE: If you are a beneficiary designated to receive policy proceeds in a single sum and wish to have information regarding any optional methods of settlement which may be available to you, please consult your ABC agent or the Office through which you are submitting this statement.

Claimant's
Signature _____   Age _____

Address _____
           (Please print)   (Street)

           _____
                         (City)

Date _____   _____
                                          (State)

before the insured's death. For example, a term life insurance policy may have reached the end of its term and expired. Thus, the claim examiner must examine the terms of the policy to determine the length of the period for which the policy provided coverage. If, for any reason, coverage was not in force when the insured died, then the insurer will deny liability to pay the policy proceeds.

Identification of the Insured

The claim examiner compares the insured's identification in the claim form and in the proof of loss document with the identifying information contained in the company's policy records to confirm that the person who died was the person insured by the policy. This step protects the insurance company against fraudulent and mistaken claims.

A claim is considered to be a ***fraudulent claim*** when the claimant intentionally attempts to collect policy proceeds by providing false information to the insurer. For example, if the person insured by a policy is still living and the beneficiary submits a forged death certificate in order to collect the policy proceeds, the beneficiary is committing fraud. Note that laws throughout Canada and the United States prohibit the filing of a fraudulent claim and impose both criminal and civil penalties on anyone who files such a claim.

A claim is considered to be a ***mistaken claim*** when a claimant makes an honest mistake in presenting a claim to the insurer. The beneficiary might, for example, mistakenly believe that the policy insured the deceased person when it actually insured someone else. The long-term nature of a life insurance policy sometimes accounts for a misidentification of the insured. A policy may have been issued decades before the claim was submitted. As shown in Figure 13-2, the majority of life insurance policies are in force for at least 20 years before a claim is submitted. The applicant, the sales agent, and others involved in issuing the policy might have died, moved away, or otherwise become unavailable. The policy may have been issued before the beneficiary was born, and policyowners often change a beneficiary designation while a policy is in force. As a result, the beneficiary, who may be unfamiliar with the policy's terms, could mistakenly submit a claim.

The claim examiner must also compare the insured's sex and date of birth as shown on the company's policy records to the sex and date of birth or age at death as stated on the death certificate and the claim form. If the information provided contains any discrepancies, then the claim examiner may ask the claimant to provide additional documents. For example, the claimant might be required to provide the insurer with the insured's birth certificate as proof of age. If the insured's age or sex were misstated in the company's records, the examiner must

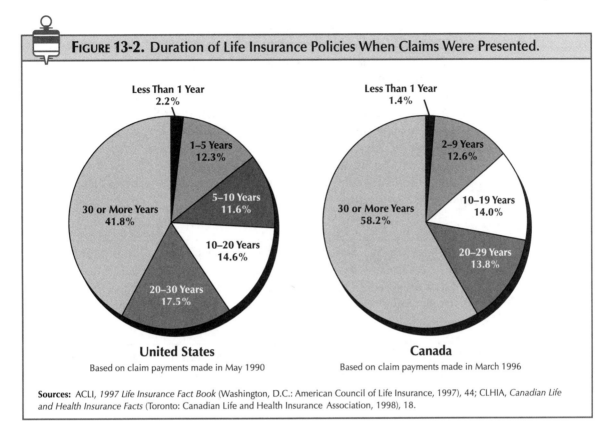

FIGURE 13-2. Duration of Life Insurance Policies When Claims Were Presented.

United States
Based on claim payments made in May 1990

Less Than 1 Year 2.2%
1–5 Years 12.3%
5–10 Years 11.6%
10–20 Years 14.6%
20–30 Years 17.5%
30 or More Years 41.8%

Canada
Based on claim payments made in March 1996

Less Than 1 Year 1.4%
2–9 Years 12.6%
10–19 Years 14.0%
20–29 Years 13.8%
30 or More Years 58.2%

Sources: ACLI, *1997 Life Insurance Fact Book* (Washington, D.C.: American Council of Life Insurance, 1997), 44; CLHIA, *Canadian Life and Health Insurance Facts* (Toronto: Canadian Life and Health Insurance Association, 1998), 18.

account for that discrepancy when she calculates the amount of the death benefit that is payable. You will recall that life insurance policies typically contain a misstatement of age or sex provision, which describes such benefit amount adjustments.

Verification of the Loss

The claim examiner also must examine the proof of loss document provided by the claimant in order to verify that the insured has died. In most cases, the death certificate or other proof of loss document submitted by the claimant provides all of the information the claim examiner needs to verify the loss. Later in the chapter, we describe situations in which the claimant is unable to provide proof of loss because the insured has disappeared.

Verification of Policy Coverage

The claim examiner must review the terms of the insurance policy to determine what type of coverage it provides. The claim examiner also must consider whether the policy contains any exclusions that might affect her decision about paying the claim. As we have noted, life insurance policies often contain provisions that limit the insurer's liability if the insured dies as a result of specified causes. The most common of these exclusions is the suicide exclusion clause. If the cause of the insured's death is excluded from coverage, then the insurer is not liable to pay the policy death benefit and will deny the claim. Policies that contain such an exclusion typically provide that if the insured dies as a result of the excluded cause, then the insurer's liability will be limited to returning the premiums paid for the policy. Some policies limit the insurer's liability to the amount of the policy's cash surrender value.

EXAMPLE Shondra Gillespie was insured by a life insurance policy that contained a typical two-year suicide exclusion period and that provided an accidental death benefit. Shondra died as the result of a fall from a fourth-floor window 18 months after the policy was issued.

ANALYSIS The claim examiner must determine why Shondra fell. If the fall was the result of an accident, then the insurer is liable to pay both the basic death benefit and the accidental death benefit. If Shondra committed suicide, however, then the insurer's liability is limited to the amount of premiums paid for the policy because Shondra died as a result of suicide during the policy's suicide exclusion period.

Identifying the Proper Payee

Once the claim examiner has determined that the claim is valid, she must identify the person who is entitled to receive the policy proceeds. Notice that the sample claim form shown in Figure 13-1 contains several questions that request information about the claimant. Although the claimant is typically the beneficiary of the policy, the claimant might claim the policy proceeds as the assignee of a collateral assignment or as the personal representative of the insured's estate. In any case, the claim examiner must review the company's policy records to determine who is entitled to the policy proceeds. (See Figure 13-3 for a graphic illustration of how the claim examiner determines who is entitled to policy proceeds.) If an assignment was in effect when the insured died, then the assignee is entitled to all or a portion of the policy proceeds. If no assignment was in effect and the primary beneficiary survived the insured, then proceeds are payable to the primary beneficiary. If the primary beneficiary predeceased the insured, then proceeds are payable to the contingent beneficiary. If no named beneficiary survives the insured, then proceeds are typically payable to

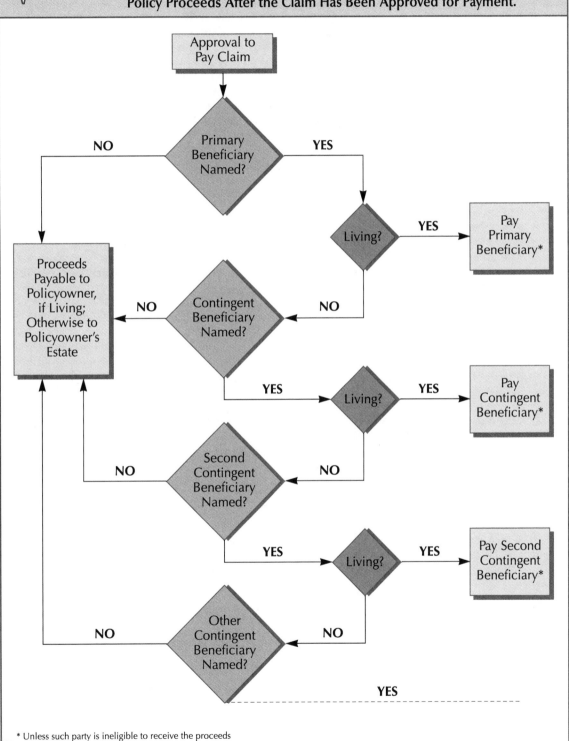

FIGURE 13-3. Primary Steps in Determining the Correct Beneficiary of Life Insurance Policy Proceeds After the Claim Has Been Approved for Payment.

* Unless such party is ineligible to receive the proceeds

"Pull harder, Henry! I just cancelled the accidental death benefit rider on my life insurance policy!"

Reprinted with permission of Phil Interlandi and Bituminous Casualty Corporation.

the policyowner; if the policyowner was also the person insured by the policy, then proceeds are payable to the policyowner-insured's estate.

In the vast majority of claims, the claim examiner is able to determine quickly who is entitled to policy proceeds. Sometimes, however, the claim examiner must investigate the claim further in order to determine the proper recipient of policy proceeds. We describe three such situations that require further investigation by the claim examiner—common disasters, short-term survivorship, and conflicting claimants.

Common Disasters. Sometimes, the insured and the beneficiary die in the same accident, but no proof is available to show that one person survived the other. This situation is referred to as a *common disaster* because the accident or disaster was *common* to more than one person. The claim examiner must investigate because the beneficiary is entitled to the policy proceeds only if she survived the insured. If the beneficiary survived the insured but died before the insurer pays the policy proceeds, then those proceeds are generally payable to the beneficiary's estate.

If no proof exists as to whether the insured died before the beneficiary died, how can the claim examiner determine who should receive the policy proceeds? Laws throughout Canada and the United States govern how insurance companies are to determine survivorship questions in common disaster situations. These survivorship laws state the following general rule.

> If the insured and the beneficiary die at the same time or under circumstances that make it impossible to determine which of them died first, then policy proceeds are payable as if the insured survived the beneficiary.

Let's look at an example to illustrate how this general rule of law affects the payment of life insurance policy proceeds.

EXAMPLE Duffy Drago and his wife, Ally, died in an airplane crash and the evidence did not show which of them died first. Duffy was insured under a policy that he owned; Ally was the primary beneficiary and Duffy's mother was the contingent beneficiary. Ally was insured under a policy that she owned; Duffy was the primary beneficiary, and Ally's father was the contingent beneficiary. Although Ally's father survived her, Duffy's mother died several years before the crash.

ANALYSIS Because no evidence exists as to the order in which Duffy and Ally died, we must apply the general rule stated in the survivorship laws to each policy.

- **Duffy's policy.** The insured, Duffy, is deemed to have survived the primary beneficiary, Ally. Thus, the policy proceeds are payable to the contingent beneficiary, if she survived the insured. Because Duffy's mother predeceased him, the policy proceeds are payable to Duffy's estate.

- **Ally's policy.** The insured, Ally, is deemed to have survived the primary beneficiary, Duffy. Thus, the policy proceeds are payable to the contingent beneficiary, if he survived the insured. Because Ally's father survived her, the policy proceeds are payable to him.

Short-Term Survivorship. The survivorship laws do not affect how policy proceeds are paid in those cases in which the beneficiary survives the insured. If the beneficiary survives the insured by any length of time—even if only for a few minutes—the right to receive the policy proceeds generally vests in the beneficiary when the insured dies. That means that if the beneficiary survives the insured but dies before receiving the policy proceeds, then the proceeds are payable to the beneficiary's estate. The policyowner, however, may prefer that the proceeds be paid to someone other than the beneficiary's heirs if the beneficiary survives the insured by only a short time.

Some life insurance policies include a common disaster clause that deals with this potential problem. A *common disaster clause,* also known as a *time clause,* states that the beneficiary must survive the insured by a specified period, such as 30 or 60 days, in order to receive the policy proceeds. If the beneficiary survives the insured by the stated time, then the beneficiary's right to the policy proceeds vests. If the beneficiary does not survive the stated time, then the policy proceeds are paid as if the beneficiary predeceased the insured. As a result, the policy proceeds are more likely to be distributed as the policyowner had intended.

EXAMPLE When she died, Maddie Brady was insured under a policy that included a typical 30 day common disaster clause. Her husband, Patrick, was the policy's primary beneficiary and her mother was the contingent beneficiary. Maddie and Patrick died as the result of an automobile accident. Maddie died within a few minutes of the accident, and Patrick died two hours later.

ANALYSIS Because the beneficiary survived the insured, the survivorship laws do not govern this situation. Therefore, we must look at the terms of the policy, which includes a 30 day common disaster clause. Because Patrick died only two hours after Maddie died, he did not survive her by the required 30 days. Therefore, the policy proceeds are payable as if Patrick died before Maddie. Thus, the proceeds are payable to the contingent beneficiary, Maddie's mother.

Conflicting Claimants. In most cases, policy proceeds are payable to the primary beneficiary, who is the only person who claims those proceeds. Even if several people claim the proceeds of a policy, the insurance company and the various claimants are usually able to agree on how the proceeds should be paid. But what does the insurer do if it receives several claims and cannot determine from its policy records who is entitled to the proceeds? If the insurer pays the proceeds to one claimant, it could later be required to pay the proceeds a second time if the other claimant in fact had a superior claim to the proceeds.

| EXAMPLE | Both Sylvia Smith and Jack Jones submitted a claim for the proceeds of an insurance policy on the life of Bobby |

Smith. The insurance company decided that Sylvia was the proper beneficiary and paid the proceeds to her. Jack filed a lawsuit against the insurance company seeking to recover the policy proceeds. The court found that Jack was entitled to the policy proceeds.

| ANALYSIS | The court verdict in favor of Jack means that the insurance company must pay the policy proceeds to him. Because |

Sylvia probably will not agree to refund the policy proceeds to the insurer, the insurer will have paid the proceeds twice.

Laws throughout the United States and Canada provide a remedy to insurance companies that are faced with conflicting claims to policy proceeds. In the United States, when an insurance company cannot determine the correct beneficiary for the policy proceeds, or fears that a court might disagree with its opinion as to the correct beneficiary, the company may use the remedy of interpleader. **Interpleader** is a procedure under which an insurance company that cannot determine which claimant is entitled to receive policy proceeds may pay such proceeds to a court and ask the court to decide the proper recipient. If the case involves conflicting claimants, the court will hold the policy proceeds and release the insurance company from the court proceedings, thus releasing the insurer from any further liability. The court then examines the evidence, determines who is entitled to the proceeds, and pays those proceeds to that claimant.

Similar procedures are available to insurance companies in Canada. In the common law jurisdictions, the insurance company's remedy in such a case is to pay the policy proceeds into court. The court then releases the insurer, examines the evidence, decides who is the proper recipient, and pays the proceeds to that claimant. Notice that this procedure, referred to as **payment into court,** is essentially the same procedure as interpleader. In Quebec, an insurance company may pay policy proceeds to the Minister of Finance when it is unable to decide between conflicting claimants. The Minister holds the proceeds until a court decides which claimant is entitled to them or until the interested parties agree among themselves who is to receive them. Payment to the Minister protects the insurer from further liability.

Determining the Amount of the Death Benefit

The next step the claim examiner takes is to calculate the amount of policy proceeds payable. For most individual life insurance policies, the claim examiner calculates the amount of proceeds payable upon the insured's death by adding together a number of items and deducting certain other items. The claim examiner first adds together the following items:

- The amount of the **basic death benefit** payable (In most cases, the basic death benefit is the policy's face amount. If the policy was in force under the reduced paid-up insurance nonforfeiture option when the insured died, then the amount of the basic death benefit payable is less than the face amount. In addition, the policy's face amount must be adjusted up or down if the insured's age or sex was misstated.)

- The amount of any **accidental death benefits** payable

- The amount of any **declared but unpaid policy dividends**

- The amount of any **accumulated policy dividends,** including interest, left on deposit with the insurer

- The face amount of any **paid-up additions**

- The amount of any **unearned premiums paid in advance** (Policyowners sometimes pay premiums before those premiums are due. A policyowner might, for example, pay two annual premiums when he purchases a policy. If the insured dies shortly before the second annual premium is payable, the insurer will usually refund the amount of the second year's premium because the insurer had not earned that premium.)

After totaling the amount of the foregoing items, the claim examiner must subtract the following items from that total.

- The amount of any **outstanding policy loans**

- The amount of any **premium due and unpaid** at the time of the insured's death (This item appears when the insured dies during the policy's grace period before the premium due has been paid.)

The result of this calculation is the total benefit amount payable. The insurer pays this total amount in a lump sum or according to the terms of a settlement option selected by the policyowner or beneficiary.

EXAMPLE When Jeff Nguyen died, he was insured under a $100,000 life insurance policy. At that time, $420 in accumulated policy dividends were on deposit with the insurer, and Jeff had an outstanding policy loan of $1,635.

ANALYSIS The total policy benefit that the insurer was liable to pay the policy beneficiary was $98,785. That amount was calculated as follows:

$100,000	Face amount of policy
+ 420	Plus: Accumulated policy dividends
− 1,635	Minus: Outstanding policy loan
$ 98,785	Amount insurer was liable to pay policy beneficiary

Payment of Policy Proceeds

The insurance company requires the recipient of life insurance policy proceeds to sign a written document, known as a *release,* in exchange for those proceeds. By signing this document, the claimant states that he has received full payment of his claim to the proceeds of a life insurance policy and that he releases—he gives up—any and all claims that he has or might have against the insurer as a result of that policy. When it obtains a valid release in exchange for life insurance policy proceeds, the insurance company is protected from having to pay the proceeds a second time to the same claimant.

In order for such a release to be valid and binding on the claimant, he must have the legal capacity required to provide the release. In general, all mentally competent adults have the required legal capacity. Claimants who are minors or who are not mentally competent generally cannot provide the insurance company with a valid release. As a result, if the insurer pays policy proceeds to such a person and does not obtain a valid release, the claimant might later have the right to demand payment of the proceeds a second time.

EXAMPLE At the time of his death, Marvin Wacht owned an insurance policy on his life. His wife, Lorraine, was the policy's primary beneficiary. Lorraine was seriously injured in the automobile accident that caused Marvin's death, and she remained unconscious for weeks. Two days after Marvin died, their son Ian notified the insurer of Marvin's death and claimed the policy proceeds on behalf of Lorraine.

ANALYSIS Although Lorraine is entitled to receive the policy proceeds, her current physical condition prevents her from being able to provide the insurer with a release in exchange for those proceeds. Unless Ian has some legal right to act on behalf of Lorraine—for example, he is her court-appointed guardian—Ian cannot provide the insurer with a valid release. If the insurer pays the proceeds and does not get a valid release, Lorraine may later recover from her injuries and demand that the insurer pay the proceeds to her. Without a valid release from Lorraine, the insurer would have to pay the proceeds a second time.

One way in which an insurance company can obtain a valid release when the beneficiary lacks the capacity to provide a release is to pay the policy proceeds to a person who has been appointed by the court as the guardian of the claimant. The court-appointed guardian has the authority to receive the policy proceeds on behalf of the claimant and to provide the insurance company with a valid release. But the procedure of having a court appoint a guardian for a claimant is an expense to the claimant, and the guardian may make decisions of which the insured would not have approved.

Some jurisdictions permit insurance companies to make limited payments for the benefit of a minor-beneficiary when these payments are made to an adult who appears to be entitled to receive these payments, such as a relative who is supporting the minor. Laws in some jurisdictions give minors who have attained a certain age the ability to give a valid release for policy proceeds or for a specified portion of those proceeds.

In some situations in which policy proceeds are payable to a minor, an insurance company may retain the policy proceeds at interest and make settlement of the proceeds and interest at a future date. This date may be either the date when the minor reaches the age of majority or the date the court appoints a guardian who can give the insurer a valid release for the proceeds.

Special Claim Situations

By following its routine claim procedures, an insurance company can establish the validity of most claims and ensure that it pays the proper amount to the correct party. Sometimes, however, the claim examiner must investigate a claim further. We have already described some special claim situations that arise if the policy contains an exclusion, such as a suicide exclusion provision. Claim examiners also pay special attention to death claims when the policy is contestable, the policy provides an accidental death benefit, the insured disappeared, or the beneficiary was responsible for the insured's death.

Policy Contests

You will recall from our discussion in Chapter 10 that if the application for life insurance contains a material misrepresentation, then the insurer has the right to avoid the insurance contract during its contestable period. Also, insurers in Canada have the right to avoid a life insurance contract at any time on the ground of fraud. If the policy's contestable period has not yet expired, the claim examiner will consider whether he has any reason to suspect that the application for the policy contains a material misrepresentation.

EXAMPLE Cherie Tanner's application for life insurance indicated that she was in good health. Six months after the policy was issued, Cherie died as the result of cancer.

ANALYSIS The policy's contestable period has not ended. Thus, the claim examiner will investigate further to determine whether Cherie had been treated for cancer before the policy was issued and failed to disclose that fact.

If the claim examiner can gather enough evidence to prove the charge of material misrepresentation in the application for insurance, the insurer will usually deny liability to pay the policy proceeds and will refund the premiums paid for the policy. Typically, the claim department will consult with the company's legal representatives before contesting a policy on the ground of material misrepresentation.

Accidental Death Benefit Claims

When an insurer receives a claim for a policy's basic death benefit and an accidental death benefit, the claim examiner will look into the cause of the insured's death in order to determine whether the death meets the policy's definition of "accidental." In order to determine the cause of an insured's death, the claim examiner may ask the claimant to provide additional proof of loss documents. Insurers sometimes request an Attending Physician's Statement (APS) from the physician who treated the insured prior to his death. Insurers also sometimes ask the claimant to provide an autopsy report. Insurers typically request these additional proof of loss documents only in cases in which (1) unusual circumstances surround the insured's death so that the claim examiner has reason to doubt the stated cause of death, (2) the policy provides additional benefits such as an accidental death benefit, or (3) the insured dies during the policy's contestable period.

If an insurer determines that the insured's death was not accidental as defined in the policy, then it will pay the policy's basic death benefit but will deny the claim for accidental death benefits. (In Chapter 9, we described accidental death benefits and the types of exclusions that typically apply.)

EXAMPLE Hilda Fallon was insured under a $100,000 life insurance policy that contained a typical accidental death benefit rider. Hilda died as a result of suicide five years after the policy was issued.

ANALYSIS When Hilda died, the policy's suicide exclusion period had expired. Thus, the insurer was liable to pay the policy's $100,000 death benefit to the named beneficiary. However, Hilda's death from suicide was not accidental, and, thus, the insurer was not liable to pay the policy's accidental death benefit.

Disappearance of the Insured

Sometimes a beneficiary files a claim for life insurance policy proceeds following the disappearance of the insured. In such situations, the claimant cannot provide the insurer with a death certificate or other document that proves the insured is dead. Without sufficient proof of an insured's death, the insurer cannot pay the policy proceeds. The claimant in such a case has the right to ask a court to declare the insured dead. If the insured disappeared under circumstances that make it likely he is dead, a court may be willing to find that the insured is dead. If, however, the insured disappeared without explanation, courts typically will find that the insured is dead or presumed dead only if (1) the insured has been missing for a specified time, typically seven years, (2) a diligent but unsuccessful search for the insured has taken place, and (3) no one has had any communication with the insured since his disappearance.

Upon receiving a court order stating that the insured is dead or is presumed dead, the insurer can pay the policy proceeds to the proper beneficiary if the policy was in force on the date of the insured's presumed death. As a result, when an insured disappears, the policyowner, beneficiary, or other interested party must continue to pay the policy's renewal premiums as they come due until the court issues an order that the insured is dead or presumed dead. The court sometimes states in its order the date on which the insured is deemed to have died. If the court establishes such a date, then the insurer will refund all premiums paid after that date. Often, however, the court order does not state the date of the insured's death; in those cases, the insured is deemed to have died on the date of the court order. If the policy lapsed for nonpayment of premium before the court order, the insurer will have no liability to pay the policy proceeds.

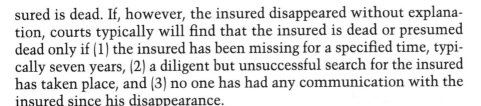

FAST FACT

Canadian insurers paid more than $2 billion in life insurance policy death benefits during 1997.[2]

Beneficiary Wrongfully Kills the Insured

Another special situation that the claim examiner occasionally faces occurs when the person who claims the proceeds of a life insurance policy is responsible for the death of the insured. Permitting someone to profit from wrongful acts is not in the public interest. As a result, laws throughout the United States and Canada disqualify the beneficiary from receiving the policy proceeds if the beneficiary wrongfully killed the insured.

Laws vary somewhat from jurisdiction to jurisdiction as to what constitutes a wrongful killing that would disqualify a beneficiary. Throughout Canada and the United States, a beneficiary who is convicted in a criminal court proceeding of intentionally killing the insured is disqualified from receiving life insurance policy proceeds. In many states and throughout Canada, a beneficiary who is convicted of a lesser offense—such as manslaughter—is also disqualified from receiving policy proceeds. Laws in Quebec are even more stringent; a beneficiary who attempts to kill the insured—even if that attempt is unsuccessful—is prohibited from receiving life insurance policy proceeds. In other words, in Quebec when a beneficiary attempts to kill the insured, the beneficiary designation is revoked; even if the beneficiary designation is not changed, the beneficiary may never collect the policy proceeds.

The fact that a beneficiary is not charged with a crime or is not convicted in a criminal proceeding of wrongfully killing the insured does not mean that the beneficiary is automatically entitled to receive the policy proceeds. Both criminal and civil court proceedings may result from a given occurrence, and these proceedings are totally separate from each other. Without regard to the outcome of a criminal court proceeding, a civil court can determine that the beneficiary wrongfully killed the insured and is disqualified from receiving the policy proceeds. Typically, a civil court proceeding in this type of case is begun by the beneficiary following the insurance company's determination that the beneficiary is disqualified because she wrongfully killed the insured. Remember that an insurer has a fiduciary obligation to pay only valid claims. If the insurer determines that a beneficiary wrongfully killed the insured, it has a duty to all of its policyowners and beneficiaries to deny the claim.

In most cases in which a beneficiary is disqualified from receiving policy proceeds, the life insurance contract is valid and the insurer is liable to pay the policy proceeds to someone, such as the contingent beneficiary. If, however, it is proven that the policy was purchased with the intention to profit from the insured's death, then the life insurance contract is void because the lawful purpose requirement was not met when the contract was created. In addition, the laws in Quebec state that the life insurance contract is void if the policyowner attempted—even if unsuccessfully—to kill the insured.

Key Terms

claim examiner	interpleader
fraudulent claim	payment into court
mistaken claim	release
common disaster clause	

Other Important Terms

claimant	claim specialist
claim approver	common disaster
claim analyst	time clause

Endnotes

1. ACLI, *1998 Life Insurance Fact Book* (Washington, D.C.: American Council of Life Insurance, 1998), 76.

2 Ibid., 127.

PART 2

Group Life Insurance, Annuities, and Health Insurance

CHAPTER 14

Principles of Group Insurance

After reading this chapter, you should be able to

- Identify the parties to a group insurance contract

- Contrast group underwriting with individual underwriting and identify the most important group underwriting considerations

- Distinguish between contributory and noncontributory group insurance plans

- Describe the operation of the probationary period and the actively-at-work requirement

- Identify situations in which a group member's coverage terminates while the group policy remains in force

- Distinguish among manual rating, experience rating, and blended rating

- Contrast insurer-administered plans with self-administered plans

Since the first modern group insurance plans were established early in the 20th century, group insurance coverage has grown rapidly. Currently, approximately 40 percent of the life insurance in force in the United States and about 50 percent of the life insurance in force in Canada is provided through group insurance.[1]

In this chapter we concentrate on those aspects of group insurance that are common to both group life and group health insurance. We begin by describing the group insurance contract. Then we describe group life and health insurance underwriting. We also describe some of the provisions that are found in group insurance policies, the process insurance companies use to set group premium rates, and the manner in which group insurance policies are administered. We describe specific group insurance products in later chapters.

Group Insurance Contracts

Although individual insurance and group insurance are similar in many ways, these insurance products also differ in many ways. The most obvious difference is that, rather than insuring one person or one family, a group insurance plan insures a number of people under a single insurance contract, called a *master group insurance contract.*

The parties to a master group insurance contract are the insurance company and the *group policyholder,* which is the person or organization that decides what types of group insurance coverage to purchase for the group members, negotiates the terms of the group insurance contract with the insurer, and purchases the group insurance coverage. Note that we have used the term *policyholder,* rather than the term *policyowner,* to refer to the party that enters into a group insurance contract. The term *policyholder* is used because the group policyholder does not have the same ownership rights in the group insurance policy that a policyowner has in an individual life insurance policy. Instead, some of these rights are granted to the insured group members. For example, each group member insured under a group life insurance policy has the right to name the beneficiary who will receive the benefit payable upon that group member's death. By contrast, an individual life insurance policy grants that right to the policyowner, rather than to the insured.

When an insurance company and a group policyholder enter into a master group insurance contract, the insurer issues a policy that contains the terms of the contractual agreement. An important part of every group insurance policy is a description of the individuals who are covered by the policy. In the United States, the individuals covered by a group insurance policy are referred to as the ***group insureds,*** and we will use that term in this text. In Canada, an individual insured under a group life insurance policy is referred to as a *group life insured;* an individual insured under a group health insurance policy is known as a *group person insured.*

The policyholder is usually responsible for handling some of the administrative aspects of the group insurance plan. For example, the policyholder typically is responsible for enrolling new group members in the plan. The group policyholder also is responsible for making all premium payments to the insurer, although the policy may require that the insured group members contribute some or all of that premium amount. If insured group members are not required to contribute any part of the premium for the coverage, then the group insurance plan is a ***noncontributory plan.*** If the group members must contribute some or all of the premium in order to be covered under the group insurance policy, then the plan is a ***contributory plan.*** A contributory group insurance policy issued to an employer to cover employees typically requires the covered employees to pay their portion of the premium through payroll deduction.

Formation of the Contract

As we described in Chapter 5, an insurance contract is an informal contract that must be formed in accordance with the rules of contract law. Thus, in order to form a valid group insurance contract, the policyholder and the insurer must meet the following requirements:

- Mutually agree to the contract's terms

- Both have contractual capacity

- Exchange legally adequate consideration

- Form the contract for a lawful purpose

The parties to a group insurance contract meet the first three of these requirements in much the same manner as do the parties to an individual insurance contract. However, the last requirement—the lawful purpose requirement—is met somewhat differently. As you will recall, the lawful purpose requirement is met for an individual insurance contract by the presence of insurable interest. Insurance laws throughout the United States and Canada exclude group life and health insurance contracts from the insurable interest requirement because the group policyholder's interest in the contract does not induce wagering contracts as does an insured's interest in an individual insurance contract. By contrast, the lawful purpose requirement is met for a group insurance contract because the policyholder enters into the contract in order to provide a benefit to covered group members.

Certificates of Insurance

Insured group members are not parties to the master group insurance contract, do not participate in the formation of the contract, and do not receive individual copies of the contract. However, insured group members have certain rights under the contract. Insurance laws throughout Canada and the United States require the insurer to provide the group policyholder with written descriptions of the group insurance plan; the group policyholder then delivers a written description to each group insured. This document, known as the **certificate of insurance,** describes (1) the coverage the group insurance contract provides and (2) the group insured's rights under the contract. As a result, an insured group member is often referred to as a **certificate holder.** Many policyholders describe the group insurance coverage in a special benefit booklet. In such a situation, the benefit booklet contains the information that would be included in a certificate, and the benefit booklet serves as the group insurance certificate.

Group Insurance Underwriting

One of the areas in which group insurance differs significantly from individual insurance is in the area of underwriting. Individual life and health insurance underwriting requires the proposed insured *individual* to meet the insurer's underwriting requirements. In contrast, group insurance underwriting generally focuses on the characteristics of the *group* and does not usually require each proposed group insured to provide individual evidence of insurability. Nevertheless, the goal of group underwriting is the same as the goal of individual underwriting—to determine whether a group of people presents an average risk and whether the group's loss experience will be predictable and acceptable to the insurer. When evaluating a group, the group underwriter also seeks to prevent antiselection and to ensure that the administrative costs involved in providing the insurance are as low as possible. Finally, the group underwriter must assign the group a risk classification and determine the appropriate premium rates to charge for the group insurance.

Group Underwriting Considerations

Each group insurance company establishes its own underwriting guidelines that define the types of group insurance coverage it will provide and the types of groups it will insure. In every case, however, the group underwriter considers specific characteristics of a group when evaluating whether the group is an acceptable risk. These risk characteristics include the reason for the group's existence, the size of the group, the flow of new members into the group, the stability of the group, the required percentage of eligible group members who must participate in the plan, the way in which benefit levels will be determined, and the activities of the group. We describe each of these risk characteristics to give you an overview of the types of characteristics that the group underwriter must consider. You should note, however, that in any given situation, the group underwriter may need to consider a variety of other characteristics of the group.

Reason for the Group's Existence

Group underwriting guidelines usually require that in order for a group to be eligible for coverage, the group must have been formed for a reason other than to obtain insurance. The likelihood of antiselection in a group formed solely to obtain group insurance coverage would be very great because people who think they would not qualify for individual insurance would be more likely to join such a group than would individuals who can obtain individual insurance.

In addition, insurance laws in the United States specify the types of groups to which a group life or health insurance policy may be issued. By contrast, insurance laws in Canada do not specify the types of groups that are eligible for group insurance. Nevertheless, insurance companies in Canada typically issue group insurance to the same types of groups that are eligible for group insurance in the United States. The groups that are eligible for coverage usually can be placed into one of the following categories: single-employer groups, labor union groups, multiple-employer groups, association groups, debtor-creditor groups, credit union groups, and discretionary groups.

Single-Employer Groups. Most group insurance policies insure the employees of a single employer. The policyholder of a single-employer group insurance contract is either the employer or the trustees of a trust fund created by the employer, and the employees are the insured group members. A *trust* is a fiduciary relationship in which one or more persons, known as the **trustees,** hold legal title to property—known as the **trust fund**—for the benefit of another person, known as the **trust beneficiary.** A *fiduciary* is a person who holds a position of special trust. Thus, when a group insurance contract is issued to the trustees of a trust, the trustees own the policy and have a fiduciary obligation to carry out the terms of the policy for the benefit of the group insureds. Because most group insurance policies insure a group of employees, our discussions of group insurance in this text will concentrate on employer-employee group insurance policies. We will sometimes refer to the group policyholder as the employer and to the group insureds as the employees.

Labor Union Groups. A group insurance contract may be issued to a labor union to insure members of the labor union. The federal *Taft-Hartley Act* in the United States prohibits employers from making premium contributions on behalf of employees who belong to a labor union covered by a group insurance contract *unless* the contract is issued to a trust established for the purpose of purchasing insurance for union members. As a result of the Taft-Hartley Act, policies insuring labor union groups in the United States usually are issued to the trustees of a trust fund, and labor union groups are often referred to as *Taft-Hartley trusts.* Labor union groups also are sometimes referred to as *negotiated trusteeships* because they are created by an agreement negotiated between one or more labor unions and the employers of union members.

Multiple-Employer Groups. A group insurance contract insuring the employees of more than one employer may be issued to a trust that is created by (1) two or more employers in the same industry, (2) two or more labor unions, or (3) one or more employers *and* one or more labor unions.

Association Groups. These groups consist of the members of an association of employers or individuals formed for a purpose other than to obtain insurance. The group policyholder is either the association or the trustees of a trust fund established for the benefit of members of one or more associations. Figure 14-1 describes some of the types of association groups that are eligible for group insurance coverage.

Debtor-Creditor Groups. These groups consist primarily of persons who have borrowed funds from a lending institution, such as a bank. The creditor is the group policyholder. Both life insurance and disability income coverages are issued to this type of group. Life insurance coverage issued to debtor-creditor groups is usually called *group creditor life insurance* or *creditor group insurance.* (This and other group life coverages are discussed in the next chapter.)

> **FAST FACT**
>
> In 1997, employee groups had 60% of the group life insurance in force in Canada. Union and association groups had 8% of the group life insurance in force. The remaining 32% insured individuals who had borrowed from credit agencies or had entered into special savings plans.[3]

FIGURE **14-1.** Types of Association Groups.

Trade Association

An association of firms that operate in a specific industry.

Association of Individuals

An association of individuals who share a common bond other than the common purpose of obtaining insurance. The following types of associations of individuals are typically eligible for group life and health insurance:

- **Professional Association.** An association of individuals who share a common occupation, such as an association of medical doctors, attorneys, or engineers.

- **Public Employee Association.** An association of individuals employed by a state, county, or city government or by a state or local school board.

- **Common Interest Association.** An association of individuals who share a common state or a common interest. Examples include associations of retired persons, participants in a specific sport, or alumni of a specific college.

Credit Union Groups. A credit union group consists of the members of one or more credit unions. The group policy usually is issued to the credit union or to the trustees of a trust fund created by one or more credit unions.

Discretionary Groups. Insurance laws in many states give the state insurance department the authority to approve the issuance of a group insurance contract covering the members of any other type of group if specified conditions are met. Such a group that does not fit within one of the previously defined categories and that the state insurance department approves for group insurance coverage is known as a *discretionary group.* In evaluating whether to approve such a group, state insurance regulators consider factors such as whether issuing the policy is in the best interest of the public and whether the policy benefits are reasonable in relation to the premiums that will be charged for the coverage.

Underwriting guidelines vary somewhat for each of the preceding types of groups. For example, group underwriting guidelines typically require the employer in an employer-employee group insurance plan to pay at least a portion of the group insurance premium. This requirement, which is imposed by law in most states in the United States, gives the employer a financial interest in the operation of the plan. By contrast, other group policyholders usually are not required to pay a portion of the group insurance premium.

Some underwriting guidelines are more stringent for some types of groups than for other types of groups. For example, antiselection by individual group members is much more likely to occur in groups such as association groups than in employer-employee groups. As a result, insurance companies often impose more stringent underwriting requirements on association groups than on employer-employee groups. An insurer might be willing to issue an employer-employee group insurance policy to a group with as few as 10 members, but it might refuse to issue an association group policy that covered fewer than 50 association members.

Size of the Group

Recall that one of the underwriter's goals is to predict the loss rate that the group will experience. The size of the group has a strong impact on the underwriter's ability to predict the group's probable loss rate. In general, the larger the group, the more likely that the group will experience a loss rate that approximates the predicted loss rate. When group insurance plans were first introduced, only groups with at least 50 members were eligible for coverage. This requirement enabled the group underwriting process to function successfully and, consequently, to enable insurers to issue coverage without requiring evidence of insurability from the group's members.

Minimum size requirements prevented many small groups from obtaining group insurance coverage. Over the years, insurers began relaxing the requirements; currently, a substantial number of the group life insurance policies in force cover groups with fewer than 10 members, though such small groups account for only a small percentage of the total amount of group life insurance in force in the United States.

As group size requirements were relaxed, underwriters also needed to modify the group underwriting process because that process functions best only when applied to large groups. The extent of modification needed depends on the group's size. For very small groups, such as groups with fewer than 15 members, group underwriting guidelines often require each individual member of the group to submit satisfactory evidence of insurability. When calculating the anticipated loss rate of a slightly larger group, such as a group with between 15 and 50 members, the underwriter often pools several groups that are of the same approximate size and are in the same business sector. By considering the expected experience of a number of small groups, the underwriter can expect the experience of those small groups taken as a whole to approximate the experience of a single large group.

Although such modifications in the group underwriting process have enabled insurers to issue coverage to all group sizes, not all insurers participate in the small group market. Many insurers establish their own minimum group size requirements and do not offer insurance to groups with fewer than the required minimum number of members.

> **FAST FACT**
>
> Canadian insurers administered more than 114,000 group life insurance policies covering 24 million insureds at the end of 1997.[4]

Flow of New Members Into the Group

Another important group underwriting requirement is that a sufficient number of new members must enter the group periodically. Young, new members are needed (1) to replace those who leave the group and, consequently, to keep the group size stable and (2) to keep the age distribution of the group stable. If a group did not add young, new members for a number of years, then the increasing age of the group's original members would adversely affect the group's age distribution, and, hence, the group's loss rate and premium rate would increase. But if young, new members are continually joining the group, the age distribution of the group should remain more stable, as should the expected loss rate. Of course, the term *young* is relative; to a group composed entirely of retired people, a new group member who is 65 would be considered young and would help keep the group's age distribution stable.

Stability of the Group

Despite the generally favorable results of changes in group membership, the insurance company must also be able to expect that the group will remain a group for a reasonable length of time and that the composition of the group will remain relatively stable. Otherwise, the costs of administering the plan would become prohibitively high. Therefore, underwriters avoid issuing coverage to groups that anticipate experiencing excessive changes in group membership. For example, a group of seasonal or temporary workers generally would not be considered an insurable group.

Participation Levels

Group insurance underwriting requirements—and insurance laws in many states—impose requirements as to the minimum percentage of eligible group members who must be covered by a group insurance plan in order for the insurance company to provide the coverage. Note that these requirements relate to participation by *eligible group members*. Each group insurance policy defines which group members are eligible for coverage. We describe these eligibility requirements later in the chapter.

Minimum participation requirements are designed to guard against the effects of antiselection and to avoid discrimination. The specific participation requirement that is imposed usually depends on whether the group insurance plan is a noncontributory plan or a contributory plan.

The laws of most states require that a noncontributory plan cover all eligible employees—to do otherwise would be discriminatory.

Therefore, 100 percent participation is required in noncontributory plans. The provincial insurance laws in Canada do not impose minimum participation requirements on group insurance policies. Nevertheless, group insurance companies in Canada typically require 100 percent participation in noncontributory plans.

By contrast, 100 percent participation is not required in contributory plans. An employer may not require employees to participate in a contributory group insurance plan, and some group members will probably decide not to enroll in the plan. In order to minimize antiselection, however, most insurers and the laws of some states require that at least 75 percent of the eligible employees in a contributory group insurance plan participate in the plan. A higher percentage of employees may participate in the plan, but a percentage of participation lower than 75 percent will cause the group to lose its eligibility for coverage. Without this requirement, the insurance company could not rely on the group underwriting process because an unusually large percentage of group members might be individuals who were uninsurable on an individual basis.

Determination of Benefit Levels

The group policyholder typically works with the insurer to establish a fair and nondiscriminatory method to determine the benefit levels provided to the group insureds. This method of determining benefit levels is then incorporated into the master group insurance contract. Thus, the group insureds do not select their coverage amounts individually. This step is necessary to avoid antiselection. Otherwise, those group members who are in poor health and unable to secure individual insurance would probably select larger benefit amounts than healthy members would select.

Some group policies allow covered group members to select additional coverage from a schedule of optional coverages. In most such situations, the group insurer minimizes the effects of antiselection by (1) limiting the optional coverages that the group plan can offer and (2) retaining the right to reject an insured group member's election of the optional coverage if the benefit levels of such optional coverages are high and the insured group member cannot provide satisfactory evidence of insurability.

Activities of the Group

A group is assigned a risk classification—standard, substandard, or declined—based on the group's normal activities. If the group's activities are not expected to contribute to a greater-than-average loss rate among its members, then the group is classified as a standard risk. Most employer-employee and association groups qualify as standard risks.

If a group's activities are expected to lead to a higher-than-average loss rate among its members, then the group is classified as a substandard risk and is charged a higher premium rate than is a group classified as a standard risk. For example, a group consisting of coal miners may be classified as a substandard risk because of the hazards involved in mining.

If the group's normal activities are extremely dangerous, some insurance companies will decline the group for coverage. For example, many insurers would decline to issue group life insurance coverage to a group consisting entirely of race car drivers.

The extent to which a group's activities affect that group's risk classification depends on the type of coverage provided by the group insurance policy. Activities that significantly affect a group's *morbidity* risk often have little effect on the group's *mortality* risk. Consequently, a group that is assigned a substandard health insurance rating might be assigned a standard rating for a group life insurance policy.

Group Insurance Policy Provisions

Certain provisions are included in every group insurance policy, whether it provides life or health insurance coverage. These standard policy provisions define which group members are eligible for group insurance coverage, identify the policy's grace period, establish when the policy and a group member's coverage become incontestable, and govern when the group insurance policy terminates and when a group insured's coverage terminates.

Eligibility Requirements

As we noted earlier in the chapter, each group policy describes who is eligible for coverage under the policy. Group insurance policies are permitted by law to define eligible employees as those employees in a specified class or those in specified classes. These classes must be defined by requirements that are related to conditions of employment, such as salary, occupation, or length of employment. For example, most group insurance policies state that an employee must work full-time in order to be eligible for coverage; thus, part-time workers are excluded from the class of eligible employees.

Some group insurance policies provide coverage both for group members and for the dependents of covered group members. Group insureds who are covered as dependents typically do not have the same rights as do group insureds who are covered as employees. For example, a covered dependent typically does not have the right to name the beneficiary of his coverage; instead, the policy usually specifies that the beneficiary of any dependent group life coverage is the group member. Further, if dependent coverage is optional, then the eligible group members—not their dependents—have the right to elect or reject that coverage.

Provisions in many group insurance policies contain requirements that new group members must meet in order to be eligible for coverage. The most common of these eligibility provisions are the actively-at-work provision and the probationary period. An ***actively-at-work provision*** requires that in order to be eligible for coverage, an employee must be actively at work—rather than ill or on leave—on the day the insurance coverage is to take effect. If the employee is not actively at work on the day the coverage is to take effect, then the employee is not covered by the group insurance policy until she returns to work.

A ***probationary period*** is the length of time—typically, from one to six months—that a new group member must wait before becoming eligible to enroll in the group insurance plan. A probationary period requirement can reduce a plan's administrative costs when new employees work for only a short period before terminating their employment. Under a noncontributory group insurance plan, a new employee who has met all other eligibility requirements is automatically covered at the end of the probationary period. By contrast, if the plan is contributory, then the probationary period is typically followed by an eligibility period. The ***eligibility period,*** which is also called the *enrollment period,* usually extends for 31 days and is the time during which a new group member may first enroll for group insurance coverage. As part of the enrollment process, the employee must sign a written authorization allowing the employer to make payroll deductions from her salary to cover the amount of her premium contributions; contributory group insurance coverage will not become effective until the employee completes such an authorization. An employee who declines coverage when she first becomes eligible for that coverage or who drops out of the plan ordinarily must submit satisfactory evidence of insurability in order to be allowed to join the plan at a later date.

EXAMPLE Felipe and Conchita Romero recently relocated to a different city and will soon begin working at new jobs. They both will be eligible for coverage under group life insurance policies provided by their employers. Both policies provide similar coverage, and both include a 30-day probationary period. The primary difference is that Felipe's coverage is noncontributory, whereas Conchita's coverage is contributory. They want to determine when their group insurance coverages will become effective.

ANALYSIS | Felipe's noncontributory coverage will automatically become effective on the first day following the end of the 30-day probationary period. Because Conchita's coverage is contributory, her 30-day probationary period will be followed by an eligibility period. At any time during the eligibility period, she may enroll for the coverage and sign a written authorization allowing her employer to deduct her group insurance premium contributions from her salary. Thus, once the 30-day probationary period is over, Conchita's coverage will become effective as soon as she signs the authorization within the eligibility period.

Grace Period Provision

Group life and health insurance policies typically contain a 31-day grace period provision. As in the case of an individual insurance policy, the insurance coverage provided by a group insurance policy remains in force during the grace period. If the group policyholder does not pay the premium by the end of this period, the group policy will terminate. Unlike the grace period provision in an individual insurance policy, the grace period provision in a group insurance policy specifies that if the policy terminates for nonpayment of premiums, then the group policyholder is legally obligated to pay the premium for the coverage provided during the grace period.

Incontestability Provision

State and provincial insurance laws require group insurance policies—like individual insurance policies—to include an incontestability provision that limits the period during which an insurance company may use statements in the group insurance application to contest the validity of the master group insurance contract. Generally, the incontestability provision in a group insurance policy limits the period during which the insurer may contest the contract to two years from the date of issue. With one exception, this two-year contestable period is the maximum period permitted by law in the United States and Canada. The exception is that in Canada an insurer may contest a group insurance contract at any time if the application contained a fraudulent misrepresentation. Material misrepresentation occurs much less frequently in group insurance applications than in individual insurance applications. As a result, insurance companies rarely contest the validity of group insurance contracts.

The incontestability provision also allows an insurance company to contest an individual group member's coverage without contesting the validity of the master group contract itself. Individuals insured under a group insurance policy usually are not required to provide evidence of insurability in order to be eligible for group coverage. Sometimes, however, group insureds are required to provide such evidence. If a group insured makes material misrepresentations about his insurability in a written application, then the incontestable clause allows the insurer to contest the group insured's coverage on the ground of material misrepresentation in the application. The period during which the insurer has the right to contest the validity of a group insured's coverage is usually one or two years after the date of that group insured's application.

EXAMPLE Joey Matsuoko was required to fill out a medical questionnaire in order to be eligible for group medical expense coverage. In completing the questionnaire, Joey made material misrepresentations about his health. Eleven months later, Joey filed a claim for medical expense benefits. While investigating the claim, the insurance company discovered Joey's material misrepresentations. The group policy contained a two-year contestable period.

ANALYSIS The insurer discovered the material misrepresentations within two years after Joey's coverage became effective. As a result, the insurer had the right to contest the validity of Joey's coverage on the basis of those material misrepresentations. The validity of the master group insurance contract was not affected by Joey's material misrepresentations.

Termination Provisions

As we have described, the coverage an individual insurance policy provides is effective as long as the individual insurance policy is in force; coverage terminates when the individual policy terminates. Similarly, under many types of group insurance contracts, a group member's coverage terminates when the master group policy terminates. However, a group insured's coverage also may terminate even though the group insurance policy remains in effect. The following sections describe group insurance policy provisions that govern (1) when the group insurance policy will terminate and (2) when a group insured's coverage will terminate.

Termination of the Group Insurance Policy

According to the terms of most group insurance policies, the group policyholder may terminate the policy at any time by notifying the insurer in writing that it has decided to terminate the policy. For example, if the group policyholder is able to obtain comparable coverage from another insurance company at a lower premium, then the policyholder is likely to switch carriers rather than renew the more expensive policy.

If certain conditions are met, the insurance company also has the right to terminate the group insurance policy on any premium due date. The terms of the policy state the conditions that must be met in order for the insurer to terminate the policy. You will recall, for example, that group insurers often establish participation requirements; if the group's participation level falls below the required minimum, the insurance company has the right to terminate the policy. To terminate the policy, the insurer must provide the group policyholder with advance written notification that the policy will terminate on a specified renewal premium due date.

Termination of a Group Insured's Coverage

Group insurance policies contain provisions that describe when a group insured's coverage terminates. Most group insurance policies provide that a group insured's coverage will terminate if the group insured (1) ceases to be a member of a class of persons eligible for coverage, (2) terminates her employment or group membership, or (3) fails to make a required contribution to the premium. As we describe in later chapters, group life insurance policies contain a provision that gives certain group insureds whose coverage terminates the right to convert their group coverage to individual coverage; group medical expense insurance policies in the United States give a group insured the right to continue group coverage for a stated period of time.

Group Insurance Premiums

We have noted that the group policyholder is responsible for paying the premiums to the insurance company, though group members must contribute to that premium payment if the group insurance plan is a contributory plan. In the following sections, we discuss how the insurer establishes the premium rates to charge for a group's coverage, how specific premium amounts are calculated, and how excess premiums can be refunded.

Premium Rates

Insurance companies typically establish group insurance premium rates on a case-by-case basis; that is, an insurer evaluates each group and establishes a premium rate that will be adequate to pay the group's claims and will be equitable to the policyholder. In order to establish premium rates that meet these criteria, the insurer must determine what costs it will incur in (1) providing the benefits promised by the group insurance policy and (2) administering the group insurance plan. An insurer can estimate these costs for a specific group insurance policy by using manual rating, experience rating, or a blend of manual and experience rating.

Unlike individual insurance premium rates, the premium rate for a group insurance policy usually is recalculated every year that the policy remains in force. The insurer generally guarantees the group's premium rate for only one year and may change the premium rate at the beginning of each policy year or on any premium due date; it may not, however, change the premium rate more than once in any 12-month period. Next, we will describe how insurers use manual rating, experience rating, and blended rating to establish the initial premium rate to charge a group and to calculate in succeeding years the renewal premium rates that the group will be charged.

Manual Rating

Manual rating is a method insurers use to calculate group insurance premium rates without considering the particular group's prior claims and expense experience. Rather, the insurance company uses its own past experience—and sometimes the experience of other insurers—to estimate the group's expected claims and expense experience.

Insurance companies typically use manual rating to set the initial premium rates to charge groups that have not previously been insured and to set both initial premium rates and renewal premium rates for small groups. In both cases, the groups have no prior claims or expense experience on which the insurer can rely to set the premium rate. The claims experience of a small group is generally unreliable because the group is not large enough for the insurer to determine whether its prior experience is a result of chance or actually reflects the group's average experience.

Experience Rating

Experience rating is a method of setting group insurance premium rates under which the insurer considers the particular group's prior claims and expense experience. Group insurance companies typically use experience rating to set renewal premium rates for large groups. In many cases, insurers also use experience rating to set the initial premium rate to charge a large group that is currently insured by another insurance company. In such a case, the insurer is able to obtain information about the group's prior experience.

Blended Rating

Some groups are too small for an insurer to rely fully on experience rating, yet they are large enough for the insurer to consider their claims and expense experience to be significant. In such situations, the insurer will use **blended rating**—a method that uses a combination of experience rating and manual rating to set the group's premium rate. The larger the group is, the more credibility the insurer will assign to the group's own experience and the less the insurer will rely on manual rating.

Additional Premium Rate Considerations

Setting a group's premium rate is often a complicated process. In addition to determining whether or to what extent a group's own experience can be used, an insurer must also consider a number of other factors when setting premium rates. For example, the insurer must consider the benefits provided by the group plan. In addition, the amount of administrative expense an insurer incurs in connection with group insurance coverage varies widely from one group to another and depends, to a great extent, on how much of the plan's administration the policyholder will handle. We discuss group insurance administration later in this chapter. For now, keep in mind that many factors enter into an insurer's premium rate calculations. In later chapters, as we describe the benefits provided by group life and health insurance policies, we note how specific coverage factors affect a group's premium rate.

Premium Amounts

Group insurance premiums are typically payable monthly. As we have described, the insurance company establishes the premium rate for a group insurance policy at the beginning of each policy year. That premium rate is typically calculated on the basis of a stated benefit unit. For example, the premium rate for group life insurance is usually based on a benefit unit of $1,000. In other words, the premium rate is stated as a rate per $1,000 of death benefit provided by the group life insurance policy.

Although the *premium rate* is generally guaranteed for one year, the *premium amount* payable each month varies, depending on the amount of insurance in force that month. A group life insurance policy, for example, requires a monthly premium amount that is equal to the premium rate per $1,000 of coverage multiplied by the number of benefit units ($1,000 of coverage) in force that month. Thus, if an employer hires several new employees one month, the premium amount the employer pays to the insurer will increase; the premium rate per $1,000 of coverage, though, does not change during the year.

EXAMPLE The Weaver Company provides $25,000 of noncontributory group life insurance coverage for each of its full-time employees. The current monthly premium rate for this coverage is $0.35 per $1,000 of coverage. In January, Weaver had 10 full-time employees. In March, Weaver hired two new full-time employees, who became eligible for group life insurance coverage in April. Calculate the premium amounts payable each month from January through April.

ANALYSIS In January, February, and March, Weaver provided $25,000 of group life insurance coverage to 10 employees. Thus, the premium amount payable in each of those 3 months was $87.50.

$ 25,000	Coverage per employee
× 10	Times: Number of employees
$250,000	Equals: Total group coverage
$ 0.35	Monthly premium rate
× 250	Times: Number of coverage units ($250,000 ÷ $1,000)
$ 87.50	Equals: Monthly premium payments

In April, Weaver provided $25,000 of group life insurance coverage to 12 employees. Thus, the premium amount payable in April was $105.

$ 25,000	Coverage per employee
× 12	Times: Number of employees
$300,000	Equals: Total group coverage
$ 0.35	Monthly premium rate
× 300	Times: Number of coverage units ($300,000 ÷ $1,000)
$ 105	Equals: Monthly premium payment

Premium Refunds

At the end of each policy year, a portion of the group insurance premium may be refunded to the group policyholder. Group insurance premium refunds are similar to the policy dividends provided for participating individual life insurance policies and are usually called *dividends* by those companies that also issue individual participating policies. Companies that do not issue participating policies generally call these premium refunds *experience refunds.*

The insurer determines the amount of a premium refund on the basis of its evaluation of the group's claim and expense experience. If the group is large enough, the evaluation is based on that group's experience alone. If the group is small, the evaluation is based on a blend of the experiences of that group and of similar small groups. If the group incurred fewer claims or if the insurer incurred lower administrative expenses than anticipated when the insurer established the group's premium rate, then the insurer will refund a portion of the premium paid for the coverage.

All premium refunds are payable to the group policyholder, even if the plan is contributory. If the amount of the refund to the policyholder of a contributory plan is greater than the portion of the group premium that was paid out of the policyholder's funds, then the excess must be used for the benefit of the individual participants in the plan. For example, when an employer receives a premium refund that is larger than the amount the employer paid out of its own funds, the employer may apply the excess refund to pay a portion of the employees' contributions during the next year or to pay for additional benefits for covered employees.

Group Plan Administration

Another distinguishing characteristic of group insurance is that a number of people can be insured at a cost that is relatively low compared to the cost of individual insurance. Insurers are able to provide relatively low-cost group coverage because of the expense savings inherent in the operation of group insurance policies. These savings result from the fact that the expenses an insurer incurs in administering a group insurance policy are much lower than those incurred in administering individual policies. Of course, the cost of administering one group insurance policy is usually higher than the cost of administering one individual policy; but, the cost of administering one group insurance policy covering 50 people is lower than the cost of administering 50 individual policies. For example, underwriting and policy issue costs are generally lower for group insurance because the insurer usually underwrites the group as a whole rather than each individual member, and it issues a master policy rather than many individual policies. In addition, sales costs are much lower for one group policy than for a number of individual policies. Expenses are also lower because the group policyholder often handles many of the clerical duties that the insurer must perform for each individual policy.

The administration of a group insurance plan is primarily a matter of record keeping. For example, some of the necessary records for a group life insurance plan include the name of each plan participant, the amount of insurance on each participant, and the name of each beneficiary. If the insurance company maintains these records, the plan is an **insurer-administered plan.** If the group policyholder keeps the records, the plan is a **self-administered plan.** In either case, the insurer receives monthly reports regarding the composition of the group and any changes in the group.

Key Terms

master group insurance contract
group policyholder
group insureds
noncontributory plan
contributory plan
certificate of insurance
certificate holder
trust
trustee
trust fund
trust beneficiary

fiduciary
discretionary group
actively-at-work provision
probationary period
eligibility period
manual rating
experience rating
blended rating
insurer-administered plan
self-administered plan

Other Important Terms

group life insured
group person insured
single-employer groups
labor union groups
Taft-Hartley Act
Taft-Hartley trusts
negotiated trusteeships
multiple-employer groups
association groups

debtor-creditor groups
group creditor life insurance
creditor group insurance
credit union groups
eligible group members
enrollment period
dividends
experience refunds

Endnotes

1. ACLI, *1998 Life Insurance Fact Book* (Washington, D.C.: American Council of Life Insurance, 1998), 18, 126.

2. Ibid., 18.

3. CLHIA, *Canadian Life and Health Insurance Facts* (Toronto: Canadian Life and Health Insurance Association, 1998), 7.

4. Ibid., 6.

5. Ibid., 4, 8.

6. ACLI, 18.

CHAPTER 15

Group Life Insurance

After reading this chapter, you should be able to

- Identify the primary regulators of group life insurance in the United States and Canada

- Describe the purpose and operation of benefit schedules in group life insurance policies

- Identify the party who designates the beneficiary of a group member's life insurance coverage

- Describe an insured group member's conversion rights when the member's group life insurance coverage terminates

- Contrast the operation of the misstatement of age provision included in individual life insurance policies and the provision included in group life insurance policies

- Identify the features of group term insurance plans, group accidental death and dismemberment plans, group permanent plans, and group creditor life insurance plans

*I*n terms of coverage amounts, group life insurance is the fastest growing line of life insurance in North America. In 1950, group life insurance accounted for about 20 percent of the total amount of life insurance coverage in force. During the 1970s alone, however, the amount of group life insurance in force in the United States tripled, and today group life insurance accounts for over 40 percent of the total amount of life insurance in force; in Canada, the amount of group life insurance in force exceeds the amount of individual life insurance in force. (See Figure 15-1, which illustrates the growth of group life insurance coverage in the United States and Canada.)

We begin our discussion of group life insurance by describing how group life insurance is regulated in the United States and Canada and some of the provisions that are typically included in group life insurance policies. Then we describe the types of group life insurance policies that are available. Finally, we describe how group creditor life insurance policies differ from other forms of group life insurance.

Regulation of Group Life Insurance

As an insurance product, group life insurance is subject to state and provincial insurance laws and regulations. Because group life insurance is often provided by employers as an employee benefit in the United States and Canada, group life insurance is also subject to federal, state, and provincial laws that relate to employer-employee relations. In the following sections, we first describe the regulation of group life insurance products that are provided as employee benefits. Then, we describe the state and provincial insurance regulations that specifically apply to group life insurance.

Regulation of Employee Benefits

State, provincial, and federal legislatures throughout the United States and Canada have enacted laws designed to ensure that all employees are treated equally in the workplace. Employers in any given state or province must comply with that jurisdiction's employment laws, as well as with all applicable federal laws. Employment laws prohibit discrimination regarding hiring, advancement, wages, and other terms and conditions of employment. Terms and conditions of employment

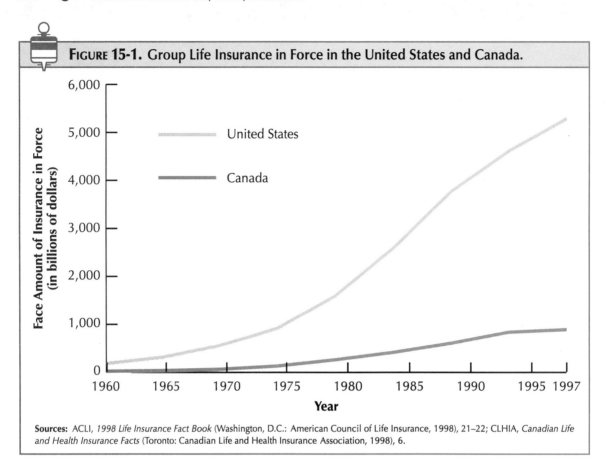

FIGURE 15-1. Group Life Insurance in Force in the United States and Canada.

Sources: ACLI, *1998 Life Insurance Fact Book* (Washington, D.C.: American Council of Life Insurance, 1998), 21–22; CLHIA, *Canadian Life and Health Insurance Facts* (Toronto: Canadian Life and Health Insurance Association, 1998), 6.

include employer-sponsored plans that provide employee benefits—such as group insurance plans—and, consequently, employers must ensure that employee benefit plans comply with these laws.

In addition, a number of U.S. federal laws directly regulate group insurance plans. For example, the federal *Age Discrimination in Employment Act (ADEA)* protects older workers from being discriminated against because of their age. The ADEA prohibits employers with 20 or more employees from discriminating on the basis of age against individuals who are age 40 and older. Because the cost of providing group insurance benefits to older workers is greater than the cost to provide the same benefits to younger workers, employers sometimes reduce the level of benefits provided to older workers. The ADEA permits employers to reduce the level of certain group insurance benefits—including life insurance benefits—for older workers, as long as the employer's premium contributions for those benefits at least equal its contributions for the benefits provided to younger workers. Retired workers are not protected by the ADEA, and most employers do not provide post-retirement life insurance coverage to their employees. Another federal law, the *Americans with Disabilities Act (ADA) of 1990,* requires that disabled employees of certain employers have equal access to the life and health insurance coverages that are available to other employees.

Most employer-employee group life and health insurance plans in the United States must comply with the federal **Employee Retirement Income Security Act (ERISA)**, which was designed to ensure that certain minimum plan requirements are contained in employee welfare benefit plans. ERISA defines a **welfare benefit plan** as any plan or program that an employer establishes to provide specified benefits to plan participants and their beneficiaries. Figure 15-2 lists the benefits that subject a welfare benefit plan to ERISA's requirements. Note that employer-employee plans that provide life or health insurance benefits must comply with ERISA. ERISA also contains detailed provisions that regulate employer-sponsored retirement plans. We describe how ERISA regulates group retirement plans in Chapter 17.

ERISA requires welfare benefit plans to be established and maintained in accordance with a written plan document. Among other things, this written document must describe

- The benefits that are provided by the plan

- How the plan will be funded

- The procedure that will be followed to amend the plan

The written plan document must also name one or more fiduciaries who are responsible for controlling and managing the operation of the benefit plan. ERISA sets out detailed standards that plan fiduciaries must meet. Above all, fiduciaries must carry out their duties by acting

FAST FACT

By the end of 1997, group life insurance provided more than $5 trillion in coverage for U.S. consumers. Canadians had more than $881 billion in group life insurance coverage.[1]

FIGURE 15-2. Employee Benefits That Subject a Welfare Benefit Plan to ERISA.

- Medical, surgical, or hospital care benefits

- Sickness, accident, disability, death, or unemployment benefits

- Vacation benefits

- Daycare benefits

- Scholarship funds

- Prepaid legal services

- Apprenticeship or training programs

- Certain benefits, which include severance benefits and housing benefits, described in the federal Labor Management Relations Act solely for the benefit of plan participants. A plan fiduciary who fails to carry out a fiduciary duty can be held personally liable for the amount of any losses that result from that breach of duty. In some cases, criminal penalties may also be imposed on plan fiduciaries who fail to carry out their fiduciary duties.

ERISA imposes a variety of disclosure and reporting requirements on employee welfare benefit plans. A summary plan description must be provided to each plan participant and to the federal Department of Labor (DOL). If the plan is changed significantly, each participant and the DOL must receive a summary of material modification. An annual report must be filed with the Internal Revenue Service (IRS). Other reports are required in other situations, such as when a plan terminates. The **plan administrator**—who is usually named in the written plan instrument—is responsible for ensuring that the welfare benefit plan complies with ERISA's disclosure and reporting requirements.

State and Provincial Regulation of Insurance

The states and provinces regulate the contents and operation of group life insurance policies in much the same way that they regulate individual insurance policies. In the United States, most states have enacted laws based on the *NAIC Group Life Insurance Model Act (NAIC Model Act)* and, thus, state regulation of group life insurance is fairly uniform. Provincial regulation of group life insurance is also fairly uniform. In Canada's common law jurisdictions, the insurance laws that are based on the Uniform Life Insurance Act regulate both individual and group life insurance policies. In Quebec, individual and group life insurance policies are regulated by the Quebec Civil Code and by insurance regulations. In addition to these provincial insurance laws and regulations, some aspects of group life insurance are governed by the *CLHIA Group Life and Group Health Insurance Guidelines (CLHIA Group Guidelines)*.

As we noted in Chapter 14, state insurance laws list the types of groups that are eligible for group insurance coverage. In addition, state and provincial insurance laws—and the CLHIA Group Life Guidelines—require insurers to include certain provisions in their group life insurance policies. In the next section, we describe many of these required policy provisions.

Group Life Insurance Policy Provisions

In Chapter 14, we described some of the features of a typical group insurance policy. Group life and health insurance policies, for example, typically include provisions that concern eligibility requirements, grace periods, incontestability, and the conditions under which the policy will terminate and under which a group insured's coverage will terminate. A number of other provisions are also typically included in group life insurance policies, and many of these provisions are very similar to provisions found in individual life insurance policies. In this section, we describe some additional provisions that are typically included in group life insurance policies. These provisions relate to (1) benefit amounts, (2) beneficiary designation, (3) conversion, (4) misstatement of age, and (5) settlement options.

Benefit Amounts

Every group life insurance policy must identify the amount—or the method the insurer will use to determine the amount—of each group insured's life insurance coverage. A group life insurance policy typically includes a schedule, known as a *benefit schedule,* that defines the amount of life insurance the policy provides for each group insured.

Two types of group life insurance benefit schedules are most common in employer-employee plans. One type of benefit schedule bases the amount of coverage on a specified formula. For example, the amount of coverage provided for each employee covered by the group life insurance plan is often a specified multiple of the employee's salary. The other type of benefit schedule specifies an amount of coverage either (1) for all group insureds or (2) for each class of group insureds. For example, the group contract may state that every employee has $30,000 worth of group life insurance coverage. Alternatively, the amount of coverage may vary according to the employee's job classification, such as one amount for senior executives, a second amount for managers, and a third amount for nonmanagement personnel. Note that the policy cannot describe coverage amounts on an individual basis, because that would violate group underwriting guidelines which seek to prevent antiselection. Instead, coverage amounts must be established using an objective factor, such as job classification or salary level. (See Figure 15-3, which provides some illustrations of the types of benefit schedules that may be included in group life insurance policies.)

If the group life insurance policy provides for coverage of dependents, then the policy includes a separate benefit schedule that defines the amount of coverage provided for each covered dependent. Such a bene fit schedule may specify that a flat amount of coverage is provided for all covered dependents, or the benefit schedule may specify one amount for the group member's spouse and a lower amount of coverage for all covered dependent children. Insurance company requirements and the laws of many jurisdictions require that the amount

FAST FACT
The average amount of coverage provided to Canadians insured under group life insurance policies was $36,700 by year-end 1997.[2]

Figure 15-3. Examples of Group Life Insurance Policy Benefit Schedules.

Benefit Schedule Based on Annual Earnings

Annual Earnings	Amount of Life Insurance
Less than $20,000	$ 20,000
$20,001 to $30,000	30,000
$30,001 to $40,000	50,000
$40,001 to $50,000	75,000
$50,001 and over	100,000

Benefit Schedule Based on Job Classification

Job Classification	Amount of Life Insurance
Company officers	$200,000
Managers	100,000
Supervisors	50,000
Nonmanagement personnel	30,000

of coverage provided on dependents be less than the amount provided for the insured group member.

Beneficiary Designation

Under the terms of a group life insurance policy—*unless* it is a creditor group life policy—each insured group member has the right to name a beneficiary who will receive the insurance benefit that is payable when that group insured dies. (We describe creditor group life policies later in the chapter.) The insured group member, rather than the group policyholder, must make this beneficiary designation, and the group insured has the right to change the beneficiary designation. If the policy provides for dependent coverage, then the insured group member also has the right to designate the beneficiary of such coverage; alternatively, the group policy may specify that the insured group member is automatically designated as the beneficiary of any coverage provided on the member's dependents.

The beneficiary designation rules and restrictions that apply to individual life insurance beneficiary designations also apply to group life insurance beneficiary designations. The only other restriction on the insured group member's right to name the beneficiary is that he may not name the group policyholder as beneficiary *unless* the plan is a group creditor life plan.

As we noted in Chapter 11, group life insurance policies sometimes include a facility-of-payment clause and/or a preference beneficiary clause. According to the NAIC Model Act, only sums of up to $2,000 may be paid under a facility-of-payment clause; any remaining policy proceeds must be paid to the designated beneficiary or to the estate of the group insured.

Conversion Privilege

The NAIC Model Act and the CLHIA Group Guidelines require group life insurance policies to include a conversion privilege. The *conversion privilege* allows a group insured whose coverage terminates for certain reasons to convert her group insurance coverage to an individual policy of insurance, without presenting evidence of her insurability.

The rights of a group insured to convert her group life insurance coverage vary depending on the reason for the termination of that coverage. Two general situations arise in which a group insured's group life insurance coverage terminates: (1) coverage terminates because the group insured ceases to be eligible for coverage—she terminates employment, leaves the group, or ceases to be a member of an eligible class—or (2) coverage terminates because the group life insurance policy terminates. We describe the group insured's conversion privilege in each of these situations, and we describe how the required conversion privilege differs in the United States and Canada.

Insured's Eligibility for Group Insurance Terminates

When a group insured's coverage terminates because he terminates employment or ceases to be a member of an eligible class, the NAIC Model Act and the CLHIA Group Guidelines require that he be given the right to purchase individual life insurance from the original insurer without providing evidence of insurability. In order to exercise the conversion privilege, the group insured must complete an application for an individual life insurance policy and pay the first premium within 31 days after his group coverage terminates. The NAIC Model Act, unlike the CLHIA Group Guidelines, requires the conversion privilege to be available to group insureds who are age 65 or older.

In general, the group insured is allowed to purchase any type of individual life insurance policy that the insurer is then issuing; but the amount of coverage the group insured may purchase is limited. Some group life insurance policies allow the group insured to convert up to the amount of insurance he received under the group policy. In accordance with the NAIC Model Act and the CLHIA Group Guidelines, many group life insurance policies state that the face amount of the individual policy may not exceed the difference between (1) the amount of the group insured's coverage under the original group life policy and (2) the amount of group coverage for which the insured will become entitled within the 31-day conversion period. In addition, the CLHIA Group Guidelines permit group life insurance policies issued in Canada to limit the face amount of the individual policy to a maximum of $200,000.

EXAMPLE Amin Bhutta, age 35, terminated his employment with the Maroon Company and immediately began working for the Jade Company. Under Maroon's group life insurance policy, Amin had group life coverage of $100,000. Jade's group life insurance policy will provide him with $60,000 of life insurance coverage. Amin would like to convert his Maroon group life insurance to an individual plan.

ANALYSIS The terms of Maroon's group life insurance policy determine the maximum amount of group life coverage that Amin will be allowed to convert to an individual life insurance policy without providing evidence of insurability. According to both the NAIC Model Act and the CLHIA Group Guidelines, the Maroon policy may limit this amount to a maximum of $40,000, which is the difference between the amount of coverage Amin had under the Maroon policy and the amount he will become entitled to receive under the Jade policy.

The premium rate the insured is charged for the individual life insurance policy is the standard premium rate that the insurance company charges an insured of the group insured's sex and attained age for the type of individual policy that the group insured is purchasing.

Group Life Insurance Policy Terminates

According to the NAIC Model Act, each group insured also must be granted the right to convert her group insurance coverage to individual coverage if the group life insurance policy terminates and the group insured was covered under the policy for at least 5 years before the termination of the policy. In such a situation, each insured group member is given a 31-day conversion period during which she may purchase an individual policy without submitting evidence of insurability. The maximum amount of coverage each group member can purchase is equal to the lesser of either (1) $10,000 or (2) the amount of coverage in force under the group plan minus the amount of group coverage for which the insured becomes entitled within 31 days of the policy's termination.

| EXAMPLE | Jocelyn Carver, Alexandra Shire, and Sam Melendez were employed by the Troup Company when it went out of |

business, and all were insured under Troup's employer-employee group life policy when that policy terminated. Jocelyn and Alexandra both had been insured for 10 years and had $20,000 of coverage; Sam's $20,000 coverage had been effective for 2 years. Alexandra and Sam obtained new jobs within 2 weeks and became eligible for $15,000 of group life insurance coverage. Jocelyn decided to leave the work force and return to school.

| ANALYSIS | Sam is not eligible to convert his group life insurance coverage because he was not covered by Troup's plan for at |

least 5 years. By contrast, Jocelyn and Alexandra had been insured under Troup's group life insurance policy for at least 5 years when it terminated; thus, they have the right to purchase individual life insurance without providing evidence of insurability. Jocelyn may purchase up to $10,000 of individual coverage because she is not entitled to be insured under a new group life insurance policy. Alexandra may purchase up to $5,000 of individual coverage—the difference between the amount of her coverage under Troup's policy ($20,000) and the amount of group coverage to which she became entitled under her new employer's policy ($15,000).

In Canada, the CLHIA Group Guidelines require group life insurance policies that include a waiver of premium benefit for disabled plan members to provide that if the group life policy terminates, then disabled plan members' insurance will continue as though the policy remained in effect.

Extension of Death Benefit

The NAIC Model Act requires group life insurance policies to contain a provision that, in effect, extends coverage on a group insured during the 31-day conversion period, even if the group insured does not exercise his conversion privilege. If the group insured dies during the 31-day conversion period and has not been issued an individual policy, then the insurer must pay a death benefit. The death benefit payable is the largest amount that the insurer would have issued as an individual policy to the group insured. Thus, if any individual described in the previous two examples died during the 31-day conversion period without being issued an individual policy, the insurer would be liable to pay a death benefit equal to the amount of insurance the individual was entitled to convert to individual coverage. Although such a provision is not required in Canada, group life insurance policies issued by Canadian insurers usually contain a similar provision.

Misstatement of Age

We noted in Chapter 10 that the misstatement of age provision included in individual life insurance policies specifies that the insurer will adjust the amount of the death benefit payable to reflect a misstatement of the insured's age. By contrast, the amount of the benefit payable following a group insured's death is specified in the group life insurance policy's benefit schedule. As a result, the misstatement of age provision in most group life insurance policies specifies that if the amount of the premium required for the plan is incorrect as the result of a misstatement of a group member's age, then the insurer will retroactively adjust the amount of the premium required for the coverage to reflect the member's correct age.

Settlement Options

When a person insured under a group life insurance policy dies, the beneficiary of the group insured's coverage usually receives the death benefit in a lump sum. Sometimes optional modes of settlement are also available. If so, the group life insurance policy gives the group insured and/or the beneficiary the right to choose a settlement option. All of the usual modes of settlement are generally made available. However, in order for a group insured or beneficiary to select the life income option, the amount of the death benefit payable usually must be at least a stated minimum.

Group Life Insurance Plans

Over 99 percent of all group life insurance policies are yearly renewable term (YRT) insurance plans. Group accidental death and dismemberment plans are also commonly issued, either as separate plans or in addition to other group life insurance coverage. Some permanent group life insurance plans are issued, but these plans are rare and typically provide coverage for group members who have retired. As we describe these various types of group life insurance plans, we will describe some aspects of how these plans are treated for federal income tax purposes.

Group Term Life Insurance

The YRT insurance coverage under group life insurance policies is similar to YRT coverage under individual policies. Evidence of insurability is not required from the group insureds each year when the coverage is renewed. These term policies do not build cash values, and the insurer has the right to change the premium rate each year.

When employers pay the premiums to provide their employees with group term insurance, the employees receive a financial benefit. Federal income tax laws sometimes consider the amount of such premiums paid as taxable income to the employees who are provided such coverage. In Canada, premiums paid by an employer for an employee's group term life insurance coverage are treated as taxable income to the employee. In the United States, with specific exceptions, an employee can receive up to $50,000 of noncontributory group term insurance coverage without paying income tax on the amount of the premium the employer paid for the coverage. (This exclusion from taxable income does not apply to certain employees as defined in U.S. federal income tax laws.) Thus, the group insured must pay income taxes on premiums paid by the employer for amounts of group term life insurance over $50,000. In both Canada and the United States, premiums an employer pays for group term life insurance coverage for its employees usually are treated as a business expense that the employer may deduct from its taxable income.

Group YRT insurance is sometimes used to fund other employee benefit plans that supplement the benefits provided by a group life insurance plan. For example, survivor income benefits are usually funded by group YRT insurance. A ***survivor income plan*** provides periodic benefit payments to specified dependents who survive a covered group member. Most survivor income plans provide monthly installment payments that are based on the amount of the group insured's salary prior to his death and on the number of his surviving dependents. For example, the plan may state that the monthly benefit payable equals (1) 20 percent of the insured's monthly salary if the insured is survived by only a spouse or only dependent children or (2) 30 percent of the insured's monthly salary if the insured is survived by both a spouse and at least one dependent child. The benefits paid to a surviving spouse usually continue until the earlier of (1) a specified time after the spouse remarries or (2) the spouse reaches age 65. The benefit paid on behalf of a surviving unmarried child usually continues until the child reaches age 19, unless the child is a full-time student, in which case the benefit is paid until the child is no longer a full-time student or until the child reaches age 23, whichever occurs first.

The premiums paid by an employer for survivor income coverage are treated for federal income tax purposes in the manner we described earlier with respect to other group term life coverage. Thus, in the United States, the amount of coverage necessary to provide the specified income benefits must be calculated. If this coverage amount, along with any other group term benefit amount, exceeds $50,000, then the employee must pay income tax on the premium amounts that the employer pays for the excess coverage.

"Generally our group insurance policies specify a term of more than forty days."

Accidental Death and Dismemberment Plans

Accidental death and dismemberment (AD&D) benefits may be included as part of a group life or group health policy, or they may be issued under a separate group insurance policy. The low cost of AD&D benefits makes them an attractive addition to group insurance plans, especially to employer-employee group plans. When the accidental death benefit is added to a group term life insurance plan, the accidental death benefit amount is usually equal to the amount of the death benefit provided under the basic group term insurance plan. Many accidental death and dismemberment plans also provide an additional travel accident benefit that covers only accidents occurring while the employee is traveling for the employer.

Accidental death and dismemberment policies are also often part of the group life insurance plans purchased by travel groups, automobile clubs, or transportation companies, such as railroads and airlines.

Group Permanent Plans

Group plans that provide permanent life insurance are less popular than group term insurance plans primarily because they do not receive the favorable income tax treatment that group term life insurance plans receive. Nevertheless, group permanent life insurance plans are sometimes used by employers to help their employees purchase life insurance coverage that will continue after retirement, when their group term insurance coverage typically ends. In most situations, group permanent insurance is offered as a *supplemental coverage,* which means that group members are offered the coverage on an optional basis as an addition to their group term life insurance coverage. Covered employees are usually required to pay a significant portion of the premium for such supplemental coverages. Therefore, participation levels in group permanent plans are generally much lower than are the participation levels that insurers require under other contributory group insurance plans.

The specific characteristics of group permanent coverage vary from plan to plan. We describe the primary characteristics of the three most commonly offered group permanent life insurance plans: (1) group paid-up plans, (2) level premium whole life plans, and (3) group universal life plans.

Group Paid-Up Plans

Group life insurance purchased under a group paid-up plan combines paid-up whole life insurance with decreasing amounts of term insurance. These plans are contributory plans under which

- The employee's premium contribution is used as a net single premium to purchase paid-up whole life insurance

- The employer's premium contribution is used to purchase the amount of group term insurance required to bring the employee's total coverage up to a predetermined amount

The total amount of paid-up insurance on each participating employee increases each year, and the amount of group term insurance that the employer must purchase for participating employees decreases each year.

The premium paid by the employer for the term portion of the coverage is eligible for the same favorable income tax treatment that group YRT premiums receive. Although the employee receives no tax benefits in connection with the premiums used to purchase permanent insurance, that insurance is in force for the employee's lifetime and stays in force after the employee retires or leaves the group.

Level Premium Whole Life Plans

Some insurance companies make level premium whole life insurance available on a group basis. Level premium coverage is usually written on a limited-payment whole life plan, such as whole life paid-up at age 65. Because these policies build cash values, employers often use them to provide retirement income benefits for employees.

If the group whole life insurance plan is noncontributory, then the employee's rights in the policy's values usually are not vested. As a result, if the employee leaves the group, then his coverage under the group plan terminates and any accumulated cash value belongs to the employer. If the group plan is contributory, then the employee has a vested right in the policy up to the amount of the employee's premium contributions. A small portion of the employer's premium contribution may be tax deductible.

Group Universal Life Plans

Shortly after individual universal life plans were introduced, group insurers began offering group universal life plans. Employers can use these plans to help employees establish life insurance coverage that will continue after the employees retire.

In many ways, group universal life plans function much more like individual insurance policies than like group insurance policies. Under most group universal life plans, an insured group member chooses the amount of premium she wishes to pay; the employer usually does not pay any portion of the premium. In turn, the amount of the policy's cash value depends on the premium amount the group insured pays. Group members can use these products as savings vehicles in the same manner that individual universal life policyowners can.

Group underwriting principles may be used, although if the available coverage amounts are high, as they often are, group members may be required to provide some evidence of insurability in order to be eligible for the coverage. Group members can also change their coverage amounts, although increases in coverage amounts may require evidence of insurability.

If the group is large enough, the mortality charges assessed under a typical group universal life policy are based on the group's own claims experience. The expense charges for group universal life plans are often lower than comparable charges for individual plans because the group policyholder handles some of the administrative aspects of the plan.

Group universal life plans differ from most other group life insurance plans in that under a group universal life plan, an individual has *portable coverage,* which means that an insured employee who leaves the group can continue his coverage under the group plan. In most other types of group life insurance plans, an individual who leaves the group and wishes to retain the coverage can do so only by converting her group insurance coverage to an individual insurance policy.

Group Creditor Life Insurance

Group creditor life insurance is insurance issued to a creditor, such as a bank, to insure the lives of the creditor's current and future debtors. Unlike other group life insurance policies, group creditor life policies designate the policyholder—the creditor—as the beneficiary to receive the benefit payable when a group insured dies. At any given time, the amount of insurance on each group insured is equal to the amount of the outstanding debt that person owes to the policyholder-creditor. In several states, the amount of insurance as well as the duration of a covered loan may be subject to maximum limits, regardless of the amount of the debt.

The premium for group creditor life insurance coverage is usually paid by the debtor, although it may be paid entirely by the creditor or shared by the creditor and the debtor. State and provincial insurance laws impose limits on the premiums that debtors may be charged for such coverage. For example, most states set a maximum premium rate that debtors may be charged for such coverage. This maximum is usually expressed in terms of a stated maximum premium amount per $1,000 of insurance coverage. If the debtor is required to pay a portion of the premium, he must be given the right to refuse to purchase the group creditor coverage. As a rule, the terms of a credit transaction may require the debtor to secure the loan with some form of insurance coverage. The creditor, however, is prohibited from requiring the debtor to purchase such coverage from the creditor as a condition of obtaining credit. In other words, the debtor may be required to purchase coverage but has the right to purchase that coverage from any source he chooses.

> **FAST FACT**
>
> At the end of 1997, $212 billion of credit life insurance was in force in the United States.[5]

Key Terms

Employee Retirement Income
    Security Act (ERISA)
welfare benefit plan
plan administrator
benefit schedule

conversion privilege
survivor income plan
portable coverage
group creditor life insurance

Other Important Terms

Age Discrimination in
    Employment Act (ADEA)
Americans with Disabilities Act
    (ADA) of 1990
NAIC Group Life Insurance
    Model Act

CLHIA Group Life and Group
    Health Insurance Guidelines
supplemental coverage

Endnotes

1. ACLI, *1998 Life Insurance Fact Book* (Washington, D.C.: American Council of Life Insurance, 1998), 18; CLHIA, *Canadian Life and Health Insurance Facts* (Toronto: Canadian Life and Health Insurance Association, 1998), 4.

2. CLHIA, 7.

3. ACLI, 76.

4. Ibid., 18.

5. Ibid., 19.

CHAPTER 16

Annuities and Individual Retirement Savings Plans

After reading this chapter, you should be able to

- Define the term *annuity* and recognize examples of an annuity

- Distinguish between an immediate annuity and a deferred annuity

- Identify the rights of the owner of a deferred annuity during the annuity's accumulation period and during its payout period

- Identify the three general types of payout options available to the owner of an annuity and distinguish between those payout options

- Distinguish between a fixed annuity and a variable annuity

- Recognize the differences between life insurance mortality rates and annuity mortality rates

- Identify the three variations of life annuities that insurers commonly offer

- Recognize the individual retirement plans that qualify for favorable income tax treatment in the United States and Canada

*I*n this chapter, our focus shifts from life insurance policies to annuities and various individual retirement products marketed by insurance companies. Annuities are often described as the flip side of life insurance because annuities protect against the financial risk of outliving one's financial resources, whereas life insurance protects against the financial risk of death.

In the most general terms, an ***annuity*** is a series of periodic payments. Most of us make and receive such periodic payments. For example, your monthly rent or mortgage payments constitute an annuity, and salaries paid on a regular, periodic basis are annuities. In the financial services industry, the term ***annuity*** means a contract under which one party—the insurer—promises to make a series of periodic payments in exchange for a premium or series of premiums.

Historically, annuities have been considered to be an insurance product; thus, by law, only insurance companies could issue annuities. Other providers of financial services—for example, stockbrokers, banks, and savings and loan institutions—now market annuity products issued by insurers, and some of these providers would like to begin issuing annuities.

As you will learn, annuities are complex products that can contain a variety of features. Nevertheless, every annuity product we describe in this chapter is, in its most basic form, a contract that provides a series of periodic benefit payments. We begin this chapter by describing some general features of annuities. Then we describe various individual annuity products that insurance companies have designed to help individuals save money, generally on a favorable income tax basis, for use in their later years.

The Annuity Contract

As we described in Chapter 5, a contract is a legally enforceable agreement that consists of a promise or set of promises. The terms of an annuity contract govern the rights and duties of the contracting parties. The parties to an annuity contract are (1) the insurer that issued the contract and (2) the person, known as the ***contractholder,*** who applied for and purchased the contract. As with a life insurance contract, the insurer issues a policy to the contractholder; the policy contains all of the terms of the contractual agreement entered into by the parties.

Insurers sell annuities on both an individual and a group basis. Thus, the contractholder can be either an individual or an organization that purchases the annuity on behalf of a group of individuals. (See Figure 16-1 for a comparison of the amounts of individual and group annuities in force.) For now, we will describe only individual annuities; we discuss group annuities in the next chapter when we describe group retirement income plans.

As part of the contractual agreement between the parties to an annuity, the contractholder pays a single premium or a series of premiums to the insurer. Premiums insurers receive for annuities generally are referred to as *annuity considerations*. The insurer pools the money it has received from a large group of contractholders, and it invests those pooled funds. The insurer uses the pooled funds and investment earnings on those funds to make periodic annuity benefit payments as they come due. Note that this pooling of funds is the same method insurers use to provide themselves with the funds to pay life insurance policy proceeds as they come due.

An insurer uses a combination of factors to calculate the amount of the periodic annuity benefit payments that it will be liable to pay under an annuity policy. Every annuity calculation, however, is based on the following basic mathematical concept.

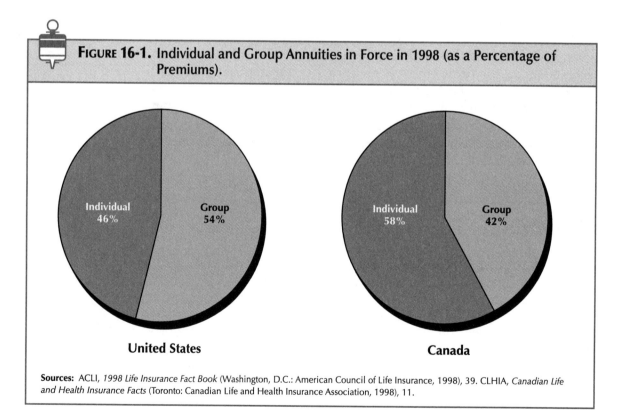

Figure 16-1. Individual and Group Annuities in Force in 1998 (as a Percentage of Premiums).

United States

Individual 46%   Group 54%

Canada

Individual 58%   Group 42%

Sources: ACLI, *1998 Life Insurance Fact Book* (Washington, D.C.: American Council of Life Insurance, 1998), 39. CLHIA, *Canadian Life and Health Insurance Facts* (Toronto: Canadian Life and Health Insurance Association, 1998), 11.

> A sum of money, known as the ***principal,*** that is invested for a certain *period of time* at a stated *rate of interest* can be paid out in a series of periodic payments—in an annuity—over a stated *period of time.*

Note that this equation contains four variables: (1) the amount of the principal invested, (2) the time over which the principal accumulates at interest, (3) the interest rate earned on the investment, and (4) the number and timing of periodic annuity payments. If we know the value of these variables, we can calculate the amount of each periodic annuity payment.

Although actual annuity contract calculations are beyond the scope of this text, let's look at a simple example that illustrates how this basic concept works.

EXAMPLE | Three years ago, Jill Black deposited $10,000 into a savings account that earns an annual interest rate of 5 percent. On the same day, Perry Watson deposited $20,000 into a savings account that also earns an annual interest rate of 5 percent. Both Jill and Perry plan to liquidate their accounts over a two-year period by withdrawing an equal amount on the first day of each month. Compare the amount of Jill's monthly withdrawal to the amount of Perry's monthly withdrawal.

ANALYSIS | The interest rate and the time periods are the same in both situations. But the amount of Perry's principal is two times the amount of Jill's principal. Without making any calculations, we can determine that Perry will be able to withdraw a larger amount from his account each month than Jill will be able to withdraw from her account.

This example illustrates the mathematical concept that if we change the amount of one of the variables in an equation, we change the result of the mathematical calculation. In our example, *increasing* the amount of the principal results in an *increase* in the amount of the periodic annuity payment.

By the same token, changing the interest rate also changes the result of the calculation. For example, if we *increase* the interest rate, the amount of the periodic annuity payment will *increase,* because the higher the interest rate, the larger the amount of investment income we will earn. And the more investment income we earn, the larger will be the total amount of money we will have available to fund the periodic annuity payments.

Increasing the time over which the principal amount is invested *increases* the amount of the investment income earned and, thus, *increases* the amount of the resulting periodic annuity payment. However, *increasing* the number of periodic annuity payments in a given time period *decreases* the amount of the periodic annuity payments.

EXAMPLE Assume that Perry Watson has decided to withdraw the funds in his account in a series of equal payments over a two-year period. He's considering whether to make withdrawals semiannually or monthly.

ANALYSIS The fewer the number of withdrawals that Perry makes, the larger that the amount of each withdrawal will be. As a result, if Perry decides to withdraw the account's funds in a series of semi-annual payments, he will receive larger annuity payments than he would receive if he had elected to receive a series of monthly payments.

For purposes of introducing you to annuities, we have provided illustrations that greatly simplify the description of how annuities operate. Now that you have a general understanding of some of the mathematical principles underlying the operation of annuities, we will examine some of their finer points. We begin by looking at ways in which annuities can be classified.

Classifications of Annuities

We can classify every annuity according to various criteria. In order to understand how a given annuity operates, we have to know the following information:

- How the annuity was purchased

- How often periodic annuity benefits are to be paid

- When annuity benefit payments are scheduled to begin

- The number of annuitants covered by the annuity policy

- Whether annuity values are guaranteed or variable

How Annuities Are Purchased

Most annuities today are purchased as single-premium annuities. A *single-premium annuity* is an annuity that is purchased by the payment of a single, lump-sum premium. Benefit payments under a single-premium annuity may begin shortly after the premium is paid or may begin many years after the premium is paid.

An annuity also can be purchased by paying periodic premiums over a period of years. Periodic premiums can be paid on either (1) a level-premium basis or (2) a flexible-premium basis. Under a *periodic level-premium annuity,* the contractholder pays equal premiums for the annuity at regularly scheduled intervals, such as monthly or annually, until some predetermined future date. Premiums might, for example, be payable annually for a stated number of years.

Under a *flexible-premium annuity,* the contractholder pays premiums on a periodic basis over a stated period of time; the amount of each premium payment, however, can vary between a set minimum amount and a set maximum amount. For example, the policy might allow the contractholder to pay any premium amount between $250 and $10,000 each year. The contractholder can also choose not to pay any premium in a given year; the only requirement is that any premium amount paid each year must fall within the stated minimum and maximum. Flexible-premium annuities are sold far more often today than are periodic level-premium annuities. (The CD-ROM included in the back cover contains a sample flexible-premium annuity.)

The operation of an annuity is basically the same regardless of whether the premium is paid in one sum or in a series of payments. The premium payment method, however, affects the length of time that the insurer holds the principal at interest. And the longer the insurer holds a given premium, the larger will be the investment earnings generated by that principal.

> **FAST FACT**
>
> Canadians owned about 3.1 million individual annuity contracts at year-end 1997.[1]

How Often Benefits Are Paid

The frequency of periodic annuity benefit payments depends on the length of the annuity period. An *annuity period* is the time span between each of the payments in the series of periodic annuity benefit payments. The annuity period is typically either one month or one year, but other options, such as quarterly or semiannual, are also available. For example, an annuity policy that provides for a series of annual benefit payments has an annuity period of one year and is referred to as an *annual annuity*. An annuity policy that provides for an annuity period of one month is referred to as a *monthly annuity*.

When Benefit Payments Begin

The date on which the insurer begins to make the annuity benefit payments is known as the annuity's **maturity date** or the *annuity date*. An annuity can be classified as either an immediate annuity or a deferred annuity, depending on when the insurer is to begin making periodic annuity benefit payments.

Immediate Annuities

An **immediate annuity** is an annuity under which benefit payments are scheduled to begin one annuity period after the annuity is purchased. Remember, an annuity period is typically one month or one year. Thus, if an immediate annuity contains an annuity period of one year, then the maturity date on which periodic annuity benefit payments will begin is one year after the annuity was purchased. In essence, an immediate annuity is an annuity for which benefit payments are scheduled to begin within 12 months after its purchase. Also, because benefit payments begin soon after an immediate annuity is purchased, an immediate annuity is generally purchased with a single premium; such a policy is known as a *single-premium immediate annuity (SPIA)*.

Deferred Annuities

A **deferred annuity** is an annuity under which periodic benefits are scheduled to begin more than one annuity period—that is, more than 12 months—after the date on which the annuity was purchased. Although a deferred annuity typically specifies the date on which benefit payments are scheduled to begin, the contractholder usually can change this date at any time before those benefit payments begin. People often purchase deferred annuities during their working years in anticipation of the need for retirement income later in their lives.

The period during which the insurer makes annuity benefit payments is known as the **payout period** or *liquidation period*. The period between the contractholder's purchase of a deferred annuity and the onset of the payout period is known as the **accumulation period**. Because a deferred annuity has an accumulation period, the contractholder generally can choose to pay for the annuity either in a single premium or in a series of periodic premiums. Although most deferred annuities are purchased as *single-premium deferred annuities (SPDAs)*, insurers also sell *flexible-premium deferred annuities (FPDAs)*. Note that every annuity purchased with the payment of periodic premiums is by definition a deferred annuity.

EXAMPLE	When she was 48 years old, Jan Isaacson received a lump sum of $50,000. She used that amount to purchase a deferred annuity that will provide her with a benefit payment each month during her retirement years, beginning when she reaches age 65.

ANALYSIS	The information given in this example tells us that Jan purchased a single-premium deferred annuity. The annuity has an accumulation period of 17 years—the time between Jan's purchase of the annuity at age 48 and the time she begins receiving benefits at age 65. The annuity period is one month; therefore, the annuity is a monthly annuity.

The insurer's obligations and the rights of the contractholder differ depending on whether a deferred annuity is in its accumulation period or its payout period. Let's look at how a deferred annuity operates during these two periods.

Accumulation Period. During a deferred annuity's accumulation period, the insurer invests the premiums paid by the contractholder. Thus, during the accumulation period, the deferred annuity builds an accumulated value. An annuity's ***accumulated value*** is equal to the net amount paid for the annuity, *plus* interest earned, *less* the amount of any withdrawals. The manner in which the policy provides for investment earnings on the accumulated value depends on whether the deferred annuity is a fixed-benefit annuity or a variable annuity. We describe these distinctions later in the chapter.

$$\begin{array}{c} \text{Accumulated} \\ \text{value of a} \\ \text{deferred annuity} \end{array} = \left(\begin{array}{c} \text{Net amount} \\ \text{paid for annuity} \end{array} \right) + \text{Interest} - \text{Withdrawals}$$

The contractholder typically can make withdrawals from a deferred annuity's accumulated value in accordance with the policy's withdrawal provision. The ***withdrawal provision*** grants the contractholder the right to withdraw all or a portion of the annuity's accumulated value during the accumulation period. Most annuity policies allow the contractholder to withdraw a stated percentage of the annuity's accumulated value each year without charge. If the contractholder withdraws more than that stated percentage in one year, then the insurer generally imposes a ***withdrawal charge.*** Withdrawals of less than a stated minimum amount are typically not permitted.

Throughout the accumulation period, the contractholder also has the right to surrender the policy for its *cash surrender value*—the accumulated value *less* any surrender charges included in the policy. A *surrender charge* is typically imposed if the policy is surrendered within a stated number of years after it was purchased. The amount of any surrender charge that is imposed usually declines over time. An insurer usually imposes these surrender charges during the early years of an annuity policy in order to recoup the costs it incurred in issuing the policy.

$$\text{Cash surrender value of a deferred annuity} = \left(\begin{array}{c} \text{Accumulated} \\ \text{value} \end{array} \right) - \left(\begin{array}{c} \text{Surrender} \\ \text{charges} \end{array} \right)$$

Deferred annuity policies usually provide a *survivor benefit;* if the annuitant or contractholder dies before annuity benefit payments begin, the annuity's accumulated value is paid to a beneficiary designated by the contractholder. Insurers usually do not impose surrender charges when the accumulated value is paid as a survivor benefit.

Payout Period. When an annuity matures, the insurer uses the annuity's accumulated value to fund the periodic annuity benefit payments. Thereafter, all provisions relating to the policy's accumulated value—including the withdrawal provision and the survivor benefit provision—become inoperable, and the terms of the payout option provision govern the parties' rights and obligations under the policy. The *payout option provision* in an annuity policy lists and describes each of the payout options from which the contractholder may select. In the next section, we describe some of the payout options typically available under an annuity policy.

When Benefit Payments End

The length of the payout period depends on the payout option that the contractholder selects. Under the three general types of payout options available, the annuity benefits will be paid as either (1) a life annuity, (2) an annuity certain, or (3) a temporary life annuity.

Life Annuity

A *life annuity* is an annuity that provides periodic benefit payments for *at least* the lifetime of a named individual. Some life annuities also provide further payment guarantees. The various forms of life annuities and commonly available payment guarantees are described later in this chapter.

The terminology used to describe the people connected with an annuity varies widely throughout the insurance industry. The named individual whose lifetime is used as the measuring life in a life annuity is often referred to as the **annuitant,** and we will use that terminology in this text. Note that the annuitant is not always the owner of the annuity, although in most situations the annuity contractholder and the annuitant are the same person. Just as we distinguish between the insured and the policyowner of a life insurance policy, we also need to distinguish between the annuitant and the contractholder. Additional confusion over annuity terminology results from the use of the term *beneficiary* in an annuity. We will use the term **annuity beneficiary** to mean the person or party that the contractholder names to receive any survivor benefits that are payable during the accumulation period of a deferred annuity. We will use the term **payee** to refer to the person who receives the annuity benefit payments during the payout period. Generally, the payee is also the contractholder.

EXAMPLE   Pat Carmichael is 53 years old and has just received an early retirement package from her employer. Part of that package was a $50,000 lump-sum payment. Pat has accepted a position with another employer and has used the $50,000 to purchase a deferred annuity that will make payments to her beginning when she retires at age 65. She named her daughter, Colleen, to receive the policy's survivor benefit.

ANALYSIS   Pat purchased the annuity, and, thus, she is the contractholder. Because annuity benefits will be paid to Pat throughout her lifetime, she is also the annuitant and the payee. Finally, because Colleen will receive any survivor benefits payable if her mother dies before the annuity benefit payments begin, Colleen is the annuity beneficiary.

We will come back to the topic of life annuities later in the chapter. For now, let's return to our discussion of how annuities are classified.

Annuity Certain

An annuity can be purchased to provide periodic payments over a period of time that is unrelated to the lifetime of an annuitant. An **annuity certain** is an annuity that is payable for a stated period of time, regardless of whether an individual person lives or dies. The stated period over which the insurer will make benefit payments is called the **period certain.** At the end of the period certain, annuity payments cease. The annuity certain is useful when a person needs an income for a specified period of time. An annuity certain also might be purchased to provide income during a specified period until some other source of income, such as a pension, becomes payable.

EXAMPLE Midori Hayakawa is a 50-year-old office manager who plans to retire at age 60. She will not begin receiving pension benefits from her employer-sponsored pension plan until she reaches age 65. Thus, she wants to purchase an annuity that will provide her with periodic benefit payments during the five-year period following her retirement before she begins receiving her pension benefits.

ANALYSIS Midori wants to begin receiving annuity benefit payments in ten years, when she retires at age 60. Thus, she should purchase a ten-year deferred annuity. Midori wants to receive annuity benefit payments only until she will begin to receive her pension benefits. Thus, she should elect a payout option under which annuity benefits are paid as a five-year annuity certain.

Temporary Life Annuity

A *temporary life annuity* provides periodic benefit payments until the end of a specified number of years or until the death of the annuitant, whichever occurs *first*. Once the stated period expires *or* the annuitant dies, the annuity benefits cease. For example, under the terms of a five-year temporary life annuity, five years is the *maximum* length of time during which annuity benefits will be payable. If the annuitant dies before the end of that five-year period, no further annuity benefits will be payable. Although temporary life annuities are not sold very often, they are sometimes purchased to fill a gap between the end of an earning period and the time some other anticipated income, such as a pension, begins.

Number of Annuitants

The examples we have looked at so far have all involved situations in which a life annuity was based on the life of one annuitant and benefits were paid to a named individual. It is possible, however, to purchase a life annuity that provides an income to more than one individual.

When a couple purchases a life annuity, they usually want the annuity to provide benefit payments throughout both of their lives. A *joint and survivor annuity,* which is also known as a *joint and last survivorship annuity*, provides a series of payments to two or more individuals, and those payments continue until both or all of the individuals die. The terms of a joint and survivor annuity policy determine whether the amount of each periodic benefit payment remains the same after the death of one of the annuitants. For example, the annuity might provide that the amount of the periodic benefit payment will remain the same until the last annuitant dies, or the annuity might provide that the amount of the periodic benefit will be reduced by a stated amount, such as 50 percent, following the death of the first annuitant. Of course, the premium amount required to fund the annuity will vary, depending on the amount of benefits that are to be paid out—the larger the expected amount of benefit payments, the larger the premium required to pay for the annuity.

Whether Annuity Values Are Guaranteed or Variable

People who purchase annuities have different purposes in mind for the funds they place in an annuity. Annuity contractholders also have different capacities for assuming a financial risk when they place money in their annuities. Thus, many insurers offer two general options to annuity purchasers: (1) the insurer will guarantee to pay at least a stated interest rate on the annuity funds it holds or (2) the insurer will pay interest at a rate that is not guaranteed; instead, the interest rate will vary according to the earnings of certain investments held by the insurer.

Fixed-Benefit Annuities

A *fixed-benefit annuity* is an annuity under which the insurer guarantees that at least a defined amount of monthly annuity benefit will be provided for each dollar applied to purchasing the annuity. Most fixed-benefit annuities specify that once the insurer begins paying annuity benefits, the amount of each benefit payment will not change. A few fixed-benefit annuities, however, specify that benefit payments may increase if the insurer's investment earnings exceed those the insurer expected when it calculated the benefit amount.

If the fixed-benefit annuity is an *immediate annuity*, then the amount of the annuity benefit payments is known when the insurer issues the annuity policy. The purchaser pays a single premium amount, and the insurer calculates the annuity benefit amount that will be provided by that premium amount.

If the fixed-benefit annuity is a *deferred annuity*, then the annuity policy includes a chart of annuity values, similar to that shown in Figure 16-2. This chart lists the amount of annuity benefit that is guaranteed for each $1,000 of accumulated value. According to the

> **FAST FACT**
>
> During 1997, U.S. life insurance companies issued 3.8 million individual fixed annuities. Most of them—95%—were deferred annuities.[2]

Figure 16-2. Guaranteed Values of a Fixed-Benefit Annuity.

		Minimum Monthly Payment Rates for Each $1,000 of Accumulated Value		
		Payments Guaranteed for		
Age*	Payments for Life Only	10 Years	15 Years	20 Years
40	$4.13	$4.12	$4.11	$4.09
45	4.36	4.34	4.32	4.28
50	4.65	4.62	4.58	4.52
55	5.05	4.99	4.91	4.81
60	5.56	5.45	5.32	5.14
65	6.27	6.07	5.82	5.48
70	7.33	6.89	6.38	5.76
75 & over	8.95	7.89	6.87	5.92

* Age on birthday preceding the due date of the first payment.

chart in our figure, for example, if the annuity's accumulated value on the maturity date is $20,000 and the annuitant is age 40, then the insurer will pay the annuitant $82.60 per month (20 × $4.13 = $82.60) for the remainder of the annuitant's life. Note, however, that the amounts listed in the policy are the minimum guaranteed benefit amounts. These are the benefit amounts that the insurer is comfortable guaranteeing when it issues a fixed-benefit annuity. At the annuity maturity date, the insurer reevaluates its investment experience and the current investment climate and, if the investment climate is more favorable than expected, then the insurer will pay a larger amount per $1,000 of accumulated value than the annuity guaranteed.

A fixed-benefit deferred annuity policy also describes the manner in which the insurer will credit investment earnings to the policy's accumulated value. When the annuity is purchased, the insurer typically guarantees that the accumulated value will be credited with a stated interest rate for at least a stated time, usually from one to five years. Such an annuity also specifies that, after that initial time, the interest rate credited will not fall below a stated rate, such as 3 percent. The actual interest rate that the insurer will apply after the initial period, however, will be greater than the guaranteed rate if the insurer's investment earnings justify the higher rate. Often, the policy specifies that the interest rate that will be credited will be tied either to a published index or, more commonly, to the insurer's overall investment results.

When an insurer provides interest rate guarantees in an annuity policy, the insurer agrees to assume the investment risk of the policy.

The insurer places the funds in relatively secure investments, such as bonds and preferred stocks, as part of its general investment account. If the general investment account performs well, the insurer can pay interest rates that are higher than the rates guaranteed in its policies while still achieving profits from the investment account. The insurer, however, takes the risk that if its investments perform poorly and its investment returns are less than the minimums guaranteed in its policies, then the insurer will lose money.

Variable Annuities

A *variable annuity* is an annuity under which the amount of the policy's accumulated value and the amount of the monthly annuity benefit payment fluctuate in accordance with the performance of a separate account. The individual who purchases a variable annuity assumes the investment risk of the policy. Because the insurer makes no guarantees regarding the investment earnings or the amount of a variable annuity's benefit payments, the insurer retains no risk under the policy. Instead, the purchaser benefits from all gains that result from profitable investments and incurs all losses from unprofitable investments. Because of this investment risk transfer, federal laws in the United States treat variable annuities as securities that must comply with federal securities laws. As we described in Chapter 8, federal securities laws require insurers to register variable life insurance and variable annuity products with the SEC, and they require sales agents to be licensed as registered representatives before selling variable products.

The mechanism that allows this investment risk transfer from the insurer to the purchaser is the separate account. A *separate account*—known as a *segregated account* in Canada—is an investment account that is completely separated from the insurer's general investment account. Insurers typically offer a number of separate accounts, and they follow a different investment strategy for each separate account. For example, some separate accounts may focus on investments in high-growth stocks, while other separate accounts may concentrate on investments in specific types of bonds. The value of the separate account increases or decreases depending on the performance of the account's investments. Typically, variable annuity contractholders can select from a variety of separate accounts and may periodically transfer funds from one separate account to another.

The owner of a variable deferred annuity invests in a separate account during the annuity's accumulation period by purchasing accumulation units in the selected separate account. *Accumulation units* represent ownership shares in the selected account. The number of accumulation units that a given premium will purchase depends on the value of the separate account when the premium is paid. Thus, if the value of the investments held in a separate account fund is low, the value of each accumulation unit will also be low; as a result, more accumulation units can be purchased for a given amount of premium than when the investment value of the fund is high. As premiums are paid throughout the accumulation period, the total number of accumulation units gradually increases.

EXAMPLE Will Howard purchased a variable deferred annuity and selected Separate Account A as the investment vehicle for his annuity. Over a three-month period, the value of an accumulation unit in Separate Account A was as follows:

January:	$2.00
February:	$3.00
March:	$2.50

Will paid a premium of $600 in each of those three months.

ANALYSIS In January, the $600 premium purchased 300 accumulation units ($600 ÷ $2.00 = 300). In February, the $600 premium purchased 200 accumulation units ($600 ÷ $3.00 = 200). In March, the $600 premium purchased 240 accumulation units ($600 ÷ $2.50 = 240). Over the three-month period, the $1,800 that Will paid in premiums was sufficient to purchase a total of 740 accumulation units (300 + 200 + 240).

Accumulation units are used to value an annuity only during the accumulation period of a variable deferred annuity. During the payout period of a variable annuity, the amount of the periodic annuity benefit payable is calculated on the basis of *annuity units.* The number of annuity units that can be purchased for each dollar applied depends on a number of factors, including the current value of the separate account and the length of the payout period. Further, the periodic benefit amount payable for each annuity unit varies over the payout period depending on the current value of an annuity unit. For an individual contractholder, then, the periodic benefit amount he will receive depends on the total number of annuity units he has purchased and the current value of each annuity unit when the benefit is paid.

EXAMPLE On the maturity date of Will Howard's variable deferred annuity, his total premiums had purchased a total of 100,000 accumulation units. On that date, the value of an accumulation unit for his separate account was $3.00. In addition, the value of an annuity unit for his separate account on the policy's maturity date was $2.50.

 On the maturity date, Will's 100,000 accumulation units will be valued at $300,000 (100,000 units × $3.00 per unit). If Will decides to receive his annuity benefits in the form of a variable annuity, the insurer will use that $300,000 to purchase 120,000 annuity units ($300,000 ÷ $2.50 = 120,000).

The insurer must periodically recalculate the value of an annuity unit based on the investment experience of the separate account. The insurer then recalculates the amount of the periodic benefit payment by multiplying the total number of annuity units times the current value of an annuity unit. Note that the total number of annuity units remains the same throughout the payout period; the value of an annuity unit varies depending on the investment experience of the separate account. Thus, the benefit amount changes as the value of the separate account changes. If the account's value increases, then the benefit amount will increase; if the account value declines, then the benefit amount will decrease correspondingly. The uncertainty of the benefit amount is the primary reason that, on the maturity date, most variable deferred annuity contractholders convert their variable annuities to fixed-benefit annuities.

More About Life Annuities

We noted earlier that time is an important variable in the operation of every annuity policy. The length of the annuity's payout period affects the amount of the periodic benefit payment that will be provided for a given premium amount. In the case of life annuities, the length of the payout period is linked to the annuitant's lifetime. Thus, with life annuities, the insurer must consider the life expectancy of the annuitant when calculating the amount of periodic annuity benefit it can provide for a specified premium amount. In this section, we describe how this life expectancy factor affects annuity benefit payments and some of the various types of life annuities.

The Life Expectancy Factor

The ability to pay life annuities was made possible by the life insurance industry's studies of mortality rates and its development of mortality tables. As we described in Chapter 6, the results of these mortality studies have provided insurers with information as to how many people from a given group of people of the same age and gender are likely to die each year. Thus, an insurer can predict the amount of life insurance policy proceeds it will be liable to pay in a given year. Establishing accurate estimates of its probable loss rate allows the insurer to establish adequate premium rates.

Mortality studies have also provided insurers with information on how many persons in a given group of people of the same age and gender are expected to be alive at the end of any given year. ***Annuity mortality rates***—the mortality rates experienced by persons purchasing life annuities—are not identical to the mortality rates experienced by persons insured by life insurance policies. The differences result from the fact that the mortality rates experienced by annuitants of a given age and gender who purchase life annuities differ markedly from the mortality rates experienced by persons of that same age and gender who purchase life insurance. In general, annuitants as a group live longer than do individuals who purchase life insurance. (See Figure 16-3, which illustrates how annuity mortality rates compare to life insurance mortality rates.)

Because annuity benefits are payable while the annuitant continues to live, a life annuity protects against the personal risk of outliving

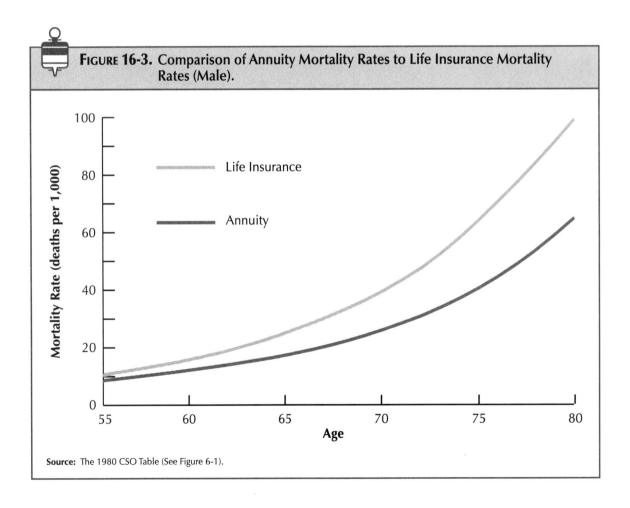

Figure 16-3. Comparison of Annuity Mortality Rates to Life Insurance Mortality Rates (Male).

Source: The 1980 CSO Table (See Figure 6-1).

one's financial resources. Thus, those people who are in good health and who anticipate a long life are more interested in purchasing life annuities than are those people who are in poor health. This form of antiselection is the opposite of the form of antiselection found in life insurance, where those people who are in poor health or who have some other reason to expect a shorter-than-normal lifespan are more interested in purchasing life insurance than are those people who are in good health. Also, in contrast to the operation of life insurance premium rates, life annuity premium rates decrease as mortality rates increase. In other words, the higher the mortality rate for a group of annuitants, the lower the premium rate that the insurer will charge for those annuities. As a result of these facts, if insurers used life insurance mortality tables to calculate premium rates for life annuities, then the premiums they collected would be inadequate to provide the lifetime annuity benefits promised.

As we described in Chapter 6, mortality rates vary by both age and gender. Mortality statistics show that females as a group may anticipate living longer than males as a group. Because females as a group live longer than males, insurers generally must pay life annuity benefits to females as a group for a longer period of time than they pay life annuity benefits to males as a group. Consequently, annuity premium rates are generally higher for females than for males of the same age. In other words, insurers compensate for a female annuitant's lower mortality risk by charging her a higher premium rate than they charge a male of the same age.

In recent years, insurers have received public pressure to charge the same premium rates for both females and males. The legislatures and courts are examining whether the use of sex-based premium rates is a form of unlawful discrimination on the basis of sex. Some jurisdictions have enacted laws requiring that insurers use the same premium rates for both men and women for some types of insurance. Hence, some insurers use unisex annuity mortality tables and charge females and males the same premium rates for life annuities.

Types of Life Annuities

When the annuitant of a life annuity dies during the payout period, the insurer's liability for additional annuity benefit payments depends on the type of annuity. The three variations of life annuity that insurers commonly offer are (1) the straight life annuity, (2) the life income annuity with period certain, and (3) the life income with refund annuity. Our discussion in this section will focus on how life annuity benefits are paid and what liability the insurer has if the annuitant dies during the payout period. Recall from our earlier discussion that if the annuitant or contractholder dies during the accumulation period, the insurer typically must pay the annuity's accumulated value to the beneficiary as a survivor benefit.

Straight Life Annuity

The *straight life annuity* provides periodic payments for only as long as the annuitant lives. Upon the death of the annuitant, the insurer has no further liability under the annuity policy. Because of the uncertainty of when an annuitant will die, the purchaser of a straight life annuity runs the risk that she may pay a great deal more in premiums than she will receive in benefit payments. Many people are unwilling to accept such a risk, and thus they purchase life annuities that contain more guarantees than are contained in a straight life annuity.

Life Income Annuity with Period Certain

A *life income annuity with period certain* guarantees that annuity benefits will be paid throughout the annuitant's life and guarantees that the payments will be made for at least a certain period, even if the annuitant dies before the end of that period. The contractholder selects the guaranteed period, which is often five or ten years, and names a contingent payee. If the annuitant dies before the period certain has expired, then the contingent payee becomes entitled to receive the periodic benefit payments throughout the remainder of the period certain. If the annuitant dies after the expiration of the period certain, benefit payments cease.

EXAMPLE   Jameel Stegall purchased a life income annuity with a 10-year period certain. He named himself as the annuitant and the payee. He named his wife, Alma, as contingent payee. Jameel died 7 years after benefit payments began.

ANALYSIS   Alma will receive the periodic benefits throughout the remainder of the 10-year period certain—she will receive periodic benefits for 3 years. After the expiration of the 10-year period certain, no more benefit payments will be made. Had Jameel lived 15 years after annuity benefits began, he would have received benefit payments throughout his life, and Alma would have received no benefits after his death.

Life Income with Refund Annuity

The *life income with refund annuity,* also known as a *refund annuity,* provides annuity benefits throughout the lifetime of the annuitant and guarantees that at least the purchase price of the annuity will be paid in benefits. This guarantee means that if the annuitant dies before the total of the benefit payments made equals the purchase price, a refund will be made to a contingent payee designated by the contractholder. The amount of the refund is equal to the difference between the purchase price of the annuity and the amount that has been paid in benefits.

EXAMPLE Anwar Lake paid a single premium of $120,000 for a refund annuity that would provide an annuity benefit of $10,000 per year during his lifetime. He named his wife, Maria, as the contingent payee. Anwar died 7 years after benefit payments began; at the time of his death, he had received benefits totalling $70,000.

ANALYSIS Maria will be entitled to a refund of $50,000, which is the difference between the $120,000 purchase price and the $70,000 paid in benefits during Anwar's lifetime. Had Anwar lived for 15 years after benefit payments began, he would have received more in benefits than he paid for the annuity (15 years × $10,000 per year = $150,000). In that case, Maria would not have received a refund payment following Anwar's death.

The refund annuity is available in two forms: (1) the *cash refund annuity* under which the refund is payable in a lump sum and (2) the *installment refund annuity* under which the refund is payable in a series of periodic payments.

Comparison of Premium Rates

Premium rates for the straight life annuity are the lowest of the three types of life annuities that we have described. When guarantees are added into a life annuity policy, the amount of the premium charged for the annuity will necessarily increase. (See Figure 16-4, which provides sample annuity benefit amounts that could be provided by various types of annuities for the same single premium amount.)

Annuity Contract Provisions

Many of the provisions that typically are included in individual life insurance policies are also included in individual annuity contracts. (See Chapter 10 for a description of the standard life insurance policy provisions.) The following provisions generally are included in all types of individual annuity contracts:

FIGURE 16-4. Sample Annuity Benefit Amounts Available Under Various Forms of Life Annuities.

Type of Annuity*	Monthly Benefit Amount
Straight life annuity	$86
Life income annuity: 10-year period certain	83
Life income annuity: 20-year period certain	78
Life income with refund annuity	83

* Each annuity is an immediate annuity purchased by a 65-year-old woman for a single premium payment of $10,000.

- An *entire contract provision*, which states that the entire contract consists of the annuity contract, the application if it is attached to the contract, and any attached riders. The provision is basically the same as that included in individual life insurance policies.

- A *free-look provision* or *free-examination provision*, which gives the contractholder a stated period of time—usually ten days—after the contract is delivered in which to examine the policy. During the free-look period, the contractholder has the right to cancel the contract and receive a full refund of all premiums paid. The provision is basically the same as that included in individual life insurance policies.

- An *incontestability provision*, which varies depending on the types of questions contained in the application for the annuity. Typically, the application for an annuity does not contain questions relating to the insurability of the applicant, and, thus, the applicant does not make representations on which the insurer bases its decision to issue an annuity. In such cases, the incontestability provision included in the annuity contract states that, once the contract becomes effective, the insurer may not contest the validity of the contract. Some insurers offer supplementary benefit riders, such as a waiver of premium for disability benefit rider. The applicant for such a rider generally must provide evidence of insurability, and the annuity or the rider includes an incontestability provision that gives the insurer a specified period—such as one or two years—in which to contest the validity of the coverage provided by the rider based on a material misrepresentation in the application.

- A *misstatement of age or sex provision*, which states that if the annuitant's age or sex was misstated, then the annuity benefits payable will be those that the premiums paid would have purchased for the correct age or sex. Recall that the annuitant's age and sex affect the amount of periodic annuity benefits payable only if those benefits are to be paid as a type of life annuity. Thus, if the insurer discovers during the payout period of a life annuity that the annuitant's age or sex was misstated, then the insurer will adjust the amount of succeeding annuity benefit payments to reflect the correct age or sex. In other words, the insurer adjusts the amount of future life annuity benefit payments to reflect the correct age or sex and to compensate for any prior overpayments or underpayments in annuity benefits.

FAST FACT

In 1997, Canadian life insurers received over $17 billion in annuity considerations, which represented about half of their total premium income.[6]

- An *assignment provision*, which is like the assignment provision included in individual life insurance policies in that it describes the roles of the insurer and the contractholder when the contract is assigned. Unlike individual life policies, individual annuity contracts generally state that if the contract is part of specified types of qualified retirement plans, then the contract may not be sold, assigned, transferred, or pledged as collateral for a loan or for any other purpose to any other person.[5] This prohibition against the assignment of specified types of qualified retirement plan contracts is required by federal tax laws, and, thus, such contracts are not assignable. We describe qualified retirement plans in the next chapter.

- A *settlement options provision* or *payout options provision*, which identifies and describes each of the payout options the contractholder may elect for the payment of annuity benefits. Throughout this chapter, we have described the various methods by which annuity benefits may be paid.

Depending on the type of annuity contract, additional provisions are included in individual annuity contracts. Earlier in the chapter, we described some unique features of deferred annuity contracts, which generally include the following provisions:

- A *beneficiary provision*, which gives the contractholder the right to name the beneficiary who will receive any survivor benefits payable if the annuitant or contractholder dies before annuity benefit payments begin.

- A *withdrawal provision*, which gives the contractholder the right to withdraw all or part of the annuity's accumulated value during the accumulation period.

- A *surrender provision,* which gives the contractholder the right to surrender the annuity for its cash surrender value during the accumulation period.

Although most annuities are single-premium or flexible-premium annuities, annuities may be purchased with the payment of fixed, scheduled premium payments. Such fixed-premium annuities generally include the following additional provisions:

- A *grace period provision,* which gives the contractholder the right to pay any premium within a specified period following the premium due date.

- A *reinstatement provision,* which gives the contractholder the right to reinstate the contract to fully paid-up status by paying all unpaid and outstanding premiums.

Like participating individual life insurance policies, participating individual annuity policies must include a *dividends provision,* which describes the contractholder's right to share in the insurer's divisible surplus, if any, and the dividend payment options available to the contractholder. Most participating annuity policies note that the insurance company does not expect to pay policy dividends. Instead, insurers usually increase the interest rate they pay on participating annuities above the minimum rate guaranteed in the policies and, thus, they allow the owners of participating annuities to share in the insurers' gains.

Regulation of Annuities

In both the United States and Canada, the states and provinces regulate the insurance companies that issue annuity policies as they regulate companies that issue life insurance policies. In order to issue annuities within a given jurisdiction, the insurer must be licensed as a life insurance company by that jurisdiction. The annuity policies that are issued must comply with all of the applicable state or provincial laws and regulations. The agents who sell annuity policies also must be licensed as life insurance agents by the applicable jurisdiction.

In the United States, an additional level of regulation has been imposed on variable annuities, which are subject to regulation by the federal Securities and Exchange Commission (SEC). As we noted in Chapter 2, the SEC has determined that variable annuities are securities contracts that are subject to federal regulation. Insurers that issue variable annuities must, therefore, comply with federal securities laws in addition to all applicable state insurance laws. A sales agent who markets variable annuities (1) must be licensed by the appropriate state as a life insurance agent and (2) must be registered with the National Association of Securities Dealers (NASD) as a registered representative, in accordance with federal registration requirements.

Taxation of Annuities

As illustrated in Figure 16-5, annuities are an increasingly popular product in the United States, and annuities now represent the largest portion of the premium receipts of U.S. life insurance companies. The popularity of annuities to U.S. consumers is in part the result of favorable federal income tax treatment. A product that qualifies as an annuity in accordance with federal tax laws provides a way for an individual to invest money over time and defer the payment of income taxes on his investment earnings. The investment income that the purchaser is earning on his premium payments is generally not subject to taxation until the investment income is actually paid out by the insurer to the named recipient. However, unless the annuity is also a qualified individual retirement plan—which we describe later in the chapter—the premiums paid for an individual annuity are not deductible from the individual's income for federal income tax purposes.

For purposes of federal income taxes, each annuity benefit payment is considered to consist of the following two parts:

1. One portion of each benefit payment is considered a return of principal, which is not taxable because the purchaser has already paid income taxes on that amount.

2. The remainder of each benefit payment is considered taxable investment income because the purchaser has never paid income taxes on the policy's investment earnings.

By contrast, Canada's tax laws do not provide this favorable treatment for annuities. Investment earnings from an annuity are taxable as income throughout the life of the annuity. The one exception is an annuity used to fund a qualified retirement plan, which we describe in the next section.

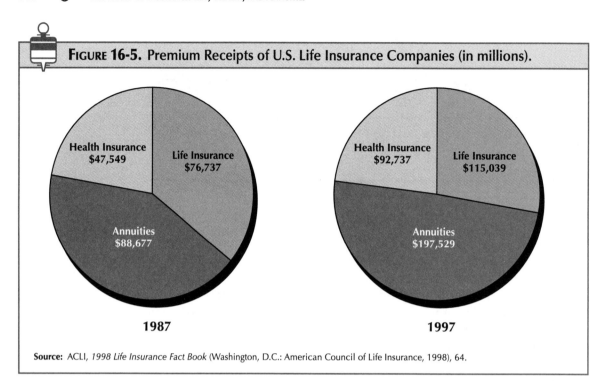

FIGURE 16-5. Premium Receipts of U.S. Life Insurance Companies (in millions).

1987

1997

Source: ACLI, *1998 Life Insurance Fact Book* (Washington, D.C.: American Council of Life Insurance, 1998), 64.

Individual Retirement Savings Plans

The governments of both the United States and Canada have enacted laws that provide federal income tax advantages to certain individuals who deposit funds into government-qualified retirement savings plans. These laws are designed to encourage taxpayers to establish savings plans for their retirement. In this section, we describe some of these qualified individual retirement savings plans, focusing on the plans that may be marketed by life insurance companies. Many individuals also participate in group retirement plans established by their employers. We describe these group retirement plans in the next chapter.

For federal income tax purposes, the amounts that certain individuals deposit into qualified retirement savings plans—up to a stated maximum—are usually deductible from their gross incomes in the year in which those funds were deposited into the plans. In other words, a taxpayer who meets specific criteria can reduce his current taxable income by making a contribution to a qualified retirement savings plan; he can, thus, defer the payment of federal income taxes until he withdraws the funds from the retirement account. In addition, the investment earnings on a qualified account generally are not taxed until the funds are withdrawn.

The advantage to this deferred taxation of the funds paid into a qualified retirement plan results from the fact that income tax rates generally increase as the amount of an individual's taxable income increases. Deposits into a qualified account are made during the individual's working years, when his income is generally higher than it will be once he retires. Because deposits are tax deductible, the individual reduces the amount of his taxable income during his working years. Withdrawals from the qualified account are made during the individual's retirement years, when his income is usually lower than it was during his working years. As a result, the withdrawals presumably will be taxed at a lower rate than the tax rate the individual would have paid on those amounts during his working years.

Figure 16-6 illustrates how the growth of income will differ depending on whether an account qualifies as a retirement savings plan. This illustration assumes that a person invests $1,000 a year into her account and that she earns 6 percent interest each year on the accumulated funds. Note that our illustration greatly oversimplifies the calculation of the person's income tax liability.

If the account qualifies as a retirement savings plan, her annual $1,000 investment is tax deductible and her investment earnings are not taxed each year. Instead, she will pay income taxes only when she withdraws funds from the account. By contrast, if the account does not qualify as a retirement savings plan, she must pay $280 in taxes (assuming a 28 percent tax rate) on that $1,000 ($1,000 × 0.28 = $280).

FAST FACT

During 1997, Canadians paid premiums of $9.9 billion for individual annuities.[7]

FIGURE 16-6. Comparison of the Accumulated Funds from an Annual Investment of $1,000 into a Qualified Account and a Nonqualified Account.

Years Held	Qualified Account Fund at Year End	Nonqualified Account Fund at Year End
1	$ 1,060	$ 751
5	5,975	4,094
10	13,972	9,153
15	24,673	15,402
20	38,993	23,124
25	58,156	32,664
30	83,802	44,450
35	118,121	59,011
40	164,048	77,002
45	225,508	99,229
50	307,756	126,691

* Contributions and earnings are taxed at a rate of 28 percent a year in the nonqualified account. A rate of return of 6 percent is assumed for both accounts.

As a result, she is able to invest only $720 into her account ($1,000 − $280 = $720). In addition, her investment earnings of $43 ($720 × 0.06) are also taxed at 28 percent, leaving her with after-tax investment income of $31 ($43 − [$43 × 0.28]). As the figure illustrates, the tax treatment of these two accounts makes a significant difference in the total amount of funds that accumulate.

United States

In the United States, two types of individual retirement savings plans qualify to receive favorable federal income tax treatment: individual retirement arrangements (IRAs) and Keogh (HR 10) plans. Federal laws (1) define which individuals may establish each type of qualified plan, (2) place limits on the amounts a taxpayer may contribute to each type of qualified plan, and (3) establish rules for the taxation of plan withdrawals.

Individual Retirement Arrangements

An *individual retirement arrangement (IRA)* is a retirement savings account that is established by an individual and that meets certain requirements to qualify for favorable federal income tax treatment. An IRA may take one of two forms:

1. An *individual retirement account* is a trust account created in the United States for the exclusive benefit of an individual and his beneficiaries; the trustee must be a bank, investment company, stock brokerage, or similar organization. Note that such organizations use the acronym IRA to refer to an individual retirement account.

2. An *individual retirement annuity* is an individual annuity issued by an insurance company. Insurers use the acronym IRA to refer to an individual retirement annuity.

To avoid confusion in terminology, we will use the acronym IRA to refer to both types of individual retirement arrangements. When individual differences exist, we distinguish between an individual retirement annuity and an individual retirement account. Our discussion focuses on individual retirement annuities issued by life insurance companies.

The sponsoring financial institution handles the administrative aspects of an individual retirement savings plan. For example, the insurance company that issues an individual retirement annuity ensures that the annuity meets the legislative requirements to qualify as an individual retirement arrangement and obtains approval from the Internal Revenue Service (IRS) that the plan qualifies. The insurer invests the funds deposited into the individual retirement annuity and manages the account. Individual retirement annuity funds may be placed in any of several special types of investments, such as stocks, bonds, or real estate.

The tax treatment of an IRA varies depending on whether it is a regular IRA or a Roth IRA. Since 1974, certain taxpayers have been able to establish and make contributions to a *regular IRA*. The following is a summary of the current federal tax treatment of a regular IRA:

1. Anyone who is less than age 70½ and who has earned income may contribute up to $2,000 per year of earned income into a regular IRA.

2. Individuals who are not participants in another qualified retirement plan may deduct the amount of the qualified contributions to a regular IRA from their taxable incomes.

3. Taxation of investment earnings is deferred until funds are withdrawn. With only a few exceptions, however, penalties are imposed on withdrawals made before the taxpayer attains age 59½.[8]

4. Taxpayers must begin making annual withdrawals of at least a specified minimum amount when they reach age 70½, and after that time they may not make additional contributions to their IRAs.

EXAMPLE Devon Smithby worked for a small printing company that did not provide a pension plan for its employees. For ten years, beginning when he was 56, Devon deposited $2,000 a year into a regular individual retirement account (IRA). At age 73, Devon retired from the printing company and began making monthly withdrawals from his IRA.

ANALYSIS Devon did not have to pay income taxes on the money he deposited into his IRA at the time of his investment. He was required to pay taxes on both the principal and the investment earnings when he withdrew the money from the IRA. Devon also had to pay a penalty because he did not begin making withdrawals from his IRA until two and one-half years after he turned 70½.

Since January 1, 1998, taxpayers have been able to establish a special type of IRA, known as a *Roth IRA*. This new type of IRA operates in much the same way as a regular IRA. For example, federal tax laws impose limits on the amount of contributions a taxpayer may make into a Roth IRA, and investment earnings that accumulate in a Roth IRA are not subject to income taxation until those earnings are withdrawn from the IRA. The primary differences in the tax treatment of a Roth IRA and a regular IRA are as follows:

1. No current tax deduction is allowed for contributions to a Roth IRA. Thus, Roth IRA contributions are made with after-tax dollars whereas regular IRA contributions are made with pre-tax dollars.

2. Qualified withdrawals from a Roth IRA that the taxpayer has held for at least five years are not subject to income taxation. Qualified withdrawals include withdrawals taken after age 59½ and withdrawals by a qualified first-time home buyer.

3. Unlike regular IRAs, Roth IRAs are not subject to minimum distribution requirements.

Keogh Plans

Another type of qualified plan is available to individuals who are self-employed. A **Keogh plan,** also known as an *HR 10 plan,* is a qualified individual retirement arrangement that may be established by a person who is self-employed and that is sponsored by a financial institution, such as an insurance company or an investment company. Life insurers market individual annuity contracts that qualify as Keogh plans. As in the case of an IRA, the sponsoring financial institution handles the administrative aspects of the Keogh; it obtains IRS approval that the plan qualifies for favorable income tax treatment, invests the funds deposited into the account, and manages the account. Also, funds in a Keogh plan may be placed in any of several types of investments, such as stocks, bonds, or real estate. Investment earnings are not taxable until they are withdrawn from the plan.

The owner of a qualified Keogh account has the right to deposit a stated percentage of her annual earned income—up to a legislatively defined maximum amount—into the account each year and to deduct that amount from her taxable income. Withdrawals from a Keogh account are taxable as income. As with IRAs, the taxpayer may have to pay penalties on withdrawals if she fails to meet the legislatively defined requirements for making withdrawals. These withdrawal penalties are designed to encourage taxpayers to use their Keogh account funds as retirement income.

Canada

In Canada, a qualified retirement account, known as a **registered retirement savings plan (RRSP),** can be established by any gainfully employed individual, including an individual who is covered by an employer-sponsored pension plan. An individual who establishes an account that qualifies as an RRSP can deduct from his gross taxable income the amount of his annual contribution to the RRSP—up to a stated maximum. Although any individual can establish an RRSP, the contribution amount that an individual can deduct from his gross income for income tax purposes varies depending on whether the individual is an active participant in a qualified pension plan. An individual who is not covered by a qualified pension plan may deduct a larger contribution amount from his gross income than can an individual who does participate in a qualified pension plan. The amount of the contribution to an RRSP that an individual may deduct each year is generally a stated percentage of his annual earned income, subject to the stated maximums.

An individual establishes an RRSP by depositing money into an approved account, which is provided by an insurance company, trust company, or other financial organization authorized to issue investment contracts. Funds an individual deposits into an RRSP account may be placed in a number of different investment vehicles, and the investment income earned on those funds is not taxed until the funds are withdrawn. Individuals who establish RRSP accounts must begin withdrawing the accumulated funds by the time they reach age 69.

> ### FAST FACT
>
> At the end of 1997, registered retirement savings plan (RRSP) accumulated assets totaled about $235.1 billion. More than $39 billion of that total was held by Canadian life insurance companies.[9]

Key Terms

annuity
contractholder
principal
single-premium annuity
periodic level-premium annuity
flexible-premium annuity
annuity period
maturity date
immediate annuity
deferred annuity
payout period
accumulation period
accumulated value
withdrawal provision

withdrawal charge
cash surrender value
surrender charge
survivor benefit
payout option provision
life annuity
annuitant
annuity beneficiary
payee
annuity certain
period certain
temporary life annuity
joint and survivor annuity
fixed-benefit annuity

Key Terms (continued)

variable annuity
separate account
segregated account
accumulation units
annuity units
annuity mortality rates
straight life annuity
life income annuity with period
  certain
life income with refund annuity

cash refund annuity
installment refund annuity
individual retirement
  arrangement (IRA)
individual retirement account
individual retirement annuity
Keogh plan
registered retirement savings
  plan (RRSP)

Other Important Terms

annuity considerations
annual annuity
monthly annuity
annuity date
single-premium immediate
  annuity (SPIA)
liquidation period
single-premium deferred annuity
  (SPDA)
flexible-premium deferred
  annuity (FPDA)
joint and last survivorship
  annuity
refund annuity
entire contract provision
free-look provision
free-examination provision

incontestability provision
misstatement of age or sex
  provision
assignment provision
tax-sheltered annuity
settlement options provision
payout options provision
beneficiary provision
withdrawal provision
surrender provision
grace period provision
reinstatement provision
dividends provision
regular IRA
Roth IRA
HR 10 plan

Endnotes

1. CLHIA, *Canadian Life and Health Insurance Facts* (Toronto: Canadian Life and Health Insurance Association, 1998), 11.

2. ACLI, *1998 Life Insurance Fact Book* (Washington, D.C.: American Council of Life Insurance, 1998), 39.

3. Ibid.

4. Ibid., 63.

5. One exception to this rule is that a tax-sheltered annuity may be used as collateral for a loan from the insurer that issued the annuity. A *tax-sheltered annuity* is a special type of qualified retirement plan that specified employers may establish for their employees.

6. CLHIA, 20.

7. Ibid., 6.

8. Beginning in 1998, taxpayers younger than 59½ may make penalty-free withdrawals from a regular IRA in order to pay qualified higher education expenses or to buy, build, or rebuild a main home.

9. CLHIA, 12.

CHAPTER 17

Group Pension and Retirement Savings Plans

After reading this chapter, you should be able to

- Identify the requirements that are imposed by law on qualified employer-sponsored retirement plans in the United States and Canada

- Identify how qualified retirement plans in the United States and registered retirement plans in Canada are treated for federal income tax purposes

- Distinguish between a defined benefit pension plan and a defined contribution pension plan

- Distinguish between a profit sharing plan and a thrift and savings plan

- Identify the features of various retirement plan funding vehicles that are provided by life insurance companies

- Describe the features of the Canadian Old Age Security (OAS) Act, the Canada Pension Plan, and the Quebec Pension Plan

- Describe the features of the United States Social Security system

In the last chapter, we described individual annuity products and noted that individuals often purchase such products to provide themselves with an income after they retire. Individual annuities are not the only source of retirement income, however. Often, people receive retirement income from various government programs and from private retirement plans—group retirement plans sponsored by employers and unions. Life insurance companies are involved in the funding and administration of many private retirement plans in the United States and Canada.

Just as group life and health insurance plans provided as employee benefits are subject to government regulation, so are many private retirement plans. In turn, those private retirement plans that meet various government requirements are granted special income tax benefits. When establishing a retirement plan, employers and unions usually want to ensure that the plan will qualify for favorable income tax treatment. In order to meet this customer need, life insurance companies design their group retirement products to meet applicable regulatory requirements.

In this chapter, we first examine the various government regulations that apply to group retirement plans and the benefits that meeting such requirements provide to plan sponsors and plan participants. We then describe the types of group retirement plans that are available and how insurance companies are often involved in the funding and administration of these retirement plans. We conclude the chapter by describing some of the government-sponsored retirement plans that operate in Canada and the United States.

Regulation of Retirement Plans

In order to encourage employers and unions to establish private retirement plans, the federal income tax laws in the United States and Canada contain incentives that provide economic benefits to both the **plan sponsors**—the employers and unions that establish plans—and the **plan participants**—the employees and union members who are covered by the plans. In the United States, a retirement plan that meets the legal requirements to receive these tax benefits is known as a **qualified plan.** In Canada, such a plan is referred to as a **registered plan** because, before the plan is established, it must be approved by and registered with Revenue Canada in order to receive favorable income tax treatment.[1] Although plan sponsors in the United States are not required to obtain advance approval from the Internal Revenue

Service (IRS) in order to receive favorable tax treatment, most plan sponsors elect to obtain advance approval in order to ensure that the plan meets the requirements of a qualified plan.

The requirements that a retirement plan must meet in order to qualify for favorable tax treatment are spelled out in a variety of laws. Because of the scope and complexity of these laws, our discussion is designed to give you only a general overview of how the regulation of retirement plans has affected plan design. We first describe the laws that regulate retirement plans in the United States, and then we describe the laws in Canada.

United States

The majority of retirement plan legislation in the United States is provided by the *Employee Retirement Income Security Act (ERISA)*. In Chapter 15, we described how ERISA regulates employee welfare benefit plans. ERISA also contains provisions designed to establish equitable standards that all retirement plans must meet. The following are some of the requirements that ERISA imposes on retirement plans:

- Nondiscrimination requirements prohibit a qualified retirement plan from discriminating in favor of highly paid employees.

- A retirement plan must contain specified minimum *vesting* requirements that define when a plan participant is entitled to receive partial or full benefits under the plan even if he terminates employment prior to retirement. In all cases, a participant's right to receive benefits funded by his own contributions vests immediately in the participant; those contributions belong to the participant. ERISA imposes time limits within which a plan participant's right to receive benefits funded by employer contributions must vest.

- A variety of requirements are imposed on the investment of plan assets in order to ensure the safety of those assets. For example, plan assets typically must be held and invested by either an insurance company or a trustee.

- The plan sponsor is required to report certain information about the plan's provisions to governmental agencies and to plan participants.

- Individuals who administer the plan and hold plan assets are deemed to be fiduciaries, and they must comply with various statutory guidelines in carrying out their duties.

ERISA also amended the federal tax laws as those laws apply to qualified retirement plans. Although tax laws tend to be amended fairly frequently, we can make the following generalizations about the federal income tax treatment of contributions to and earnings from a qualified retirement plan:

- Within stated limits, the contributions that an employer makes to a qualified plan are considered a business expense and are deductible from the employer's current taxable income.

- The contributions an employer makes to a qualified plan on behalf of a plan participant are *not* considered current taxable income to the participant. Instead, a plan participant's payment of income taxes on the employer's contributions is deferred until she actually receives benefits from the plan.

- The investment earnings on plan contributions—whether the contributions are made by the employer or the employee—are allowed to accrue tax-free. As in the case of employer contributions, plan participants pay income taxes on these investment earnings only when they actually receive benefits from the plan.

Some retirement plans, known as **contributory plans,** require that employees also make contributions to fund the plan. In the United States, employees generally are not able to deduct the amount of their contributions to an employer-sponsored retirement plan from their taxable income. For this reason, many retirement plans in the United States are **noncontributory plans** that do not require employee contributions. There are exceptions to these rules, however, and we describe some of those exceptions later in the chapter.

Canada

The Canadian federal government and all the provincial governments have each enacted a **Pension Benefits Act** that governs the terms and operation of private pension plans. The federal *Pension Benefits Standards Act* governs private pension plans of employers that are subject to federal legislative control. Pension plans established by all other employers are subject to the applicable provincial act. Note that these statutes regulate pension plans, which are a specific type of retirement income plan. We distinguish among the various types of retirement plans later in the chapter.

The Pension Benefits Acts require that when an employer establishes a pension plan and makes contributions to that plan, the employer must register the plan with a specified government agency. In order to qualify for registration, the plan must comply with a number of requirements similar to the requirements that ERISA imposes on qualified retirement plans in the United States. The specific requirements, however, vary from province to province. The following are some of the general types of requirements that a plan must meet in order to qualify for registration under a Pension Benefits Act:

- The plan must contain specified minimum vesting requirements.

- Plan benefits must be *portable,* which means that benefits can be moved from one registered plan to another. Note that this requirement, which is not found in ERISA, has had a significant effect on the design of registered pension plans in Canada.

- Plan assets must be invested in accordance with standards specified in the applicable Pension Benefits Act.

The Pension Benefits Acts typically require that the terms of the plan be communicated in writing to covered employees. In addition, the plan sponsor must file annual information returns with the applicable governmental agencies and is responsible for ensuring that the plan continues to meet all statutory requirements.

In order to qualify for favorable federal income tax treatment in Canada, a retirement income plan must be approved by and registered with Revenue Canada. The registration requirements vary, depending on the type of retirement plan. One notable requirement is that in order to be approved by and registered with Revenue Canada, a pension plan must first be registered in accordance with the applicable Pension Benefits Act. Those retirement plans that meet the requirements for registration with Revenue Canada are eligible to receive the following tax benefits:

- Employer contributions, within specified limits, are deductible from the employer's current taxable income.

- Employer contributions are not included in the employee's current taxable income.

- Within specified limits, employee contributions are deductible from the employee's current taxable income. An individual taxpayer may contribute to a variety of registered retirement plans

FAST FACT

During 1997, Canadians paid premiums of $7.2 billion for group annuities.[2]

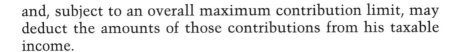

and, subject to an overall maximum contribution limit, may deduct the amounts of those contributions from his taxable income.

- Investment earnings are allowed to accrue tax-free until participants receive plan benefits.

Types of Retirement Plans

Three general types of qualified (registered) retirement plans are established by employers in the United States and Canada: (1) pension plans, (2) profit sharing plans, and (3) qualified (registered) retirement savings plans. The distinctions between these types of plans are important because the statutory requirements imposed on retirement plans vary somewhat depending on the type of plan. Keep in mind, however, that these statutory requirements are complex, and our discussion is intended to give you only a general overview. The specific provisions of any given retirement plan govern the operation of the plan.

Pension Plans

The term *pension plan* can have a variety of meanings, depending on the context in which it is used. For purposes of our classification system, a **pension plan** is an agreement under which an employer establishes a plan to provide its employees with a *pension*—a lifetime monthly income benefit that begins at retirement. The employer obligates itself to fund, in advance, at least a portion of the pension plan's promised benefits each year. Although pension plans typically provide other types of benefits to covered employees, the primary goal of a pension plan is to provide periodic retirement income benefits in the form of a life annuity to plan participants. Most employer-sponsored pension plans in the United States are qualified pension plans, and in the employee benefits area, the term *qualified plan* is often used to refer to a qualified pension plan. In Canada, such a plan is known as a **registered pension plan (RPP).** Although employers can select from various types of pension plans, each qualified (registered) pension plan can be categorized as either a defined benefit plan or a defined contribution plan.

Defined Benefit Pension Plans

A **defined benefit pension plan** defines the amount of the benefit that a participant will receive at retirement. The plan sponsor guarantees that a participant who has met the other requirements of the plan will be entitled to this specified benefit. The retirement benefit is usually described in terms of a monthly annuity, and the plan sponsor is obligated to deposit enough assets into the plan to provide the promised benefits.

The services of an actuary are typically required to determine the amount of contributions needed to fund the plan. The actuary determines the amount of these contributions by making estimates of employee mortality, employee turnover, future salaries, administration expenses, and plan investment earnings. Contributions made on behalf of all participants are typically pooled into one fund for investment and are allocated to individual plan participants as they retire in accordance with the plan's provisions.

Defined Contribution Pension Plans

A **defined contribution pension plan** describes the annual contribution that the employer will deposit into the plan on behalf of each plan participant. Usually, this contribution is a specified percentage of the participant's salary or wages. Contributions are allocated to each participant's account and are invested and accumulated on behalf of each plan participant. When a plan participant retires, the total amount allocated to that person is available either in a lump sum or in the form of a monthly annuity, depending on the provisions of the plan. The amount of the annuity benefit that each retiree receives depends upon the size of the fund that has been accumulated during her working years.

In recent years, plan sponsors have tended to establish pension plans as defined contribution plans rather than as defined benefit plans. (See Figure 17-1, which illustrates recent patterns of contributions to defined benefit and define contribution plans in the United States.) The primary reason behind this trend involves the costs required to fund a pension plan. When an employer establishes a defined contribution plan, it knows in advance what it will cost to fund the plan each year. By contrast, an employer that is funding a defined benefit plan must rely on actuarial estimates of what it will cost each year to fund the plan. In addition, the employer's costs may increase beyond what it estimated if the plan's investment experience is unfavorable. Other factors also influence an employer's decision as to whether to establish a defined benefit plan or a defined contribution plan. For example, ERISA imposes more complex requirements on defined benefit plans than it imposes on defined contribution plans.

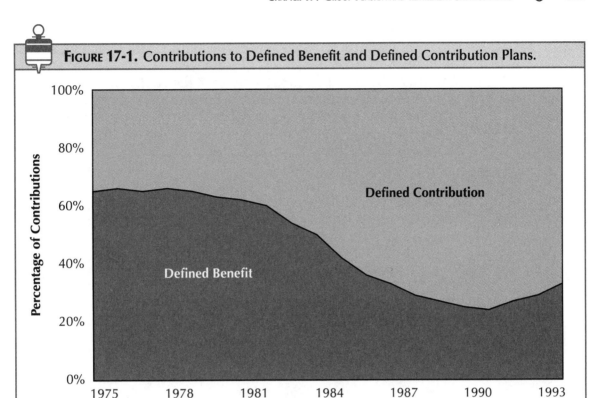

FIGURE 17-1. Contributions to Defined Benefit and Defined Contribution Plans.

Source: ACLI, *1997 Life Insurance Fact Book* (Washington, D.C.: American Council of Life Insurance, 1997), 24.

Profit Sharing Plans

A *profit sharing plan* that qualifies for favorable tax treatment is typically a type of retirement savings plan that is funded primarily by employer contributions payable from the employer's profits. In Canada, a qualified profit sharing plan is referred to as a *deferred profit sharing plan (DPSP)*. Although a qualified profit sharing plan functions in most respects like a defined contribution pension plan, the employer's contributions to a profit sharing plan are usually based on company profits, and the amount of those contributions may change from year to year. If conditions warrant it, the employer may not make any contribution in some years. By contrast, an employer's contributions to a pension plan must be made every year in accordance with a formula stated in the plan.

Although employers are permitted some latitude with respect to the amount of their plan contributions, laws in the United States and Canada impose certain conditions that qualified profit sharing plans must meet. Qualification rules in the United States require that employer contributions (1) must be substantial and recurring and (2) cannot unduly benefit highly paid employees. To qualify as a DPSP in Canada, a plan that defines the amount of the employer's contributions "by reference to profits" must provide that at least 1 percent of those profits will be contributed to the plan. If the plan defines the amount of the employer's contributions "out of profits," then limitations are imposed that are not as stringent as the 1 percent requirement.

Most profit sharing plans are noncontributory plans, though some plans in the United States allow employee contributions. Current laws in Canada prohibit employees from making contributions to a DPSP. Thus, in order to qualify for favorable tax treatment, DPSPs must be established as noncontributory plans.

Qualified Retirement Savings Plans

Some qualified retirement savings plans are funded primarily by employee contributions. Such plans are designed to encourage employees to save for their own retirement. Because different plans are offered in the United States and Canada, we discuss separately the qualified retirement savings plans available in these countries.

United States

In the United States, an employer may offer a ***thrift and savings plan*** to encourage employees to save for retirement. A thrift and savings plan operates in much the same way as a profit sharing plan. The primary difference is that an employer is obligated to make contributions to a thrift and savings plan on behalf of an employee if that employee makes a specified contribution to the plan. In contrast, under a profit sharing plan, the employer generally has no obligation to make plan contributions if its profits do not warrant it.

An account is established for each plan participant, and all contributions made on behalf of a participant are credited to that account and are invested in accordance with the terms of the plan document. The amount of an employee's contributions to a thrift and savings plan are subject to statutory limitations; the amount of an employer's contribution usually is equal to the amount contributed by the employee or is a percentage of that amount, subject to a specified maximum. For example, the plan document often specifies that an employee may contribute a percentage of his salary to the plan, subject to specified minimums and maximums, and that the employer will match that contribution up to a stated maximum percentage of the employee's salary.

EXAMPLE   The Compton Company sponsors a qualified thrift and savings plan that allows full-time employees to participate by contributing from 1 to 10 percent of their monthly salaries. Compton will match any employee contribution up to a maximum of 3 percent of the employee's salary. Irene Kowalsky, Wilbur Jensen, and Lorie Chen are all full-time employees. During the month of April, Irene made no plan contribution; Wilbur contributed 2 percent of his $2,000 monthly salary, and Lorie contributed 10 percent of her $3,000 monthly salary.

ANALYSIS   Wilbur's 2 percent contribution ($40) will be credited to his account, and Compton will make a matching contribution of $40. Lorie's 10 percent contribution ($300) will be credited to her account, and Compton will make a matching contribution of 3 percent of Lorie's $3,000 monthly salary ($90). Because Irene made no contribution to the plan, Compton will make no contribution on her behalf.

For federal income tax purposes, an employee who contributes to a qualified thrift and savings plan is not able to deduct the amount of that contribution from her current taxable income. In order to provide an incentive to employees to participate in such plans, tax laws in the United States allow employees to contribute to a special type of thrift and savings plan, known as a ***401(k) plan,*** on a before-tax basis. In other words, when an employee contributes to a 401(k) plan, the amount of her contribution is not included in her current gross taxable income. Instead, the employee will be taxed when she withdraws funds from her 401(k) plan. In order to participate in a 401(k) plan, an employee must enter into a salary reduction arrangement that permits the employer to deduct the amount of the employee's plan contribution from her salary.

EXAMPLE   Chad Green has become eligible to participate in a qualified thrift and savings plan. His friend, Iris Major, has become eligible to participate in a 401(k) plan. Chad and Iris earn the same salary—which is $30,000 a year—and they have each decided to contribute $2,000 a year to the plan.

ANALYSIS   Iris can contribute to her 401(k) plan on a before-tax basis. As a result, her $2,000 plan contribution will reduce the amount of her gross taxable income to $28,000. Chad's contribution to a qualified thrift and savings plan has no effect on the amount of his gross taxable income.

Another type of qualified retirement plan may be established by any employer that had no more than 100 employees during the preceding year. Under such a plan, known as a ***Savings Incentive Match Plan for Employees (SIMPLE plan),*** a SIMPLE IRA (individual retirement account or annuity) is established for each participating employee. The employee agrees to reduce his compensation by a stated percentage each pay period and to have the employer contribute that amount to the employee's SIMPLE IRA. Contribution limits are specified, and those limits generally are higher than the limits imposed on other types of IRAs but are lower than the limits placed on other qualified retirement plans described in this chapter. Note that the salary reduction contributions made on behalf of an employee are not considered current taxable income to the employee. The sponsoring employer also must make plan contributions on behalf of the employee, but only within specified limits.

All contributions to a SIMPLE IRA account must be fully vested in the employee. Unlike other types of qualified plans, SIMPLE plans are not required to include nondiscrimination requirements, and the regulatory reporting requirements are much less complex than those imposed on other types of qualified plans. As a general rule, withdrawals from a SIMPLE IRA must comply with the same requirements imposed on withdrawals from other types of IRAs.

Canada

As we noted in Chapter 16, an individual who wishes to establish a retirement savings program in Canada can purchase a Registered Retirement Savings Plan (RRSP) and, within stated limits, can deduct the amount of his annual plan contributions from his taxable income for federal income tax purposes. Many employers in Canada sponsor group RRSPs to help their employees save for retirement. A ***group RRSP*** is an employer-sponsored registered retirement savings plan in which an account is established for each participating employee. Employees and employers are permitted to make plan contributions within specified limits, and any employer contributions are treated as if they were made by the employee. As a result, all funds deposited into an individual's account are immediately vested with the employee, and for income tax purposes the employee can deduct the amount of all contributions—employee and employer—from his current taxable income.

Nonqualified Retirement Savings Plans

Because of the favorable tax treatment they receive, many U.S. employers have established qualified (registered) plans. Nevertheless, in

"Listen, Ogden, if I want to spend my retirement income on fashion swim-wear, that's my business!"

some situations, employers also have established retirement plans that do not qualify for all the tax benefits available to qualified and registered plans. The primary advantage to a plan sponsor of establishing such a nonqualified retirement savings plan is that the plan sponsor is relieved from complying with much of the complex legislation and stringent requirements that govern qualified (registered) plans. For example, an employer that establishes a nonqualified plan is able to provide additional benefits to certain classes of employees, such as highly paid executives, that the employer is unable to provide under a qualified plan.

EXAMPLE The Acorn Company is a closely held corporation that has established a profit sharing plan under which the two owners share in the company's annual profits. According to the terms of the plan, any year in which profits exceed a stated dollar amount, the company will pay the owners' shares of the profits into the plan. The company's 12 employees are not eligible to participate in the profit sharing plan.

ANALYSIS This profit sharing plan benefits only the two owners of the company, who receive plan benefits in the form of cash. The plan does not meet the requirements of a qualified plan. As a result, the cash benefits are taxable to the owners in the year in which they receive those benefits.

In the following sections, we describe nonqualified retirement plans in the United States and Canada.

United States

Because of the complexity of the laws governing qualified retirement plans, many employers—especially small employers—are unable to undertake the task of complying with those laws. In order to make retirement plans more available to the employees of these businesses, the federal tax laws were amended to provide tax benefits to participants in an employer-sponsored plan known as a *simplified employee pension (SEP) plan.* When an employer establishes a SEP, the employer makes contributions into an individual retirement account or individual retirement annuity for each participating employee. In order to participate in the plan, an employee must establish an IRA into which the employer will deposit its contributions. Note that it is the employee—not the employer—who establishes and owns the IRA. Because the employee owns the IRA into which the employer makes contributions, the employee is immediately vested in all amounts that are deposited into the account.

The amount of an employer's contribution into these IRAs, subject to legislatively defined maximums, is deductible as a business expense from the employer's taxable income. Although the amount of an employer's contribution on behalf of an employee is considered to be taxable income to the employee, the employee is generally allowed to take a tax deduction that offsets the amount of the employer's contribution. The maximum deductible amount contributed into an IRA through a SEP is considerably higher than the maximum deductible amount permitted with an individually established IRA. Because of the higher deductible amounts available through a SEP, many self-employed individuals also have established SEPs.

Employers generally establish SEPs because they are easy to administer and they reduce the amount of paperwork normally associated with establishing a qualified pension plan. Nevertheless, the employer must ensure that the plan meets various statutory requirements concerning the eligible employees who must be covered by the plan and the contribution amounts that can be made on behalf of specific classes of employees.

Canada

Some Canadian employers have established *employees' profit sharing plans (EPSPs)* that are nonregistered savings plans; typically, both the employer and the employees contribute to such a plan. Contributions to EPSPs must be allocated each year to individual accounts on behalf of plan participants. For income tax purposes, employer contributions to EPSPs typically are deductible by the employer as a business expense. However, in order for the employer to receive this tax deduction, the plan must provide that employer contributions will be made by reference to profits, which means that the employer must contribute at least 1 percent of its profits to the plan. A plan participant may not deduct the amount of her contributions to an EPSP and must pay income tax each year both on the employer's contributions and on the investment income credited to her account. As a result, a participant generally is not taxed on amounts that she receives from an EPSP.

> **FAST FACT**
>
> About 42% of eligible workers in Canada participate in employer-sponsored pension plans.[4]

Components of a Retirement Plan

A retirement plan consists of three components: (1) the plan, which describes how benefits will be funded and paid to participants; (2) a method for administering the plan; and (3) the funding vehicle into which the plan assets are invested. Insurance companies are involved in activities related to all three of these components—designing and developing retirement plans, administering retirement plans, and providing retirement plan funding vehicles.

The Plan

The plan sponsor must determine the type of plan to establish and the terms of that plan, which are spelled out in the written *plan document.* The plan document must contain a number of provisions. For example, the plan document specifies the eligibility requirements that employees must meet in order to participate in the retirement plan. The plan document must specify the amount of time that must pass before a plan participant is partially or fully vested. The plan document also must specify the times at which a plan participant is eligible to receive benefits payable from plan assets and, in most cases, the formula that will be used to determine the amount of benefits that plan participants will receive.

Plan Administration

The plan sponsor usually names a *plan administrator* who becomes responsible for a variety of aspects of the plan's operation. Although the plan administrator usually is a named individual, the administrator may be the sponsoring employer or it may be a board or committee established by the employer. The plan administrator, for example, is responsible for maintaining service records on all participants. These records ensure that the plan's eligibility and vesting requirements are met. Records are also needed to determine the amount of benefits payable to participants. The plan administrator uses these records to prepare all required reports for governmental agencies and for providing the plan participants with information about the plan.

In many cases, the services of various professionals are required to operate a retirement plan according to its terms; the plan administrator is responsible for hiring these professionals. For example, we noted earlier that the services of an actuary are typically required to determine the amount of contributions that are needed to fund a defined benefit plan. The plan administrator may also need to obtain the services of other professionals, such as accountants, attorneys, and consultants. Life insurers often provide such administrative services for retirement plans. In some cases, a life insurer provides only administrative services to a plan. In other cases, the insurer provides both administrative services and a funding vehicle for the plan.

Funding Vehicles

Contributions to fund a retirement plan must be invested. A *funding vehicle* is the means for investing the plan's assets as they are accumulated. This funding vehicle might be an annuity, a life insurance contract, a mutual fund, or some other type of investment. The plan sponsor is required by law to adhere to certain standards of prudence in handling and investing plan assets.

Although the plan sponsor may invest the assets directly, the sponsor generally seeks investment services from financial services companies that specialize in providing such services. For example, life insurance companies, banks, and investment companies provide investment services to the sponsors of retirement plans. Each type of financial services company offers various funding vehicles to appeal to the varying needs of plan sponsors. Funding vehicles offered by life insurance companies can provide guarantees against certain financial and mortality risks and are, therefore, attractive to many plan sponsors.

Life insurers offer a variety of products that are designed as retirement plan funding vehicles, and insurers are quite flexible in tailoring their products to meet the specific needs of a plan sponsor. In this section, we describe the types of retirement plan funding vehicles that are offered by life insurance companies, including group deferred annuities, deposit administration contracts, immediate participation guarantee contracts (IPGs), separate account contracts, and guaranteed investment contracts (GICs). Keep in mind, however, that the funding vehicle of a given retirement plan usually has been tailored specifically for that plan. As a result, it may be difficult to classify a given funding vehicle. In addition, a retirement plan may combine two or more types of funding vehicles. For example, some retirement plans include both an insurance contract and a noninsurance contract; such combination arrangements are referred to as *split-funding contracts.*

Group Deferred Annuities

A **group deferred annuity** operates much like a group insurance plan. A life insurance company issues a master policy to the plan sponsor and issues certificates to each individual plan participant. Each year, the insurer uses the contributions made on behalf of each plan participant to purchase a single-premium deferred annuity for that plan participant. When the plan participant retires, benefit payments from these deferred annuities will provide the scheduled retirement benefits. Because contributions are used to purchase annuities in the years prior to a plan participant's retirement, group deferred annuities require premium payments and are known as *fully insured products.* In recent years, very few group deferred annuity contracts have been issued, as pension plan sponsors have increasingly turned to contracts that provide greater flexibility in terms of contributions and greater participation in investment experience.

Deposit Administration Contracts

Under a **deposit administration contract,** the plan sponsor places plan assets in the insurance company's general investment account. When a plan participant retires, the insurer withdraws sufficient funds from the general account to purchase an immediate annuity for the plan participant. The insurance company usually provides the plan sponsor with guarantees against investment loss, as well as guarantees regarding minimum investment returns. Further, the insurer usually guarantees, in advance, the price of the immediate annuity to be purchased at the time of a plan participant's retirement. When the immediate annuity is purchased, the insurance company guarantees the amount of the periodic annuity benefit that will be paid to the plan participant.

Immediate Participation Guarantee Contracts

Plan assets placed in an **immediate participation guarantee (IPG) contract** are also placed by the life insurance company in an investment account on behalf of the plan sponsor. However, IPG contracts do not provide the full guarantees against investment loss or the guarantees regarding the minimum investment returns that are provided through deposit administration contracts. Instead, an IPG contract is designed to allow the plan sponsor to share in the gains or losses experienced by the life insurance company as it invests and pays benefits from the investment account. Many IPG contracts, however, guarantee that the plan sponsor will not share in losses greater than a stated amount. When a plan participant retires, funds may be withdrawn to purchase an immediate annuity for that retiree, or the retirement benefit may be paid directly each month from the investment account to the retired person.

Separate Account Contracts

Under a **separate account contract,** which is sometimes called an *investment facility contract,* the insurance company invests plan assets in common stocks, short-term money market investments, mutual funds, bonds, real estate, or other specialized investments. The insurer follows a different investment strategy for each separate account, and the plan sponsor chooses the account or accounts in which the plan contributions are to be placed. Separate account contracts usually do not make any guarantees regarding investment performance.

Guaranteed Investment Contracts (GICs)

Under a basic **guaranteed investment contract (GIC),** the insurer accepts a single deposit from the plan sponsor for a specified period of time, such as five years. The contract guarantees that at least a specified interest rate will be paid on deposited funds during that period. Interest earned may be accumulated until the period expires, or the earned interest may be paid out annually. At the end of the period, the account balance—including any accumulated interest—is returned to the plan sponsor. Numerous variations of this basic GIC have been developed to (1) allow the plan sponsor to make monthly contributions rather than a single deposit, and (2) allow the principal and interest to be paid out in installments as benefit payments to plan participants. A GIC may also be called a *guaranteed interest contract* or a *guaranteed income contract.*

Under the terms of both separate account contracts and GICs, the plan sponsor is permitted to purchase an immediate annuity from the insurer at the time of a plan participant's retirement, although the plan sponsor is not required to purchase such an annuity.

Government-Sponsored Retirement Plans

The governments of both Canada and the United States have established plans that provide monthly retirement income benefits to qualified residents. Because many employer-sponsored pension plans determine the amount of plan benefits by factoring in the amount of benefits that will be payable under government-sponsored plans, you should understand how these government plans operate. We first examine the retirement plans provided by government programs in Canada, and then we describe those provided by government programs in the United States.

Canada

Pensions are provided to Canadian retirees through three separate government plans: (1) the Old Age Security Act, which is in effect throughout Canada; (2) the Canada Pension Plan, which operates in all Canadian provinces except Quebec; and (3) the Quebec Pension Plan, which operates only in Quebec.

Old Age Security Act

The federal *Old Age Security (OAS) Act* provides a pension to virtually all Canadian residents who are age 65 or older. The right to receive a pension under the OAS Act is not dependent on a person's preretirement wages, current employment, or marital status. Each retired person who has reached age 65 and has met certain residency requirements receives the same pension amount; this pension amount is tied to the Canadian Consumer Price Index and increases along with increases in that index. The money to fund these pensions is taken from federal government general tax revenues.

Canada Pension Plan and Quebec Pension Plan

The *Canada Pension Plan (CPP)* is a federal program that provides a pension for wage earners who have contributed money into the plan during their working years. The CPP covers workers in all provinces except Quebec, which has elected to establish its own provincial plan. The *Quebec Pension Plan (QPP)* is a plan that functions in the same manner as the CPP except that the QPP applies only to wage earners in Quebec. The CPP and QPP are closely coordinated and tend to operate as one plan. For example, contributions made into one of these plans can be transferred to the other plan if an individual moves into or out of Quebec. In addition to pension benefits, the CPP and the QPP provide survivorship benefits, lump-sum death benefits, benefits for orphans, and long-term disability income benefits.

Participation in these plans is mandatory for employees covered by the plans, and virtually all employees and self-employed persons in Canada are covered. Benefits are funded through compulsory contributions from employees and their employers. Each covered worker

> **FAST FACT**
>
> As of January 1, 1996, total accumulated assets for Canadian pension plans were valued at $485 billion.[5]

must contribute a stated percentage of his earned income, subject to a specified maximum annual amount. The worker's employer must contribute the same percentage as the worker contributes each year. A self-employed person must contribute a higher percentage of his earned income because his contributions will not be matched by an employer's contributions.

The amount of the monthly benefit paid following retirement is related to the amount contributed into the plan by or on behalf of the individual; the amount is also limited to a legislatively established maximum amount. Benefit amounts paid under the CPP and the QPP are adjusted each year to reflect any cost-of-living increases.

United States

In the United States, government pensions are provided under several programs, including (1) the Civil Service Retirement Act, (2) the Railroad Retirement Act, and (3) the Old Age, Survivors, Disability and Health Insurance (OASDHI) Act or, as it is better known, *Social Security*. Nearly all people employed in the United States are covered under Social Security, including those employed by the armed forces. The only sizable groups not covered are those federal civil service workers who are covered by the Civil Service Retirement Act, railroad workers who are covered by the Railroad Retirement Act, and some state and municipal civil service workers. Participation in the Social Security system is not mandatory for state civil service workers at this time, and several states provide their own retirement programs for their civil service workers. Other states, however, have voluntarily joined the Social Security system, and their civil service employees are covered by the Social Security program. Because Social Security covers far more people than do the other government pension plans, we limit our discussion to the pension plan provided through Social Security.

> **FAST FACT**
>
> In the United States, ½ of all full-time, private-sector workers and ¾ of all government civilian employees are enrolled in retirement plans other than Social Security.[6]

Social Security provides a monthly income benefit to people who have contributed to the system during their income-earning years. Social Security retirement benefits are available to covered persons who are age 62 or older, although people retiring before age 65 typically receive a lesser monthly benefit amount than they would receive if they retired at age 65 or older. Social Security benefits may also be paid to surviving spouses and dependent children of covered workers who have died, as well as to covered persons who become disabled. The federal government administers the Social Security system and makes frequent changes in the system's funding and benefits.

The Social Security plan is funded by mandatory contributions from covered workers and their employers. During their working years, each covered worker must contribute a stated percentage of her earned income, up to a specified maximum yearly contribution amount. An individual's employer contributes an amount equal to that contributed by the employee. A self-employed participant must contribute a higher percentage of earnings than does an employee because a self-employed person's contributions are not matched by any employer contributions.

The amount of monthly benefit a person receives depends on the wages earned during the contribution period and is also subject to a specified maximum amount. However, the amount of retirement benefit is periodically increased to reflect increases in the cost of living, as measured by the Consumer Price Index (CPI) in the United States.

Key Terms

plan sponsors
plan participants
qualified plan
registered plan
vesting
contributory plans
noncontributory plans
Pension Benefits Act
pension plan
registered pension plan (RPP)
defined benefit pension plan
defined contribution pension plan
profit sharing plan
deferred profit sharing plan (DPSP)
thrift and savings plan
401(k) plan
Savings Incentive Match Plan for Employees (SIMPLE plan)
group RRSP

nonqualified retirement savings plan
simplified employee pension (SEP) plan
employees' profit sharing plan (EPSP)
plan document
plan administrator
funding vehicle
group deferred annuity
deposit administration contract
immediate participation guarantee (IPG) contract
separate account contract
guaranteed investment contract (GIC)
Old Age Security (OAS) Act
Canada Pension Plan (CPP)
Quebec Pension Plan (QPP)
Social Security

Other Important Terms

Employee Retirement Income
   Security Act (ERISA)
Pension Benefits Standards Act
portable plan benefits
pension
qualified plan
split-funding contracts

fully insured products
investment facility contract
guaranteed interest contract
   (GIC)
guaranteed income contract
   (GIC)

Endnotes

1. Revenue Canada is the federal department that is responsible for Canadian tax, trade, and border administration.

2. CLHIA, *Canadian Life and Health Insurance Facts* (Toronto: Canadian Life and Health Insurance Association, 1998), 11.

3. ACLI, *1998 Life Insurance Fact Book* (Washington, D.C.: American Council of Life Insurance, 1998), 28.

4. CLHIA, 12.

5. Ibid.

6. ACLI, 27.

CHAPTER 18

Medical Expense Coverage

After reading this chapter, you should be able to

- Identify the most common types of basic medical expense coverage and describe the benefits that each provides

- Identify the purpose of expense participation features in major medical expense policies and give examples of commonly used expense participation methods

- Recognize the types of medical expenses that major medical policies commonly cover and those that are commonly excluded from coverage

- Identify and describe the most common types of specified expense coverage

- Distinguish between the features of the Medicare program and the Medicaid program in the United States

- Describe how medical expense coverage is provided in Canada

- Explain how insurers price health insurance

ost people cannot afford to pay the full costs of their medical treatment should they become seriously ill, nor can most people afford a loss of income when they are unable to work because of an illness or injury. Life and health insurance companies market a range of individual and group health insurance products designed to protect against the risk of financial loss insureds are likely to experience as the result of an illness or injury. The remainder of this text is devoted to health insurance products, which provide two types of coverage:

1. **Medical expense coverage** provides benefits to pay for the treatment of an insured's illnesses and injuries. This chapter describes medical expense insurance coverage.

2. **Disability income coverage** provides income replacement benefits to an insured who is unable to work because of sickness or injury. We describe disability income coverage in the next chapter.

In the United States and Canada, most people are covered by some form of medical expense insurance. Medical expense insurance coverage in the United States is provided to individuals and groups primarily by a private system of commercial life and health insurance companies and other private health insurance providers. Government-sponsored medical expense insurance programs are designed to cover only specified people, including the elderly and the poor. Figure 18-1 shows the percentages of individuals in the United States who have various types of health insurance coverage.

By contrast, virtually everyone residing in Canada has medical expense insurance coverage provided by government-sponsored programs. Life and health insurance companies market products designed to supplement the coverages provided by governmental programs, but such private coverage represents only a small portion of the medical expense insurance coverage in force in Canada.

Medical Expense Coverage in the United States

Both private health insurance plans and government-sponsored plans provide medical expense insurance coverage in the United States. First,

FIGURE 18-1. Health Insurance Coverage in the United States, 1997.

Type of Coverage	Percentage of Total U.S. Population
Covered by some form of health insurance	83.9%
Private health insurance coverage	70.1%
Employment-based health insurance coverage	61.4%
Government-provided coverage	24.8%
Medicare coverage	13.2%
Medicaid coverage	10.8%
Military plan coverage	3.2%
No health insurance coverage	16.1%

Source: U.S. Census Bureau, March 1998 Current Population Survey. Available online at http://www.census.gov/hhes/hlthins/hltin97/hi97t1.html.

we describe the medical expense plans that commercial insurance companies traditionally have provided. Then we describe government-sponsored medical expense plans.

Traditional Medical Expense Insurance

Insurance companies have developed a range of medical expense products designed to provide benefits for specified expenses an insured incurs. Traditionally, medical expense insurance products have provided ***indemnity benefits,*** or *reimbursement benefits*, which are stated as a maximum dollar amount the insurer will reimburse the insured for each covered expense the insured incurs. When an insured receives medical care, he is responsible for paying the medical care provider's charges and then seeking reimbursement for covered expenses from the insurance company by filing a claim for policy benefits. In this chapter, we describe traditional medical expense insurance policies that provide indemnity benefits. Note, however, that most medical expense insurance coverage today is provided by ***managed care plans,*** which are medical expense plans that combine the financing and delivery of health care within a system that manages the cost, accessibility, and quality of care. We describe managed care plans, including health maintenance organizations (HMOs) and preferred provider organizations (PPOs), in Chapter 22.

In this section, we describe three broad categories of traditional medical expense coverage: basic medical expense coverage, major medical expense coverage, and a number of supplemental coverages.

Basic Medical Expense Coverage

When insurance companies first offered medical expense policies, most policies provided *basic medical expense coverage,* which consisted of separate benefits for each specific type of covered medical care cost. The following list describes some of the most common types of basic medical expense coverage and the benefits that each coverage provides:

- *Hospital expense coverage* provides benefits for specified hospital expenses such as room and board, medications, laboratory services, and other fees associated with a hospital stay.

- *Surgical expense coverage* provides benefits for the costs of inpatient and outpatient surgical procedures.

- *Physicians' expense coverage* provides benefits for charges associated with physicians' visits both in and out of the hospital.

Each type of coverage may be provided under a separate policy, or several coverages can be provided under one policy. Basic medical expense coverage is often offered as *first-dollar coverage*—the insurer begins to reimburse the insured for eligible medical expenses without first requiring an out-of-pocket contribution from the insured. However, basic medical expense coverage often provides limited benefits and does not cover many types of medical expenses.

As individuals and group policyholders began to seek a broader range of benefits, basic medical expense coverages became less popular. Nevertheless, many types of basic medical expense coverage are still offered, either separately or in conjunction with a major medical policy.

Major Medical Insurance

Most traditional medical expense plans today are *major medical insurance plans,* which provide substantial benefits for hospital expenses, surgical expenses, and physicians' fees—just like the separate basic coverages we discussed in the previous section. Major medical insurance, however, can provide coverage for expenses that the separate basic coverages may not have covered. Although major medical plans focus mainly on providing benefits for medical services related to illness and accidents, most plans now also offer benefits for preventive care.

Major medical policies generally provide either a maximum benefit amount, such as $1 million, or specify an unlimited maximum benefit amount. In the past, the maximum benefit amount available under a major medical policy sometimes was applied to each covered sickness or injury. Most major medical policies now specify a lifetime

> ### FAST FACT
>
> In 1995, U.S. health insurers paid a total of $282 billion for medical care benefits and disability claims. Canadian insurers paid more than $5 billion in health insurance benefits that year.[1]

maximum benefit amount—the coverage ceases once the insured person has received that maximum amount in medical care benefits.

Types of Major Medical Coverage. Two types of major medical coverage are commonly available: (1) supplemental major medical and (2) comprehensive major medical. A *supplemental major medical policy* is issued in conjunction with an underlying basic medical expense insurance policy, such as a hospital expense plan. The supplemental policy is designed to provide benefit payments for expenses that exceed the benefit levels of the underlying basic plan and, often, for expenses that are not covered by the underlying plan.

A *comprehensive major medical policy* is a combination into one policy of the coverages provided by both a supplemental major medical policy and an underlying basic medical expense policy. A comprehensive major medical policy provides substantial medical expense coverage under one policy, and that policy covers most of the medical expenses the insured may incur. Today, the majority of medical expense insurance policies are issued as comprehensive major medical policies.

Covered Expenses. The benefits provided by major medical coverage include payment for many different types of medical treatments, supplies, and services. Major medical policies usually cover a wider range of medical expenses than do basic medical expense policies. The covered services and treatments typically include all or some of the following medical expenses:

- Hospital charges for room and board in a semiprivate room

- Miscellaneous hospital charges, such as laboratory fees, X-rays, medications, and the use of an operating room

- Surgical charges

- Anesthetics and oxygen

- Physical, occupational, and speech therapy

- Surgeons' and physicians' fees and services of registered nurses

- Specified outpatient expenses, such as laboratory fees, X-rays, and prescription drugs

Major medical policies allow the insured to seek medically necessary treatment from any licensed provider of recognized medical

"It only hurts when I pay my deductible."

Reprinted with permission of Phil Interlandi and Bituminous Casualty Corporation.

services. As long as the policy covers the medical services or treatments, the insurer will reimburse the insured for any eligible expenses, less the deductible and coinsurance amounts. We describe deductibles and coinsurance later in the chapter.

Usual, Customary, and Reasonable Fees. Major medical policies typically use the phrase *usual, customary, and reasonable* to describe the amount of any eligible expense that the insurer will reimburse under the policy. The **usual, customary, and reasonable (UCR) fee** is the maximum dollar amount of a given covered expense that the insurer will consider as eligible for reimbursement. To determine the UCR for a specific medical procedure in a given geographic area, insurers often analyze statistics from a national study of fees charged by medical providers. Using these statistics, insurers chart a range of fees for each geographic area in which services are provided. Each insurer sets its maximum benefit amount for each covered medical procedure by applying a predetermined formula to the range of fees charted for that procedure. Then, when an insured submits a claim requesting payment of the fee for the procedure, the insurer pays all or part of the claim, depending on whether the amount of the claim is within the usual, customary, and reasonable fee limits.

For example, a group insurer may determine that it will pay UCR fees falling below the 90th percentile of the fee range for an appendectomy in a specific state. If a medical provider charges fees for an appendectomy that are high enough to be in the top 10 percent of fees charged for appendectomies in that state, then the insurer will not pay the amount above the 90 percent level. The insured group member is responsible for paying fees that exceed the UCR amount. By contrast, if the medical provider's fees in this case were at the 85 percent level, the insurer would consider the entire fee eligible for coverage. The insurer, however, would not reimburse the insured for more than the actual amount of the fee.

Expense Participation. Major medical policies usually require the insured to share in paying for his medical expenses. This requirement encourages insureds to keep medical expenses to a minimum, and that, in turn, helps reduce the costs of the coverage. The two most common expense participation methods are deductibles and coinsurance, and most major medical policies include both a deductible and a coinsurance feature.

A *deductible* is usually a flat dollar amount of eligible medical expenses, such as $200 or $500, that the insured must incur out of her own pocket before the insurer will begin making any benefit payments under the policy. Most health insurance policies contain a *calendar-year deductible,* which is a deductible that applies to any eligible medical expenses an insured incurs during a given calendar year. The amount of the deductible specified in group major medical policies is generally lower than the amount specified in individual major medical policies.

The second expense participation feature, the *coinsurance provision,* states that once the insured has paid the deductible amount, he then must pay a specified percentage of all the remaining covered medical expenses. For example, many policies include a 20 percent coinsurance requirement under which the insured pays 20 percent of all covered medical expenses after paying the deductible amount. Most major medical policies limit the amount of money the insured must pay under the coinsurance provision by including a stop-loss provision. The *stop-loss provision* specifies that the policy will cover 100 percent of the insured's eligible medical expenses after he has incurred a specified amount of out-of-pocket expenses, such as $5,000, in deductible and coinsurance payments. Let's look at some examples to learn more about how deductibles and coinsurance provisions work.

FAST FACT

In 1995, hospital, surgical, physician, and major medical insurance claims in the United States totaled $98 billion under group policies and $8.8 billion under individual policies.[2]

EXAMPLE | Jeff Kowalski is covered by a comprehensive major medical policy that specifies a $500 calendar-year deductible and includes a 20 percent coinsurance provision with a $5,000 stop-loss provision. During 1998, Jeff incurred a total of $200 in covered medical expenses following an accident in the month of December. During 1999, Jeff incurred a total of $400 in covered medical expenses.

ANALYSIS | Because Jeff did not meet the $500 calendar-year deductible in either 1998 or 1999, he must pay the entire $600 in expenses incurred during those years.

EXAMPLE | Karen Anderson is covered by a comprehensive major medical policy that specifies a $500 calendar-year deductible and includes a 20 percent coinsurance provision with a $5,000 stop-loss provision. Karen incurred a total of $1,500 in covered medical expenses in January 1998 when she was hospitalized for treatment of an illness. In May 1998, Karen was hospitalized and incurred covered medical expenses of $30,000.

ANALYSIS | Let's look first at Karen's January expenses. After paying $500 in order to meet her policy's deductible, Karen then had to pay 20 percent of the remaining balance of $1,000. Karen's coinsurance equaled $200 (0.20 × $1,000). After paying both the deductible and coinsurance, Karen's out-of-pocket expenses totaled $700. The insurer paid the remaining $800.

$1,500	**Total covered expenses**
− 500	**Less: deductible**
$1,000	
− 200	**Less: coinsurance paid by Karen**
$ 800	**Amount insurer paid**

When Karen incurred additional expenses in May, she had already met the calendar-year deductible, but the policy's coinsurance provision required her to pay 20 percent of the remaining covered expenses, which totalled $6,000 (0.20 × $30,000). That amount, however, exceeded the policy's $5,000 stop-loss amount. Karen had already paid $700 in deductible and coinsurance amounts, and, thus, she had to pay only $4,300 of the covered expenses she incurred in May ($5,000 − $700). The insurer paid the remaining $25,700.

$30,000	**Total covered expenses**
− 4,300	**Less: coinsurance paid by Karen**
$25,700	**Amount insurer paid**

Exclusions. Major medical policies commonly exclude from coverage any medical expenses that result from the following treatments:

- Cosmetic surgery other than corrective surgery required as a result of an accidental injury or other medical reasons

- Treatment for injury or sickness that occurs while the insured is in military service or that results from an act of war

- Treatment for intentionally self-inflicted injuries

- Treatment that is provided free-of-charge in a government facility or that is paid for by other organizations

- Routine dental treatments, routine eye examinations, and corrective lenses

Supplemental Medical Expense Coverages

Insurance companies provide a range of supplemental medical expense coverages that provide benefits to reimburse the insured for the costs of (1) treatment for an illness that is specified in the supplemental policy or (2) medical supplies or treatments that are specified in the policy. The types of supplemental medical expense coverage that are most commonly offered to groups are dental expense coverage, prescription drug coverage, and vision care coverage. Another common type of supplemental coverage—dread disease coverage—is usually available only through individual insurance policies. Finally, we describe critical illness coverage, long-term care coverage, and Medicare supplement coverage, which are commonly offered on both a group and an individual basis.

Dental Expense Coverage

Basic medical expense coverage and major medical coverage typically do not provide benefits for expenses incurred in obtaining routine dental work and dental treatments. **Dental expense coverage** is a type of medical expense coverage that provides benefits for routine dental examinations, preventive work, and dental procedures needed to treat tooth decay and diseases of the teeth and jaw.

Most dental expense policies include both a deductible and a co-insurance feature. Because early detection and treatment of dental problems can result in significantly lower expenses overall, most dental policies provide full coverage for routine examinations and preventive work in order to encourage insureds to obtain regular dental checkups.

Prescription Drug Coverage

Prescription drug coverage provides benefits for the purchase of drugs and medicines that are prescribed by a physician and are not available over-the-counter. Usually, the insured pays a small amount toward the cost of each prescription. This amount, known as a *copayment*, is often between $5 and $10. The pharmacist then submits a claim for the remainder of the cost of the prescription directly to the organization that provides the coverage or to an organization that administers the prescription benefits. By contrast, some plans require the insured to pay deductibles and coinsurance and to complete a claim form in order to obtain plan benefits.

Vision Care Coverage

Vision care coverage provides the insured with benefits for expenses incurred in obtaining eye examinations and corrective lenses. Most policies that provide vision care coverage provide coverage for one routine examination of the insured per year. Policies also specify the maximum amount of the benefit the insurer will pay for eyeglass lenses and frames or contact lenses.

Dread Disease Coverage

Dread disease coverage provides benefits for medical expenses incurred by an insured who has contracted a specified disease. The most commonly offered coverage is cancer insurance. Coverage can supplement basic medical expense coverage and can serve the same purpose as supplemental major medical coverage if the insured should incur medical expenses as a result of having the disease named in the policy. Some states, however, do not allow the sale of dread disease coverage.

Critical Illness Coverage

Some insurers now offer *critical illness (CI) coverage* that pays a lump-sum benefit if the insured is diagnosed with a critical illness while the policy is in force. The conditions that are considered critical illnesses covered by the policy are specified in the policy and usually include heart attack, stroke, and life-threatening cancer. Other conditions generally are listed, but the specific conditions covered vary from insurer to insurer. CI coverage typically includes a return of premium benefit that is payable if the insured dies without having a critical illness. CI coverage may be offered as a policy rider or as either an individual or a group policy.

Long-Term Care Coverage

Long-term care (LTC) coverage provides medical and other services to insureds who, because of their advanced age or the effects of a serious illness or injury, need constant care in their own homes or in a qualified nursing facility. LTC coverage is a relatively new product that is still evolving as insurance companies gain experience with providing this coverage. The market for this coverage is growing rapidly as the population ages and medical advances enable many people to live longer than they would have lived in the past. In order to encourage taxpayers to purchase LTC coverage, U.S. federal income tax laws now allow taxpayers to deduct premiums paid for LTC coverage as a medical expense, subject to certain limitations.

The specific benefits provided by long-term care policies vary widely depending on the policy. (Figure 18-2 lists the typical coverages offered by the leading sellers of long-term care coverage.) Most policies provide coverage for services that range from skilled nursing care to custodial care, such as help in performing normal activities of daily living. Benefit levels also vary depending on the policy, but most policies contain an inflation protection feature under which benefit levels increase as inflation drives up the cost of living.

Medicare Supplement Coverage

In the United States, the Old Age, Survivors, Disability, and Health Insurance (OASDHI) program, popularly known as *Social Security*, provides medical expense coverage under the *Medicare* program. (We describe Medicare coverage in the next section of this chapter.) Insurance companies offer both individual and group health insurance products designed to supplement the coverage offered under Medicare. The policies, known as **Medicare supplements** or *Medigap policies*, often reimburse the insured for his out-of-pocket expenses, such as Medicare's deductible amount and coinsurance payments.

Government-Sponsored Medical Expense Coverage

In the United States, medical expense insurance benefits are provided through several government programs. The most important of these programs are Medicare and Medicaid.

FIGURE 18-2. Typical Coverages Offered by Leading Sellers of Long-Term Care Insurance, 1995.

Services	Nursing home care Home health care Alternate care Assisted living Hospice care Respite care
Other Benefits/Services	Care coordination/case management Homemaker/chore assistance Bed reservation Medical equipment coverage Spousal discount
Daily Benefit	$40–$250/day nursing home care $40–$250/day home health care
Benefit Eligibility	Medical necessity, or ADLs, or cognitive impairment
Maximum Benefit Period	Unlimited/lifetime
Deductible Period	0–100 days
Pre-Existing Condition	6 months None if disclosed during application
Renewability	Guaranteed
Alzheimer's Disease Coverage	Yes
Age Limits for Purchasing	18 to 99 years
Waiver of Premium	Yes
Free-Look Period	30 days
Inflation Protection	Yes
Nonforfeiture Benefit	Shortened benefit period, return of premium, or reduced paid-up coverage

Source: Health Insurance Association of America, Long-Term Care Market Survey, 1996. Used with permission.

Medicare

The federal Social Security Act was amended in 1965 to create a health insurance plan primarily for the elderly and disabled people. This plan, known as **Medicare,** now insures a large segment of the population. The following people are eligible for Medicare benefits:

- Those age 65 or over and eligible for Social Security retirement benefits

- Those entitled for at least two years to receive Social Security disability income benefits

- Those entitled to receive retirement benefits under the Railroad Retirement Act

- Those who are afflicted with—or are the dependent of a person afflicted with—kidney disease that requires either dialysis or a transplant

Medicare is a two-part program. *Medicare Part A* provides basic hospital insurance coverage to all eligible individuals. Coverage under Part A is automatically extended to all eligible persons. Benefits under Part A of Medicare cover the costs of the insured's (1) hospitalization, (2) confinement in an extended-care facility after hospitalization, and (3) home health care services. Part A includes both a deductible and a coinsurance provision.

Medicare Part B coverage is voluntary. Individuals who are eligible to receive Part A benefits have the option of purchasing coverage under Part B, which provides supplementary medical insurance. In order to receive Part B coverage, an individual must pay a monthly premium. The amount of the premium changes yearly, and, in 1999, the premium increased from $43.80 per month to $45.50 per month.

Medicare Part B provides benefits for physicians' professional services, whether the services are performed in a hospital, a physician's office, an extended-care facility, or the insured's home. Benefits are also payable for other services, including ambulance services, medical supplies, outpatient services, diagnostic tests, and other services necessary for the diagnosis or treatment of an illness or injury. Part B includes an annual deductible and a coinsurance feature.

Medicare Part A is financed primarily by a payroll tax imposed on employers and workers who are covered by the Social Security program. Medicare Part B is financed through premiums paid by covered individuals and from the federal government's general revenues. Although the federal government is responsible for administering the Medicare program, it has delegated this task to third parties. These third parties—called *intermediaries* when they administer Part A benefits and *carriers* when they administer Part B benefits—administer the benefit payments. Some insurance companies serve as Medicare intermediaries and carriers.

Many persons who are eligible for Medicare are also insured under private insurance plans. Some persons, for example, are covered as retirees under employer-employee plans. Others have purchased Medicare supplement coverage, which we described earlier in the chapter. Federal laws contain extensive rules concerning coordination of benefits between Medicare and the private plans in these cases. These rules define the individuals for whom Medicare will be the primary payor of medical expense benefits and those people for whom Medicare will be the secondary payor of benefits. Private medical expense plans also contain provisions that are designed to integrate the plans' benefits with the benefits provided by Medicare to prevent insureds from receiving more in benefit payments than the actual costs incurred for their medical care. (We describe these provisions in Chapters 20 and 21.)

Medicaid

Medicaid is a joint federal-state program that provides hospital and medical expense coverage to people who are poor. The state and federal governments jointly fund the program. Each state, however, administers its own program and establishes its own eligibility criteria. In addition, each state determines the services that its Medicaid plan will cover and the benefit amounts payable for covered services. As a result, Medicaid plans vary widely from state to state. However, each state plan must meet certain minimum standards and must include certain provisions in order to be eligible to receive federal matching funds.

Federal laws mandate that Medicaid programs provide certain services, including physicians' and hospital services, laboratory tests, and home health visits. Unlike Medicare and most private health insurance plans, Medicaid plans must cover long-term custodial nursing-home care. States have the option of including coverage for prescription drugs, dental care, and vision care. Federal laws also mandate that persons who receive certain federal benefits must be eligible for Medicaid assistance. For example, persons receiving Supplemental Security Income (SSI) benefits must be eligible for Medicaid coverage. Persons who are blind or disabled also must be eligible for Medicaid.

Unlike Medicare, which may be either the primary or secondary payor of benefits, Medicaid is always the secondary payor of benefits. Medicaid benefits typically are paid only after benefits payable from all other available sources have been paid.

Medical Expense Coverage in Canada

Each Canadian province and territory provides a medical expense insurance plan for its residents. The goal of these provincial plans is to provide an acceptable, basic level of health care to all provincial residents. Insured services vary somewhat from one provincial plan to another. Generally, however, covered services consist of the following:

- Hospital services that are medically necessary to maintain health, prevent disease, or diagnose or treat an injury, illness, or disability

- Physician services, which include specifically defined medical services provided by medical practitioners

- Surgical-dental services, which include specifically defined surgical-dental procedures performed in a hospital

Some provincial plans also provide certain residents with additional coverages, including benefits for preventive dental care and prescription drugs. Although the provincial health insurance plans cover a variety of medical expenses, not all medical expenses are covered. Some people want a higher level of benefits than the government plans provide. Provincial laws allow commercial insurers to offer health insurance coverages to supplement the coverages provided by the provincial health plans. As a result, many employers offer extended health care coverage to their employees under group health insurance policies offered primarily by traditional health insurance companies. Individual health insurance policies are also available.

The benefits provided under supplemental, extended health care insurance policies vary widely. Many policies, for example, provide supplemental hospital benefits. The hospital benefit provided by the provincial government plans is based on the cost of a bed in a hospital ward; a supplemental policy usually provides a benefit to make up the difference in cost between a bed in a ward and a semiprivate room. Private health insurance policies often include coverage of the cost of prescription drugs and out-of-country emergency care. Some policies also cover vision care expenses, such as the cost of eyeglasses or corrective lenses, and dental care expenses, such as preventive dental care. Supplemental health insurance policies may also cover any number of other miscellaneous medical expenses. For example, many health insurance policies provide benefits to reimburse the insured for expenses incurred for ambulance services, hearing aids, private-duty nursing care, and care in a convalescent home.

Many of the features of major medical policies described earlier in this chapter are also found in policies in Canada. For example, policies issued in Canada typically include expense participation features—deductibles and coinsurance. The deductible amount, however, tends to be much lower in Canada than in the United States. Policies issued in both countries contain the same types of exclusions; in Canada, however, policies also exclude all services that the provincial health plans cover. Unlike major medical policies issued in the United States, health insurance policies issued in Canada usually contain no overall maximum benefit amount.

Pricing Health Insurance

In order to provide the funds it will need to pay health insurance claims as they come due, an insurance company must collect premiums from the people to whom it provides health insurance coverage. As in the case of life insurance, the insurance company uses those premiums to create a fund from which to pay benefits as claims are incurred.

The fundamental principles underlying the pricing of health insurance are the same as those underlying life insurance pricing. That is, health insurance premiums must be adequate to provide the promised benefits and must be equitable to all policyowners. Nevertheless, life insurance and health insurance have significant differences, and most of these differences affect how insurance companies price these two products. Before we describe how health insurance is priced, let's look at some of these differences between life insurance and health insurance.

- Whereas the amount payable for a life insurance claim is definitely defined by the policy, the amount payable for a health insurance claim is often much less definite. For example, medical expense claims range from fairly small amounts to very large amounts, depending on the severity of the covered illness or injury.

- An insurer is likely to pay a number of covered claims from each person insured by a health insurance policy, but it will pay only one death claim for each person insured by a life insurance policy.

- Inflation, changes in the economy, and changes in medical practice affect the amount of benefits paid for health insurance claims much more dramatically than such factors affect life insurance claims.

- Because of the variation in medical costs in different geographic areas, certain health insurance premiums must be calculated separately for different geographic areas. By contrast, life insurance premium rates at given ages generally do not vary by geographical location within North America.

As described in an earlier chapter, insurers use morbidity rates to calculate health insurance premium rates, just as they use mortality rates to calculate life insurance premium rates. The insurance company uses this information about morbidity rates to calculate its **claim costs**—the costs the insurer predicts that it will incur to provide the policy benefits promised. For example, medical expense insurance typically provides benefits to pay the following types of expenses: (1) hospital expenses, (2) surgical expenses, (3) physicians' fees, and (4) major medical expenses. The insurer must estimate its claim costs for each type of benefit provided. (Figure 18-3 shows the percentages of private medical expense claim payments by category of services in 1995.)

Let's look at how an insurer might project its claim costs for benefits it will pay for hospital room and board expenses.

$$\text{Claim costs} = \begin{pmatrix} \text{Frequency of the} \\ \text{expected claim} \end{pmatrix} \times \begin{pmatrix} \text{Average amount} \\ \text{of each claim} \end{pmatrix}$$

The *frequency* of the expected claim is the number of claims for hospital room and board expenses that the insurer will receive.

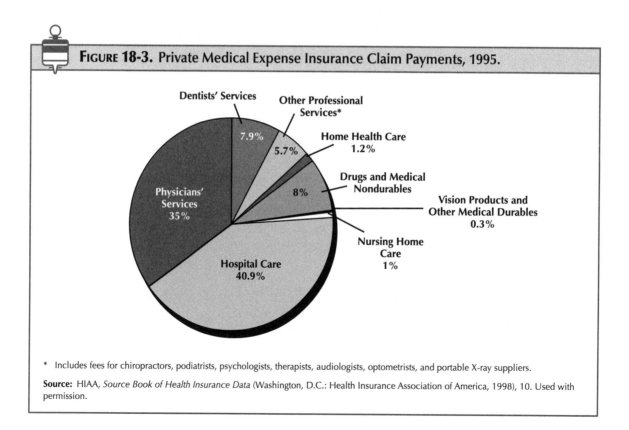

FIGURE 18-3. Private Medical Expense Insurance Claim Payments, 1995.

Dentists' Services — 7.9%
Other Professional Services* — 5.7%
Home Health Care — 1.2%
Physicians' Services — 35%
Drugs and Medical Nondurables — 8%
Vision Products and Other Medical Durables — 0.3%
Nursing Home Care — 1%
Hospital Care — 40.9%

* Includes fees for chiropractors, podiatrists, psychologists, therapists, audiologists, optometrists, and portable X-ray suppliers.

Source: HIAA, *Source Book of Health Insurance Data* (Washington, D.C.: Health Insurance Association of America, 1998), 10. Used with permission.

EXAMPLE The Hathaway Insurance Company expects to receive 100 claims for hospital room and board. The average amount of each claim will be $1,600.

ANALYSIS Hathaway's claim costs for hospital room and board will equal $160,000 (100 claims × $1,600 per claim).

The insurer uses its projected claim costs to calculate the net annual premium rates that will be sufficient to pay the promised health insurance benefits. The insurer then adds a loading factor that it estimates will be sufficient to cover all of its expenses and unforeseen contingencies. Because the risk is more uncertain for health insurance than for life insurance, insurance companies usually include in their loading for health insurance premiums a greater amount for unforeseen contingencies than they include in their loading for life insurance premiums. Recall that the net annual premium plus the loading equals the gross annual premium that the insurer will charge for a policy.

Insurers generally calculate health insurance premium rates on an annual basis. If premiums are payable more frequently than annually, then the insurer will add a small amount to the gross annual premium to cover the additional expenses incurred in collecting premiums on this more frequent basis.

A number of states require gross premiums for health insurance policies to be "reasonable." As a measure of "reasonableness," insurers are generally required to calculate the anticipated loss ratio for a group of similar policies, and this loss ratio typically must be at least a minimum stated percentage. The *loss ratio* is the ratio of benefits an insurer paid out for a block of policies to the premiums the insurer received for those policies. The loss ratio measures the percentage of total premiums the insurer received for a block of policies and that the insurer paid out in policy benefits. Note that even if the loss ratio for a block of policies remains level over time, the amount of premiums required for those policies will increase if policy benefit costs increase.

Key Terms

medical expense coverage
disability income coverage
indemnity benefits
managed care plans
basic medical expense coverage

hospital expense coverage
surgical expense coverage
physicians' expense coverage
first-dollar coverage
major medical insurance plans

Key Terms (continued)

supplemental major medical
   policy
comprehensive major medical
   policy
usual, customary, and
   reasonable (UCR) fee
deductible
calendar-year deductible
coinsurance provision
stop-loss provision
dental expense coverage

prescription drug coverage
copayment
vision care coverage
dread disease coverage
critical illness (CI) coverage
long-term care (LTC) coverage
Medicare supplement
Medicare
Medicaid
claim costs
loss ratio

Other Important Terms

reimbursement benefits
Social Security
Medigap policies
Medicare Part A

Medicare Part B
intermediaries
carriers
claim frequency

Endnotes

1. HIAA, *Source Book of Health Insurance Data* (Washington, D.C.: Health Insurance Association of America, 1998), 28; CLHIA, *Canadian Life and Health Insurance Facts* (Toronto: Canadian Life and Health Insurance Association, 1998), 15.

2. HIAA, 29.

3. Ibid.

4. Health Care Financing Administration, *Highlights National Health Expenditures, 1997* (Washington, D.C.: Health Care Financing Administration, 1998). Available online at http://www.hcfa.gov/stats/nhe-oact/nhe.htm.

5. CLHIA, 13.

CHAPTER 19

Disability Income Coverage

After reading this chapter, you should be able to

- Identify the various definitions of "total disability" that have commonly been included in disability income insurance policies and distinguish among those definitions

- Identify the criteria used to classify disability income coverage as either short-term coverage or long-term coverage

- Explain the purpose of including an elimination period in a disability income insurance policy and identify the length of the typical elimination period

- Identify and describe some supplemental benefits that may be included in a disability income insurance policy

- Recognize the causes of disability that a disability income insurance policy may exclude from coverage

- Identify three types of specialized disability coverage that are designed to meet the needs of closely held businesses for disability coverage of owners, partners, and key people

- Identify and describe the disability income coverage provided by government-sponsored plans in the United States and Canada

Most people worry about how they would pay their bills if they were unable to work because of an illness or injury. In fact, when a person is unable to work because of disability, the financial effect on the individual and his family is likely to be much greater than if the individual had died. When a wage-earner dies, his family is left without a source of income. In case of disability, however, the wage-earner and his family not only lose a source of income, but they also may be faced with additional expenses resulting from the disability.

Often, people who are unable to work because of sickness or injury qualify to receive income replacement benefits under government-sponsored programs. (We describe these government-sponsored programs later in this chapter.) However, many people who are unable to work or who suffer a loss of income because of injury or illness do not qualify to receive benefits under government-sponsored programs. For these individuals, commercial insurance companies provide *disability income coverage* that provides a specified, periodic income replacement benefit to an insured who becomes unable to work because of an illness or an accidental injury.

We begin this chapter by describing how various disability income policies define total disability. Then we describe some other features of disability income policies, including the benefit period, the elimination period, the benefit amount, supplemental benefits that are available, and some common policy exclusions. We next describe some specialized forms of disability insurance available to meet the needs of businesses for disability coverages. The chapter concludes with a description of government-sponsored disability income coverages in the United States and Canada.

Definition of Total Disability

In order to receive periodic income benefits under a disability income policy, the insured person must have a disability that meets the policy's definition of total disability. Each disability income policy specifies the definition of *total disability* that the insurer will use to determine whether a covered person is entitled to receive disability income benefits. Although a complete listing of every definition of total disability that is or has been used would be impossible to construct, we describe the definitions that commercial insurance companies have most commonly included in disability income policies.

Any Occupation

At one time, disability income policies defined total disability as a disability that prevented the insured from performing the duties of *any occupation*. Because a strict interpretation of this definition would prevent most people from ever qualifying for disability income benefits, most insurers now define total disability more liberally.

Current Usual Definition

The definition of total disability included in most disability income policies issued today provides that an insured is considered totally disabled if at the start of disability, the disability prevents him from performing the essential duties of his *regular occupation*. At the end of a specified period after the disability begins, usually two or five years, an insured is considered totally disabled only if the disability prevents him from working at *any occupation for which he is reasonably fitted by education, training, or experience.*

EXAMPLE Samuel Tyler, a surgeon, is insured under a disability income policy that contains the current usual definition of total disability; the policy's definition of total disability changes after the insured has been disabled for two years. Samuel was involved in an accident and lost his right arm. Although Samuel is unable to perform surgery, he has been hired to teach in a medical college.

ANALYSIS Because Samuel's injury prevents him from working as a surgeon, he meets the policy's initial definition of total disability and, thus, will be eligible to receive disability income benefits for up to two years. At the end of that time, Samuel will no longer be considered totally disabled because his disability does not prevent him from working at an occupation for which he is reasonably fitted by his education and training.

Policies that use this definition of total disability, however, may also state that the insured is not considered to be totally disabled if he is working in a gainful occupation. Thus, no total disability income benefits are payable if the person insured by such a policy voluntarily returns to work at any occupation.

Own Previous Occupation

Some insurers have further liberalized the definition of total disability that is included in disability income policies sold to members of certain professional occupations. This definition, which is included more often in individual policies than in group policies, specifies that an insured is totally disabled if she is unable to perform the essential duties of her *own previous occupation*. In fact, policies using this "own previous occupation" definition specify that benefits will be paid even while the insured is gainfully employed in another occupation, as long as she is prevented by disability from engaging in the essential duties of her own previous occupation.

EXAMPLE Suppose that Samuel Tyler from our last example is insured under a disability income policy that contains this "own previous occupation" definition of total disability. Because of his accident, Samuel is unable to perform surgery and has begun teaching at a medical school.

ANALYSIS Samuel is unable to perform surgery and, thus, will never be able to work in his own previous occupation. Therefore, the insurance company will pay Samuel the full disability income benefit until the end of the policy's benefit period.

Income Loss

A type of disability income coverage, often called **income protection insurance,** has gained popularity since the late 1970s, primarily in the upper-income professional market. The definition of total disability included in income protection policies specifies that an insured is disabled if he suffers an income loss caused by the disability. As a result, such a policy provides an income benefit both while the insured is totally disabled and unable to work and while he is able to work but, because of a disability, is earning less than he earned before being disabled. The policy specifies both (1) a maximum benefit amount that will be paid when an insured is completely unable to work and (2) a method for determining the amount of lost income when the disabled insured is working but is earning less than he previously earned.

| EXAMPLE | Suppose that Samuel Tyler from our last example is insured under an income protection policy. Because of his |

accident, Samuel is no longer able to perform surgery and has begun teaching at a medical school. The salary he receives as a professor is considerably less than his income as a surgeon.

| ANALYSIS | Under an income protection policy, Samuel will be paid a policy benefit based on the difference between his salary |

as a professor and his income as a surgeon. The payments will continue until the end of the policy's maximum benefit period.

Presumptive Disabilities

Disability income policies may also classify certain conditions as presumptive disabilities. A **presumptive disability** is a stated condition that, if present, automatically causes the insured to be considered totally disabled; thus, the insured will receive the full income benefit amount provided under the policy, even if she resumes full-time employment in a former occupation. Presumptive disabilities include total and permanent blindness, loss of the use of any two limbs, and loss of speech or hearing.

Benefit Period

Each disability income policy specifies a **benefit period**—the time during which the insurer will pay income benefits. Disability income coverages are classified as either short-term or long-term, depending on the length of the benefit period. Different criteria are used to classify the benefit period of group and individual coverages.

- **Short-term group disability income coverage** provides a maximum benefit period of less than one year; such coverage commonly specifies a maximum benefit period of 13, 26, or 52 weeks. **Long-term group disability income coverage** provides a maximum benefit period of more than one year; the maximum benefit period commonly extends to the insured's normal retirement age or to age 70.

- Individual disability income coverage is seldom offered with a maximum benefit period of less than one year. Thus, **short-term individual disability income coverage** provides a maximum benefit period of from one to five years. **Long-term individual** *disability income coverage* provides a maximum benefit period of at least five years. The maximum benefit period provided by individual long-term coverage commonly extends until the insured reaches age 65; in some cases, benefits are provided for the insured's lifetime.

Elimination Period

Although some forms of disability income coverage are designed to provide benefits beginning on the first day of an insured's disability, most policies specify an elimination period. An **elimination period,** often referred to as a *waiting period,* is the specific amount of time that the insured must be disabled before becoming eligible to receive policy benefits.

Like the deductible amount found in medical expense policies, the purpose of the elimination period is to reduce the cost of coverage. By specifying an elimination period, the insurer can substantially reduce the expenses involved in processing and paying claims for disabilities that last for only a very short time. This expense savings is reflected in the cost of the coverage; the longer the elimination period, the lower the cost for otherwise equivalent disability income coverage.

The length of the elimination period included in both short-term and long-term individual disability income policies is typically from 30 days to 6 months. The elimination period in a group policy is typically related to the length of the maximum benefit period. Most group *short-term* disability income policies specify no elimination period for disabilities caused by accidents and an elimination period of 1 week for disabilities caused by sickness. Most group *long-term* disability income policies specify an elimination period of from 30 days to 6 months, though such plans also typically coordinate their short-term and long-term coverages. That is, the length of the elimination period before long-term benefits are payable is designed to ensure that short-term coverage ends before long-term benefits become payable.

> **FAST FACT**
>
> More than 1.7 million Canadians had short-term disability income coverage at the end of 1997. Almost 5.3 million Canadians had long-term disability income coverage.[2]

Benefit Amount

As a general rule, the benefit amount available through disability income coverage is *not* intended to replace fully an individual's pre-disability earnings. Instead, disability income benefits are limited to an amount that is lower than the individual's regular earnings when not disabled. Without restrictions on the income amounts available through disability income coverage, a disabled insured could receive as much income as he received when working. In such a case, the disabled insured has no financial incentive to return to work and might prolong the period of disability.

Disability income benefit amounts, however, should not be so low that a disabled insured must suffer a drastic reduction in income and lifestyle; the purpose of insurance is, after all, to provide protection against the economic consequences of loss. Therefore, the benefit amount paid to a disabled insured should bear a relationship to the amount of the individual's income before disability.

Disability income providers use two methods to establish the amount of disability income benefits that will be paid to a disabled person: (1) an income benefit formula or (2) a flat benefit amount. The method used generally depends on whether the coverage is provided by a group or an individual policy and on whether the coverage is short-term or long-term.

Income Benefit Formula

Group disability income policies typically include an income benefit formula that the insurer uses to determine the amount of the periodic benefit that is payable to a disabled insured. The income benefit formula usually expresses the disability income benefit amount as a stated percentage of the insured's pre-disability earnings and considers all sources of disability income that the disabled insured receives. The amount of the stated percentage varies from policy to policy. The percentage typically included in group long-term disability income policies ranges from 60 to 75 percent. For example, the formula may specify that the insured will receive a disability income benefit amount equal to 75 percent of her pre-disability earnings and that the benefit amount will be reduced by the amount of any disability income benefit she receives from another source. Group short-term policies often specify a higher percentage than do group long-term policies, and it is not uncommon for group short-term policies to provide from 90 to 100 percent income replacement benefits.

Flat Amount

Individual disability income policies usually specify a flat benefit amount that the insurer will periodically pay to an insured who becomes totally disabled. The specified benefit amount is based on the amount of the insured's income when the policy was purchased. The specified benefit amount typically is paid to a disabled insured regardless of any other income benefits the insured receives during the disability.

Insurers carefully limit the maximum amount of disability income benefit that a particular applicant can purchase. When determining the maximum amount of disability income available to an applicant, the insurer considers the following factors:

- The amount of the applicant's usual earned income, before taxes

- The amount of the applicant's unearned income, such as dividends and interest, that will continue during a disability

- Additional sources of income available to the applicant during a disability, such as disability income benefits provided through group disability income coverage and government-sponsored disability income programs

- The applicant's current income tax bracket, because the applicant's usual earned income is taxable income, whereas disability income benefits provided under an individual policy usually are not taxable income

In general, the maximum amount of disability income benefit that insurers will provide to an applicant is 50 to 70 percent of her usual pre-tax earnings at the time of the application for the policy. Note that the amount of an insured's disability income benefit will be lower than the amount of after-tax income the insured earned before she was disabled.

Supplemental Benefits

In addition to providing benefits when the insured is totally disabled, disability income coverage may provide other benefits. These supplemental benefits may be automatically included with the basic coverage or may be available on an optional basis for an additional premium amount. The supplemental benefits that we will describe are partial disability benefits, future purchase option benefits, and cost-of-living adjustment (COLA) benefits.

Partial Disability Benefits

Some disability income policies provide benefits for periods when the insured person has a *partial disability*—a disability that prevents the insured either from performing some of the duties of his usual occupation or from engaging in that occupation on a full-time basis. The amount of the disability income benefit paid when an insured has a partial disability is described in the policy. Typically, this amount is either a specified flat amount, often 50 percent of the total disability income benefit amount, or an amount established according to a formula specified in the policy. Using the formula method, the amount of the income benefit will vary according to the percentage of income that the insured has lost because of the partial disability.

Future Purchase Option Benefit

A disability income policy that specifies a flat benefit amount may contain a *future purchase option benefit,* which grants the insured the right to increase the benefit amount in accordance with increases in the insured's earnings. This benefit provision generally specifies that these increases can be made only if the insured can prove a commensurate increase in income; further, the amount of such increases is generally limited to a specified maximum. The insured, however, usually does not need to provide evidence of insurability in order to increase the benefit amount.

Cost-of-Living Adjustment Benefit

A *cost-of-living adjustment (COLA) benefit* provides for periodic increases in the disability income benefit amount that the insurer will pay to a disabled insured; these increases usually correspond to increases in the cost of living. When a policy or rider provides a COLA benefit, it usually defines an *increase in the cost of living* in terms of a standard index, such as the Consumer Price Index (CPI).

Exclusions

Disability income policies often specify that income benefits will not be paid to a disabled insured if the insured's disability results from certain causes. The causes of disability that may be excluded from coverage include the following:

- Injuries or sicknesses that result from war, declared or undeclared, or any act of war

- Intentionally self-inflicted injuries

- Injuries received as a result of active participation in a riot

- Occupation-related disabilities or sickness for which the insured is entitled to receive disability income benefits under some government program, such as workers' compensation

Specialized Types of Disability Coverage

In addition to disability income coverage, insurers market several specialized types of disability coverage. These specialized coverages are designed to provide benefits for specific expenses—other than loss of income—that may result from an insured's disability. As described in Chapter 4, closely held businesses are subject to certain financial risks if an owner, partner, or key person dies. Likewise, such businesses could suffer a financial loss if an owner, partner, or key person becomes unable to work because of a disability. We describe three types of disability coverage that are available to closely held businesses: (1) key person disability coverage, (2) disability buyout coverage, and (3) business overhead expense coverage.

Key Person Disability Coverage

Just as businesses that rely on the work of a key person may need to purchase key person life insurance, businesses also may need *key person disability coverage,* which provides benefit payments to the business if an insured key person becomes disabled. When a key person is unable to work because of disability, the business loses the person's services and, thus, loses money. Such losses can be offset by key person disability benefits.

Disability Buyout Coverage

In Chapter 4, we described buy-sell agreements and how they can be funded by life insurance policy death benefits. A buy-sell agreement also may include provisions concerning the purchase of a partner's or owner's interest in the business should the partner or owner become disabled. *Disability buyout coverage* provides benefits designed to fund the buyout of a partner's or owner's interest in a business should he become disabled. Insight 19-1 describes the importance of disability coverage.

Business Overhead Expense Coverage

Should a business owner become disabled, she still may incur expenses to operate the business. For example, office rent or mortgage payments continue and office utility bills come due. Some insurers sell *business overhead expense coverage* that provides benefits designed to pay the disabled insured's share of the business' overhead expenses. Policies typically define *overhead expenses* as usual

Insight 19-1. | **An Agent's Personal Approach to Disability Insurance.**

Years ago, my father and uncle owned a retail business. When my diabetic uncle became disabled and eventually died, my father continued the business and supported my uncle's family until he had to close the business two years later. If my father and uncle had protected their business with a disability buyout policy, their business could have survived.

My father later opened a family hardware business, which also was uninsured. I took over the business when my parents retired. The demands of running the business burned me out; I contracted a severe case of mononucleosis and was bedridden for more than a year. My husband and I instantly were without one-half our income. My parents eventually sold the business.

Statistics claiming that there is a far greater chance of being dis-abled than dying tell only part of the story. Advances in medical science have caused a dramatic decrease in premature death from hypertension, heart disease, cerebro-vascular disease, and diabetes. People who are stricken with any of these diseases and survive will become a disability statistic rather than a mortality statistic.

The odds of a disability occur-ring at least once between ages 25 and 55, lasting 90 days or longer, are 43 percent. A study in *Dental Economics* said that about one-third of all dentists will be disabled for 3 months or longer before they reach 65. The same study con-cluded that long-term disabilities rank as the leading factors in mortgage foreclosures and per-sonal bankruptcies. A joint LIMRA/ *U.S. News & World Report* study showed that of the 3.4 million small businesses with fewer than 50 employees in the United States, 75 percent owned no disability coverage. Less than 20 percent of the working population have long-term disability (LTD) protection.

Many agents find disability buy-out [insurance] tough to close. I think disability is a logical sale. I explain that my client's equity in the business is income he did not take out to enable the business to grow. I tell him that it is hard to get the money from the business to his family if he dies, and even harder if he becomes disabled.

Agents have a responsibility to their clients. I owe it to my clients to protect them, their businesses, their livelihoods, and their families. I owe it to them to introduce what it is like to be in business and lose that business. •

Source: Excerpt from address by Candace G. Kaplan, RHU, CFP, at the 1995 Million Dollar Round Table Annual Meeting. Reprinted with permission of MDRT.

and necessary business expenses, including employee salaries, rent, telephone, electric and gas utilities, and other expenses required to keep the business open.

Government-Sponsored Disability Income Programs

In both the United States and Canada, government-sponsored programs provide disability income benefits to specified individuals.

United States

U.S. workers who are under age 65 and who have paid a specified amount of Social Security tax for a prescribed number of quarter-year periods are eligible to receive *Social Security Disability Income (SSDI)* benefit payments if they become disabled. For purposes of SSDI, *disability* is defined as a person's inability to work because of a physical or mental sickness or injury; this sickness or injury must have lasted or be expected to last for at least one year, or it must be expected to lead to the person's death.

Social Security provides a disabled worker with a monthly disability income benefit equal to the monthly benefit that would normally have become payable when the worker retired. SSDI benefit payments do not begin until the insured has been disabled for at least 5 months and, hence, begin approximately 6 months after the onset of disability. Benefit payments continue until (1) 2 months after the disability ends, (2) the insured worker dies, or (3) the insured worker reaches age 65, when regular Social Security retirement income benefits become payable.

The spouse and dependent children of a disabled worker may also receive an income benefit while the worker is disabled. Their income benefits are equal to a percentage of the amount received by the disabled worker. Benefits, however, are subject to an overall family maximum benefit amount.

Canada

Several government-sponsored programs in Canada provide disability income benefits to covered residents. Short-term disability income benefits are available under the federal *Unemployment Insurance Act* for all employees who have worked a stated minimum number of weeks during the preceding 52-week period. These taxable benefits are available for up to 15 weeks after a short waiting period if absence from work was caused by accident, sickness, or pregnancy. The benefit amount is a percentage of the worker's average weekly earnings, up to a stated maximum amount. The plan is financed by compulsory employer and employee contributions and is administered by Human Resources Development Canada.

Employers can reduce their premium contributions by establishing a qualified, private disability income plan, and many employers have established such plans. For individuals who are covered under such a private plan that provides weekly benefits for short-term disabilities, the private plan is always the "first payor" before benefits are available under the federal Unemployment Insurance Act. We will describe the requirements that such private plans must meet to comply with the Unemployment Insurance Act more fully in Chapter 23.

Long-term disability income benefits are provided through the Canada Pension Plan (CPP) and the Quebec Pension Plan (QPP). To qualify for disability income benefits under one of these plans, a worker must (1) have made contributions to the plan for a stated

> **FAST FACT**
>
> In 1997, Canadians received more than $3 billion in disability income benefits.[4]

minimum number of years, (2) be under the age of 65, and (3) be afflicted with a *severe and prolonged disability.* A *severe disability* is defined as a disability that prevents the worker from engaging in any substantially gainful occupation. A *prolonged disability* is defined as a disability that is expected to be of long, continued, and indefinite duration or that is likely to result in the covered worker's death.

A disabled worker who meets the foregoing requirements receives a monthly income benefit. The amount of the benefit is based on the amount of the worker's pre-disability earnings and the amount he contributed to the plan. These taxable benefit payments begin 4 months after the onset of the disability and continue until the person (1) is no longer disabled, (2) dies, or (3) reaches age 65, when normal retirement benefits provided through the CPP or QPP become payable. Dependent children of disabled workers are also eligible to receive income benefits under both the CPP and the QPP.

Key Terms

disability income coverage
total disability
income protection insurance
presumptive disability
benefit period
short-term group disability
   income coverage
long-term group disability
   income coverage
short-term individual disability
   income coverage
long-term individual disability
   income coverage

elimination period
partial disability
future purchase option benefit
cost-of-living adjustment
   (COLA) benefit
key person disability coverage
disability buyout coverage
business overhead expense
   coverage
overhead expenses
Social Security Disability
   Income (SSDI)

Other Important Terms

waiting period
Unemployment Insurance Act

severe disability
prolonged disability

Endnotes

1. American Insurance Network. Available online at http://www.americaninsurance.com/disability.html.

2. CLHIA, *Canadian Life and Health Insurance Facts* (Toronto: Canadian Life and Health Insurance Association, 1998), 13.

3. HIAA, *Source Book of Health Insurance Data* (Washington, D.C.: Health Insurance Association of America, 1998), 41.

4. CLHIA, 18.

CHAPTER 20

Traditional Group Health Insurance Plans

After reading this chapter, you should be able to

⬤ Identify and describe the provisions that are typically included in group health insurance policies

⬤ Calculate the amount of benefits payable when an insured is covered by two group health insurance policies that both contain a coordination of benefits (COB) provision

⬤ Identify the factors that group underwriters use to determine a group's expected morbidity rate

⬤ Identify and describe three funding mechanisms used in connection with fully insured group health insurance plans

⬤ Explain why an employer might decide to self-insure a group health insurance plan

⬤ Describe the operation of a self-insured group health insurance plan, including the uses of stop-loss insurance and plan administration

The health insurance coverages we described in the previous two chapters are provided under both individual and group health insurance policies. Most health insurance issued by commercial insurers is provided by group health insurance policies. In this chapter, we describe the features of traditional group health insurance plans provided by commercial insurance companies in both Canada and the United States.

Group Health Insurance Policies

As we described in Chapter 14, a group health insurance policy is a contract between the insurer and the group policyholder that purchased the group insurance coverage. The insured members of the group are not parties to this contract and are not given individual policies. Instead, each insured group member is given a certificate or a benefit booklet that provides information about his group health insurance coverage.

Group medical expense insurance policies specify the types of medical expenses they cover, the benefit maximums (if any), the deductible amount, and the coinsurance features. Group disability income policies specify the elimination period, the method of determining the amount of the disability income benefit, and the maximum benefit period.

In addition to providing coverage for eligible group members, most employer-employee group medical expense policies provide that an insured employee's family and dependents are eligible for group insurance coverage. Such dependent coverage is generally available at the option of the insured group member, who usually must pay an additional premium amount for dependent coverage. By contrast, most group disability income plans do not provide coverage for dependents of group members. (Figure 20-1 shows the types of coverages provided by group health insurance policies in 1995.)

An insurer can provide all of a group's coverage under one group health insurance policy, or the insurer can issue separate master policies to the group for each type of coverage provided. In the latter instance, for example, an insurer could issue both a group major medical policy and a group disability income policy to the group policyholder. In addition, a group policyholder can choose to purchase insurance coverage from more than one provider.

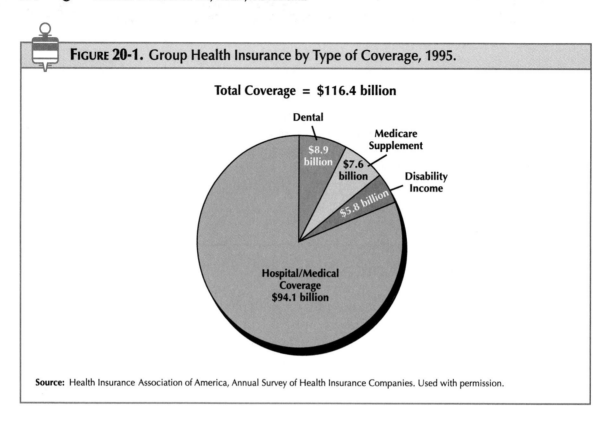

FIGURE 20-1. Group Health Insurance by Type of Coverage, 1995.

Total Coverage = $116.4 billion

Dental

Medicare Supplement

Disability Income

$8.9 billion

$7.6 billion

$5.8 billion

Hospital/Medical Coverage $94.1 billion

Source: Health Insurance Association of America, Annual Survey of Health Insurance Companies. Used with permission.

Group Health Insurance Policy Provisions

You will recall from our discussion in Chapter 14 that certain provisions are included in both group life and group health insurance policies. In that chapter, we described the eligibility requirements often included in group life and health insurance policies, as well as the grace period provision, the incontestability provision, and the termination provisions that group policies typically contain. In this section, we describe some additional provisions that insurers typically include in group health insurance policies in the United States and Canada. These provisions are (1) the pre-existing conditions provision, (2) the conversion provision, (3) the coordination of benefits provision, and (4) the physical examination provision.

Pre-Existing Conditions Provision

Group health insurance policies—both medical expense and disability income policies—often contain a *pre-existing conditions provision* stating that benefits are not payable for pre-existing conditions until the insured has been covered under the policy for a specified length of time. Group policies usually define a **pre-existing condition** as a condition for which an individual received medical care during the three months immediately prior to the effective date of her coverage. A group policy also usually specifies that a condition will no longer be considered pre-existing—and, thus, the condition will be eligible for coverage—if (1) the insured has not received treatment for that condition for 3 consecutive months *or* (2) the insured has been covered under the policy for 12 consecutive months.

According to most group policies, the insurer will waive the requirements of the pre-existing conditions provision for any group member who was eligible for coverage when the policy became effective *if* (1) the group was previously covered by a group health insurance policy issued by another insurer *and* (2) the group member was covered by that prior policy. Thus, if a group policyholder decides to switch insurance carriers, the pre-existing conditions provision in the new carrier's policy will not apply to group members who were covered under the earlier plan.

In 1996, the U.S. Congress enacted the *Health Insurance Portability and Accountability Act (HIPAA)*, which imposes a number of requirements on employer-sponsored group health insurance plans, health insurance companies, and health maintenance organizations. As a general rule, the requirements imposed by HIPAA are designed to provide wider access to health insurance coverage and to provide greater portability of benefits between group health insurance plans. Specifically, HIPAA places restrictions on the pre-existing conditions provision included in group health benefit plans. These limits are designed to allow group insureds who have a pre-existing condition to change jobs without losing coverage for the condition. A discussion of HIPAA appears in Chapter 23.

Conversion Provision

The laws of most states in the United States require group medical expense insurance policies to include a conversion provision. Although group medical expense policies in Canada are not required to include a conversion provision, many Canadian group medical expense policies include such a provision. The **conversion provision** grants an insured group member who is leaving the group a limited right to purchase an individual medical expense insurance policy without presenting evidence of insurability. The right is limited in that the insurer can refuse to issue the individual policy if the coverage would result in the insured group member becoming overinsured. For example, an employee who is changing jobs and will be eligible for group medical expense insurance from his new employer would probably be overinsured if he were also issued an individual medical expense insurance policy.

When an insured group member elects to convert his group coverage to an individual health insurance policy, he will find that the individual health insurance policy differs from the group health insurance policy in several respects. For example, the insured will generally be charged a higher premium rate for the individual policy than he paid for group coverage and the benefits provided by the individual policy will probably be more restricted than those provided by the group policy. Requirements regarding the specific coverages that a conversion policy must provide vary from jurisdiction to jurisdiction.

Coordination of Benefits Provision

The *coordination of benefits (COB) provision* is designed to prevent a group member who is insured under more than one group medical expense insurance policy from receiving benefit amounts that are greater than the amount of medical expenses the insured actually incurred. Many people are eligible for coverage under more than one group medical expense plan. For example, spouses who both work typically are eligible for coverage under their own employers' group policy and under their spouses' group policy. If benefits payable under such duplicate coverage were not coordinated, the insured could receive full benefits from both policies and, consequently, would profit from an illness or injury.

The COB provision prevents duplicate benefit payments by defining the group health plan that is the primary provider of benefits and the plan that is the secondary provider for insured group members who have duplicate group medical expense coverage.

A plan defined in the COB provision as the primary provider of benefits is the plan that is responsible for paying the full benefit amounts promised under the plan. Once the plan designated as the primary plan has paid the full benefit amounts promised, then the insured can submit the claim to the secondary plan, along with a description of the benefit amounts the primary plan paid. The provider of the secondary plan will then determine the amount payable for the claim in accordance with the terms of that plan.

A plan's COB provision may take one of several approaches to determining the amount of benefits payable when the plan is functioning as the secondary provider of benefits. Under the most common approach, the secondary provider first calculates the amount of the insured individual's total allowable expenses and the amount of those expenses that the insurer would pay if it were the primary provider. *Allowable expenses* are those reasonable and customary expenses that the insured incurred and that are covered under at least one of the insured's group medical expense plans. The secondary provider then looks at the amount the primary provider paid. If payment of the full benefit amount provided by the secondary plan would result in the insured receiving more in benefit payments from both plans than the total amount of allowable medical expenses, then the secondary plan will pay only the difference between the amount of allowable expenses incurred and the amount the insured already received from the primary plan. Under this type of COB provision, the insured individual typically pays no portion of her covered medical expenses; the primary plan pays all benefits in excess of the deductible and coinsurance requirements, and the secondary plan pays the portion of allowable medical expenses not paid by the primary plan—the secondary plan will reimburse the insured for any deductible and coinsurance amounts paid by the insured.

EXAMPLE Sean Poe is covered by two group medical expense plans; both plans include a coordination of benefits provision. Each plan also specifies a $100 deductible and a 20 percent coinsurance requirement. Sean incurred $5,100 in allowable medical expenses.

ANALYSIS The plan designated as the primary plan will pay benefits equal to $4,000. The calculations used to determine this benefit amount are as follows.

$5,100	Total allowable expense
− 100	Less: deductible
$5,000	
− 1,000	Less: coinsurance (0.20 × $5,000)
$4,000	Amount the primary plan will pay

Because both plans contain the same deductible and coinsurance features, Sean's secondary plan would normally also provide her with a $4,000 benefit payment. Under the COB provision, however, the secondary plan will provide Sean only a $1,100 benefit payment; that is, the secondary plan will pay the difference between the total allowable expenses ($5,100) and the amount the primary plan paid in benefits ($4,000). Sean incurs no out-of-pocket costs.

Some group medical expense insurance policies contain another type of coordination of benefits provision, generally called a nonduplication of benefits provision. A *nonduplication of benefits provision* is a COB provision that, if included in a secondary provider's plan, limits the amount payable by the secondary plan to the difference, if any, between the amount paid by the primary plan and the amount that would have been payable by the secondary plan had that plan been the primary plan. Nonduplication of benefits provisions require the insured individual to pay a portion of the cost of covered medical expenses and, thus, more strictly limit the amount of benefits payable than do the COB provisions we discussed previously.

EXAMPLE Let's return to our example of Sean Poe's duplicate group medical expense coverage. Remember that both plans contain the same deductible and coinsurance features. In this example, however, assume that the plan designated as Sean's secondary plan contains a nonduplication of benefits provision.

ANALYSIS As in the earlier example, the primary plan would pay a $4,000 policy benefit. Under the nonduplication of benefits provision, however, the secondary plan would provide no benefit amount because the primary plan had already paid the full $4,000 benefit amount to which Sean was entitled under the secondary plan.

Most COB provisions include a number of rules to determine which plan is primary. First, the COB provision usually states that when an insured is also covered by another group plan that does not include a COB provision, the plan without a COB provision will be the primary provider of benefits; the plan with the COB provision will be secondary. In addition, if more than one group plan covering an individual includes a COB provision, then the primary provider is usually defined as the plan under which the insured is covered as an employee rather than as a dependent.

EXAMPLE Jeanette and Norm Langer are married and have a young daughter, Lacey. Both Jeanette and Norm work full time for employers that provide group medical expense coverage to employees and their spouses and dependents. Which plan is considered the primary payor for Jeanette and Norm?

ANALYSIS In order to determine which plan is the primary payor for Jeanette and Norm, we must know whether the plans contain a COB provision. If one plan includes a COB provision and the other plan does not, then the plan without the COB provision will always be considered the primary payor for both Jeanette and Norm. Alternatively, if both plans contain a COB provision, then Jeanette's primary provider is her employer's plan, and her secondary provider is the plan provided by Norm's employer; Norm's primary provider is his employer's plan, and his secondary provider is the plan provided by Jeanette's employer.

If an individual is covered as a dependent under more than one group plan, two methods are commonly used to define which plan is the primary payor. The first method, known as the *birthday rule* or the *earlier birthday method*, states that the plan covering the employee whose birth date falls earlier in the calendar year will be considered the primary provider of benefits for a dependent. Under the second method, the primary provider of benefits for a dependent child is the one that provides benefits for a male employee rather than a female employee.

EXAMPLE | In our example, Jeanette Langer's birthday falls in March, and Norm Langer's birthday falls in September. Which plan is considered the primary payor for their daughter Lacey?

ANALYSIS | According to the birthday rule, the plan provided by Jeanette's employer would be considered the primary provider of benefits for Lacey. Under the second method, the plan provided by Norm's employer would be considered the primary payor for Lacey.

Note that the employees' actual ages are not a factor in determining the primary provider under the birthday rule. If only one plan has adopted the birthday rule or if neither plan has adopted the birthday rule, then the plan that provides benefits to a dependent of a male will be primary. In some states, insurers are required by law to use the earlier birthday method.

Physical Examination Provision

The **physical examination provision** is included in most group disability income policies and grants the insurer the right to require an insured who has submitted a disability income claim to be examined by a doctor of the insurer's choice, at the insurer's expense. Such an examination allows the insurer to verify the validity of the insured's claim. The provision also usually grants the insurer the right to require that a disabled insured undergo medical examinations at regular intervals so that the insurer can verify that the insured is still disabled.

Group Health Insurance Underwriting

When an insurer evaluates a group for group health insurance coverage, the insurer applies the group underwriting principles described in Chapter 14. Usually, the group as a whole—rather than the individual members of the group—must meet the insurer's underwriting requirements. If the size of the group is small, however, the insurer may require the individual members of the group to submit evidence of insurability. We describe individual health insurance underwriting in the next chapter.

The group's risk classification—standard, substandard, or declined—will be established on the basis of the group's expected morbidity rate. As noted in an earlier chapter, *morbidity rates* describe the incidence of sickness and accidents that may be expected to occur among a given group of people. The expected morbidity rate for a group reflects a number of factors, including the following:

- **The nature of the industry in which the group members work.** Some industries, for example, present greater occupational hazards to employees than do other industries.

- **The age distribution of the group.** Morbidity rates generally increase as the group members get older.

- **The distribution of males and females in the group.** Females generally experience higher morbidity rates than do males of the same age.

If a sufficient amount of previous claim experience information is available, the group underwriter will use the group's own morbidity experience to estimate the group's expected morbidity experience. As in group life insurance, there are three possible rating methods: *manual rating, experience rating,* and *blended rating.* In calculating manually rated premiums, the insurance company generally derives the amount of its projected annual claim costs from the actual morbidity experience of all those groups it expected to have normal morbidity. In calculating experience rated premiums, the morbidity experience of a particular group is the basis for that group's net annual premiums. Sometimes an insurer combines the experience of several small groups to produce experience rated premiums.

Funding Mechanisms

The way in which a group insurance plan's claim costs and administrative expenses are paid is known as the plan's **funding mechanism.** A number of funding mechanisms are available for group insurance plans. Some group health insurance plans are **fully insured plans**—the group policyholder makes monthly premium payments to the insurance company, and the insurance company bears the responsibility for all claim payments. At the other extreme, a *fully self-insured plan* is a plan for which the employer takes complete responsibility for all claim payments and related expenses. Other funding mechanisms fall between these two extremes.

Although various funding mechanisms may be used for any type of employee benefit plan, most group life insurance plans and most group long-term disability income plans are fully insured plans. Group medical expense insurance plans, by contrast, are much more likely to use alternative funding methods. In this section, we describe some of the various methods used to fund group health insurance coverages. You should note, however, that many different approaches to plan funding are available.

Fully Insured Plans

A fully insured group insurance plan is a plan for which the insurance company bears the risk of paying claims and the risk that claims may be excessive. For example, even if the dollar amount of the claims submitted exceeds the dollar amount of premiums collected, the insurer must pay the claims. On the other hand, if the group experiences fewer claim expenses than anticipated, the insurer can earn a larger profit.

A fully insured plan is the traditional funding arrangement for a group health insurance plan. The insurer issues the group health insurance policy on a one-year renewable term basis, and each year's premium pays for just that year's coverage. New premium rates are charged each year based on the sex and attained ages of the insured members of the group. These group health insurance premium rates are typically guaranteed for 12 months. At the end of the policy year, the insurance company may establish new premium rates for the group.

Insurers and employers have developed a number of alternatives to this traditional arrangement of paying premiums in advance to fund a group health insurance plan. These alternatives enable employers to reduce the total cost of providing the health insurance for employees by modifying the manner in which premiums are paid. The employer, however, must still pay premiums for the group insurance policy, and the insurer remains responsible for paying all covered claims.

Retrospective Rating Arrangements

Under a *retrospective rating arrangement,* the insurer agrees to charge the group policyholder a lower monthly premium than it would normally charge for the group health insurance plan based on the group's prior claim experience. The group policyholder agrees that it will pay an additional amount to the insurer if at the end of the policy year, the group's claim experience has been unfavorable. By reducing its monthly premium cost, the employer is able to increase the amount of funds it has available to it throughout those months. A retrospective rating arrangement also usually includes an experience refund feature. If the group's claim experience during the policy year is favorable, the insurer will pay the group policyholder an experience refund.

Premium Delay Arrangements

A *premium delay arrangement* allows the group policyholder to postpone paying monthly group insurance premiums for a stated period of time beyond the expiration of the policy's grace period. As a result, the group policyholder has the use of those funds during the premium delay period. Typically, the group policyholder has the right to delay premium payments up to 60 or 90 days beyond the end of the grace period. When the group insurance contract terminates, the group policyholder must pay any deferred premiums.

Minimum Premium Plans

Under a *minimum premium plan (MPP),* the group policyholder deposits into a special account funds that are sufficient to pay a stated amount of expected claims. For example, the group policyholder may deposit the amount needed to pay 80 or 90 percent of expected claims. The insurer administers the plan and pays claims from that special account until the allocated funds are exhausted. Thereafter, the insurer is responsible for paying claims from its own funds, and it charges the group policyholder a premium for the coverage it provides. By using this funding arrangement, the premium that the insurer charges for the coverage it provides can be greatly reduced; the amount of premium taxes is also thereby reduced.

Self-Insured Plans

Many employers are taking an active role in providing health insurance benefits by choosing to partially or fully self-insure, or self-fund, the medical expense or disability income coverage they provide for their employees. As a result, the employers bear some or all of the risk of paying claims and the risk that claims may be excessive.

Many employers, for example, fully self-insure short-term disability income coverage for their employees by means of a salary continuation plan. A *salary continuation plan* typically provides 100 percent of the insured employee's salary, beginning on the first day of the employee's absence due to sickness or injury and continuing for some specified time.

Alternatively, many medical expense benefit plans are partially self-insured; the employer is financially responsible for paying a certain level of claims, and the risk for claims above that level is transferred to a traditional health insurance provider. For example, an employer might self-insure the plan's basic medical expense benefits and purchase supplemental major medical insurance coverage from an insurance company.

Many employers believe that self-insuring can help them to better control increasing health care costs. In a typical fully-insured plan, the group health insurer must set premium rates that will be adequate to (1) pay claims incurred; (2) cover the insurer's expenses, which can include agent commissions, overhead costs (such as salaries and rent), and state premium taxes; and (3) provide some profit to the insurer. By self-insuring health insurance coverage for employees, an employer may avoid some of these costs that are built into insurance premium rates. For example, the employer can avoid paying agent commissions, state premium taxes, and the insurer's overhead expenses. Another benefit an employer may receive from self-insuring is an improved cash flow because the employer retains the money it would have paid in premiums and can earn interest on that money.

Self-insured plans offer another advantage to some employers in the United States. Because self-insured plans are exempt from state laws that apply to insurance policies, employers that self-insure have more freedom in designing their group insurance plans. For example, insurance laws in many states require health insurance policies to include certain coverages. The cost of those mandated coverages must be reflected in any plan an insurer offers in those states. A self-insured plan is not subject to these state insurance laws, and, thus, an employer offering a self-insured plan does not have to include state-mandated coverages. Many self-insured plans in the United States, however, are subject to regulation by the federal Employee Retirement Income Security Act (ERISA). We describe both state regulation of health insurance and ERISA in Chapter 23.

Stop-Loss Coverage

If a self-insured group experiences several catastrophic medical claims in one year, the employer may not have the financial resources to pay all of the claims. For this reason, many employers that self-insure purchase **stop-loss insurance** from an insurance company so that they can place a maximum dollar limit on their liability for paying health insurance claims. Several forms of stop-loss coverage are available. Under **individual stop-loss coverage** or *specific stop-loss coverage*, the stop-loss insurer pays a portion of each claim that exceeds a stated amount. Under *aggregate stop-loss coverage,* the stop-loss insurer becomes responsible for paying claims when the employer's total claims exceed a stated dollar amount within a stated period of time.

Stop-loss coverage is typically provided under a contract entered into between the stop-loss carrier (the insurer) and the employer. The contract defines the relationship between the carrier and the employer and includes a schedule of benefit payments for which the carrier will reimburse the employer. The agreement is typically for a 12-month period. Note that the stop-loss carrier does not make benefit payments directly to the insured group members; instead, the carrier reimburses the employer, which retains responsibility for making claim payments to insureds.

Plan Administration

Self-insured plans are administered by a variety of methods. Remember that when an employer purchases group insurance from an insurer, the insurer is responsible for most administrative aspects of the plan. Some employers that self-insure their plans are able to fully administer their own plans. For other employers, having an outside organization provide some or all administrative services for the plan is more cost-effective. These employers usually purchase an *administrative services only (ASO) contract* from an insurance company or other organization, such as a third-party administrator (TPA). A *third-party administrator (TPA)* is an organization other than an insurance company that provides administrative services to the sponsors of group benefit plans. Under an ASO contract, the employer pays a fee in exchange for the administrative services provided by the insurer or TPA. These fees are not subject to state premium taxes.

Key Terms

pre-existing conditions provision
pre-existing condition
conversion provision
coordination of benefits (COB)
   provision
allowable expenses
nonduplication of benefits
   provision
physical examination provision
funding mechanism
fully insured plan

fully self-insured plan
retrospective rating arrangement
premium delay arrangement
minimum premium plan (MPP)
salary continuation plan
stop-loss insurance
individual stop-loss coverage
aggregate stop-loss coverage
administrative services only
   (ASO) contract
third-party administrator (TPA)

Other Important Terms

Health Insurance Portability and
   Accountability Act (HIPAA)
birthday rule
earlier birthday method
morbidity rates

manual rating
experience rating
blended rating
specific stop-loss coverage

Endnotes

1. Health Care Financing Administration, *Highlights National Health Expenditures*, 1997 (Washington, D.C.: Health Care Financing Administration, 1998). Available online at http://www.hcfa.gov/stats/nhe-oact/nhe.htm.

2. Bureau of Labor Statistics, *Employee Benefits Survey* (Washington, D.C.: Bureau of Labor Statistics, 1998). Available online at http://stats.bls.gov/news.release/ebs.t06.htm.

3. Employee Benefits Research Institute, *EBRI Health Care Research: 1998 Findings* (Washington, D.C.: Employee Benefits Research Institute, 1999). Available online at http://207.152.182.56/health_findings.htm.

CHAPTER 21

Traditional Individual Health Insurance Policies

After reading this chapter, you should be able to

- Describe how individual health insurance policies differ from group health insurance policies

- Identify and describe the provisions that are typically included in individual health insurance policies

- Differentiate between the various renewal provisions included in individual health insurance policies

- Identify the factors that affect the degree of morbidity risk presented by an applicant and explain how each factor affects morbidity risk

Many people in the United States and Canada purchase individual health insurance policies because they are not eligible for group health insurance coverage. In this chapter, we examine the individual health insurance policy and some of the ways in which individual health insurance coverage and benefits differ from the coverage and benefits provided by group health insurance policies. We also look at the policy provisions that insurers typically include in individual health insurance policies. We end the chapter by describing individual health insurance underwriting.

Individual Health Insurance Policies

An individual health insurance policy is a contract between the insurer and the policyowner. The policy describes the coverages provided, the benefits payable, and the premium amounts and their due dates. A copy of the application for insurance the policyowner completed is attached to the policy. The policyowner and the insured are usually the same person, and the insurer typically pays benefits directly to that person or to a medical-care provider on behalf of that person.

Although insurers do not offer individual health insurance applicants the number of coverage options that are available to group policyholders, an applicant is permitted to make some choices concerning the benefit levels and renewal provisions that will be included in the individual policy. Also, insurers usually offer an applicant for an individual medical expense policy several choices concerning the amount of the policy's deductible. Insurers generally offer an applicant for an individual disability income policy several possible combinations of elimination periods and maximum benefit periods. Applicants for individual disability income policies also may be able to purchase the supplemental disability income benefits that we described in Chapter 19. The premium rate for an individual health insurance policy will vary depending on the choices the applicant makes.

Individual Health Insurance Policy Provisions

Individual health insurance policies contain many of the same provisions that are included in group health insurance policies. They also contain some unique provisions. In this section, we describe some of the provisions typically included in individual health insurance policies.

Renewal Provision

The *renewal provision* describes (1) the circumstances under which the insurer has the right to refuse to renew or the right to cancel the coverage and (2) the insurer's right to increase the policy's premium rate. Individual medical expense policies and individual disability income policies can be classified on the basis of the type of renewal provision that the policy contains. Traditionally, U.S. and Canadian insurers have used the following five general classifications of individual health insurance policies:

- Cancellable policy

- Optionally renewable policy

- Conditionally renewable policy

- Guaranteed renewable policy

- Noncancellable policy

Cancellable Policy. The renewal provision included in a *cancellable policy* grants the insurer the right to terminate the policy at any time, for any reason, simply by notifying the policyowner that the policy is cancelled and by refunding any advance premium that has been paid for the policy. Some states in the United States do not permit insurers to issue cancellable policies.

Optionally Renewable Policy. The insurer has the right to refuse to renew an *optionally renewable policy* on certain dates specified in the policy—usually either the policy anniversary date or any premium due date. The insurer is also allowed to add coverage limitations and to increase the premium rate if it does so for a class of optionally renewable policies. A *class of policies* consists of all policies of a particular type or all policies issued to a particular group of insureds. For example, a class of policies may be defined as all policies in force in a particular state or as all policies issued to insureds who are a particular age or who fall into a specific risk category.

Conditionally Renewable Policy. A *conditionally renewable policy* grants the insurer a limited right to refuse to renew an individual health policy at the end of a premium payment period. The insurer may refuse to renew such a policy only if its decision is based on one or more specific reasons stated in the policy. The reasons *cannot* be related to the insured's health. The age and employment status of the insured are often listed as reasons for possible nonrenewal. For example, an individual disability income policy may state that the insurer will renew the policy until the insured reaches a certain age or until the insured retires from gainful employment. A conditionally renewable policy also gives the insurer the right to increase the premium rate for any class of conditionally renewable policies.

Guaranteed Renewable Policy. An insurer must renew a *guaranteed renewable policy*—as long as premium payments are made—at least until the insured attains the age limit stated in the policy. Most individual guaranteed renewable policies are renewable until the insured reaches age 60 or 65; some are renewable until age 70 or for the insured's lifetime. The insurer has the right to increase the premium rate for such a policy only if it increases the premium rate for an entire class of policies.

Noncancellable Policy. A *noncancellable policy* is guaranteed to be renewable until the insured reaches the limiting age stated in the policy. In addition, an insurer does not have the right to increase the premium rate for a noncancellable policy under any circumstances; the guaranteed premium rate is specified in the policy. Disability income policies typically are noncancellable; medical expense policies are rarely noncancellable.

> **FAST FACT**
>
> In 1995, U.S. families spent nearly 7% of their disposable personal income for health insurance premiums.[1]

In the United States, the federal Health Insurance Portability and Accountability Act (HIPAA) enacted in 1996 imposes a general requirement that insurers must renew or continue an individual medical expense insurance policy in force at the option of the policyowner. We describe the requirements imposed by HIPAA in detail in Chapter 23. In the common-law jurisdictions of Canada, most individual medical expense policies are cancellable and most individual disability income policies are noncancellable. By contrast, most insurers in the province of Quebec offer individual health insurance policies in several classifications, and the applicant can choose which classification of policy to purchase.

The renewal classification of a health insurance policy affects the premium rate that the insurer will charge for the coverage. Premium rates for noncancellable policies—which provide guarantees not found in policies in other renewal classifications—are higher than the premium rates charged for otherwise equivalent policies in the other classifications.

Grace Period Provision

Individual health insurance policies contain a *grace period provision* that allows the policyowner to pay a renewal premium within a stated grace period following the premium due date. The length of the grace period varies, depending on how frequently renewal premiums are payable. For example, policies for which renewal premiums are paid monthly typically contain a 10-day grace period. The grace period is usually 31 days if premiums are payable less often than monthly, although many insurers provide a 31-day grace period even when premiums are payable monthly. Coverage remains in force during the grace period.

Reinstatement Provision

Individual health insurance policies typically include a **reinstatement provision** stating that if certain conditions are met, the insurer will reinstate a policy that has lapsed for nonpayment of premiums. The policyowner usually must pay any overdue premiums and must complete a reinstatement application. The insurer has the right to evaluate the reinstatement application and to decline to reinstate the policy on the basis of statements in that application. If the insurer does not complete the evaluation within a stated number of days—in most states, 45 days—after receiving the reinstatement application, or if the insurer accepts an overdue premium without a reinstatement application, then the policy is usually considered to be automatically reinstated. Coverage under a reinstated policy is limited to accidents that occur after the date of reinstatement and to sicknesses that begin more than 10 days after the date of reinstatement. Thus, the insurer can protect against antiselection by excluding from coverage those losses that occur after the policy lapses and before it is reinstated.

Incontestability Provision

Although individual medical expense policies and individual disability income policies both include an incontestability provision, the provisions are not identical. Most individual medical expense policies contain a provision entitled *time limit on certain defenses*. This time limit on certain defenses provision, commonly referred to as the **incontestability provision** or *incontestable clause*, states that after the policy has been in force for a specified period, usually two or three years, the insurer cannot use material misrepresentations in the application either to void the policy or to deny a claim *unless* the misrepresentations were fraudulent. This provision typically states the following:

Incontestability. After coverage on a covered person has been in force during the lifetime of that person for two years, only fraudulent misstatements in the application shall be used to void the coverage on that person.

No claim for a covered charge that is incurred after those two years will be denied because of a pre-existing condition, unless that pre-existing condition was excluded from coverage, by name or specific description, on the date that charge was incurred.

This provision does not have any effect on nor does it bar any other defenses under this policy.

The word *defenses* refers to any reasons that the insurer may use to deny liability under the policy. Thus, the provision specifically notes that the insurer retains the right to deny a claim on the basis of another policy provision. For example, the insurer may deny a claim on the basis that the expenses are specifically excluded from coverage.

Most individual disability income policies include an incontestability provision which states that after the policy has been in force for a stated period, usually one or two years, the insurer cannot contest the policy's validity on the ground of material misrepresentation in the application. Note that this incontestability provision does not include a reference to fraudulent misstatements. Consequently, the incontestability provision included in individual disability income policies is essentially the same as the incontestability provision included in individual life insurance policies in the United States.

> **FAST FACT**
>
> The number of people in the United States with individual health insurance coverage decreased from 10.2 million people in 1990 to 7 million people in 1995.[2]

Pre-Existing Conditions Provision

Most individual health insurance policies include a ***pre-existing conditions provision*** stating that until the insured has been covered under the policy for a certain period, the insurer will not pay benefits for a pre-existing condition. A ***pre-existing condition*** is usually defined in individual health policies as an injury that occurred or a sickness that first appeared or manifested itself within a specified period—usually two years—before the policy was issued *and* that was not disclosed on the application. Note especially the second part of this two-part definition. A condition that is disclosed on the application is never considered pre-existing for purposes of this exclusion. The insurer has the opportunity to evaluate such a condition and, thus, can specifically exclude the condition from the policy's coverage. If the insurer does not exclude a disclosed condition from the policy's coverage, then the policy will cover that condition. Any specific exclusions, however, remain in effect throughout the life of the policy. A sample pre-existing conditions provision follows.

> **Pre-existing conditions.** Benefits for a charge that results from a covered person's pre-existing condition, as defined in this policy, will be provided only if that charge is a covered charge and is incurred by that person after coverage for that person has been in force for two years. However, if a condition is excluded from coverage by name or specific description, no benefits will be provided for any charges that result from that condition even after those two years.

EXAMPLE Mark Schulman was treated for a back injury one year before he applied for an individual medical expense policy. Six months before completing the application, Mark was diagnosed with, and treated for, allergies. When he completed the application, Mark disclosed that he had been treated for allergies, but inadvertently omitted the fact that he had been treated for the back injury. The insurer issued the policy, which did not specifically exclude allergies from coverage.

ANALYSIS Because Mark did not disclose that he had been treated for a back injury, that condition is considered a pre-existing condition and the insurer has the right to exclude the condition from coverage for two years after the policy issue date. Thus, if Mark has continuing problems related to the back injury and submits claims related to his back injury during the first two years after the policy was issued, the insurer can deny benefits because of the pre-existing condition provision. In contrast, Mark's allergies are not considered a pre-existing condition because that condition was disclosed on the application. When evaluating Mark's application, the insurer decided not to exclude allergies from the policy's coverage. Thus, expenses incurred for treatment of allergies will be covered throughout the life of the policy.

In most states and throughout Canada, two years is the maximum period during which an insurer is permitted to exclude pre-existing conditions from coverage. Insurers, however, are permitted to specify a shorter exclusion period because a shorter exclusion is more favorable to the insured. In the United States, the federal Health Insurance Portability and Accountability Act (HIPAA) prohibits insurers from including a pre-existing conditions provision in individual health insurance policies issued to specified individuals.

You should also remember from the discussion in the previous section that when an applicant fails to disclose a condition on the application for insurance, the policy's incontestable clause may apply. The insurer first will consider whether that nondisclosure constitutes a material misrepresentation and, thus, provides a ground for the insurer to avoid the policy. If the insurer decides that the misrepresentation was not material, then it will apply the policy's pre-existing conditions provision.

Claims Provisions

Individual health insurance policies typically include provisions that define both the insured's obligation to provide timely notification of loss to the insurer and the insurer's obligation to make prompt benefit payments to the insured. In Canada, for example, the policy usually requires the insured to notify the insurer of a claim in writing within 30 days from the date the claim arose and to furnish the insurer with proof of the loss within 90 days from the date the claim arose. The insurer must pay benefits within 60 days of receipt of proof of loss for a medical expense claim and within 30 days of receipt of proof of loss for a disability income claim. Policies issued in the United States contain similar requirements.

Physical Examination Provision

The *physical examination provision* included in individual disability income insurance policies is similar to the physical examination provision included in most group disability income insurance policies. After an insured submits a claim, the insurer has the right to have the insured examined by a doctor of the insurer's choice, at the insurer's expense. The insurer, therefore, has the ability to verify the validity of disability income claims.

Legal Actions Provision

Individual health insurance policies typically include a *legal actions provision,* which limits the time during which a claimant who disagrees with the insurer's claim decision has the right to sue the insurer to collect the amount the claimant believes is owed under the policy. The length of this time period varies from jurisdiction to jurisdiction, but it typically ranges from one to three years after the claimant provides the insurer with proof of the loss.

Change of Occupation Provision

Many individual disability income insurance policies contain a *change of occupation provision* that permits the insurer to adjust the policy's premium rate or the amount of benefits payable under the policy if the insured changes occupation. As we describe in the next section, the insured's occupation has a direct effect on her morbidity risk. The change of occupation provision typically permits the insurer to reduce the maximum benefit amount payable under the policy if the insured changes to a *more* hazardous occupation. If the insured changes to a *less* hazardous occupation, the provision permits the insurer to reduce the policy's premium rate.

For example, if a teacher were to enter the more dangerous occupation of coal miner, then the insurer would reduce the maximum benefit amount available under the policy to the benefit amount that the premium charged would have purchased for a coal miner; the policy's premium rate would not change. Alternatively, if a coal miner were to change occupations and become a teacher, the insurer would reduce the premium rate to the premium rate that would be charged to a teacher for the same level of benefits; the policy's maximum benefit amount would remain the same. All benefit amount and premium rate changes take effect as of the time the insured changes occupation.

Overinsurance Provision

Many individual health insurance policies contain an *overinsurance provision* that is intended to prevent an insured from profiting from a sickness or injury. This provision states that the benefits payable under the policy will be reduced if the insured is overinsured. An *overinsured person* is one who is entitled to receive either (1) more in benefits from his medical expense policies than the actual costs incurred for treatment or (2) a greater income amount during disability than he earns while working.

An overinsurance provision takes effect *only* if the insurer was not notified of the other coverage at the time of application. In cases of overinsurance, the insurer reduces the amount of the benefits that would otherwise be payable under the policy and refunds any premium amount paid for the excess coverage.

Individual Health Insurance Underwriting

Individual health insurance underwriters evaluate each application to determine the degree of morbidity risk represented by the proposed insured. This process of evaluating the degree of risk presented by a proposed insured is very similar to the process that insurance companies use to evaluate applications for life insurance.

Morbidity Factors

The primary factors that affect the degree of morbidity risk presented by a proposed insured are the individual's age; current and past health; sex; occupation; avocations; work history; and habits and lifestyle. We examine how each of these factors affects an individual's morbidity risk.

Age

Morbidity rates generally increase with age. As people grow older, they are more likely to become ill, and the average duration of their illnesses increases. Further, the length of time required to recuperate from an injury also increases with age.

Health

An individual's health history and current health are both important factors in determining morbidity risk. Many illnesses have a tendency to recur, and an individual's future health is strongly affected by her past and current illnesses and injuries.

Sex

A person's sex has an effect on the degree of that person's morbidity risk. Because females generally experience a higher morbidity rate than males of the same age, the cost of providing health insurance coverage to females is generally higher than the cost of providing coverage to males.

Occupation

A person's morbidity risk also depends on his occupation. Factors about a person's occupation that affect the degree of morbidity risk include the hazards inherent in the occupation, the stability of the occupation, and the amount of recovery time that people in that occupation usually need to resume their normal job duties. In order to reflect these differences in morbidity, health insurance underwriters establish several occupational classes and rank these classes according to morbidity rate. An individual's risk classification and corresponding premium rate correspond to the individual's occupation class. Figure 21-1 includes an example of an insurer's occupational rating classes, which range from least hazardous to most hazardous. Note

---

Figure 21-1. An Insurer's Occupational Rating Classes.

Class 1	*Standard:* This class includes people in the least hazardous occupations. Examples include attorney, bookkeeper, insurance agent, librarian, pharmacist, and secretary.
Class 2	This class generally includes the following people: (a) People who work in certain nonhazardous occupations in which even a minor injury can result in disability. Examples include most people who work in the allied medical professions, laboratory workers, and musicians. (b) People who have office and overall supervisory responsibility in manufacturing plants or at construction sites. Examples include architect and supervising plant manager.
Class 3	This class generally includes (a) blue-collar workers or people doing light manual labor, (b) people who drive passenger or light delivery vehicles, and (c) forepersons who directly supervise manual laborers on the job and who may occasionally assist in manual activity. Examples include athletic coach, house painter, plumber, taxi driver, and waitpersons.
Class 4	*Most Hazardous:* This class includes people in the most hazardous insurable occupations. Examples include boilermaker, locomotive engineer, and structural steelworker.
Uninsurable	This class includes people who are exposed to unusual hazards and are uninsurable for any coverage. Examples include blaster, underground miner, test pilot, and war correspondent.

Least Hazardous (top) → *Most Hazardous* (bottom)

Source: Ernest L. Martin, *Intro to Underwriting* (Atlanta: LOMA, 1999), 50. Used with permission.

---

that health insurers consider some occupations, such as experimental aircraft testing, to be so risk prone that applicants who work in those occupations are usually classified as uninsurable.

Avocations

An individual's avocations also have a strong bearing on his potential health insurance risk. Engaging in certain sports or hobbies may expose an individual to a significant chance of injury or disease. For example, a mountain climber is more prone to accidental injury than is a stamp collector. Hence, the manner in which a person spends leisure time may have a bearing on his exposure to health risks.

Work History

An individual's work history can also have a bearing on her morbidity risk. For example, a person with a number of gaps in her work record or who has a history of temporary jobs might be deemed to be a poor risk for disability income coverage because such a person might lack the incentive to recover from a disability. The person may, for one reason or another, prefer not to work and, should she become disabled, might be inclined to prolong the disability in order to continue receiving disability income benefits and to avoid returning to work. Such an individual's morbidity risk is likely to be greater than the morbidity risk of an individual with a history of regular employment.

Habits and Lifestyle

A person's habits and lifestyle can expose him to a high degree of risk of accidental injury or illness. For example, an individual who has a recent criminal record may present a higher degree of risk than does an individual who has never been convicted of a crime. Further, individuals who have alcohol or drug problems are also more likely to present health insurance claims than are individuals who do not abuse drugs or alcohol.

The degree of risk inherent in various lifestyles is often difficult to measure, and health insurance underwriters must be careful when assigning an individual a higher degree of morbidity risk on the basis of habits and lifestyle. Many jurisdictions have enacted antidiscrimination legislation to prevent health insurance underwriters from classifying individuals as substandard risks and charging them higher premium rates solely on the basis of certain lifestyles. Many jurisdictions, for example, specifically prohibit insurers from considering an applicant's sexual orientation during the underwriting process.

Risk Classifications

Underwriters evaluate each applicant for individual health insurance in order to determine the degree of morbidity risk presented by the proposed insured. Using this evaluation, the underwriter will usually place the applicant into one of three categories of risk—standard, substandard, or declined.

Standard Risk

An applicant who is classified as a standard risk will be issued a policy at standard premium rates. The policy will not contain any special exclusions or reductions in benefits. Most applicants for individual health insurance are classified as standard risks.

Substandard Risk

Those applicants who may be expected to present a higher-than-average morbidity risk are classified as substandard health insurance risks. Rather than decline such applicants for coverage, health insurers have developed several ways to modify health insurance policies to compensate for the extra risk represented by applicants in this category.

In some situations, health insurers charge a higher premium rate to applicants who are classified as substandard risks. Alternatively, a health insurer might compensate for the extra risk by modifying the benefits available under the policy. For example, a policy issued to a substandard risk might include a longer elimination period or a lower maximum benefit amount than a policy issued to a standard risk. Finally, if an applicant presents a specific and definable extra morbidity risk, the insurer might attach an exclusion rider to the policy issued to that applicant. An *exclusion rider,* which is also called an *impairment rider,* specifies that benefits will not be provided for any loss that results from the condition specified in the rider. In this way, health insurers can often provide coverage at standard premium rates to an applicant who would otherwise be charged a higher rate because she has a known health problem or engages in certain activities that increase morbidity risk. For example, an insurer may be able to offer an individual who has a history of back disorders an individual disability income policy at standard premium rates by excluding from coverage any disability that results from the back disorders. (See Figure 21-2, which shows a sample exclusion rider.)

Declined Risk

Applicants are declined coverage if they have very poor health or engage in extremely dangerous occupations or activities. Additionally, health insurers may decline to issue disability income coverage to applicants who would not suffer a substantial income loss during a disability either because the applicant has adequate disability income coverage through another provider or because a large percentage of the applicant's income would continue during a disability.

Many jurisdictions have issued regulations that prohibit insurers from declining coverage to physically disabled persons, unless such action can be supported by morbidity statistics. When insuring a disabled person, however, insurers are permitted to exclude coverage of the person's existing disability.

FIGURE 21-2. Sample Exclusion Rider.

ABC Life Insurance Company
New York, NY 00000
WAIVER-RIDER

In consideration of the premium at which this policy is issued, it is agreed and understood, by and between the company and the insured, that the terms of this policy shall not apply to any disability or loss on the part of Doris Holden caused directly or indirectly, wholly or in part, anything in the policy to the contrary notwithstanding, by or from the following:

Any disease of or injury to the lumbosacral region of the spine or its underlying nerve structures, including intervertebral discs, any complication thereof, treatment or operation therefor.

In all other respects the provisions and conditions of the policy remain unchanged.

Attached to and forming
part of the policy number:

000000

This rider is effective at
12:00 noon standard time on:
September 19, 1999

Heather R. King

Secretary

BJ Nemitt

President

Issued to: Doris Holden

Accepted by Insured: **Date:**

_____

Countersigned at: Authorized Representative:

_____

Key Terms

renewal provision	incontestability provision
cancellable policy	pre-existing conditions provision
optionally renewable policy	pre-existing condition
class of policies	physical examination provision
conditionally renewable policy	legal actions provision
guaranteed renewable policy	change of occupation provision
noncancellable policy	overinsurance provision
grace period provision	overinsured person
reinstatement provision	exclusion rider

Other Important Terms

time limit on certain defenses	impairment rider
incontestable clause	

Endnotes

1. HIAA, *Source Book of Health Insurance Data* (Washington, D.C.: Health Insurance Association of America, 1998), 28.
2. Ibid., 40.

CHAPTER 22

Managed Care Plans

After reading this chapter, you should be able to

- Identify and describe the features of a managed care plan

- Identify and describe the characteristics of a health maintenance organization (HMO) and the various fee structures that HMOs use to compensate network providers

- Identify and describe the various types of open panel HMOs and closed panel HMOs

- Recognize some of the ways in which preferred provider organizations (PPOs) differ from HMOs

- Identify the features of an open-ended HMO and a gatekeeper PPO

Over the last few decades, the way in which medical expense coverage is provided in the United States has changed dramatically. In the earlier chapters in this section, we described traditional medical expense insurance plans that provide indemnity benefits for covered losses as defined in the insurance policy. Currently, most insureds in the United States are covered by some type of managed care plan rather than a traditional medical expense insurance plan. By *managed care* we mean a method of integrating the financing *and* delivery of health care within a system that manages the cost, accessibility, and quality of care.

Managed care plans differ from traditional health insurance plans in a number of ways, including the specific benefits provided, the manner in which an insured obtains medical care services, and the manner in which the health care provider is paid for rendering services. This chapter will describe the operation of a number of managed care plans, concentrating on health maintenance organizations (HMOs), preferred provider organizations (PPOs), and variations of such plans. First, we describe some characteristics that distinguish managed care plans from traditional medical expense plans.

Concepts of Managed Care

One of the primary distinctions between managed care plans and traditional medical expense insurance plans has to do with insureds' access to medical care. In a traditional indemnity insurance plan, insureds are free to choose any licensed physician or hospital for their medical needs. By contrast, managed care plans negotiate contracts with selected health care providers, and insureds are referred to that network of providers. An insured may choose any provider who is a part of that network.

The health care providers' involvement in risk sharing is another unique feature of managed care plans. Under a traditional indemnity plan, the risk insured—the cost of medical care for illness or accident—is shared between the insured person and the insurer. The more often a given insured seeks medical care, the more money the insured and the insurer must pay health care providers. The physician or hospital that treats the insured person, however, bears none of the financial risk of the insured's illness or accident. The doctor or hospital is paid for services each time the insured uses those services. In fact, the more a person insured under such a traditional *fee-for-service plan* visits a health care provider, the more the provider can benefit financially.

Managed care plans broaden the circle of financial risk sharing to include health care providers. The philosophy of these plans is that providers should share in the financial risk of an insured's poor health and should not be rewarded for an insured's excessive use of medical services. Instead, health care providers should be encouraged to deliver the necessary care in a cost-effective way. Managed care plans achieve risk sharing by negotiating fee arrangements with health care providers and making other contractual agreements that encourage cost-effective care. The nature of these fee arrangements depends on the type of managed care plan.

Another feature that can be found in varying degrees in all managed care plans is **utilization management,** which is a process by which a plan manages an insured's use of medical services and assures that she receives necessary, appropriate, high-quality care in a cost-effective manner. Utilization management combines and broadens utilization review and case management techniques—both of which we discuss below. **Utilization review (UR)** is a process by which a plan evaluates the necessity and quality of a patient's medical care. Although the specific details of utilization review vary from plan to plan, the basic components are generally the same. Most utilization review programs include preadmission certification, concurrent review, and retrospective review.

- **Preadmission certification.** Before any nonemergency hospital stay, an insured must contact the UR organization to obtain preadmission certification. The insured must provide information such as the purpose of the hospitalization and expected length of stay. Then the UR agent analyzes the situation and determines whether hospitalization or some other type of care is most appropriate and what the length of a hospital stay should be. In some cases, the UR agent contacts the insured's physician to get more information. In case of an emergency hospitalization, the insured or the insured's physician must generally notify the UR organization within 48 hours after the insured is hospitalized. Failure to obtain preadmission certification most often results in reduced payment of medical expenses.

- **Concurrent review.** Concurrent review takes place while the patient is in the hospital. Once the patient has been admitted, the UR staff monitors her condition by visits or telephone calls to the patient's physician in which they discuss treatment and prognosis and begin to plan for the patient's discharge from the hospital.

<hr>

FAST FACT

By 1998, enrollments in managed care plans sponsored by U.S. insurance companies totaled almost 132 million people.[1]

- **Retrospective review.** Retrospective review involves much of the same analysis that takes place in preadmission certification and concurrent review—except that it takes place after the patient has been discharged from the hospital. Although retrospective review may uncover some erroneous charges or billing errors, its main purpose is to help insurers spot trends and identify areas or providers that have excessive costs.

Case management is an extension of utilization review and is a process by which a plan evaluates not only the medical necessity of care—as in utilization review—but also alternative treatments or solutions for medical care. Case management is most often used in situations in which the patient has an illness or injury that is likely to require very expensive treatment. A case manager, who is usually a registered nurse, works with the patient, the patient's family, and physicians to develop a treatment plan. The case manager is familiar with the patient's insurance plan and tries to achieve the best possible use of the patient's insurance coverage, along with any private and community programs that might be available. The case manager can help stretch the benefit dollars to achieve the most appropriate care without exhausting the patient's financial resources. Figure 22-1 is an example of how one insurance company used case management.

The Health Care Coverage Continuum

Because of the variety of managed care plans that have developed, classifying any specific plan is not easy. Although some plans fit neatly into a classification as a traditional indemnity insurance plan or a managed care plan, many plans on the market today are hybrids. That is, they contain some aspects of managed care plans and some aspects that are more common to traditional indemnity plans.

The health care coverage continuum in Figure 22-2 illustrates this point. On the far left side of the continuum are traditional indemnity insurance plans; on the far right are pure managed care plans. The various types of managed care systems are positioned in between with, for example, PPOs closer to traditional indemnity plans and HMOs closer to pure managed care. The plans on the right side of the continuum incorporate more elements of managed care than do those on the left. As you learn more about managed care plans, you will begin to understand how each product fits on this continuum. For now, just review the continuum and use it as a reference tool to help you put these plans in perspective as you read the remainder of this chapter.

Positioning a plan on the continuum requires more than just looking at the plan's title—you must study its exact features. The boundaries

FIGURE 22-1. Case Example: Rehabilitation of "Tom".

Case Management Steps	Case Highlights
Early Identification	• Case identified due to diagnosis of spinal cord injury
Assessment	• 27-year-old male with spinal cord injury and resultant quadriplegia • Review of patient's clinical status and treatment plan • Evaluation of facility qualifications to care for patient requiring highly specialized care • Long-range goals established
Intervention	• Coordination of services and transfer of patient to regional center for spinal cord injury patients
Managing the Care Plan	• Weekly communication established with the rehabilitation team to review patient's progress • Acquisition of durable medical equipment • Coordination of discharge plan
Case Closure	• Cost savings of $26,000 through negotiation of length of stay and acquisition of durable medical equipment • Patient benefits; early discharge to an appropriate home environment with necessary services and equipment • Patient moved to the final phase of rehabilitation, independent living, in a timely manner

Source: "Case Management: Meeting the Challenge of High Cost Illness," by Carol Delaney and David Aquilina, reprinted with permission from the *Employee Benefits Journal* Volume II Number 1, March 1987 published by the International Foundation of Employee Benefit Plans, Brookfield, WI. Statements or opinions expressed in this article are those of the author and do not necessarily represent the views or positions of the International Foundation, its officers, directors, or staff.

FIGURE 22-2. Health Care Coverage Continuum.

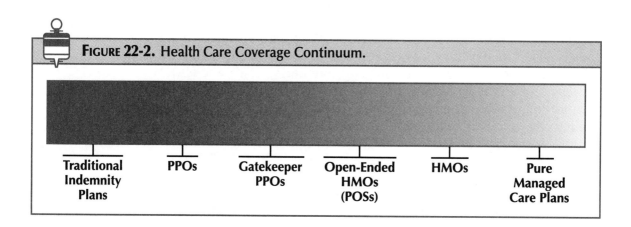

Traditional Indemnity Plans — PPOs — Gatekeeper PPOs — Open-Ended HMOs (POSs) — HMOs — Pure Managed Care Plans

between the different types of plans are not rigid, and, as the various systems and providers continue experimenting with new forms and ideas, classifying these plans will probably become even more difficult.

Health Maintenance Organizations

A *health maintenance organization (HMO)* is a health care financing and delivery system that provides comprehensive health care services for subscribing members—often referred to as *subscribers*—in a particular geographic area. Note that HMOs combine both the financing and the delivery aspects of health care services—an HMO is both an insurer and a provider of health care services. Although HMOs have been in existence since 1929, they have become popular only within the last few decades. HMO membership increased from 6 million people in 1976 to more than 67 million people in 1996. (See Figure 22-3.)

HMOs can be owned or sponsored by many different types of organizations: by national HMO organizations, by commercial insurers, and even by medical schools and hospitals. HMOs can be operated as either not-for-profit or for-profit organizations. Although for-profit HMOs well outnumber not-for-profit HMOs, the not-for-profit HMOs represent more subscribers than those HMOs operated for profit.

Characteristics of HMOs

As financing and delivery systems, HMOs are concerned not only with the payment of an insured's medical expenses but also with arranging for doctors, hospitals, clinics, and other medical care organizations and personnel to provide medical care to HMO subscribers. Although various types of HMOs have developed, most HMOs share some common characteristics.

Comprehensive Care

HMO subscribers are eligible to receive comprehensive health care services, including inpatient and outpatient treatment in a hospital. In an effort to reduce the incidence and severity of illnesses, HMOs emphasize the practice of preventive care, including routine physical examinations, diagnostic tests, pre-natal and well-baby care, and immunizations. By contrast, traditional indemnity plans generally do not emphasize preventive care.

FIGURE 22-3. HMO Enrollments, 1976 to 1996.

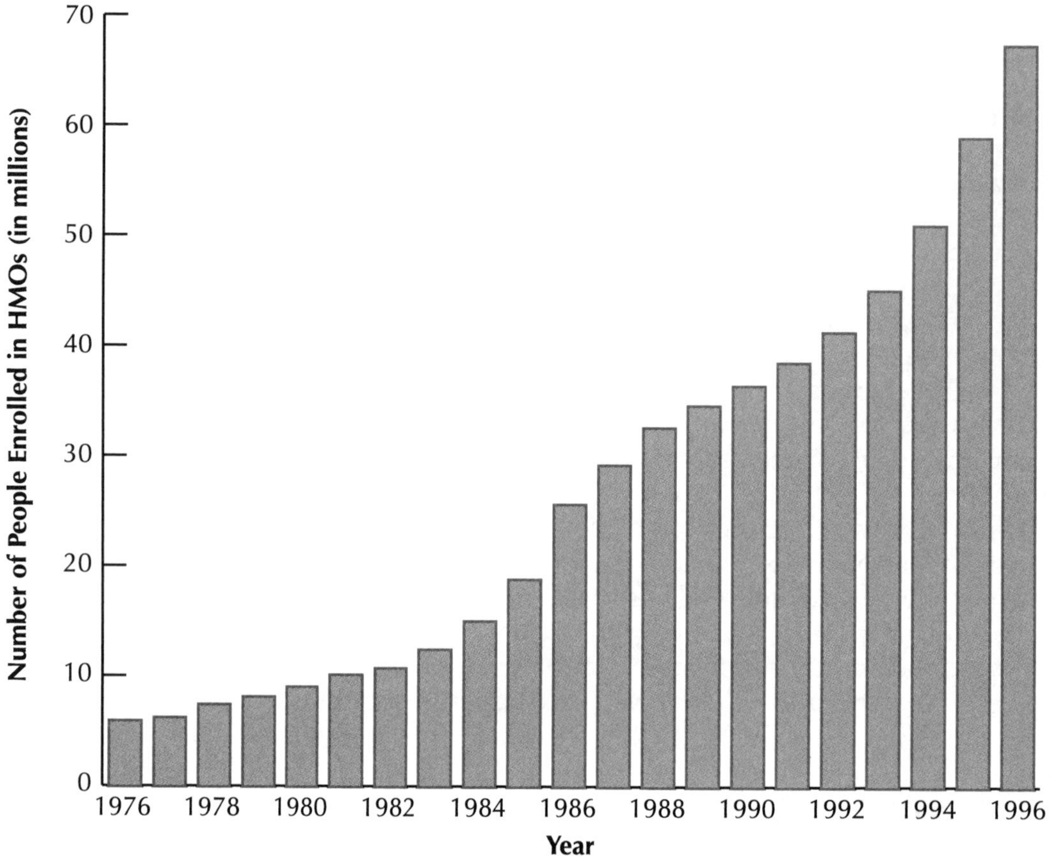

Source: American Association of Health Plans, "Managed Care Facts," *AAHP Online,* January 1998, http://www.aahp.org/menus/index.cfm?CFID=29950&CFTOKEN=96824522. Used with permission.

Prepaid Care

In a traditional HMO, subscribers receive comprehensive health care in exchange for the payment of a fixed, periodic—usually monthly—fee. Most HMOs also require the subscriber to pay an additional fee—known as a *copayment*—for certain medical services. For example, an HMO might specify that a subscriber must pay $10 for each visit to a doctor. From a provider's point of view, HMO subscribers receive prepaid care because the provider receives a stated amount per subscriber, regardless of the amount of services he provides to subscribers. You will recall that the insurer bears the financial risk under a traditional medical expense insurance plan. By contrast, HMOs shift all or part of the financial risk to the health care providers. As we will describe in the following sections, the method an HMO uses to compensate

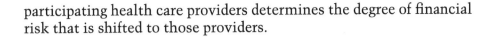

participating health care providers determines the degree of financial risk that is shifted to those providers.

Networked Providers and Negotiated Fees

HMOs contract with physicians and hospitals to make up a network of health care providers. HMO subscribers must choose their medical care providers from within this network. The HMO generally does not cover medical services or health care provided by physicians or hospitals that are not a part of the HMO's network. By contracting with specific physicians and hospitals, HMOs achieve certain advantages.

- They can better control the quality of the providers that treat their subscribers.

- They can negotiate fees for the medical services provided to their subscribers and, thus, reduce the cost of providing those services.

Unlike traditional indemnity plans, HMOs negotiate fee arrangements with physicians and hospitals belonging to the HMO network. Physicians, in turn, control how HMO subscribers use health care services and, thus, play an important role in controlling expenses in an HMO. We will discuss several fee structures that may be used to compensate physicians who provide services to HMO subscribers.

Capitation. Under a *capitation* arrangement, the provider is paid the same amount each month for a subscriber regardless of how often the subscriber receives medical attention or of the cost of that medical attention. (You might see the acronym *PMPM*, which stands for per member per month, used in relation to capitation payments.) However, the capitation payment may not be the same for all HMO subscribers. For example, an HMO might have a higher capitation payment for infants up to age 18 months than for teenagers because infants typically have more doctor visits in the first two years of life than most teenagers have in a two-year period.

Salary. Some types of HMOs compensate physicians with a predetermined salary. The salaries are usually based on average salaries of local physicians in the same field or specialty. Many physicians who receive a salary may also receive certain types of performance-based bonuses or incentive pay. Because salaries, like capitation payments, are stated fixed amounts, the HMO is able to reduce the amount of its financial risk.

Discounted Fee-for-Service. When an HMO uses the *discounted fee-for-service payment structure,* it pays physicians a certain percentage of their normal fees. For example, if the HMO pays physicians 90 percent of their normal fees, the HMO achieves a 10 percent "discount" on those physicians' fees. The physicians agree to accept the discounted fee as payment in full for their services. The discounted fee arrangement is similar to traditional health insurance in that it places most of the financial risk on the organization that provides the health insurance—in this case, the HMO. For that reason, it is not as widely used as some of the other fee structures.

Fee Schedule. The *fee schedule payment structure* allows the HMO to place caps or limits on the dollar amounts that it will reimburse providers for covered medical procedures and services. The HMO will pay no more than the specified maximum fee for each procedure. In using a fee schedule payment structure, the HMO transfers more risk to physicians and other providers than when using a discounted fee-for-service payment structure because the HMO remains responsible for only a limited portion of the subscriber's medical fees. The physician has to absorb the cost for that portion of a fee that exceeds the maximum allowable fee and may not bill the patient for the balance of the fee.

Intensive Use of Managed Care Techniques

HMOs typically use a variety of managed care techniques that enable them to reduce the costs of providing health care to their subscribers. For example, traditional HMOs require subscribers to select a primary care physician from the network of providers. The *primary care physician (PCP)* is usually a general or family practitioner who serves as the subscriber's personal physician and first contact with the HMO. If additional care is needed, the PCP may refer the subscriber to specialists within the network. Because PCPs must authorize all services delivered by another network physician or provider, they are often called *gatekeepers.*

Utilization management is also a very important managed care technique used by HMOs to determine the most appropriate care for the patient, the most appropriate provider of that care, and the most cost-efficient setting in which the patient can receive that care.

Types of HMOs

In this section, we identify several different types, or models, of HMOs. While some HMOs can be easily classified, others possess characteristics of more than one model, making them difficult to classify. The descriptions of the models we present will provide you with a foundation of knowledge about HMOs.

"If Frank makes it through the maze, I figure he's ready to handle the job of choosing a managed care provider for our employee benefits plan."

Reprinted with permission of Phil Interlandi and Bituminous Casualty Corporation.

HMOs usually can be broadly classified as either open panel HMOs or closed panel HMOs. In an *open panel HMO,* any physician or provider who meets the HMO's specific standards can contract with the HMO to provide services to the members. In a *closed panel HMO,* physicians either must belong to a special group of physicians that has contracted with the HMO or must be employees of the HMO.

Open Panel

An open panel HMO can be classified as either an individual practice association (IPA) model or a direct contract HMO.

Individual Practice Association. An *individual practice association (IPA) model* is an arrangement in which the HMO enters into a contract with an *IPA,* which is an association of physicians that agrees to provide services for the HMO's subscribers. The physicians are generally independent practitioners who have established their own offices with their own supplies and support staff. They provide services for their own patients as well as the HMO's subscribers. Because physicians in an IPA operate out of their own offices, the HMO is not required to establish offices for its physicians. As a result, IPAs are generally easier to establish than some other HMO models because they require less start-up capital and can offer a broad range of medical specialties.

The HMO most often compensates the IPA based on a capitation payment structure; the IPA is then responsible for compensating all the physicians who belong to the association. The IPA generally uses either the capitation payment structure or the discounted fee-for-service payment structure. Most often, primary care physicians are compensated on a capitation basis, and specialists are compensated on a discounted fee-for-service basis.

In an IPA model HMO, much of the financial risk of providing medical care to HMO members rests with the IPA and its participating physicians. Because the HMO typically compensates the IPA through a capitation arrangement, the IPA has only those funds available to use to compensate doctors and nurses and to pay all other costs of providing any medical care that HMO subscribers need during the period. Some HMOs require subscribers to pay a small copayment for an office visit or a deductible amount in connection with certain services, but the bulk of the financing comes from the capitation arrangement. Thus, the IPA assumes the financial risks of an unusually high rate of illness among its subscribers and of overutilization of medical services by subscribers.

Direct Contract HMO. Under the *direct contract HMO* arrangement, the HMO contracts directly with physicians to provide medical services for HMO members—no association or middleman organization is involved. Direct contract HMOs generally contract with both primary care physicians and specialists. These physicians work out of their own offices, use their own staffs and facilities, and continue to see their own patients as well as the HMO members.

Like IPAs, direct contract HMOs can use either the capitation or discounted fee-for-service payment systems. In order to minimize financial risk to the HMO, most direct contract HMOs use the capitation payment system.

Closed Panel

Two types of HMOs can be classified as closed panels. These HMOs either directly employ physicians or contract with physicians' group practices.

Staff Model. In a *staff model HMO,* the physicians are actually employees of the HMO and generally operate out of offices in the HMO's facilities. These physicians are paid a salary and sometimes receive bonuses or incentive payments related to their performance. The staff model HMO may also own or contract with hospitals, laboratories, pharmacies, and other organizations to provide non-physician medical services.

A staff model HMO is usually the most difficult and costly type of HMO to start up because of both the capital costs needed to build facilities and the large fixed expenses related to physicians' salaries. In addition, the financial risk rests primarily on the HMO rather than on the physicians. But, because it offers the HMO greater control over physicians, the staff model HMO can often manage utilization of health care services better than other models can.

Group Model. A *group model HMO* functions much as a staff model HMO, except that the physicians are employees of a physicians' group practice, rather than employees of the HMO. The physicians in such a group practice generally share office space, support staff, and medical equipment at a common health center or clinic. Kaiser Permanente is one of the oldest and most widely known group model HMOs in the United States. A group model HMO that contracts with more than one group practice of physicians is called a *network model HMO.*

Group model HMOs most often pay a negotiated capitation rate to each physicians' group practice. The group practice, in turn, generally compensates the individual physicians in the group with salaries based on their performance, their area of expertise, and the amount of administrative work they must perform. As a result, the financial risk is borne primarily by the physicians' groups.

Mixed Models

As we mentioned, many HMOs do not fit neatly into only one of the models we have described. Some HMOs combine certain characteristics of two or more of the models and are known as *mixed model HMOs.* The number of mixed model HMOs is growing. In fact, as of January 1997, 40 percent of all HMOs were mixed models. Figure 22-4 shows the distribution of HMOs by type of model.

Preferred Provider Organizations

A *preferred provider organization (PPO)* is an organization that negotiates contracts between health care providers and health care purchasers—such as employers, third-party administrators (TPAs), insurance companies, and unions. The PPO does not provide health care directly; rather, it acts as a broker or middleman by contracting with health care providers to deliver medical services to a specific

FIGURE 22-4. Distribution of HMOs by Model Type.

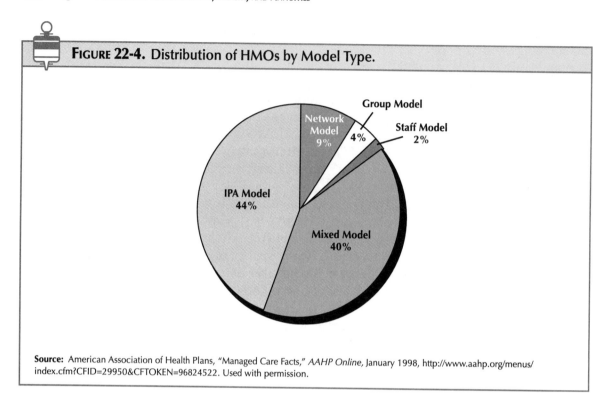

Source: American Association of Health Plans, "Managed Care Facts," *AAHP Online,* January 1998, http://www.aahp.org/menus/index.cfm?CFID=29950&CFTOKEN=96824522. Used with permission.

group of covered individuals. PPOs are thus able to combine some advantages of both traditional indemnity plans and HMOs.

PPOs can be sponsored or organized in a number of ways; some are sponsored by groups of physicians or hospitals, others are sponsored by Blue Cross or Blue Shield plans, TPAs, or employers. Insurance companies, however, are the dominant sponsors of PPOs in the United States.

Like HMOs, PPOs use a network of health care providers. But unlike HMOs, PPOs do offer some coverage for members who choose to use the services of non-network—or out-of-network—providers. To encourage plan members to see the preferred providers in the PPO network, PPOs pay a higher portion of those medical expenses incurred with PPO providers than they pay for services provided by out-of-network providers. For example, the plan may cover 90 percent of the cost of a certain medical expense—usually without a deductible—if the insured sees a preferred provider. On the other hand, if the insured chooses to see a provider that is not in the network, the plan may cover only 70 percent of the expense and may also specify deductibles and other out-of-pocket amounts that the insured must pay.

PPO networks generally include both primary care physicians and specialists. The PPO negotiates discounted fees with the providers and generally requires the providers to follow strict utilization management procedures in order to achieve cost-effective patient

FAST FACT

Since 1990, enrollments in PPOs have increased by 154%.[2]

care. In return for discounting their fees, the physicians generally are able to increase their patient bases because of the new PPO members. Many PPOs also offer physicians the benefit of faster claim processing and payment than is available under traditional medical expense insurance plans.

PPOs resemble traditional indemnity plans in that they typically compensate health care providers on a fee-for-service basis. As a result, PPOs do not accept the financial risk of providing health care services to insureds—they pass it on to either the insurer or the policyholder. However, many PPOs have now started to include risk-sharing arrangements in their contracts with providers in an attempt to achieve greater cost savings and more control over utilization.

When PPOs first began operating, most providers in the networks were either physicians or hospitals. Specialty PPOs have since developed and provide coverages such as physical therapy, dental care, pharmaceutical products, laboratory services, chiropractic services, and psychological care.

Hybrid Plans

As we have noted, the distinctions between various types of managed care plans are fading as these plans continue to evolve. Some HMOs have adopted features that more closely resemble traditional indemnity plans, and many PPOs have adopted additional managed care features. In this section, we describe two of these hybrid plans—open-ended HMOs and gatekeeper PPOs. (Figure 22-5 shows the distribution of the various types of medical expense plans in 1997.)

Open-Ended HMOs

In order to give subscribers more freedom to choose their health care providers, a new type of HMO was designed. This type of HMO, known as an **open-ended HMO** or a *point of service (POS) plan*, has some features of a traditional HMO and some features that more closely resemble a traditional indemnity plan. When a subscriber to an open-ended HMO needs medical care, she may use the HMO providers as in a traditional HMO. The subscriber, however, may choose to use a provider that does not participate in the HMO. In such a case, the HMO operates more like a traditional indemnity plan. The HMO reimburses the subscriber for her covered medical expenses, but the subscriber typically must pay higher deductible and coinsurance amounts than she would pay under a traditional indemnity plan. Thus, the subscriber has the option of going out of the

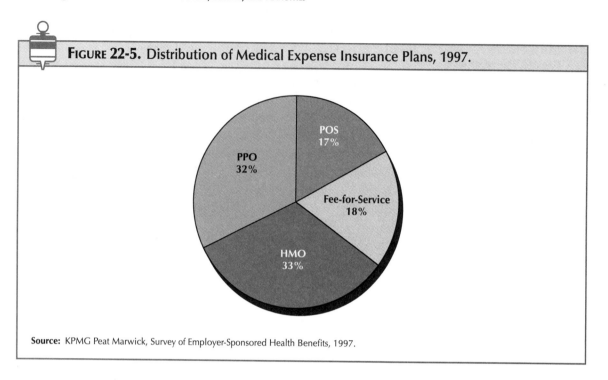

FIGURE 22-5. Distribution of Medical Expense Insurance Plans, 1997.

Source: KPMG Peat Marwick, Survey of Employer-Sponsored Health Benefits, 1997.

HMO network of providers, but the plan contains financial incentives to encourage subscribers to use network providers.

Gatekeeper PPOs

In an effort to control costs and utilization of health care services, PPOs have begun to adopt more features of managed care plans. A *gatekeeper PPO* is a PPO that requires plan members to select a primary care physician from within the PPO's network of physicians. The primary care physician operates as a gatekeeper to control utilization of medical care by authorizing certain medical services and referring plan members to specialists within the PPO's network. As in a traditional PPO, when a plan member needs medical care, he may select any provider. However, the out-of-pocket costs a member incurs are lowest if he obtains medical care through his primary care physician and obtains referrals for specialists within the PPO network.

Another way that gatekeeper PPOs differ from traditional PPOs concerns how participating providers are compensated. Recall that PPOs typically compensate participating providers on a discounted fee-for-service basis. By contrast, gatekeeper PPOs typically compensate primary care physicians on a capitation basis. Thus, gatekeeper PPOs transfer more of the financial risk to providers than do traditional PPOs.

Key Terms

managed care
utilization management
utilization review (UR)
preadmission certification
concurrent review
retrospective review
case management
health maintenance
   organization (HMO)
copayment
capitation
discounted fee-for-service
   payment structure
fee schedule payment structure
primary care physician (PCP)

gatekeeper
open panel HMO
closed panel HMO
individual practice association
   (IPA) model
direct contract HMO
staff model HMO
group model HMO
network model HMO
mixed model HMO
preferred provider organization
   (PPO)
open-ended HMO
gatekeeper PPO

Other Important Terms

fee-for-service plan
subscribers
individual practice association
   (IPA)

point of service (POS) plan

Endnotes

1. HIAA, *Source Book of Health Insurance Data* (Washington, D.C.: Health Insurance Association of America, 1998), 50.

2. AAHP, "Managed Care Facts" (Washington, D.C.: American Association of Health Plans, 1998). Available online at http://www.aahp.org/menus/index.cfm?CFID=29950&CFTOKEN=96824522.

CHAPTER 23

Regulation of Health Insurance

After reading this chapter, you should be able to

- Describe the roles of the federal and state governments in regulating health care coverage in the United States

- Identify the types of provisions that most states require insurers to include in health insurance policies

- Describe how the states regulate HMOs and PPOs

- Identify and describe the primary federal laws that regulate health insurance plans in the United States

- List the criteria that Canada's provincial hospital and medical expense plans must meet in order to qualify for federal financial assistance

- Identify the criteria that a private disability income plan must meet in order to be registered as a qualified plan in Canada and the advantage of registering as a qualified plan

- Recognize the requirements that provincial insurance laws impose on health insurance policies

- Describe how health insurance policy premiums and benefits are treated for income tax purposes in the United States and Canada

Although regulation of health insurance is very similar in the United States and Canada, the methods of regulation the two countries use are different. These differences result from the distinctions in how health insurance is provided in the two countries. In this chapter, we first describe health insurance regulation in the United States, then we describe regulation in Canada.

Regulation in the United States

As we described in Chapter 2, the states have enacted laws and regulations that govern a wide range of insurance company operations. State laws, for example, regulate the licensing of insurers and their agents, seek to ensure the solvency of insurers, and regulate the advertising and sale of insurance policies. In this chapter, we focus on those state laws that are unique to health insurance regulation. We also describe federal laws that affect health insurance plans.

State Regulation of Health Insurance

The National Association of Insurance Commissioners (NAIC) has adopted a number of model laws designed to regulate individual and group health insurance. Some of these model laws are listed in Figure 23-1. The vast majority of states have enacted laws patterned on the *NAIC Uniform Individual Accident and Sickness Policy Provision Law* (Individual Health Insurance Model Law). As a result, the regulation of *individual* health insurance is somewhat uniform. In contrast, however, state regulation of *group* health insurance is much less uniform because many states have not closely patterned their group health insurance laws on the *NAIC Group Health Insurance Definition and Group Health Insurance Standard Provisions Model Act* (Group Health Insurance Model Act).

Policy Provisions

In Chapters 20 and 21, we described some of the provisions that insurers typically include in health insurance policies. State insurance laws require that many of these provisions be included in health insurance policies.

FIGURE 23-1. NAIC Model Laws Designed to Regulate Health Insurance.

- **Uniform Individual Accident and Sickness Policy Provision Law**—Contains requirements as to certain individual health insurance policy provisions

- **Group Health Insurance Definition and Group Health Insurance Standard Provisions Model Act**—Defines groups that are eligible for insurance and contains requirements as to certain group health insurance policy provisions

- **Model Newborn Children Bill**—Mandates coverage for newborn children of an insured under policies that make coverage available to dependent children of insureds

- **Group Health Insurance Mandatory Conversion Privilege Model Act**—Requires group health insurance contracts to give insureds the right to convert their group health insurance coverage to an individual health insurance policy if their employment terminates or if the group contract is terminated

- **Group Coordination of Benefits Regulations and Guidelines**—Establish uniformity in the use of overinsurance provisions to avoid claim delays and misunderstandings that otherwise result from the use of inconsistent provisions among several carriers

---

- Most states require that a stated minimum grace period be included in both individual and group health insurance policies.

- Most states require individual and group health insurance contracts to include an incontestable clause (time limit on certain defenses provision).

- If a pre-existing conditions provision is included in an individual or group health insurance policy, most states limit the time within which such a condition can be excluded from coverage. As we describe later in the chapter, federal law now imposes strict limitations on the operation of pre-existing conditions exclusions in medical expense plans.

- The states regulate the cancellation and renewal provisions that may be included in individual health policies.

- Individual health insurance policies typically must include a reinstatement provision, and group health insurance policies must contain a conversion provision.

- Almost all of the states have laws regulating the coordination of benefits (COB) provision typically included in group health policies. The states also regulate overinsurance provisions commonly included in individual health policies.

Regulations Unique to Group Health Insurance

About half of the states require that a minimum number of persons—usually five or ten—be insured under a group health insurance contract. Many states, however, have no minimum size requirement. In these states, the insurer can rely solely on its own underwriting requirements to decide how small a group it will insure.

Most states have laws that prohibit a group insurance policy from being delivered in the state unless the group meets certain eligibility requirements. These requirements vary from state to state. The NAIC Group Health Insurance Model Act states that a group health insurance contract can be issued to an employer, a creditor, a labor union, a trust established by an employer or union, an association, a credit union, or a discretionary group.

Mandated Benefits

Laws in most states require individual and group health insurance policies to provide specific benefits. The benefits that are mandated, however, vary widely from state to state. In some states, these laws apply only to policies that are issued within the state. In other states, the laws apply to any policy that insures a resident of the state. The benefits that have been mandated include, among others, coverage of newborn children; treatment of alcoholism and drug addiction; coverage of services provided by medical practitioners such as chiropractors, psychologists, and podiatrists; and coverage of certain diagnostic tests, such as mammograms.

Regulation of Alternative Providers

In addition to regulating the insurance industry and traditional health insurance plans, the states regulate HMOs, PPOs, and other alternative health care plans. Most states have enacted comprehensive laws to regulate all aspects of how HMOs operate. These laws are usually patterned on the *NAIC Model Health Maintenance Organization (HMO) Act*, which requires each such organization to qualify to operate as an HMO before beginning operations. In order to qualify, an HMO must provide certain basic health care services and must meet a number of statutory requirements designed to ensure the financial and operational viability of the plan. Most states also regulate PPOs with laws and regulations designed to ensure that insureds have reasonable access to medical services and that those services adequately meet their medical needs.

Other state laws have affected the development of alternative methods to provide health care. For example, some states regulate hospital rates; such regulation affects a health insurance plan's ability to negotiate discounted rates with those providers. Many states

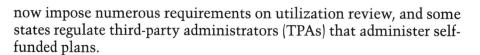

now impose numerous requirements on utilization review, and some states regulate third-party administrators (TPAs) that administer self-funded plans.

Taxation

Health insurers are subject to state, as well as federal, taxes. Most states impose a premium tax on insurance premiums received by insurers operating within the state. Note that the tax is on *insurance* premiums. Self-funded health insurance plans pay no premiums and, thus, do not pay premium taxes. Likewise, the states generally do not tax premiums paid to Blue Cross and Blue Shield plans and HMOs. Some states, however, have begun to consider extending the taxation of premiums to these other types of benefit plans.

In states that impose an income tax, an employer may deduct as a business expense any group health insurance premiums it paid on behalf of its employees. Employees generally are not taxed on premiums paid on their behalf or on medical expense benefits provided by employer contributions. As a general rule, disability income benefits are considered taxable income to an employee if the employer paid the premiums for the coverage.

Federal Regulation of Health Insurance

Throughout the 1990s, Congress gradually expanded federal regulation of health insurance. For many years, federal regulation of health insurance generally was limited to regulation of health insurance plans provided as an employee benefit. Currently, several federal laws apply to group health benefit plans as well as to health insurers and managed care plans. In this section, we describe these federal laws, which are summarized in Figure 23-2.

Age Discrimination in Employment Act

As we described in Chapter 15, the *Age Discrimination in Employment Act (ADEA)* protects workers who are age 40 and older from being discriminated against because of their age. Although an employer may in some cases be able to reduce the level of group life insurance benefits provided to older employees, the ADEA requires an employer to make the same medical expense coverage available to workers who are age 65 and older and their dependents as are available to younger workers and covered dependents. All active employees, regardless of age, must be eligible for the same medical expense coverages and cannot be required to pay more for that coverage than

FIGURE 23-2. Some U.S. Federal Laws That Regulate Health Care Coverage.

Legislative Act	Who Must Comply	Protected Class	Effect of Legislation on Health Care
ADEA	Employers that have 20 or more employees	Employees age 40 and over	All active employees, regardless of age, must be eligible for the same health care coverages, and older employees cannot be required to pay more for that coverage than younger employees pay.
Title VII of the Civil Rights Act	Employers that have 15 or more employees and that are engaged in interstate commerce	All employees	Pregnancy Discrimination Act (an amendment to the Civil Rights Act) requires group health plans sponsored by employers subject to the act to provide coverage for pregnancy, childbirth, and related medical conditions on the same basis as they provide coverage for other medical conditions.
Family and Medical Leave Act	Employers that have 50 or more employees	Employees, upon the birth or adoption of a child, or who need to provide care for a seriously ill family member, or who are ill themselves	Workers must be allowed to take up to 12 weeks of unpaid leave during any 12-month period for qualifying events. Employers are required to continue to make group health benefits available to workers while they are on leave.
ERISA	Employers that sponsor welfare benefit plans to provide benefits listed in the act (medical, surgical, hospital, disability, death, unemployment benefits, etc.)	Employees covered under welfare benefit plans	ERISA requires group health care plans to have a written plan document, to have a summary plan description, and to file an annual report with the IRS, and establishes standards of conduct for plan fiduciaries.
COBRA	Employers that have 20 or more employees	Employees and certain dependents whose health care coverage is lost due to a qualifying event	COBRA requires that certain persons whose group health coverage would otherwise terminate be allowed to continue group coverage at their own expense for a stated period following a qualifying event.
HMO Act of 1973	Federally qualified HMOs and employers that have 25 or more employees and that make contributions to an employee health care plan	*Not applicable*	The HMO Act encouraged the establishment and development of HMOs by providing grants and low-interest loans to start up HMOs that met federal qualification requirements; created requirements for federal qualification; requires employers in certain situations to provide employees with the option of participating in either a federally qualified HMO or the employer's group health plan.
HIPAA	Employer-sponsored group medical expense insurance plans and insurers that issue individual medical expense insurance coverage	*Not applicable*	Individuals who own medical expense coverage generally have the right to renew that coverage by paying premiums as they come due. Specified individuals are guaranteed the right to purchase individual medical expense coverage. By limiting the pre-existing condition exclusion that group medical expense plans may include, HIPAA increased the portability of medical care coverages.

younger employees pay. Retired employees are not protected by the ADEA and may be treated differently than active employees. As a result, employee benefits are typically reduced or eliminated following retirement.

The ADEA allows employers to reduce disability income benefits of workers and dependents who are age 65 and older if the reduction is justified on the basis of cost. A cost justification occurs when the cost of providing benefits for older workers is more than the cost of younger workers' benefits. An insured short-term disability income plan may reduce the level of benefits for those age 65 and older if it is cost justified. The level of long-term disability income benefits can also be reduced for those workers who become disabled at age 65 or older.

Civil Rights Act of 1964

The federal *Civil Rights Act of 1964* is one of the broadest federal antidiscrimination statutes. Title VII of the Civil Rights Act prohibits employment discrimination on the basis of race, color, sex, religion, or national origin. The Act applies to employers that are engaged in interstate commerce and that have 15 or more employees. The federal Equal Employment Opportunity Commission (EEOC), which administers the Civil Rights Act, has issued guidelines concerning sex discrimination. These guidelines prohibit employee fringe benefit plans, including group health insurance plans, from discriminating on the basis of sex.

A 1978 amendment to the Civil Rights Act, known as the *Pregnancy Discrimination Act,* requires employers to treat pregnancy, childbirth, or related medical conditions the same as any other medical condition. As a result, group health plans sponsored by an employer subject to the Act must provide coverage for pregnancy, childbirth, and related medical conditions. In addition, employees' wives who are covered by a group health plan must receive the same medical expense coverages as do female employees.

Family and Medical Leave Act

The federal *Family and Medical Leave Act* requires employers with 50 or more employees to allow workers to take up to 12 weeks of unpaid leave within any 12-month period in specified situations. A covered worker is entitled to unpaid leave upon the birth or adoption of a child, to care for a seriously ill family member, or while the worker is ill. The Act also requires that employers continue to provide group health insurance to workers while they are on family and medical leave.

Employee Retirement Income Security Act

You will recall that employer plans providing health care benefits must comply with the *Employee Retirement Income Security Act (ERISA)*. Whether a plan is fully insured or self-funded, if the plan provides a benefit listed in the Act, then the plan must comply with the Act. Review our discussion in Chapter 15 of the reporting and disclosure requirements that ERISA imposes on employee benefit plans.

A significant feature of ERISA is that it preempts or supersedes state laws that regulate employee benefit plans. In other words, the terms of ERISA take precedence over any state laws that regulate employee welfare benefit plans. ERISA's preemption provision, however, leaves to the states the authority to regulate insurance, banking, and securities. Thus, state insurance laws apply to an employee benefit plan only if the plan is insured. The state laws we described earlier relating to required policy provisions, size or eligibility of the group, and mandated benefits apply to group insurance policies, but not to uninsured, self-funded group health insurance plans.

Consolidated Omnibus Budget Reconciliation Act

The *Consolidated Omnibus Budget Reconciliation Act (COBRA)* generally applies to employers with 20 or more employees and requires each group medical expense insurance plan to allow employees and certain dependents to continue their group coverage for a stated period of time following a qualifying event that causes the loss of group medical expense coverage. For example, when an employee terminates his employment, he ceases to be a member of the group and, thus, is no longer eligible to participate in the group insurance plan. As a result of COBRA, termination of employment that results in loss of coverage is a qualifying event; the employee must be allowed to continue his group medical expense coverage for up to 18 months following termination of employment. The employee's spouse and dependent children also may continue their group coverage for up to 18 months. In addition, the spouse and dependent children of a covered employee are given the right to continue their group medical expense coverage for up to 36 months following either the employee's death or a divorce or legal separation from the employee. COBRA also gives a dependent child who ceases to be an eligible dependent under a group medical expense plan the right to continue group coverage for up to 36 months.

A person who elects to continue group medical expense coverage under COBRA must pay the full cost of continuation coverage. In addition, the insurer can add an administrative fee of 2 percent. Thus,

> **FAST FACT**
>
> In 1996, more than 28% of the employees and dependents who were eligible for COBRA coverage elected that coverage.[3]

the premium is generally 102 percent of the actual premium that would be charged for the person's group medical expense coverage if he were eligible for the group coverage.

The plan administrator of a group medical expense plan must notify covered individuals of their rights under COBRA when they become covered under the plan and when a qualifying event occurs. Upon the occurrence of a qualifying event, the affected individuals have a specified time within which they can elect to continue their group medical expense insurance coverage. This continuation coverage must be identical to that provided to individuals who are eligible for coverage under the group plan.

Health Insurance Portability and Accountability Act

The *Health Insurance Portability and Accountability Act (HIPAA)* imposes a number of requirements on employer-sponsored group medical expense insurance plans, including indemnity insurance plans and managed care plans. Group health plans that provide accident-only coverage or only disability income coverage are exempt from HIPAA. Some of HIPAA's requirements overlap requirements imposed by state insurance laws, but HIPAA does *not* preempt state insurance laws that are more favorable to insureds than the minimum requirements imposed by HIPAA. HIPAA also imposes requirements on insurers that issue individual medical expense insurance coverage.

Regulation of Individual Medical Expense Policies. HIPAA imposes a general requirement that insurers must renew or continue an individual medical expense insurance policy in force at the option of the policyowner. Insurers, however, have the right to discontinue or not renew coverage of an individual under any of the following conditions:

- Nonpayment of premium

- The individual has committed fraud or made an intentional misrepresentation of a material fact under the terms of the coverage

- The insurer ceases to offer the coverage by complying with statutory requirements, which involve notification of insureds and offering them the option to purchase any other individual medical expense insurance policy the insurer is then offering in their state of residence

- Coverage is offered under a network health care plan; the insured no longer resides, lives, or works in the network's geographic service area; and the insurer terminates such coverage uniformly without regard to any factor related to the health of covered individuals

- Coverage is available only through one or more associations; the insured is no longer an association member; and the insurer terminates such coverage uniformly without regard to any factor related to the health of covered individuals

HIPAA also requires the guaranteed availability of individual medical expense coverage to certain individuals who have had group medical expense coverage. An insurer is prohibited from declining to cover such eligible individuals and may not impose any pre-existing condition exclusion on the coverage of eligible individuals. Health insurers, however, are exempt from this requirement if the state in which they conduct business implements an acceptable alternative mechanism by which such eligible individuals may obtain coverage. Currently, 48 states have implemented an acceptable alternative mechanism.

Regulation of Group Medical Expense Plans. HIPAA imposes a number of requirements on group medical expense plans, including indemnity plans and managed care plans.

- In order to increase the portability of medical care coverages, HIPAA places limits on the pre-existing condition exclusion that group insurance plans may include. These limits are designed to allow group insureds who have a pre-existing condition to change jobs without losing coverage for the condition. HIPAA defines a *pre-existing condition* as a physical or mental condition for which medical advice, diagnosis, care, or treatment was recommended or received within the six-month period preceding the date an individual enrolls in a group plan. Note that the maximum look-back period for purposes of defining a pre-existing condition under HIPAA is six months.

- HIPAA requires a group health benefits plan to provide a special enrollment period for specified individuals who declined coverage when they first became eligible for it. The individuals eligible for such special enrollment are individuals who declined coverage because they were covered at the time by another health plan but no longer are eligible for that coverage.

- HIPAA prohibits group health benefits plans from establishing eligibility rules for group health coverage based on specified factors, including health status, medical condition, claims experience, genetic information, and disability. Group medical expense plans also may not require a higher premium contribution from any individual than is required of similarly situated individuals based on the specified factors.

"Heavens no, I go through enough of that just waiting
to see what will happen with health care reform."

Reprinted with permission of Phil Interlandi and Bituminous Casualty Corporation.

- Insurers that offer group health benefit coverages must renew such coverage at the option of the group policyholder. Although HIPAA permits insurers to increase the premium rates charged for such renewal coverage, insurers must provide group policyholders with continued access to group coverage except for reasons such as non-payment of premium, fraud or other intentional misrepresentation of a material fact by a group policyholder, or the insurer no longer offers group coverage in the state.

Mental Health Parity Act

The federal *Mental Health Parity Act* imposes requirements on group health plans, health insurance companies, and HMOs that offer mental health benefits. Policies that provide mental health benefits may not set an annual or lifetime maximum mental health benefits limit that is lower than any such limits for medical and surgical benefits. A policy that does not impose an annual or lifetime limit on medical and surgical benefits may not impose such a limit on mental health benefits.

Newborns' and Mothers' Health Protection Act of 1996

The federal *Newborns' and Mothers' Health Protection Act of 1996* imposes requirements on health insurance policies that provide benefits for maternity and newborn care. Such policies must provide coverage for at least a 48-hour hospital stay following a normal vaginal delivery and at least 96 hours for a cesarean section. Note that this law does not require policies to provide benefits for maternity and newborn care; instead, the law imposes specific requirements on plans that do provide such benefits.

Women's Health and Cancer Rights Act of 1998

The federal *Women's Health and Cancer Rights Act of 1998* requires health insurance policies that provide coverage for mastectomies to provide certain mastectomy-related benefits or services. According to this law, insureds who receive benefits in connection with a mastectomy and who elect to have breast reconstruction following the mastectomy are entitled to receive benefits for the reconstruction.

Health Maintenance Organization Act of 1973

The *Health Maintenance Organization (HMO) Act of 1973* was passed to encourage the establishment and development of health maintenance organizations. It provided federal funds to HMOs that met the requirements to become federally qualified. (See Figure 23-3, which lists benefits that federally qualified HMOs are required to provide.) Today, HMOs have the option of becoming federally qualified, and many HMOs seek such qualification. In order to become federally qualified, an HMO must comply with a range of requirements established by the HMO Act and subsequent amendments to that Act. These requirements include standards concerning plan solvency, plan design and benefits, and plan administration.

Taxation

For federal income tax purposes, employer contributions to fund a group health insurance plan are deductible as a business expense by the employer. In most cases, the employer's contributions to such a plan are not considered taxable income to the employee. One exception arises when a self-funded group health plan fails to meet the nondiscrimination requirements of the federal tax laws. These nondiscrimination requirements were enacted to ensure that highly compensated employees do not receive an inordinately large portion of the benefits provided by an employee benefit plan. If a plan is dis-

FIGURE 23-3. Benefits That Federally Qualified HMOs Are Required to Provide.

Physician services
Inpatient and outpatient hospital services
Medically necessary emergency health services
Preventive health services
Short-term outpatient mental health care
Medical treatment and referral for alcohol and drug abuse and addiction
Home health services
Diagnostic laboratory services
Diagnostic and therapeutic radiological services

criminatory, then part of the benefits that highly compensated employees receive are considered taxable income to those employees.

Medical expense benefits that individuals receive are not considered taxable income to the employees, whether these benefits are provided under group or individual policies. By contrast, disability income benefits provided by employer contributions to a group or individual insurance plan are taxable income to the employee. Disability income benefits are not taxable income when received under an individual disability income policy purchased by the insured. Individuals who itemize their federal income tax deductions may be able to deduct from their taxable incomes the amount of any individual or group medical expense insurance premiums they pay.

Regulation in Canada

As we noted in Chapter 2, regulation of insurance in Canada is shared by the federal and provincial governments. Both the federal and provincial governments regulate the operation of insurance companies. Laws in each province and territory regulate the licensing of insurers and their agents, as well as how insurers conduct their business within the province or territory. Federal and provincial laws seek to ensure the solvency of insurers. In the remainder of this chapter, we describe federal and provincial laws that are unique to health insurance.

Earlier, we described government-sponsored medical expense and disability income programs. The establishment of these programs profoundly affected how health care is provided to Canadians and, thus, how health insurance is provided. We will first describe the federal laws governing these government-sponsored health care plans. Then we will describe how the provinces regulate health insurance policies issued by commercial insurers.

Federal Regulation of Health Insurance

In Chapter 18, we described the health care plans that the Canadian provinces and territories sponsor and that the federal and provincial governments fund jointly. The federal *Canada Health Act* establishes the following criteria that provincial hospital and medical expense plans must meet in order to qualify for federal financial assistance:

- The plan must be administered on a nonprofit basis by the province or a provincial agency.

- The plan must be comprehensive, covering specified health services provided by hospitals, medical practitioners, and dentists.

- The plan must provide universal coverage—that is, the plan must cover virtually all residents of the province.

- Plan benefits must be portable—coverage must be available to insured persons who move between provinces and to those who are temporarily absent from the province.

- The plan must provide insured services on a nondiscriminatory basis and must operate on a basis that does not preclude reasonable access to services.

In Chapter 19, we described the short-term disability income benefits provided to covered residents under the federal *Unemployment Insurance Act*. In order to encourage the continuance of private disability income plans, the Unemployment Insurance Act allows employers to register qualified, private disability income plans with Human Resources Development Canada. In order to qualify for registration, a private plan must meet the following criteria:

- Benefits must begin no later than the 15th day of disability and must continue for at least 15 weeks.

- The benefit level must be at least 60 percent of insurable earnings.

- Employees must become eligible for benefits after completing no more than three months of continuous service.

A plan that meets these criteria qualifies the sponsoring employer to receive a partial reduction in unemployment insurance premium contributions. The Unemployment Insurance Act also grants a partial reduction in premium contributions for an employer that provides employees with a paid sick-leave plan that meets certain criteria.

Finally, in Chapter 19, we described the long-term disability income benefits provided through the Canada Pension Plan (CPP) and the Quebec Pension Plan (QPP). We described the retirement income benefits provided by the CPP and the QPP in Chapter 17.

Provincial Regulation of Health Insurance

When the provinces and territories established their hospital insurance plans, they also enacted legislation that prohibited private insurers from providing benefits for services that the provincial plans cover. Likewise, the introduction of provincial medical expense plans legislated private insurers out of the basic health insurance market entirely. Private insurers had to terminate all of their basic surgical, medical, and diagnostic insurance plans, and they had to amend their major medical plans to remove coverage of any services provided by the government plans.

Supplemental health insurance policies issued by insurance companies are regulated by the provincial insurance laws. In addition, the insurance industry in Canada in effect regulates itself by agreeing to abide by a variety of guidelines issued by the Canadian Council of Insurance Regulators (CCIR) and the Canadian Life and Health Insurance Association (CLHIA). In this section, we describe how the provincial insurance laws and the various guidelines regulate health insurance policies.

Provincial Insurance Laws

Provincial legislation governing health insurance contracts is similar in all of the common-law jurisdictions because they have each adopted, with some minor variations, the **Uniform Accident and Sickness Insurance Act (Uniform A&S Act)** developed by the CCIR. In the province of Quebec, health insurance policies are governed by the Quebec Civil Code and by various insurance regulations that specifically govern health insurance policies. In most respects, however, the regulation of health insurance is similar throughout Canada.

The provincial insurance laws require an insurer to include certain information in each health insurance policy. Each policy, for example, must identify the person insured and the length of the period of coverage. These statutory requirements vary somewhat between group and individual health insurance policies. The provincial insurance laws contain requirements relating to several provisions that are typically included in health insurance policies.

- With certain exceptions, insurers may not avoid individual health insurance policies on the ground of misrepresentation in the application after the policy has been in force for two years. One exception is that an insurer can avoid a policy at any time in the case of a fraudulent misrepresentation in the application.

- With a few exceptions, group and individual health insurance policies may not exclude a pre-existing condition from coverage after the insured person's coverage under the policy has been in force for two years.

- Most jurisdictions have enacted statutory requirements relating to the continuation of coverage when a group health insurance policy terminates; these requirements vary from jurisdiction to jurisdiction.

- Provincial insurance laws throughout Canada contain requirements concerning how disability income benefits must be paid when an insured person is overinsured.

A number of provisions that insurers typically must include in individual and group health insurance policies in the United States are not required by provincial insurance laws. For example, provincial laws do not require an insurer to reinstate an individual health insurance policy, to include a grace period provision in every policy, or to include a conversion privilege in group health insurance policies. Nevertheless, health insurance policies issued in Canada generally contain the same provisions as do policies issued in the United States. (We described these policy provisions in Chapters 20 and 21.) This fact results, at least in part, from the insurance industry's adherence to the Superintendents' Guidelines and the CLHIA Guidelines, which address a number of matters not addressed by the provincial insurance laws.

CLHIA Guidelines

The CLHIA has adopted various guidelines that relate to health insurance policies. Insurers are expected to abide by these guidelines as a condition of membership in the CLHIA. For example, the CLHIA has issued *Guidelines Governing Individual Accident and Sickness*

Insurance, which address matters such as the renewal provision included in an individual health insurance policy. In addition, the CLHIA issued *Coordination of Benefits (COB) Guidelines* to ensure that the COB provisions included in group health insurance policies throughout Canada are consistent.

The CLHIA also adopted *Group Life and Group Health Insurance Guidelines,* which provide a minimum standard for group insurance policies. The CLHIA Group Guidelines, for example, include a number of provisions designed to protect group members when the policyholder has changed insurers.

Taxation

Benefits that an individual taxpayer in Canada receives under a private medical expense insurance policy are intended to reimburse the taxpayer for his covered medical expenses. Medical expense insurance benefits, therefore, are not taxable income for purposes of federal income taxation. Premiums that a taxpayer pays for an individual medical expense policy are deductible by the taxpayer as a medical expense. Similarly, premiums that an employer pays for a group medical expense policy are deductible by the employer as a business expense, and employer-paid premiums are not considered taxable income to the covered employees. The one exception to this rule is that the province of Quebec treats contributions an employer pays on behalf of an employee under a private health insurance plan as taxable income to the employee.

Whether benefits that an individual receives under a disability income insurance policy are considered to be taxable income depends on whether the individual paid the policy's premiums. When a taxpayer receives disability income benefits under an insurance policy on which the taxpayer paid the premiums, the benefits are not considered to be taxable income. However, if the taxpayer's employer paid any part of the premiums for the disability income policy, then the benefits are considered taxable income to the employee to the extent the benefits exceed the amount of the employee's actual premium contributions.

Premiums that a taxpayer pays for disability income insurance are not deductible by the taxpayer. In contrast, premiums paid by an employer for group disability income insurance are deductible by the employer as a business expense; such premiums are not considered to be taxable income to the covered employees.

Key Terms

NAIC Uniform Individual
Accident and Sickness Policy
Provision Law
NAIC Group Health Insurance
Definition and Group Health
Insurance
Standard Provisions Model Act

Consolidated Omnibus Budget
Reconciliation Act (COBRA)
Health Insurance Portability and
Accountability Act (HIPAA)
Uniform Accident and Sickness
Insurance Act

Other Important Terms

Model Newborn Children Bill
Group Health Insurance
Mandatory Conversion
Privilege Model Act
Group Coordination of Benefits
Regulations and Guidelines
NAIC Model Health
Maintenance Organization
(HMO) Act
Age Discrimination in
Employment Act (ADEA)
Civil Rights Act of 1964
Pregnancy Discrimination Act
Family and Medical Leave Act
Employee Retirement Income
Security Act (ERISA)
pre-existing condition

Mental Health Parity Act
Newborns' and Mothers' Health
Protection Act of 1996
Women's Health and Cancer
Rights Act of 1998
Health Maintenance
Organization (HMO) Act of
1973
Canada Health Act
Unemployment Insurance Act
Guidelines Governing Individual
Accident and Sickness
Insurance
Coordination of Benefits (COB)
Guidelines
Group Life and Group Health
Insurance Guidelines

Endnotes

1. Health Care Financing Administration, *Highlights National Health Expenditures, 1997* (Washington, D.C.: Health Care Financing Administration, 1998). Available online at http://www.hcfa.gov/stats/nhe-oact/nhe.htm.

2. Health Canada, *National Health Expenditures in Canada, 1975–1996, Fact Sheets* (Toronto: Health Canada, 1997). Available online at http://www.hc-sc.gc.ca/datapcb/datahesa/hex97/ehex97.htm.

3. Employee Benefits Research Institute, *EBRI Health Care Research: 1998 Findings* (Washington, D.C.: Employee Benefits Research Institute, 1999). Available online at http://207.152.182.56/health_findings.htm.

Appendix

Model Regulation Service—July 1988

UNIFORM APPLICATION FOR
INDIVIDUAL RESIDENT/NON-RESIDENT LICENSE

(Please PRINT or TYPE)

Please read carefully and complete all necessary information.

STATE FOR WHICH APPLICATION IS SOUGHT _____ ( ) Resident ( ) Non-Resident

PART I — IDENTIFICATION

A. Social Security No. _____
    (Note: Your Social Security Number will only be used for purposes of computer identification in issuing your license. If you choose not to give this number, please check here. ( ) This will not have any impact on the issuance of your license.)

B. Date of Birth _____ / _____ / _____

C. Full Legal Name of Applicant: _____
                                  (Last)   (First)   (Middle Name)

D. Home Address: _____
                                  (Street)

    _____
          (County)   (City)   (State)   (Zip Code)

E. Business Address _____
                                 (Street)   (PO Box)

    _____
              (City)   (State)   (Zip Code)

F. Home Phone No. (___) _____ Business Phone No. (___) _____

G. If residence address has changed during last 12 months, list former resident address for past year:

    _____
                                  (Street)

    _____
              (City)   (State)   (Zip Code)

PART II — LINES OF AUTHORITY REQUESTED (Check Appropriate Spaces)

( ) Life   ( ) Accident & Health (Sickness, Disability)
( ) Property   ( ) Casualty
( ) Other (please specify) _____

                                                                  211-1

Uniform Application for Individual Resident/Non-Resident License

PART III — BACKGROUND INFORMATION

A. Do you now or have you ever held an insurance license in another state or province of Canada? If the license is still in force, attach a certification letter from the issuing state. If the license is cancelled, attach a letter of clearance from the issuing state.

B. Have you had an insurance license cancelled, refused, suspended, revoked or subject to any other disciplinary action? ( ) Yes ( ) No
If yes, provide full explanation on separate sheet of paper.

C. Have you ever been convicted of or pled nolo contendere to any felony? ( ) Yes ( ) No
If yes, attach certified copies of the final adjudication.

D. Are you an officer, director or employee of a lending institution (bank, savings and loan or other such institution which accepts deposits and lends money) or of a bank holding company or an affiliate of one of the above? ( ) Yes ( ) No
If yes, give name and address of institution. _____

PART IV — APPLICANT'S CERTIFICATION

STATE OF _____

COUNTY OF _____

The undersigned, being first duly sworn, deposes and says that he has executed and read this application; that to the best of his knowledge and belief the statements made in the application and in any attachment are true and correct, and that he has read and understands the insurance laws of the State of _____, for which application is made.

_____
Signature of Applicant

SUBSCRIBED AND SWORN to before me on this _____ day of _____, 19 ____.

_____
Notary Public

211-2

Glossary

401(k) plan. In the United States, a special type of thrift and savings plan that allows employees to contribute to the plan on a before-tax basis. [17]

absolute assignment. An assignment by which a property owner transfers all of his ownership rights in a particular property to another party. *See also* **collateral assignment.** [12]

accelerated death benefit rider. A life insurance policy rider that allows a policyowner to receive all or part of the policy's death benefit before the insured's death if certain conditions are met. Also known as a *living benefit rider.* [9]

accidental death and dismemberment (AD&D) rider. An accidental death benefit rider that provides an additional benefit payable if an accident causes the insured to lose any two limbs or sight in both eyes. [9]

accidental death benefit. A supplementary life insurance policy benefit that provides a specified death benefit amount in addition to the policy's basic death benefit if the insured dies as a result of an accident. [9]

accumulated value. The net amount paid for a deferred annuity plus interest earned less the amount of any withdrawals. [16]

accumulation at interest dividend option. A policy dividend option under which policy dividends are left on deposit with the insurer to accumulate at interest. [12]

accumulation period. The period between a contractholder's purchase of a deferred annuity and the beginning of the payout period. [16]

accumulation units. During the accumulation period of a variable deferred annuity, the separate (segregated) investment account shares owned by the contractholder. [16]

actively-at-work provision. A group insurance policy provision which requires that in order to be eligible for coverage, an employee must be actively at work—rather than ill or on leave—before insurance coverage will take effect. [14]

activities of daily living (ADLs). Activities such as eating, bathing, and dressing that, if an insured is unable to perform, demonstrate her need for long-term care and, thus, qualify her to receive long-term care benefits. [9]

actuaries. Specialists who are trained in the mathematics of insurance and are responsible for performing all of the calculations needed to ensure that an insurance company's products are mathematically sound. [6]

AD&D rider. *See* **accidental death and dismemberment rider.**

additional insured rider. *See* **second insured rider.**

additional term insurance dividend option. A policy dividend option under which the insurer uses each policy dividend as a net single premium to purchase one-year term insurance on the insured's life. Also known as *the fifth dividend option.* [12]

adjustable life insurance. A form of life insurance that allows policyowners to vary the type of coverage provided by their policies as their insurance needs change. [8]

ADLs. *See* **activities of daily living.**

administrative services only (ASO) contract. A contract under which an insurer or other organization, such as a third-party administrator, agrees to provide some or all administrative services for a self-insured group health insurance plan. [20]

adverse selection. *See* **antiselection.**

aggregate stop-loss coverage. A type of stop-loss insurance under which the stop-loss insurer is responsible for paying claims when the employer's total claims exceed a stated dollar amount within a stated period of time. [20]

aleatory contract. An agreement under which one party provides something of value to another party in exchange for a conditional promise. *See also* **commutative contract.** [5]

allowable expenses. According to the coordination of benefits provision included in most group medical expense insurance policies, those reasonable and customary expenses that the insured incurred and that are covered under at least one of the insured's group medical expense plans. [20]

Annual Return. In Canada, an accounting statement that every company subject to federal regulation must file with the Office of the Superintendent of Financial Institutions. [2]

Annual Statement. In the United States, an accounting report that was developed by the National Association of Insurance Commissioners and that each insurer prepares each calendar year and files with the insurance department in each state in which it operates. [2]

annually renewable term (ART) insurance. *See* **yearly renewable term insurance.**

annuitant. The named individual whose lifetime is used as the measuring life in a life annuity. [16]

annuity. (1) A series of periodic payments. (2) In the financial services industry, a contract under which an insurer promises to make a series of periodic payments to a named individual in exchange for a premium or series of premiums. [1, 16]

annuity beneficiary. The person or party named to receive any survivor benefits that are payable during the accumulation period of a deferred annuity. [16]

annuity certain. An annuity that is payable for a stated period of time, regardless of whether an individual person lives or dies. [16]

annuity date. *See* **maturity date.**

annuity mortality rates. The mortality rates experienced by people who purchase life annuities. [16]

annuity period. The time span between each of the payments in a series of periodic annuity benefit payments. [16]

annuity units. During the payout period of a variable deferred annuity, the separate (segregated) investment account shares owned by the contractholder. [16]

antiselection. The tendency of individuals who believe they have a greater-than-average likelihood of loss to seek insurance protection to a greater extent than do those who believe they have an average or a less-than-average likelihood of loss. Also known as *adverse selection* or *selection against the insurer.* [3]

APL provision. *See* **automatic premium loan provision.**

applicant. The person or business that applies for an insurance policy. [3]

ART insurance. *See* **yearly renewable term insurance.**

ASO contract. *See* **administrative services only contract.**

assessment method. A historical method of funding life insurance in which the participants in an insurance plan prepaid an equal portion of the estimated annual cost of the plan's death benefits. If actual costs were less than expected, then participants received refunds. If costs were more than expected, then participants paid an additional amount. [6]

assets. Things of value owned by a company or an individual. [2, 4]

assignee. A person or party to whom a property owner transfers some or all of the property owner's rights in a particular property by means of an assignment. [12]

assignment. An agreement under which one party—the assignor—transfers some or all of his ownership rights in a particular property to another party—the assignee. [12]

assignment provision. An individual life insurance and annuity policy provision that describes the roles of the insurer and the policyowner when the policy is assigned. [12, 16]

assignor. A property owner who transfers some or all of her ownership rights in a particular property to another party by means of an assignment. [12]

attained age. The current age of an insured. [7]

attained age conversion. The conversion of a term life insurance policy to a permanent plan of insurance at a premium rate that is based on the insured's age when the coverage is converted. *See also* **original age conversion.** [7]

automatic dividend option. A specified policy dividend option that an insurance company will apply if the policyowner does not choose an option. The specified option typically is the paid-up additional insurance option. [12]

automatic nonforfeiture benefit. The specified nonforfeiture benefit that becomes effective automatically when a renewal premium for a permanent life insurance policy is not paid by the end of the grace period and the insured has not elected another nonforfeiture option. The most typical automatic non-forfeiture option is the extended term insurance benefit. [10]

automatic premium loan (APL) provision. A permanent life insurance policy nonforfeiture provision which states that the insurer will automatically pay an overdue premium for the policyowner by making a loan against the policy's cash value as long as the cash value equals or exceeds the amount of the premium due. [10]

bargaining contract. A contract that is created by both contracting parties who, as equals, set the terms and conditions of the contract. *See also* **contract of adhesion.** [5]

basic medical expense coverage. Medical expense coverage consisting of separate benefits for each specific type of covered medical care cost. Basic coverage typically includes hospital, surgical, and physicians' expense coverages. [18]

beneficiary. The person or party the owner of a life insurance policy names to receive the policy benefit. [3]

beneficiary for value. According to laws that are no longer in force in the common law jurisdictions of Canada, a life insurance policy beneficiary who has vested rights to policy proceeds because the beneficiary provided the policyowner with valuable consideration. [11]

benefit period. The specified time during which disability income benefits will be paid under a disability income policy. [19]

benefit schedule. A schedule that is included in a group life insurance policy and that defines the amount of life insurance the policy provides for each group insured. [15]

bilateral contract. A contract between two parties who both make legally enforceable promises when they enter into the contract. *See also* **unilateral contract.** [5]

blended rating. A method of calculating group insurance premium rates by which the insurer uses a combination of experience rating and manual rating. [14]

block of policies. A group of policies issued to insureds who are all the same age, the same sex, and in the same risk classification. [6]

business continuation insurance plan. An insurance plan designed to enable a business owner (or owners) to provide for the business' continued operation if the owner or a key person dies. [4]

business overhead expense coverage. Disability coverage that provides benefits designed to pay a disabled insured's share of a business' overhead expenses. [19]

buy-sell agreement. An agreement in which (1) one party agrees to purchase the financial interest that a second party has in a business following the second party's death and (2) the second party agrees to direct his estate to sell his interest in the business to the purchasing party. [4]

calendar-year deductible. A deductible that applies to any eligible medical expenses the insured incurs during a given calendar year. [18]

Canada Pension Plan (CPP). A Canadian federal program that provides a pension for retirees who reside in all provinces except Quebec and who have contributed money into the plan during their working years. [17]

Canadian Council of Insurance Regulators (CCIR). A collective body formed by the provincial superintendents of insurance to discuss insurance issues and to recommend uniform insurance legislation to the provinces. [2]

Canadian Life and Health Insurance Association (CLHIA). An industry association of life and health insurance companies operating in Canada. [2]

Canadian Life and Health Insurance Compensation Corporation (CompCorp). A federally incorporated, nonprofit company established by the Canadian Life and Health Insurance Association to protect Canadian consumers against loss of benefits in the event a life or health insurance company becomes insolvent. [2]

cancellable policy. An individual health insurance policy that gives the insurer the right to terminate the policy at any time, for any reason, simply by notifying the policyowner that the policy is cancelled and by refunding any advance premium paid for the policy. [21]

capital. The portion of a company's owners' equity consisting of the amount of money invested in the company by its owners. [2]

capitation. A fee payment method used by some HMOs under which the HMO prepays a medical care provider a flat amount for each subscriber's medical care—usually on a monthly basis. [22]

case management. A process by which a managed care plan evaluates the necessity and quality of an insured's medical care and the appropriateness of alternative treatments or solutions for the insured's medical care. [22]

cash dividend option. A policy dividend option under which the insurance company sends the policyowner a check in the amount of the policy dividend the insurer's board of directors declared. [12]

cash refund annuity. A life income with refund annuity under which the refund is payable in a lump sum. [16]

cash surrender value. (1) The amount, before adjustments for factors such as policy loans, that the owner of a permanent life insurance policy is entitled to receive if the policy does not remain in force until the insured's death. Also known as *cash value* or *surrender value.* [8] (2) The amount of a deferred annuity's accumulated value, less any surrender charges, that the contractholder is entitled to receive if she surrenders the policy during its accumulation period. [16]

cash surrender value nonforfeiture option. A nonforfeiture option that allows the owner of a permanent life insurance policy to discontinue premium payments and surrender the policy for its cash surrender value. [10]

cash value. The savings element of a permanent life insurance policy, which represents the policyowner's ownership interest in the policy. *See* **cash surrender value.** [8]

CCIR. *See* **Canadian Council of Insurance Regulators.**

cede. To obtain reinsurance on insurance business by transferring all or part of the risk to a reinsurer. [3]

ceding company. In a reinsurance transaction, the insurance company that purchases reinsurance from another insurer. [3]

certificate holder. An individual who is insured under a group insurance contract and who has received a certificate of insurance. [14]

certificate of insurance. A document that a group policyholder delivers to each group insured and that describes the coverage provided by a group insurance contract and the group insured's rights under the contract. [14]

change of occupation provision. An individual disability income insurance policy provision that permits the insurer to adjust the policy's premium rate or the amount of benefits payable under the policy if the insured changes occupation. [21]

children's insurance rider. A rider that may be added to a whole life insurance policy and that provides coverage on the insured's children. [9]

CI coverage. *See* **critical illness coverage.**

claim. A request for payment of insurance policy benefits following the occurrence of a covered loss. [3]

claim analyst. *See* **claim examiner.**

claim approver. *See* **claim examiner.**

claim costs. In pricing health insurance, the costs the insurer predicts that it will incur to provide the policy benefits promised. [18]

claim examiner. An insurance company employee who is responsible for processing and paying claims for policy benefits that the insurer receives. Also known as *claim approver, claim analyst,* or *claim specialist.* [13]

claim specialist. *See* **claim examiner.**

class designation. A life insurance policy beneficiary designation that identifies a certain group of persons as beneficiaries. [11]

class of policies. All policies of a particular type that an insurer has issued or all policies an insurer has issued to a particular group of insureds. [21]

CLHIA. *See* **Canadian Life and Health Insurance Association.**

CLHIA Guidelines. A series of recommendations to insurers issued by the Canadian Life and Health Insurance Association. [2]

closed contract. A contract for which only those terms and conditions that are printed in—or attached to—the contract are considered to be part of the contract. *See also* **open contract.** [10]

closed panel HMO. A type of HMO that requires physicians either to belong to a special group of physicians that has contracted with the HMO or to be employees of the HMO in order to provide services to HMO members. [22]

closely held business. A sole proprietorship, a partnership, or a corporation that is owned by only a few individuals. [4]

COB provision. *See* **coordination of benefits provision.**

COBRA. *See* **Consolidated Omnibus Budget Reconciliation Act.**

coinsurance provision. A medical expense insurance policy provision which states that once the insured has paid the deductible amount, he then must pay a specified percentage of all the remaining covered medical expenses. [18]

COLA benefit. *See* **cost-of-living adjustment benefit.**

collateral assignment. An assignment by which a property owner temporarily assigns the monetary value of a particular property, such as a life insurance or annuity policy, as collateral for a loan. *See also* **absolute assignment.** [12]

common disaster clause. A life insurance policy provision which states that the beneficiary must survive the insured by a specified period, such as 30 or 60 days, in order to receive the policy proceeds. Also known as *time clause.* [13]

community-property state. A state in which, by law, each spouse is entitled to an equal share of the income earned by the other and, under most circumstances, to an equal share of the property acquired by the other during the period of their marriage. [11]

commutative contract. An agreement under which the parties specify in advance the values that they will exchange; moreover, the parties generally exchange items or

services that they think are of relatively equal value. *See also* **aleatory contract.** [5]

CompCorp. *See* **Canadian Life and Health Insurance Compensation Corporation.**

compound interest. Interest paid on both an original principal sum and on the interest that has accrued on that principal sum. [6]

comprehensive major medical policy. A major medical policy that combines into one policy the coverages provided by both a supplemental major medical policy and an underlying basic medical expense policy. [18]

concurrent review. A component of utilization review under which the utilization review organization monitors an insured's treatment and prognosis while she is in the hospital. [22]

conditional promise. A promise to perform a stated act if a specified, uncertain event occurs. [5]

conditionally renewable policy. An individual health insurance policy that gives the insurer a limited right to refuse to renew the policy at the end of a premium payment period. [21]

conservative mortality table. A mortality table that shows higher mortality rates than an insurer anticipates for a particular block of insurance policies. [6]

consideration. One of the requirements for the formation of a valid informal contract that is met when each party gives or promises to give something of value to the other party. [5]

Consolidated Omnibus Budget Reconciliation Act (COBRA). A U.S. federal law that generally applies to employers with 20 or more employees and requires each group medical expense insurance plan to allow employees and certain dependents to continue their group coverage for a stated period of time following a qualifying event that causes the loss of group medical expense coverage. [23]

contingency reserves. Reserves established by an insurer in addition to policy reserves to protect the insurer against unusual conditions that may occur. [6]

contingent beneficiary. The party designated to receive the proceeds of a life insurance policy following the insured's death if the primary beneficiary predeceased the insured. Also known as *secondary beneficiary* or *successor beneficiary*. [11]

contingent payee. The person or party who is to receive insurance policy proceeds in accordance with the terms of a settlement agreement following the payee's death. Also known as *successor payee*. [12]

continuous-premium whole life policy. A whole life insurance policy for which premiums are payable until the insured's death. Also known as a *straight life insurance policy* or an *ordinary life insurance policy*. [8]

contract. A legally enforceable agreement between two or more parties. [5]

contract of adhesion. A contract that one contracting party prepares and that the other contracting party must accept or reject as a whole, without any bargaining between the parties. *See also* **bargaining contract.** [5]

contract of indemnity. An insurance policy under which the amount of the policy benefit payable for a covered loss is based on the actual amount of financial loss that results from the covered loss, as determined at the time of loss. *See also* **valued contract.** [3]

contractholder. The person who applied for and purchased an annuity contract. [16]

contractual capacity. The legal capacity to make a contract. [5]

contributory plan. (1) A group insurance plan under which individual group members must contribute some or all of the premium in order to be covered under the plan. [14] (2) A retirement plan that requires plan participants to make contributions to fund the plan. [17] *See also* **noncontributory plan.**

conversion privilege. (1) A term life insurance policy provision that allows the policyowner to change (convert) the term policy to a permanent plan of insurance without providing evidence that the insured is an insurable risk. [7] (2) The right that group life insurance policies give to a group insured whose coverage terminates for certain reasons to convert his group coverage to an individual policy of insurance, without presenting evidence of his insurability. [15]

conversion provision. A group medical expense insurance policy provision that gives an in-sured group member who is leaving the group a limited right to purchase an individual medical expense policy without presenting evidence of her insurability. [20]

convertible term insurance policy. A term life insurance policy that gives the policyowner the right to convert the policy to a permanent plan of insurance. [7]

coordination of benefits (COB) provision. A group medical expense insurance policy provision that is designed to prevent a group member who is insured under more than one group medical expense policy from receiving benefit amounts that are greater than the amount of medical expenses the insured actually incurred. [20]

copayment. (1) For purposes of prescription drug coverage, a stated amount the insured must pay toward the cost of each prescription. [18] (2) A fee imposed on HMO subscribers each time they receive specified medical services. [22]

corporation. A legal entity that is created by the authority of a governmental unit and that is separate and distinct from the people who own it. [1]

cost-of-living adjustment (COLA) benefit. A supplemental benefit that is included in some disability income policies and that provides for periodic increases in the disability income benefit amount being paid to a disabled insured. [19]

CPP. *See* **Canada Pension Plan.**

credit life insurance. A type of term life insurance designed to pay the balance due on a loan if the borrower dies before the loan is repaid. [7]

critical illness (CI) coverage. Supplemental medical expense coverage that pays a lump-sum benefit if the insured is diagnosed with any of stated types of critical illnesses. [18]

cross-purchase method. A method of carrying out a partnership buy-sell agreement under which each partner agrees to purchase a proportionate share of a deceased partner's interest in the partnership. *See also* **entity method.** [4]

current assumption whole life insurance. *See* **interest-sensitive whole life insurance.**

DD benefit. *See* **dread disease benefit.**

declined risk. A proposed insured who is considered to present a risk that is too great for an insurer to cover. [3]

decreasing term life insurance. Term life insurance that provides a death benefit that decreases in amount over the policy term. [7]

deductible. A flat dollar amount of eligible medical expenses that an insured must incur out of his own pocket before the insurer will begin making benefit payments under a medical expense policy. [18]

deferred annuity. An annuity under which benefit payments are scheduled to begin more than one annuity period after the annuity is purchased. *See also* **immediate annuity.** [16]

deferred compensation plan. A plan established by an employer to provide income benefits to an employee at a later date, such as after the employee's retirement, if the employee does not voluntarily terminate employment before that date. [4]

deferred profit sharing plan (DPSP). In Canada, a profit sharing plan that qualifies for favorable federal income tax treatment. [17]

defined benefit pension plan. A pension plan that defines the amount of the benefit a plan participant will receive at retirement. *See also* **defined contribution pension plan.** [17]

defined contribution pension plan. A pension plan that describes the plan sponsor's annual contribution to the plan on behalf of each plan participant. *See also* **defined benefit pension plan.** [17]

dental expense coverage. Supplemental medical expense coverage that provides benefits for routine dental examinations, preventive work, and dental procedures needed to treat tooth decay and diseases of the teeth and jaw. [18]

deposit administration contract. A retirement plan funding vehicle under which plan assets are placed in an insurance company's general investment account and, at a plan participant's retirement, are used to purchase an immediate annuity for the participant. [17]

direct contract HMO. A type of open panel HMO that contracts directly with physicians to provide medical services for HMO members. [22]

disability buyout coverage. Disability coverage that provides benefits designed to fund the buyout of a partner's or owner's interest in a business should she become disabled. [19]

disability income benefit. A supplementary life insurance policy benefit that provides a monthly income benefit to the policyowner-insured if he becomes totally disabled while the policy is in force. [9]

disability income coverage. Health insurance coverage that provides income replacement benefits to an insured who is unable to work because of sickness or injury. [1, 18, 19]

discounted fee-for-service payment structure. A fee structure used by some HMOs under which the HMO pays physicians a certain percentage of their normal fees, thereby achieving a "discount" on those fees. [22]

discretionary group. In the United States, a group that is not a type listed in state insurance laws as being eligible for group insurance but that the state insurance department may approve for group insurance coverage if specified conditions are met. [14, 23]

dividend options. Specified methods by which the owner of a participating insurance policy may receive policy dividends. [12]

divisible surplus. The amount of an insurance company's surplus that is available for distribution to owners of participating policies issued by the company. [6]

domestic insurer. From the perspective of a particular state, an insurance company incorporated by that state. [2]

double indemnity benefit. An accidental death benefit that is equal to the face amount of the life insurance policy that provides the accidental death benefit. [9]

DPSP. *See* **deferred profit sharing plan.**

dread disease (DD) benefit. A type of accelerated death benefit under which the insurer agrees to pay a portion of a life insurance policy's face amount to the policyowner if the insured suffers from one of a number of specified diseases. [9]

dread disease coverage. Supplemental medical expense coverage that provides benefits for medical expenses incurred by an insured who has contracted a specified disease. [18]

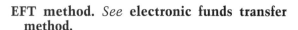

EFT method. *See* **electronic funds transfer method.**

electronic funds transfer (EFT) method. An automatic premium payment technique under which policyowners authorize their banks to pay premiums automatically on premium due dates. [12]

eligibility period. The period of time—usually 31 days—following the probationary period during which a new group member may first enroll for group insurance coverage. Also known as *enrollment period.* [14]

elimination period. The specific amount of time an individual insured by a disability income policy must be disabled before becoming eligible to receive policy benefits. Also known as *waiting period.* [19]

Employee Retirement Income Security Act (ERISA). A U.S. federal law that regulates both employee welfare benefit plans, including group life and health insurance plans established by employers, and employer-sponsored retirement plans. [15, 17]

employees' profit sharing plan (EPSP). In Canada, an employer-sponsored nonregistered retirement savings plan to which the employer and employees contribute. [17]

endorsement. A document that is attached to an insurance policy and that is a part of the insurance contract. *See also* **policy rider.** [11]

endorsement method. (1) A method of transferring ownership of a life insurance policy under which the ownership change becomes effective once the policyowner notifies the insurer, in writing, of the change and the insurer records the change in its records. [12] (2) A rarely used method of changing a life insurance policy beneficiary designation which requires the name of the new beneficiary to be added to the policy in order for the change to be effective. *See also* **recording method.** [11]

endowment insurance. Life insurance that provides a policy benefit payable either when the insured dies or on a stated date if the insured lives until then. [1, 8]

enrollment period. *See* **eligibility period.**

entire contract provision. An insurance and annuity policy provision that defines the documents that constitute the contract between the insurance company and the owner of the policy. [10, 16]

entity method. A method of carrying out a partnership buy-sell agreement under which the partnership agrees to purchase the share of any partner who dies and to distribute a proportionate share of that ownership interest to each of the surviving partners. *See also* **cross-purchase method.** [4]

EPSP. *See* **employees' profit sharing plan.**

ERISA. *See* **Employee Retirement Income Security Act.**

estate plan. A plan that considers the amount of assets and debts an individual is likely to have when she dies and how best to preserve those assets so that they can pass to the individual's heirs as she desires. [4]

evidence of insurability. Proof that a person is an insurable risk. [7]

exclusion. An insurance policy provision that describes circumstances under which the insurer will not pay policy benefits that otherwise would be payable. [10]

exclusion rider. An individual health insurance policy rider which states that benefits will not be provided for any loss that results from a condition specified in the rider. Also known as *impairment rider.* [21]

expected mortality. The number of deaths that have been predicted to occur in a group of people at a given age according to a mortality table. Also known as *tabular mortality.* [6]

experience rating. A method of calculating group insurance premium rates by which the insurer considers the particular group's prior claims and expense experience. [14]

extended term insurance nonforfeiture option. A nonforfeiture option that allows the owner of a permanent life insurance policy to discontinue premium payments and to use the policy's net cash value to purchase term insurance for the full coverage amount provided under the original policy for as long a term as the net cash value can provide. [10]

face amount. The amount of the death benefit payable under a life insurance policy. Also known as *face value.* [3]

face value. *See* **face amount.**

facility-of-payment clause. A life insurance policy provision that permits the insurance company to pay all or part of the policy proceeds either to a relative of the insured or to anyone who has a valid claim to those proceeds. [11]

family income coverage. A plan of decreasing term insurance that provides a stated monthly income benefit amount to the insured's surviving spouse if the insured dies during the term of coverage. [7]

family income policy. A whole life insurance policy that includes family income coverage. [7]

family policy. A whole life insurance policy that includes term life insurance coverage on the insured's spouse and children. [8]

fee schedule payment structure. A fee structure used by some HMOs under which the HMO places maximum limits on the dollar amounts that it will reimburse providers for covered medical procedures and services. [22]

fiduciary. A person who holds a position of special trust. [14]

field office. An insurance company's local sales office. [1]

fifth dividend option. *See* **additional term insurance dividend option.**

financial intermediary. An organization that helps to channel funds through an economy by accepting the surplus money of savers and supplying that money to borrowers who pay to use the money. [1]

financial services industry. An industry made up of various kinds of financial intermediaries that help consumers and business organizations save, borrow, invest, and otherwise manage money. [1]

first beneficiary. *See* **primary beneficiary.**

first-dollar coverage. Medical expense insurance coverage under which the insurer begins to reimburse the insured for eligible medical expenses without first requiring the insured to make an out-of-pocket contribution. [18]

first-to-die life insurance. *See* **joint whole life insurance.**

fixed-amount option. A life insurance policy settlement option under which the insurer pays equal installments of a stated amount until the policy proceeds, plus the interest earned, are exhausted. [12]

fixed-benefit annuity. An annuity under which the insurer guarantees that at least a defined amount of monthly annuity benefit will be provided for each dollar applied to purchasing the annuity. *See also* **variable annuity.** [16]

fixed-period option. A life insurance policy settlement option under which the insurer agrees to pay policy proceeds in installments of equal amounts to the payee for a specified period of time. [12]

flexible-premium annuity. An annuity that is purchased by the payment of periodic premiums that can vary between a set minimum amount and a set maximum amount. [16]

flexible-premium variable life insurance. *See* **variable universal life insurance.**

foreign insurer. (1) From the perspective of a particular state in the United States, an insurance company incorporated under the laws of another state. (2) In Canada, an insurance company incorporated under the laws of a country other than Canada. [2]

formal contract. A contract that is enforceable because the parties to the contract met certain formalities concerning the form of the agreement. *See also* **informal contract.** [5]

fraternal benefit society. An organization formed to provide social, as well as insurance, benefits to its members. [1]

fraudulent claim. A claim for which the claimant intentionally attempts to collect policy proceeds by providing false information to an insurer. [13]

fraudulent misrepresentation. A misrepresentation that was made with the intent to induce the other party to enter into a contract and that did induce the innocent party to enter into the contract. [10]

free-examination provision. *See* **free-look provision.**

free-look provision. An individual life insurance and annuity policy provision that gives the policyowner a stated time—usually ten days—after the policy is delivered in which to cancel the policy and receive a full refund of the initial premium payment. Also known as *free-examination provision*. [10, 16]

fully insured plan. A group insurance plan for which the group policyholder makes monthly premium payments to the insurance company and the insurer is responsible for making all claim payments. [20]

fully self-insured plan. A group insurance plan for which the employer takes complete responsibility for all claim payments and related expenses rather than purchasing coverage from an insurance company. [20]

funding mechanism. The method by which a group health insurance plan's claim costs and administrative expenses are paid, ranging from fully insured plans to fully self-insured plans. [20]

funding vehicle. The means for investing the assets of a retirement plan as those assets are accumulated. [17]

future purchase option benefit. A supplemental benefit that is provided by some disability income policies and that gives the insured the right to increase the policy's specified flat benefit amount in accordance with increases in the insured's earnings. [19]

gatekeeper. A term used to describe the primary care physician's role in a managed care plan; this role is to authorize all services delivered to the insured by other physicians or health care providers. [22]

gatekeeper PPO. A PPO that requires plan members to select a primary care physician from within the PPO's network of physicians. [22]

general investment account. An undivided investment account in which a life insurer maintains funds from guaranteed insurance products. [8]

GI benefit. *See* **guaranteed insurability benefit.**

GIC. *See* **guaranteed investment contract.**

GIO. *See* **guaranteed insurability benefit.**

grace period. A specified length of time within which a renewal premium that is due may be paid without penalty. [10]

grace period provision. A life insurance, health insurance, and annuity policy provision that allows the policyowner to pay a renewal premium within a stated grace period following the premium due date. [10, 14, 16, 21]

graded-premium policy. A type of modified-premium whole life policy that calls for three or more levels of annual premium payment amounts, increasing at specified points in time—such as every three years—until reaching the amount to be paid as a level premium for the rest of the life of the policy. [8]

gross premium. The premium amount an insurer charges a policyowner to keep a policy in force. The gross premium is equal to the policy's net premium and the loading. [6]

group creditor life insurance. Insurance issued to a creditor, such as a bank, to insure the lives of the creditor's current and future debtors. [15]

group deferred annuity. A retirement plan funding vehicle under which contributions made on behalf of each plan participant are used to purchase a series of single-premium deferred annuities for the participant. [17]

group insurance policy. An insurance policy that is issued to a party that is purchasing insurance coverage for a specific group of people. [1]

group insureds. The individuals who are covered by a group insurance policy. [14]

group model HMO. A type of closed panel HMO that operates much like a staff model HMO except that the physicians who provide medical services for HMO members are employees of a physicians' group practice rather than of the HMO. [22]

group policyholder. The person or organization that enters into a group insurance contract with an insurance company. [14]

group RRSP. In Canada, an employer-sponsored registered retirement savings plan in which an account is established for each participating employee. [17]

guaranteed income contract. *See* **guaranteed investment contract.**

guaranteed insurability (GI) benefit. A supplementary life insurance policy benefit that gives the policyowner the right to purchase additional insurance of the same type as the life insurance policy that provides the GI benefit on specified option dates. Also known as *guaranteed insurability option (GIO)*. [9]

guaranteed insurability option. *See* **guaranteed insurability benefit.**

guaranteed interest contract. *See* **guaranteed investment contract.**

guaranteed investment contract (GIC). A retirement plan funding vehicle under which an insurer accepts a single deposit from the plan sponsor for a specified period. The insurer invests the funds, and guarantees the plan sponsor at least a specified investment return. Also known as *guaranteed interest contract* or *guaranteed income contract*. [17]

guaranteed renewable policy. An individual health insurance policy that requires the insurer to renew the policy—as long as premium payments are made—at least until the insured attains a specified age. [21]

head office. *See* **home office.**

health insurance policy. An insurance policy that provides protection against the risk of financial loss resulting from the insured person's sickness, accidental injury, or disability. [1]

Health Insurance Portability and Accountability Act (HIPAA). A U.S. federal law that imposes requirements on employer-sponsored group medical expense insurance plans and on insurers that issue individual medical expense insurance plans. [23]

health maintenance organization (HMO). A health care financing and delivery system that provides comprehensive health care services for subscribing members in a particular geographic area. [22]

HIPAA. *See* **Health Insurance Portability and Accountability Act.**

HMO. *See* **health maintenance organization.**

home office. The headquarters of an insurance company. Also known as *head office*. [1]

home service agent. A commissioned insurance sales agent who sells a range of products and provides specified policyowner services, including the collection of renewal premiums, within a specified geographic area. [8]

home service distribution system. A method of selling and servicing insurance policies through commissioned sales agents who sell a range of products and provide specified policyowner services, including the collection of renewal premiums, within a specified geographic area. [8]

hospital expense coverage. A type of basic medical expense coverage that provides benefits for specified hospital expenses such as room and board, medications, laboratory services, and other fees associated with a hospital stay. [18]

HR 10 plan. *See* **Keogh plan.**

immediate annuity. An annuity under which benefit payments are scheduled to begin one annuity period after the annuity is purchased. *See also* **deferred annuity.** [16]

immediate participation guarantee (IPG) contract. A retirement plan funding vehicle that is similar to a deposit administration contract except that an IPG contract does not provide the full guarantees against investment losses or guarantees regarding minimum investment returns that are provided by deposit administration contracts. [17]

impairment rider. *See* **exclusion rider.**

income protection insurance. A type of disability income coverage that provides an income benefit both while the insured is totally disabled and unable to work and while he is able to work but, because of a disability, is earning less than he earned before being disabled. [19]

incontestability provision. An insurance and annuity policy provision that limits the time within which the insurer has the right to avoid the contract on the ground of material misrepresentation in the application for the policy. Individual health insurance policies typically refer to this provision as the time limit on certain defenses provision. Also known as *incontestable clause*. [10, 14, 16, 21]

incontestable clause. *See* **incontestability provision.**

increasing term life insurance. Term life insurance that provides a death benefit that increases by some specified amount or percentage at stated intervals over the policy term. [7]

indemnity benefits. Medical expense insurance plan benefits that are stated as a maximum dollar amount the insurer will reimburse the insured for each covered expense the insured incurs. Also known as *reimbursement benefits.* [18]

indeterminate premium life insurance policy. A type of nonparticipating whole life policy that specifies two premium rates—both a maximum guaranteed rate and a lower rate. The insurer charges the lower premium rate when the policy is purchased and guarantees that rate for at least a stated period of time, after which the insurer uses its actual mortality, interest, and expense experience to establish a new premium rate that may be higher or lower than the previous premium rate. Also known as *nonguaranteed premium life insurance policy* and *variable-premium life insurance policy.* [8]

individual insurance policy. An insurance policy that is issued to insure the life or health of a named person. Some policies also insure the named person's immediate family or a second named person. [1]

individual practice association (IPA) model. A type of open panel HMO that contracts with an association of physicians, known as an IPA, that agrees to provide services for the HMO's subscribers. [22]

individual retirement account. In the United States, a form of individual retirement arrangement that consists of a trust account created for the exclusive benefit of an individual and her beneficiaries; the trustee must be a bank, investment company, stock brokerage, or similar organization. [16]

individual retirement annuity. In the United States, a form of individual retirement arrangement that consists of an individual annuity issued by an insurance company. [16]

individual retirement arrangement (IRA). In the United States, a retirement savings plan that is established by an individual and that meets certain requirements to qualify for favorable federal income tax treatment. *See also* **individual retirement account** and **individual retirement annuity.** [16]

individual stop-loss coverage. A type of stop-loss insurance under which each claim in excess of a stated amount is covered by the

stop-loss insurer. Also known as *specific stop-loss coverage.* [20]

informal contract. A contract that is enforceable because the parties to the contract met requirements concerning the substance of the agreement rather than requirements concerning the form of the agreement. *See also* **formal contract.** [5]

initial premium. The first premium paid for an insurance policy. [5]

installment refund annuity. A life income with refund annuity under which the refund is payable in a series of periodic payments. [16]

insurable interest. The interest an insurance policyowner has in the risk that is insured. The owner of a life insurance policy has an insurable interest in the insured when the policyowner is likely to benefit if the insured continues to live and is likely to suffer some loss or detriment if the insured dies. [3]

insurance agent. A person who is authorized by an insurance company to represent that company in its dealings with applicants for insurance. Also known as *sales agent.* [4]

Insurance Companies Act. A Canadian federal law that governs specified insurance companies operating in Canada. [2]

insured. The person whose life or health is insured under an insurance policy. [3]

insurer-administered plan. A group insurance plan for which the insurer is responsible for handling the administrative and record-keeping aspects of the plan. *See also* **self-administered plan.** [14]

interest. Money paid for the use of money. [6]

interest option. A life insurance policy settlement option under which the insurer invests the policy proceeds and periodically pays interest on those proceeds to the payee. [12]

interest-sensitive whole life insurance. A type of indeterminate premium life insurance which provides that the policy's cash value can be greater than that guaranteed if changing assumptions regarding mortality, investment, and expense factors warrant such an increase. Also known as *current assumption whole life insurance.* [8]

interpleader. In the United States, a procedure under which an insurance company that cannot determine which claimant is entitled to receive policy proceeds may pay the proceeds to a court and ask the court to decide the proper recipient. *See also* **payment into court.** [13]

investment facility contract. *See* **separate account contract.**

IPA model. *See* **individual practice association model.**

IPG contract. *See* **immediate participation guarantee contract.**

IRA. *See* **individual retirement arrangement.**

irrevocable beneficiary. A life insurance policy beneficiary who has a vested interest in the policy proceeds even during the insured's lifetime because the policyowner has the right to change the beneficiary designation only after obtaining the beneficiary's consent. *See also* **revocable beneficiary.** [11]

joint and last survivorship annuity. *See* **joint and survivor annuity.**

joint and survivor annuity. An annuity under which the insurer agrees to make a series of benefit payments to two or more individuals until both or all of the individuals die. Also known as *joint and last survivorship annuity.* [16]

joint and survivorship life income option. A life income settlement option under which the policy proceeds are used to purchase a joint and survivor annuity. [12]

joint mortgage redemption insurance. A plan of decreasing term life insurance that insures the lives of two people and provides a death benefit amount that corresponds to the decreasing amount the two people owe on a mortgage loan. [7]

joint whole life insurance. Whole life insurance that insures two lives under the same policy and that provides a death benefit upon the death of one of the insureds payable to the surviving insured. Also known as *first-to-die-life insurance.* [8]

juvenile insurance policy. An insurance policy that is issued on the life of a child but is owned and paid for by an adult, usually the child's parent or legal guardian. [9]

Keogh plan. In the United States, a qualified IRA that may be established by a person who is self-employed and that is sponsored by a financial institution, such as an insurance company or an investment company. Also known as *HR 10 plan.* [16]

key employee life insurance. *See* **key person life insurance.**

key person. Any person or employee whose continued participation in a business is necessary to the success of the business and whose death would cause the business a significant financial loss. [4]

key person disability coverage. Disability coverage that provides benefit payments to a business if an insured key person becomes disabled. [19]

key person life insurance. Insurance that a business purchases on the life of a person whose continued participation in the business is necessary to its success and whose death would cause financial loss to the business. Also known as *key employee life insurance.* [4]

lapse. The effect on an insurance policy if a renewal premium has not been paid by the end of the grace period. [10]

last survivor life insurance. Whole life insurance that insures two lives under the same policy and that provides a death benefit payable after both insureds have died. Also known as *second-to-die life insurance.* [8]

law of large numbers. A theory of probability which states that, typically, the more times we observe a particular event, the more likely it is that our observed results will approximate the "true" probability that the event will occur. [3]

legal actions provision. An individual health insurance policy provision that limits the time within which a claimant who disagrees with the insurer's claim decision has the right to sue the insurer to collect the amount the claimant believes is owed under the policy. [21]

legal reserve system. A modern method of pricing life insurance under which the insurer (1) specifies the amount of the death benefit in advance of the insured's death, (2) collects the money needed to pay death benefits in advance of the insured's death, and (3) ensures that the premium the individual pays for a policy is directly related to the amount of risk the insurer assumes when it issues the policy. [6]

legal reserves. *See* **policy reserves.**

level premium system. A life insurance pricing system that allows the purchaser of a policy to pay the same premium amount each year the policy is in force. [6]

level term life insurance. Term life insurance that provides a death benefit that remains the same amount over the term of the policy. [7]

liabilities. A company's debts and future obligations. [2]

life and health guaranty association. An organization that operates under the supervision of a state insurance commissioner to protect policyowners, insureds, beneficiaries, and specified others against losses that result from the financial impairment or insolvency of a life or health insurer that operates in the state. [2]

life annuity. An annuity that provides periodic benefit payments for at least the lifetime of a named individual. [12, 16]

life income annuity with period certain. A life annuity that provides annuity benefits throughout the annuitant's life and guarantees that payments will be made for at least a certain period, even if the annuitant dies before the end of that period. [16]

life income option. A life insurance policy settlement option under which the insurer agrees to pay the policy proceeds in periodic installments over the payee's lifetime. [12]

life income with period certain option. A life income settlement option under which the policy proceeds are used to purchase a life income annuity with period certain. [12]

life income with refund annuity. A life annuity that provides annuity benefits throughout the annuitant's lifetime and guarantees that at least the purchase price of the annuity will be paid in benefits. Also known as *refund annuity.* [16]

life insurance policy. A policy under which the insurance company promises to pay a benefit upon the death of the person who is insured. [1]

life insured. In all provinces of Canada except Quebec, the person who is insured by a life insurance policy. [3]

limited-payment whole life policy. A whole life insurance policy for which premiums are payable only until some stated period expires or until the insured's death, whichever occurs first. [8]

liquidation. The process of selling off a business' assets for cash and using that cash to pay the business' debts; any funds remaining are distributed to the owners of the business. [4]

liquidation period. *See* **payout period.**

living benefit rider. *See* **accelerated death benefit rider.**

loading. The total amount added to a policy's net premium to cover all of the insurer's costs of doing business. [6]

long-term care (LTC) benefit. A type of accelerated death benefit under which the insurer agrees to pay a portion of a life insurance policy's face amount as a monthly benefit to the policyowner if the insured requires constant care for a medical condition. [9]

long-term care (LTC) coverage. Supplemental medical expense coverage that pays benefits for medical and other expenses incurred by insureds who, because of advanced age or the effects of a serious illness or injury, need constant care in their homes or in a nursing home. [18]

long-term group disability income coverage. Group disability income coverage that provides a maximum benefit period of more than one year. [19]

long-term individual disability income coverage. Individual disability income coverage that provides a maximum benefit period of at least five years. [19]

loss ratio. The ratio of the benefits an insurer paid out for a block of health insurance policies to the premiums the insurer received for those policies. [18]

LTC benefit. *See* **long-term care benefit.**

LTC coverage. *See* **long-term care coverage.**

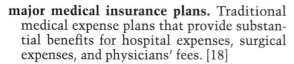

major medical insurance plans. Traditional medical expense plans that provide substantial benefits for hospital expenses, surgical expenses, and physicians' fees. [18]

managed care. A method of integrating the financing and delivery of health care within a system that manages the cost, accessibility, and quality of care. [22]

managed care plans. Medical expense plans that combine the financing and delivery of health care within a system that manages the cost, accessibility, and quality of care. [18]

manual rating. A method of calculating group insurance premium rates by which the insurer uses its own past experience—and sometimes the experience of other insurers—to estimate a group's expected claims and expense experience. [14]

market conduct laws. State insurance laws that regulate how insurance companies conduct their business within the state. [2]

master group insurance contract. An insurance contract that insures a number of people. [14]

material misrepresentation. A misrepresentation that would affect the insurance company's evaluation of a proposed insured. [10]

maturity date. (1) The date on which an insurer will pay the face amount of an endowment policy to the policyowner if the insured is still living. [8] (2) For a given annuity, the date on which the insurer begins to make annuity benefit payments. Also known as *annuity date.* [16]

McCarran-Ferguson Act. A U.S. federal law under which Congress agreed to leave insurance regulation to the states as long as Congress considered state regulation to be adequate. [2]

MDO policy. *See* **monthly debit ordinary policy.**

Medicaid. In the United States, a joint federal-state program that provides hospital and medical expense benefits to people who are poor. [18]

medical expense coverage. Health insurance coverage that provides benefits to pay for the treatment of an insured's illnesses and injuries. [1, 18]

Medicare. In the United States, a federal program that provides specified hospital and medical expense benefits primarily to the elderly and the disabled. [18]

Medicare supplement. In the United States, a medical expense policy designed to supplement the coverage provided under Medicare. Also known as *Medigap policy.* [18]

Medigap policy. *See* **Medicare supplement.**

minimum premium plan (MPP). A group health insurance funding mechanism under which the group policyholder deposits into a special account funds that are sufficient to pay a stated amount of expected claims, and the insurer administers the plan and pays claims from that special account until the funds are exhausted. Thereafter, the insurer is responsible for paying claims from its own funds, and it charges the policyholder a premium for the coverage provided. [20]

minor. A person who has not attained the age of majority and, thus, has limited contractual capacity. [5]

misrepresentation. A false or misleading statement. [10]

misstatement of age or sex provision. A provision that typically is included in life insurance and annuity policies and that describes the action the insurer will take to adjust the amount of the policy benefit if the age or sex of the insured or annuitant is incorrectly stated. [10, 16]

mistaken claim. A claim for which the claimant makes an honest mistake in presenting a claim to the insurer. [13]

mixed model HMO. An HMO that combines certain characteristics of two or more of the various types of HMO models. [22]

model bill. A sample law that is developed by a national association of state or provincial regulators and that the states or provinces are encouraged to use as a basis for their laws. In the United States, the NAIC proposes model insurance laws, and in Canada, the CCIR proposes such laws. [2, 10]

modified coverage policy. A whole life insurance policy under which the amount of insurance provided decreases by specific percentages or amounts either when the insured reaches certain stated ages or at the end of stated time periods. [8]

modified-premium whole life policy. A whole life insurance policy for which the policyowner first pays a lower premium than she would for a similar level-premium whole life policy for a specified initial period and then pays a higher premium than she would for a similar level-premium policy. [8]

monthly debit ordinary (MDO) policy. A whole life insurance policy that is marketed under the home service distribution system and is paid for by monthly premium payments. [8]

moral hazard. For underwriting purposes, the likelihood that a person may act dishonestly in an insurance transaction. [3]

morbidity tables. Charts that indicate the incidence of sickness and accidents, by age, occurring among a given group of people. [3]

mortality experience. The number of deaths that actually occur in a given group of insureds in a given year. [6]

mortality tables. Charts that show the death rates an insurer may reasonably anticipate among a particular group of insured lives at certain ages. [3, 6]

mortgage redemption insurance. A plan of decreasing term life insurance designed to provide a death benefit amount that corresponds to the decreasing amount owed on a mortgage loan. [7]

MPP. *See* **minimum premium plan.**

mutual assent. One of the requirements for the formation of a valid informal contract that is met when the parties reach a meeting of the minds about the terms of their agreement. [5]

mutual benefit method. A method used in the past to fund life insurance in which the members of a mutual benefit society agreed to pay an equal, specific amount of money after the death of any other member. Also known as *post-death assessment method.* [6]

mutual insurance company. An insurance company that is owned by its policyowners. *See also* **stock insurance company.** [1]

NAIC. *See* **National Association of Insurance Commissioners.**

NAIC Group Health Insurance Definition and Group Health Insurance Standard Provisions Model Act. An NAIC model law that defines the groups that are eligible for group insurance and contains requirements as to certain group health insurance policy provisions. [23]

NAIC Uniform Individual Accident and Sickness Policy Provision Law. An NAIC model law that has been adopted by most states and that contains requirements as to certain individual health insurance policy provisions. [23]

National Association of Insurance Commissioners (NAIC). In the United States, a nongovernmental organization that consists of the commissioners or superintendents of the various state insurance departments. [2]

net amount at risk. The difference between the face amount of a life insurance policy—other than a universal life policy—and the policy reserve the insurer has established at the end of any given policy year. For universal life insurance policies, the net amount at risk varies depending on whether the policyowner selects an Option A or an Option B plan. [6, 8]

net cash value. The amount the owner of a permanent life insurance policy will receive upon surrendering the policy for its cash surrender value. The net cash value is calculated by adjusting the amount of the cash surrender value for amounts such as paid-up additions, advance premium payments, and policy loans. [10]

net premium. The amount of money an insurer needs to receive for an insurance policy in order to provide the policy benefits. [6]

network model HMO. A group model HMO that contracts with more than one physicians' group practice. [22]

noncancellable policy. An individual health insurance policy that is guaranteed to be renewable until the insured reaches a specified age. [21]

noncontributory plan. (1) A group insurance plan under which insured group members are not required to contribute any part of the premium for the coverage. [14] (2) A retirement plan that does not require plan participants to make contributions to fund the plan. [17] *See also* **contributory plan.**

nonduplication of benefits provision. A coordination of benefits provision that, if included in a secondary provider's plan, limits the amount payable by the secondary plan to the difference, if any, between the amount paid by the primary plan and the amount that would have been payable by the secondary plan had that plan been the primary plan. [20]

nonforfeiture benefits. Benefits available to the owner of a life insurance policy that builds a cash value. [10]

nonguaranteed premium life insurance policy. *See* **indeterminate premium life insurance policy.**

nonpar policy. *See* **nonparticipating policy.**

nonparticipating policy. An insurance policy under which the policyowner does not share in the insurance company's divisible surplus. Also known as *a nonpar policy.* [6]

nonqualified retirement savings plan. In the United States, a retirement savings plan that does not meet the legal requirements necessary to qualify for favorable federal income tax treatment. In Canada, known as a *nonregistered retirement savings plan.* [17]

nonregistered retirement savings plan. *See* **nonqualified retirement savings plan.**

OAS Act. *See* **Old Age Security Act.**

Office of the Superintendent of Insurance. An administrative agency established in each of the Canadian provinces to enforce provincial insurance laws and regulations. [2]

Old Age Security (OAS) Act. A Canadian federal law under which virtually all Canadian residents who are age 65 and older receive a pension. [17]

open contract. A contract that identifies the documents that constitute the contract between the parties, but the enumerated documents are not all attached to the contract. *See also* **closed contract.** [10]

open-ended HMO. An HMO that provides medical expense benefits to a subscriber who uses a medical care provider who is not a member of the HMO's network and that contains financial incentives to encourage subscribers to use network providers. Also known as *point of service (POS) plan.* [22]

open panel HMO. A type of HMO that allows any physician or health care provider who meets the HMO's specific standards to contract with the HMO to provide services to HMO members. [22]

Option 1 plan. *See* **Option A plan.**

Option 2 plan. *See* **Option B plan.**

Option A plan. A universal life insurance policy that provides a level death benefit amount, which is always equal to the policy's face amount. Also known as *Option 1 plan.* [8]

Option B plan. A universal life insurance policy that provides a death benefit amount that, at any given time, is equal to the policy's face amount plus the amount of the policy's cash value. Also known as *Option 2 plan.* [8]

optional insured rider. *See* **second insured rider.**

optional modes of settlement. *See* **settlement options.**

optionally renewable policy. An individual health insurance policy that gives the insurer the rights to refuse to renew the policy on specified dates, to add coverage limitations, and to increase the premium rate if it does so for a class of policies. [21]

ordinary life insurance policy. *See* **continuous-premium whole life policy.**

original age conversion. The conversion of a term life insurance policy to a permanent plan of insurance at a premium rate that is based on the insured's age when the original term policy was purchased. *See also* **attained age conversion.** [7]

overhead expenses. For purposes of business overhead expense coverage, usual and necessary business expenses, including employee salaries, rent, telephone, electric and gas utilities, and other expenses required to keep the business open. [19]

overinsurance provision. An individual health insurance policy provision that is intended to prevent an insured who is considered to be overinsured from profiting from a sickness or injury. [21]

overinsured person. According to the overinsurance provision included in many individual health insurance policies, a person who is entitled to receive either more in benefits from his medical expense policies than the actual costs incurred for treatment or a greater income amount during disability than he earns while working. [21]

owners' equity. The owners' financial interest in a company, which is equal to the difference between the amount of a company's assets and the amount of its liabilities. [2]

ownership of property. The sum of all the legal rights that exist in a specific piece of property. [5]

PAC system. *See* **preauthorized check system.**

paid-up additional insurance dividend option. A policy dividend option under which the insurer uses any declared policy dividend as a net single premium to purchase paid-up additional insurance on the insured's life; the paid-up additional insurance is issued on the same plan as the basic policy and in whatever face amount the dividend can provide at the insured's attained age. [12]

paid-up additions option benefit. A supplementary benefit that is provided by some whole life insurance policies and that gives the policyowner the right to purchase single-premium paid-up additions to the policy on stated dates in the future and thus to increase the amount of coverage provided under the policy. [9]

paid-up policy. An insurance policy that requires no further premium payments but continues to provide coverage. [8]

par policy. *See* **participating policy.**

partial disability. A disability that prevents an insured from performing some of the duties of her usual occupation or from engaging in that occupation on a full-time basis. [19]

partial surrender provision. *See* **policy withdrawal provision.**

participating policy. An insurance policy under which the policyowner shares in the insurance company's divisible surplus by receiving policy dividends. Also known as *par policy.* [6]

partnership. A business that is owned by two or more people, who are known as the partners. [1]

payee. (1) The person or party who is to receive insurance policy proceeds in accordance with the terms of a settlement agreement. [12] (2) The person who receives periodic annuity benefit payments. [16]

payment into court. In the common law jurisdictions of Canada, a procedure under which an insurance company that cannot determine which claimant is entitled to receive policy proceeds may pay the proceeds to a court and ask the court to decide the proper recipient. *See also* **interpleader.** [13]

payout options provision. An annuity policy provision that lists and describes the options from which the contractholder may select how the insurer will make annuity benefit payments. [16]

payout period. The period during which an insurer makes annuity benefit payments. Also known as *liquidation period.* [16]

payroll deduction method. An automatic premium payment technique under which the policyowner's employer deducts insurance premiums directly from the employee's paycheck. [12]

PCP. *See* **primary care physician.**

Pension Benefits Act. A law enacted by the federal government and each of the provincial governments in Canada to govern the terms and operation of private pension plans. [17]

pension plan. An agreement under which an employer establishes a plan to provide its employees with a lifetime monthly income benefit that begins at their retirement. [17]

period certain. The stated period over which an insurer makes periodic benefit payments under an annuity certain. [16]

periodic level-premium annuity. An annuity that is purchased by the payment of equal premium amounts at regularly scheduled intervals until some predetermined future date. [16]

permanent life insurance. Life insurance that provides coverage throughout the insured's lifetime and also provides a savings element. [1, 8]

personal property. All property other than real property. [5]

personal risk. The risk of economic loss associated with death, poor heath, and outliving one's savings. [3]

physical examination provision. A provision that often is included in individual and group disability income insurance policies and that gives the insurer the right to require an insured who has submitted a disability income claim to be examined by a doctor of the insurer's choice, at the insurer's expense. [20, 21]

physical hazard. For underwriting purposes, a physical characteristic that may increase the likelihood that a specific individual will suffer a loss. [3]

physicians' expense coverage. A type of basic medical expense coverage that provides benefits for charges associated with physicians' visits both in and out of the hospital. [18]

plan administrator. (1) According to the Employee Retirement Income Security Act (ERISA), the individual named in a written plan instrument as being responsible for ensuring that a welfare benefit plan complies with ERISA's disclosure and reporting requirements. [15] (2) A person or party who is responsible for a variety of aspects of the operation of a retirement plan. [17]

plan document. A document that spells out the terms of a retirement plan. [17]

plan participants. The employees and union members who are covered by private retirement plans established by their employers or unions. [17]

plan sponsors. The employers and unions that establish private retirement plans for their employees and members. [17]

point of service (POS) plan. *See* **open-ended HMO.**

policy. A written document that contains the terms of the contractual agreement between an insurance company and the owner of the policy. [3]

policy anniversary. As a general rule, the date on which coverage under an insurance policy became effective. [7]

policy benefit. A stated amount of money an insurance company agrees to pay under an insurance policy when a specific loss occurs. Also known as *policy proceeds.* [3]

policy dividend. The share of an insurer's divisible surplus the insurer pays to the owner of a participating policy issued by the insurer. [6]

policy form. A standardized contract form that shows the terms, conditions, benefits, and ownership rights of a particular insurance product. [2]

policy loan. A loan that an insurer makes to the owner of a permanent life insurance policy and that is secured by the policy's cash value. [8]

policy loan provision. A permanent life insurance policy provision that grants the policyowner the right to take a loan for an amount that does not exceed the policy's net cash value less one year's interest on the loan. [10]

policy proceeds. *See* **policy benefit.**

policy prospectus. A written prospectus provided by an insurer to the potential buyer of a variable life insurance policy or a variable annuity policy. [8, 16]

policy reserves. Liabilities that represent the amount an insurer estimates it needs to pay policy benefits as they come due. Also known as *legal reserves* or *statutory reserves.* [2, 6]

policy rider. An amendment to an insurance policy that becomes a part of the insurance contract and that either expands or limits the benefits payable under the contract. Also known as *an endorsement.* [7]

policy term. The specified period of time during which a term life insurance policy provides coverage. [7]

policy withdrawal provision. A universal life insurance policy provision that permits the policyowner to reduce the amount in the policy's cash value by withdrawing up to the amount of the cash value in cash. Also known as *partial surrender provision.* [10]

policyowner. The person or business that owns an insurance policy. [3]

portable coverage. Group insurance coverage that can be continued when an insured employee leaves the covered group. [15]

POS plan. *See* **open-ended HMO.**

post-death assessment method. *See* **mutual benefit method.**

PPO. *See* **preferred provider organization.**

preadmission certification. A component of utilization review under which the utilization review organization determines whether an insured's proposed nonemergency hospital stay or some other type of care is most appropriate and what the length of an approved hospital stay should be. [22]

preauthorized check (PAC) system. An automatic premium payment technique under which the policyowner authorizes the insurance company to generate checks against the policyowner's checking or savings account to pay renewal premiums as they come due. [12]

pre-existing condition. (1) According to most group health insurance policies, a condition for which an individual received medical care during the three months immediately prior to the effective date of her coverage. [20] (2) According to most individual health insurance policies, an injury that occurred or a sickness that first appeared or manifested itself within a specified period—usually two years—before the policy was issued *and* that was not disclosed on the application for insurance. [21]

pre-existing conditions provision. An individual and group health insurance policy provision which states that benefits will not be paid for pre-existing conditions until the insured has been covered under the policy for a specified length of time. [20, 21]

preference beneficiary clause. A life insurance policy provision which states that if the policyowner does not name a beneficiary, then the insurer will pay the policy proceeds in a stated order of preference. Also known as *succession beneficiary clause.* [11]

preferred beneficiary classification. According to laws that are no longer in force in the common law jurisdictions of Canada, a life insurance policy beneficiary classification consisting of the husband, wife, children, parents, and grandchildren of the insured and who have vested rights to policy proceeds. [11]

preferred provider organization (PPO). An organization that negotiates contracts between health care providers and health care purchasers, such as employers, third-party administrators, insurance companies, and unions. [22]

preferred risk. A proposed insured who presents a significantly less-than-average likelihood of loss and who is charged a lower-than-standard premium rate. [3]

premium. A specified amount of money an insurer charges in exchange for its promise to pay a policy benefit when a specific loss occurs. [3]

premium delay arrangement. A group health insurance funding mechanism that allows the group policyholder to postpone paying monthly group insurance premiums for a stated period of time beyond the expiration of the policy's grace period. [20]

premium payment mode. The frequency at which renewal premiums are payable. [12]

premium reduction dividend option. A policy dividend option under which the insurance company applies policy dividends toward the payment of renewal premiums [12]

pre-need funeral insurance. Whole life insurance that provides funds to pay for the insured's funeral and burial, which have been arranged while the insured is living. Also known as *pre-need insurance.* [8]

pre-need insurance. *See* **pre-need funeral insurance.**

prescription drug coverage. Supplemental medical expense coverage that provides benefits for the purchase of drugs and medicines that are prescribed by a physician and are not available over-the-counter. [18]

presumptive disability. According to the terms of some disability income policies, a stated condition that if present, automatically causes the insured to be considered totally disabled and thus eligible to receive disability income benefits. [19]

primary beneficiary. The party designated to receive the proceeds of a life insurance policy following the death of the insured. Also known as *first beneficiary.* [11]

primary care physician (PCP). A physician, usually a general or family practitioner, who serves as the insured's personal physician and contact with a managed care plan. [22]

principal. A sum of money that is invested over a period of time. [16]

probability. The likelihood that a given event will occur in the future. [3]

probationary period. The length of time—typically, from one to six months—that a new group member must wait before becoming eligible to enroll in a group insurance plan, as specified in the group master contract. [14]

profit. The money, or revenue, that a business receives for its products or services *minus* the costs it incurred to produce the goods or deliver the services. [1]

profit sharing plan. A type of qualified retirement savings plan that is funded primarily by employer contributions payable from the employer's profits. [17]

property. A bundle of rights a person has with respect to something. Property can be classified as either *real property* or *personal property*. [5]

prospectus. According to U.S. federal securities laws, any communication—written or oral—that offers a security for sale and that must contain specified information. [8]

pure risk. A risk that involves no possibility of gain. *See also* **speculative risk.** [3]

QPP. *See* **Quebec Pension Plan.**

qualified plan. In the United States, a private retirement plan that meets the legal requirements to receive federal income tax benefits. *See also* **registered plan.** [17]

Quebec Pension Plan (QPP). In the Canadian province of Quebec, a provincial program that provides a pension for wage earners who reside in Quebec and who have contributed money into the plan during their working years. [17]

real property. Land and whatever is growing on or affixed to the land. *See also* **personal property.** [5]

recording method. A method of changing the beneficiary of a life insurance policy under which the change is effective when the policyowner notifies the insurer in writing of the change. *See also* **endorsement method.** [11]

redating. A practice by which an insurance company agrees to reinstate a term life insurance policy that has lapsed and to change the policy date to the date on which the policy is reinstated. [10]

reduced paid-up insurance nonforfeiture option. A nonforfeiture option that allows the owner of a permanent life insurance policy to discontinue premium payments and to use the policy's net cash value to purchase paid-up life insurance of the same plan as the original policy. [10]

refund annuity. *See* **life income with refund annuity.**

refund life income option. A life income settlement option under which the policy proceeds are used to purchase a life income with refund annuity. [12]

regional office. An insurance company office that is charged with many of the same functions and operations as the company's home office but that is geographically closer to the market it serves and generally reports to the home office. [1]

registered pension plan (RPP). In Canada, a pension plan that qualifies for favorable federal income tax treatment. [17]

registered plan. In Canada, a private retirement plan that meets the legal requirements to receive favorable federal income tax treatment. *See also* **qualified plan.** [17]

registered retirement savings plan (RRSP). In Canada, a qualified retirement account that may be established by any gainfully employed individual. [16]

reimbursement benefits. *See* **indemnity benefits.**

reinstatement. The process by which an insurer puts back into force (1) a life or health insurance policy that has been terminated for nonpayment of renewal premiums or (2) a life insurance policy that has been continued under the extended term or reduced paid-up insurance nonforfeiture option. [10]

reinstatement provision. An individual life insurance, health insurance, and annuity policy provision which states that if certain conditions are met, the insurer will reinstate a policy that has lapsed for nonpayment of premiums. In the case of individual life insurance policies, the provision also governs the reinstatement of policies that have been continued under the extended term or reduced paid-up insurance nonforfeiture option. [10, 16, 21]

reinsurance. Insurance that one insurance company purchases from another insurance company. [3]

reinsurer. An insurance company that accepts risks transferred from another insurer in a reinsurance transaction. [3]

release. A written document that a recipient of life insurance policy proceeds must sign stating that the claimant has received full payment of his claim to the policy proceeds and that he gives up any and all claims that he has or might have against the insurer as a result of that policy. [13]

renewable term insurance policy. A term life insurance policy that gives the policyowner the option to continue the coverage for an additional policy term. [7]

renewal premiums. Premiums paid for an insurance policy after the initial premium is paid. [5]

renewal provision. (1) A term life insurance policy provision that gives the policyowner the right, within specified limits, to continue the coverage for an additional policy term without providing evidence of insurability. [7] (2) An individual health insurance policy provision that describes the circumstances under which the insurer has the right to refuse to renew or the right to cancel the coverage and the insurer's right to increase the policy's premium rate. [21]

representation. A statement that is made by a contracting party and that will invalidate the contract if the statement is not substantially true. [10]

retention limit. A specified maximum amount of insurance that a life insurer is willing to carry at its own risk on any one life without transferring some of the risk to a reinsurer. [3]

retrocession. A transaction by which a reinsurer cedes risks to another reinsurer. [3]

retrospective rating arrangement. A group health insurance funding mechanism under which the insurer agrees to charge the group policyholder a lower monthly premium than it would normally charge based on the group's prior claim experience and the policyholder agrees to pay an additional amount if, at the end of the policy year, the group's claim experience has been unfavorable. [20]

retrospective review. A component of utilization review under which the utilization review organization reviews the necessity and quality of the medical care an insured received in a hospital following the hospitalization. [22]

revocable beneficiary. A life insurance policy beneficiary who has no right to the policy proceeds during the insured's lifetime because the policyowner has the unrestricted right to change the beneficiary designation during the insured's lifetime. *See also* **irrevocable beneficiary.** [11]

right of revocation. The policyowner's right to change the beneficiary designation of a life insurance policy. [11]

RPP. *See* **registered pension plan.**

RRSP. *See* **registered retirement savings plan.**

salary continuation plan. A short-term disability income insurance plan that provides 100 percent of an insured employee's salary, beginning on the first day of the employee's absence due to sickness or injury and continuing for some specified time. [20]

sales agent. *See* **insurance agent.**

Savings Incentive Match Plan for Employees (SIMPLE). In the United States, a qualified retirement plan that may be established by specified employers. An individual retirement arrangement (IRA) is established for each participating employee, and the employee agrees to reduce her compensation by a stated percentage each pay period and to have the employer contribute that amount to her IRA. [17]

second insured rider. A life insurance policy rider that provides term insurance coverage on the life of an individual other than the policy's insured. Also known as *optional insured rider* or *additional insured rider*. [9]

secondary beneficiary. *See* **contingent beneficiary.**

second-to-die life insurance. *See* **last survivor life insurance.**

Section 7702 corridor. For purposes of U.S. federal income tax laws, the required difference between a policy's face amount and the amount of the policy's cash value needed for the policy to qualify as a life insurance policy rather than an investment product. [8]

segregated account. In Canada, an investment account that is maintained separately from an insurer's general investment account and that allows the insurer to manage the funds placed in variable life insurance policies and variable annuity policies. *See also* **separate account.** [8, 16]

selection against the insurer. *See* **antiselection.**

selection of risks. *See* **underwriting.**

self-administered plan. A group insurance plan for which the group policyholder is responsible for handling the administrative and record-keeping aspects of the plan. *See also* **insurer-administered plan.** [14]

self-insurance. A risk-management technique by which a person or business accepts financial responsibility for losses associated with specific risks. [3]

SEP plan. *See* **simplified employee pension plan.**

separate account. In the United States, an investment account that is maintained separately from an insurer's general investment account and that allows the insurer to manage the funds placed in variable life insurance policies and variable annuity policies. *See also* **segregated account.** [8, 16]

separate account contract. A retirement plan funding vehicle under which plan assets are invested in an insurance company's separate accounts. Also known as *investment facility contract.* [17]

settlement agreement. A contractual agreement between an insurer and the owner or beneficiary of a life insurance policy who has selected an optional mode of settlement. The settlement agreement governs the rights and obligations of the parties after the insured's death. [12]

settlement options. Alternative methods that the owner or beneficiary of a life insurance policy can elect for the payment of policy proceeds. Also known as *optional modes of settlement.* [12]

settlement options provision. A life insurance and annuity policy provision that grants a policyowner or a beneficiary several choices as to how the insurer will distribute the policy proceeds. In the case of annuities, Also known as *payout options provision.* [12, 16]

short-term group disability income coverage. Group disability income coverage that provides a maximum benefit period of less than one year. [19]

short-term individual disability income coverage. Individual disability income coverage that provides a maximum benefit period of from one to five years. [19]

simple interest. Interest paid on a stated sum of money. [6]

SIMPLE plan. *See* **Savings Incentive Match Plan for Employees.**

simplified employee pension (SEP) plan. In the United States, an employer-sponsored pension plan under which a participating employee establishes and owns an individual retirement account or individual retirement annuity into which the employer deposits its plan contributions for the employee. Self-employed people also may establish a SEP plan. [17]

single-premium annuity. An annuity that is purchased by the payment of a single, lump-sum premium. [16]

single-premium whole life policy. A type of limited-payment whole life insurance policy that requires only one premium payment. [8]

Social Security. In the United States, a federal program that provides specified benefits, including a monthly retirement income benefit to people who have contributed to the plan during their income-earning years. [17]

Social Security Disability Income (SSDI). A U.S. government program that provides monthly income benefits to qualified disabled individuals who are under age 65 and who have paid a specified amount of Social Security tax for a prescribed number of quarter-year periods. [19]

sole proprietorship. A business that is owned and operated by one individual. [1]

solvent. Able to pay debts and policy benefits when they come due. [2]

special class rates. *See* **substandard premium rates.**

special class risk. *See* **substandard risk.**

specific stop-loss coverage. *See* **individual stop-loss coverage.**

speculative risk. A risk that involves three possible outcomes: loss, gain, or no change. *See also* **pure risk.** [3]

split-dollar life insurance plan. An agreement under which a business provides individual life insurance policies for certain selected employees, who share in paying the cost of the policies. [4]

spouse and children's insurance rider. A rider that may be added to a whole life insurance policy and that provides coverage on the insured's spouse and children. [9]

SSDI. *See* **Social Security Disability Income.**

staff model HMO. A type of closed panel HMO in which the physicians who provide medical services for HMO members are employees of the HMO and generally operate out of offices in the HMO's facilities. [22]

standard premium rates. The premium rates charged insureds who are classified as standard risks. [3]

standard risk. A proposed insured who has a likelihood of loss that is not significantly greater than average. [3]

state insurance department. The state administrative agency charged with ensuring that insurance companies operating within the state comply with all state insurance laws and regulations. [2]

statutory reserves. *See* **policy reserves.**

stock insurance company. An insurance company that is owned by the people and organizations that purchase shares of the company's stock. *See also* **mutual insurance company.** [1]

stop-loss insurance. Insurance purchased by employers that self-insure group health insurance plans so that they can place a maximum dollar limit on their liability for paying claims. [20]

stop-loss provision. A major medical insurance policy provision which specifies that the policy will cover 100 percent of the insured's eligible medical expenses after he has incurred a specified amount of out-of-pocket expenses in deductible and coinsurance payments. [18]

straight life annuity. A life annuity that provides periodic payments for only as long as the annuitant lives. [16]

straight life income option. A life income settlement option under which the policy proceeds are used to purchase a straight life annuity. [12]

straight life insurance policy. *See* **continuous-premium whole life policy.**

substandard premium rates. The premium rates charged insureds who are classified as substandard risks. Also known as *special class rates.* [3]

substandard risk. A proposed insured who has a significantly greater-than-average likelihood of loss. Also known as *special class risk.* [3]

succession beneficiary clause. *See* **preference beneficiary clause.**

successor beneficiary. *See* **contingent beneficiary.**

successor payee. *See* **contingent payee.**

suicide exclusion provision. An individual life insurance policy provision that excludes suicide as a covered risk for a specified period—usually two years—following the date the policy is issued. [10]

Superintendents' Guidelines. A series of recommendations to insurers adopted by the Canadian Council of Insurance Regulators in cooperation with the Canadian Life and Health Insurance Association (CLHIA). [2]

supplemental major medical policy. A major medical policy that is issued in conjunction with an underlying basic medical expense insurance policy. *See also* **comprehensive major medical policy.** [18]

supplementary contract. A settlement agreement between an insurer and a life insurance policy beneficiary who elects a settlement option following the insured's death. [12]

surgical expense coverage. A type of basic medical expense coverage that provides benefits

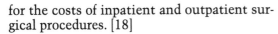

for the costs of inpatient and outpatient surgical procedures. [18]

surplus. The portion of owners' equity consisting of the amount by which the company's assets exceed its liabilities and capital. [2]

surrender charges. (1) Expense charges imposed by an insurer if the owner of a universal life insurance policy surrenders the policy for its cash surrender value. [8] (2) A charge an insurer imposes if a deferred annuity policy is surrendered for its cash surrender value within a stated number of years after it was purchased. [16]

surrender value. *See* **cash surrender value.**

survivor benefit. A benefit typically provided by deferred annuity policies under which the annuity's accumulated value is paid to a designated beneficiary if the annuitant or contractholder dies before annuity benefit payments begin. [16]

survivor income plan. A plan that supplements the benefits provided by a group life insurance policy by providing periodic benefit payments to specified dependents who survive a covered group member. [15]

tabular mortality. *See* **expected mortality.**

temporary life annuity. An annuity that provides periodic benefit payments until the end of a specified number of years or until the death of the annuitant, whichever occurs first. [16]

term life insurance. Life insurance that provides a death benefit if the insured dies during a specified period. [1, 7]

terminal illness (TI) benefit. A type of accelerated death benefit under which the insurer pays a portion of a life insurance policy's death benefit to the policyowner if the insured suffers from a terminal illness and has a physician-certified life expectancy of 12 months or less. [9]

third-party administrator (TPA). An organization other than an insurance company that provides administrative services to the sponsors of group benefit plans. [20]

third-party policy. A life insurance policy that one person purchases on the life of another person. [3]

thrift and savings plan. In the United States, a retirement savings plan to which an employer is obligated to make contributions on behalf of an employee if the employee makes a specified contribution to the plan. [17]

TI benefit. *See* **terminal illness benefit.**

time clause. *See* **common disaster clause.**

time limit on certain defenses provision. *See* **incontestability provision.**

total disability. A disability that meets the requirements of a disability benefit provision of an insurance policy or policy rider and that qualifies the policyowner or insured to receive specified disability benefits. [9, 19]

TPA. *See* **third-party administrator.**

trust. A fiduciary relationship in which one or more persons—the trustees—hold legal title to property for the benefit of another person—the trust beneficiary. [14]

trust beneficiary. The person for whose benefit a trustee holds legal title to property. [14]

trust fund. The property held in trust by one or more trustees. [14]

trustee. A person who holds legal title to property for the benefit of another person. [14]

UCR fee. *See* **usual, customary, and reasonable fee.**

underwriting. The process of identifying and classifying the degree of risk represented by a proposed insured. Also known as *selection of risks.* [3]

underwriting guidelines. General rules of risk selection that underwriters follow when classifying proposed insureds into specific risk categories. [3]

Uniform Accident and Sickness Insurance Act. A model law adopted by the Canadian Council of Insurance Regulators and enacted by all of the common law provinces of Canada to regulate health insurance contracts. [23]

Uniform Life Insurance Act. A model law adopted by the Canadian Council of Insurance Regulators to regulate life insurance policies. [10]

unilateral contract. A contract between two parties only one of whom makes legally enforceable promises when entering into the contract. *See also* **bilateral contract**. [5]

universal life insurance. Permanent life insurance that is characterized by its flexible premiums, its flexible face amounts and flexible death benefit amounts, and its unbundling of the pricing factors. [8]

universal life II. *See* **variable universal life insurance**.

UR. *See* **utilization review**.

usual, customary, and reasonable (UCR) fee. The maximum dollar amount of a given covered expense that the insurer will consider as eligible for reimbursement under a medical expense policy. [18]

utilization management. A process by which a managed care plan manages an insured's use of medical services and assures that she receives necessary, appropriate, high-quality care in a cost-effective manner. [22]

utilization review (UR). A process by which a managed care plan evaluates the necessity and quality of an insured's medical care, using techniques such as preadmission certification, concurrent review, and retrospective review. [22]

valid contract. A contract that is enforceable at law. [5]

valued contract. An insurance policy that specifies the amount of the benefit that will be payable when a covered loss occurs, regardless of the actual amount of the loss that was incurred. *See also* **contract of indemnity**. [3]

variable annuity. An annuity under which the amount of the policy's accumulated value and the amount of the monthly annuity benefit payment fluctuate in accordance with the performance of a separate account. *See also* **fixed-benefit annuity**. [16]

variable life insurance. A form of whole life insurance under which the death benefit and the cash value of the policy fluctuate according to the investment performance of a separate (segregated) account. [8]

variable-premium life insurance policy. *See* **indeterminate premium life insurance policy**.

variable universal life insurance. A type of life insurance that combines the premium and

death benefit flexibility of universal life insurance with the investment flexibility and risk of variable life insurance. Also known as *universal life II* and *flexible-premium variable life insurance*. [8]

vested interest. A property right that has taken effect and cannot be altered or changed without the consent of the person who owns the right. [11]

vesting. A retirement plan participant's right to receive partial or full plan benefits even if he terminates employment prior to retirement. [17]

vision care coverage. Supplemental medical expense coverage that provides benefits for expenses incurred in obtaining eye examinations and corrective lenses. [18]

void contract. A contract that was never enforceable at law. [5]

voidable contract. A contract that is otherwise enforceable except that one party has the right to avoid her obligations under the contract without incurring legal liability. [5]

waiting period. *See* **elimination period**.

waiver of premium for disability (WP) benefit. A supplementary life insurance policy benefit under which the insurer promises to give up its right to collect renewal premiums that become due while the insured is totally disabled. [9]

waiver of premium for payor benefit. A supplementary benefit provided by some juvenile insurance policies under which the insurer promises to give up its right to collect the policy's renewal premiums if the policyowner dies or becomes totally disabled. [9]

warranty. A statement that is made by a contracting party and that will invalidate the contract if the statement is not literally true. [10]

welfare benefit plan. According to the Employee Retirement Income Security Act, any plan or program that an employer establishes to provide specified benefits, including life and health insurance benefits, to plan participants and their beneficiaries. [15]

whole life insurance. Life insurance that provides lifetime insurance coverage at a level premium rate that does not increase as the insured ages. [8]

withdrawal charge. A charge an insurer imposes on certain withdrawals a contractholder makes from the accumulated value of a deferred annuity. [16]

withdrawal provision. A deferred annuity policy provision that gives the contractholder the right to withdraw all or a portion of the annuity's accumulated value during the accumulation period. [16]

WP benefit. *See* **waiver of premium for disability benefit.**

yearly renewable term (YRT) insurance. One-year term life insurance that is renewable at the end of the policy term. Also known as *annually renewable term (ART) insurance.* [7]

YRT insurance. *See* **yearly renewable term insurance.**

Index

S

IMPORTANT—READ CAREFULLY BEFORE REMOVING THE QUIK REVIEW CD-ROM FROM ITS JACKET. *Use of the software program on the enclosed CD is subject to the terms of the license agreement printed below. By removing the CD from the jacket, you indicate your acceptance of the following LOMA License Agreement.*

LOMA LICENSE AGREEMENT

This is a legal agreement between you (individual or company) and LOMA. By removing the CD from its jacket, you are agreeing to be bound by the terms of this agreement.

Grant of License. LOMA grants to you the right to use one copy of the enclosed Quik Review (hereinafter "the software") on a single computer. The software is in "use" on a computer when it is loaded into temporary memory (RAM) or installed into permanent memory (hard disk, CD-ROM, or other storage device) of that computer.

Copyright. The software is owned by LOMA and is protected by U.S. copyright laws and international treaty provisions. Therefore, you must treat the software like any other copyrighted material (e.g., a book or musical recording) EXCEPT that you may either make one copy of the software solely for backup or archival purposes or transfer the software to a single hard disk provided you keep the original solely for backup or archival purposes. You may not copy the written material accompanying the software. The instructional material (hereinafter "the content") contained in the software is also owned by LOMA and protected by U.S. copyright laws and international treaty provisions. It is illegal to make any copy whatsoever of the content; to install the software on a network, intranet, or web site; to download the content to another computer or device; to print screens or otherwise cause the content to be printed; or to in any other way reproduce the content contained in the software.

Other Restrictions. You may not rent or lease the software. You may not reverse engineer, decompile, or disassemble the software or in any way duplicate the contents of the code and other elements therein.

Warranty. LOMA warrants that all software provided by LOMA has been treated with a virus detection, removal, and prevention system before the LOMA software is shipped to the User. Before installing the software, it is the User's responsibility to re-check the software and verify that it is free from any virus, bug, or any other problem whatsoever that may affect User's hardware, software, network, data, database, or any other equipment, material, or operations whatsoever.

Disclaimer of Warranty. LOMA MAKES NO OTHER WARRANTY EXPRESSED OR IMPLIED INCLUDING, WITHOUT LIMITATION, NO WARRANTY OF MERCHANTABILITY OR FITNESS OR SUITABILITY FOR A PARTICULAR PURPOSE. In the event of LOMA's breach of its warranty above, User's sole remedy shall be replacement of the defective LOMA software or refund of the purchase price thereof, as determined at LOMA's sole option. UNDER NO CIRCUMSTANCES SHALL LOMA BE LIABLE TO THE USER OR ANY THIRD PARTY FOR ANY INCIDENTAL OR CONSEQUENTIAL DAMAGES WHATSOEVER.

Limitation of Liability. User agrees to indemnify and hold harmless LOMA, its employees, its agents, and their successors and assigns against any loss, liability, cost or expense (including reasonable attorneys' fees) asserted against or suffered or incurred by LOMA as a consequence of, or in the defense of, any claim arising from or based upon any alleged negligence, act or failure to act, whatsoever of LOMA, its employees, their successors, agents, heirs, and/or assigns with respect to the aforementioned software.

LOMA® is a registered trademark of LOMA (Life Office Management Association), Atlanta, Georgia, USA. All rights reserved.